WESTERN ❧ CIVILIZATION

Sources, Images, and Interpretations

Eighth Edition / From the Renaissance to the Present

DENNIS SHERMAN

John Jay College, City University of New York

McGraw Hill

*Connect
Learn
Succeed*

WESTERN CIVILIZATION: SOURCES, IMAGES, AND INTERPRETATIONS, FROM THE RENAISSANCE TO THE PRESENT, EIGHTH EDITION

Published by McGraw-Hill, a business unit of The McGraw-Hill Companies, Inc., 1221 Avenue of the Americas, New York, NY, 10020. Copyright © 2011 by The McGraw-Hill Companies, Inc. All rights reserved. Previous editions © 2008, 2004, and 2000. No part of this publication may be reproduced or distributed in any form or by any means, or stored in a database or retrieval system, without the prior written consent of The McGraw-Hill Companies, Inc., including, but not limited to, in any network or other electronic storage or transmission, or broadcast for distance learning.

Some ancillaries, including electronic and print components, may not be available to customers outside the United States.

This book is printed on recycled, acid-free paper containing 10% post-consumer waste.

1 2 3 4 5 6 7 8 9 0 DOW/DOW 1 0 9 8 7 6 5 4 3 2 1 0

ISBN: 978-0-07-338560-0
MHID: 0-07-338560-3

Vice President & Editor-in-Chief: *Michael Ryan*
Vice President EDP/Central Publishing Services: *Kimberly Meriwether David*
Editorial Director: *William Glass*
Publisher: *Chris Freitag*
Sponsoring Editor: *Matthew Busbridge*
Managing Editor: *Meghan Campbell*
Executive Marketing Manager: *Pamela S. Cooper*
Senior Project Manager: *Lisa A. Bruflodt*
Design Coordinator: *Margarite Reynolds*
Photo Research Coordinator: *Brian Pecko*
Cover Image: *Gerard Terborch (1617–1681). Curiosity. ca. 1660. Oil on canvas, 30 × 24 1/2 in. (76.2 × 62.2 cm). The Jules Bache Collection, 1949 (49.7.38). Image copyright © The Metropolitan Museum of Art/Art Resource, NY.*
Buyer: *Kara Kudronowicz*
Compositor: *Lachina Publishing Services*
Typeface: *10.5/12.5 Goudy Old Style*
Printer: *R.R. Donnelley*

All credits appearing on page or at the end of the book are considered to be an extension of the copyright page.

Library of Congress Cataloging-in-Publication Data

Western civilization : sources, images, and interpretations, from the Renaissance to the present / [edited by] Dennis Sherman. —8th ed.
    p. cm.
    Includes bibliographical references.
    ISBN-13: 978-0-07-338560-0 (alk. paper)
    ISBN-10: 0-07-338560-3 (alk. paper)
        1. Civilization, Western—History—Sources. 2. Civilization, Western—History—Textbooks.
    I. Sherman, Dennis.

    CB245.W48355 2010
    909'.09821—dc22

                                                                                        2010030948

About the Author

Dennis Sherman is Professor of History at John Jay College, the City University of New York. He received his B.A. (1962) and J.D. (1965) degrees from the University of California at Berkeley and his Ph.D. (1970) from the University of Michigan. He was Visiting Professor at the University of Paris (1978–1979; 1985). He received the Ford Foundation Prize Fellowship (1968–1969, 1969–1970), a fellowship from the Council for Research on Economic History (1971–1972), and fellowships from the National Endowment for the Humanities (1973–1976). His publications include *World Civilizations:* *Sources, Images, and Interpretations* (co-author); *The West in the World: A Mid-Length Narrative History;* a series of introductions in the Garland Library of War and Peace; several articles and reviews on nineteenth-century French economic and social history in American and European journals; and several short stories in literary reviews. He is recipient of the college's Outstanding Teacher of the Year award.

Advisory Editor
Raymond Grew, University of Michigan

To Pat, Joe, Darryl, Vera, and Raymond

In time choice, change, and obligation merge;
How quietly we listen to ourselves.

Contents

Part Two
The Early Modern Period

4 War and Revolution: 1560–1660

5 Aristocracy and Absolutism in the Seventeenth Century

6 The Scientific Revolution

Part Three
The Nineteenth Century

19　The Present in Perspective

Preface

I compiled *Western Civilization: Sources, Images, and Interpretations* with three main goals in mind. First, I wanted to show readers the variety of sources historians use to write about history. Therefore, I have included not only primary documents, but also visual and secondary sources. Second, this collection is intended to be relatively concise, so I wanted the sources to "get to the point." To do that, I have carefully edited each selection to highlight its historical meanings as efficiently as possible. Third, I sought to structure the book in a way that makes sense to the reader and does not dominate the organization of a course that may be following a textbook or using other books. To this end, I arranged the sources along chronological lines, beginning with the origins of Western civilization in the ancient Near East and gradually moving up to the present. From time to time, this chronological approach is modified, such as with the treatment of the Renaissance in one chapter, to account for the nature of the era and the organization of most courses.

This book thus provides a broad introduction to the sources historians use, the ways in which they interpret historical evidence, and the challenges they face in studying the evolution of Western civilization over the past 6,000 years. Each selection—whether a document, photograph, or map—is presented with an introduction, commentary, and questions designed to provide meaningful context and to facilitate readers' understanding of the selection's historical significance. I have also selected sources that provide a general balance among political, economic, social, intellectual, religious, and cultural history. However, different chapters highlight particular themes that are important for understanding certain eras. For example, some chapters offer more sources on social and women's history, while others might emphasize political and religious history.

A book of this size can contain only a small portion of the historical material that is available. Thus, *Western Civilization* is truly an introduction. Indeed, it is my hope that the materials presented here will serve primarily as a jumping-off point for further exploration into history and the historian's discipline.

New in This Edition

This new edition includes several changes:

- One of the most unusual and popular features of this book is the Visual Sources section in each chapter. I have enlarged several of these sections with new images, larger reproductions, greater use of color, and longer guides to the new images. Because the images are presented in ways that encourage students to "read" and analyze what they are seeing as historical documents, the new images, color, and guides make this section more useful and interesting.

- In response to reviewers' requests, I added several new primary and secondary sources.

- To reflect changing developments, the material in the final chapter has been revised with new emphasis on the significance of recent historical developments.

Otherwise, the structure, approach, and approximate length of this edition remain as in previous editions.

Structure of the Book

As the table of contents indicates, each of the book's volumes contains chapters of manageable length. All the chapters are structured in the same way.

Each chapter opens with a **chapter introduction** that previews the period of history and the topics covered. A **time line** follows, outlining the relevant dates, individuals, events, and developments focused on in the chapter. In addition, a time line at the beginning of each of the six parts in the book puts the developments covered in each chapter into a broader perspective.

Then come the three categories of historical sources. First are **primary sources,** usually written documents that give voice to the individuals who lived through the events described. These are followed by the **visual sources**—paintings, drawings, sculpture, ceramics, photographs, buildings, monuments, coins, and so forth—which provide valuable historical insights that are difficult to gain solely through written documents. Included within this category are **maps.** Finally, **secondary sources,** most written by scholars looking back on the time in question, offer interpretations of primary sources.

Each source is preceded by a **headnote,** which identifies the nature of the source, places it in historical context, and indicates its particular focus. Headnotes for visual sources—including maps—are extensive, to help readers see their unique value as historical evidence.

The headnotes end with **points to consider.** These are not simply facts that readers must search for in the selection. Rather, they are designed to stimulate thought about the selections and to indicate the uses of each source.

Each chapter then ends with **chapter questions** that challenge readers to draw major themes together.

The first chapter of each volume contains three special sections: **Using Primary Sources, Using Visual Sources,** and **Using Secondary Sources.** They offer suggestions for interpreting and using these different kinds of sources.

Finally, what immediately follows the **acknowledgments** is a section on **Using This Book,** aimed at helping readers to use all the features in this book to their best advantage.

Acknowledgments

McGraw-Hill and the author would like to thank the following reviewers for their many helpful comments and suggestions: David Bernatowicz, Cuyahoga Community College; Cynthia Carter, Florida Community College—North Campus; William E. Kinsella, Jr., Northern Virginia Community College; Suzanne Cloud Tapper, Rowan University; David Valone, Quinnipiac College.

Dennis Sherman

Using This Book

In using this book, you face a task similar to that confronting all historians: discover what people in the past thought and did, and why, and to organize this information into a chronological record. To do this, historians must search for evidence from the past, and this evidence comes in many different forms. Most sources consist of written materials, ranging from government records to gravestone inscriptions, memoirs, and poetry. Other sources include paintings, photographs, sculpture, buildings, maps, pottery, and oral traditions. Historians also use secondary sources—accounts of a particular topic or period written by other scholars. But in searching for sources, historians usually have something in mind—some particular interest or tentative conclusions that shape their search. Thus, in working with sources, historians make numerous decisions about which ones to include and emphasize, and how to interpret them. What historians write is ultimately a synthesis of the questions they posed, the sources they used, and their own ideas.

This book provides examples of all these materials and lets you try your hand at thinking as a historian does. However, working with sources takes practice. Each piece of historical evidence is usually mute. It's up to the historian (or "you") to unlock the message in the evidence—to give voice, in a sense, to the people who created that document or those paintings so long ago. The historian (or "you") therefore must be a skilled detective. Here are some guidelines to help you hone your detecting skills.

1. **What Is the Context?** Get a sense of the **context** of the source you are about to read or analyze. This book gives you three ways to do this. First, read the brief introduction to the chapter in which the source appears. This preview sketches some of the most important developments in the period covered by the chapter. It introduces the topics, issues, and questions that the sources in the chapter focus on, and places these sources in the larger historical context of the civilizations being examined.

   Second, look at the time line, which shows the period covered by the chapter and indicates the approximate dates and life spans of the developments and people depicted in the sources. Third, read the headnote—the one or two paragraphs in italics that

precede each source. These provide the immediate context to the source, introduce the source's author or creator, and indicate what the source is about.

2. **What Kind of Source Is It?** Each chapter is divided into three kinds of sources: primary, visual, and secondary. Primary sources are "first-hand" or "eyewitness" accounts of historical events or issues. Historians consider these documents their main building blocks for learning about and interpreting the past. These pieces of evidence are the most direct links possible to what people thought, how and why they acted as they did, and what they accomplished.

   The visual sources in the book—such as paintings, sculpture, photographs, and buildings—are far more than just ornamentation or examples of renowned pieces of art and architecture. These sources reveal just as much of the past as written materials do—if you know how to interpret them. The extensive headnotes accompanying the visual sources will help you with this challenge.

   Finally, secondary sources are accounts or analyses of events by someone (usually a scholar looking back on the past) who did not witness the event or live through the particular era described in the source. Secondary-source writers usually base their interpretations of what occurred on their examination of numerous primary documents and other sources. The analyses in these sources reflect the authors' choices and their own understanding of what happened. Often scholars differ on how to interpret significant historical developments.

   At times the distinction between primary and secondary sources blurs, as when the author of a source lived during the events he or she is interpreting but did not witness it directly. If a historian views such a document as an interpretation of what occurred, the document is considered a secondary source. However, if the historian treats the document as evidence of the assumptions and attitudes of the author's times, the document is considered a primary source.

3. **What Does the Source Seem to Be Saying?** All sources reveal some information (whether directly or indirectly) about people and societies of the past. As you consider each source, ask yourself: What does this document or image tell me about this topic, society,

individual, or era? The **"Consider"** questions that follow the headnote to each source will help you identify the important information contained in the sources.

4. **Who Created the Source, and Why?** To critically examine a source, ask yourself four questions. First, who created the source? Knowing the author or creator— a religious figure? scholar? worker?—may give you clues to the point expressed in the view reflected in the source. Second, what might be the author's biases and assumptions, such as political sympathies, group allegiances, or religious beliefs? Discerning these can give you valuable information that the author did not intend to convey. Third, why was the document written or created? Perhaps the author was trying to advocate a particular point of view or satisfy the wishes of a powerful group. Identifying the motivation behind the source sheds further light on its meaning. Fourth, who were the source's intended readers or viewers? Were they scholars? nobles? women? Knowing this can help you interpret a document's message or decipher the meaning of a painting.

Each kind of source—primary, visual, and secondary —poses its own challenge to historians who are trying to analyze them critically. Some primary documents, for example, may be forgeries or contain errors. There may also be inconsistencies within the document. These problems call into question the credibility of a document. The kind of primary source may limit its usefulness as well. For example, a law may not tell you anything about whether people followed it or whether it was enforced. And just because a book was published doesn't necessarily mean that it was widely read at the time. A formal written statement may reveal less about an individual's feelings and actual behavior than a diary entry can. Moreover, language constantly evolves, so the meanings of words and phrases may have changed over time. To fully understand a primary source, try to imagine yourself living during the time and in the society in which the source was first created.

Visual sources require especially careful interpretation. For example, a painter's intentions can be difficult to discern. Furthermore, a particular painting might mean something completely different to a sixteenth-century viewer than it does to a twenty-first-century viewer. Similarly, it makes a great difference whether a photograph was posed or spontaneous. Scholars differ greatly over how to interpret sources such as paintings, ceramics, and coins. Therefore, the descriptions that accompany the visual sources in this book are open to debate. They are designed primarily to show you how historians use visual materials—as unwritten evidence of what people in the past valued, thought, did, and found interesting.

Maps are a special kind of visual source. In this book, they are intended to shed light on relationships, such as the connections between geographical factors and political developments. As with other visual sources, the descriptions in the headnotes indicate some of the ways historians use maps.

With secondary sources, the authors (usually historians) often try to present a narrative of an event or era, or explain some social or political development. By its very nature, writing secondary sources means making decisions about what information to include. The author must make numerous judgment calls from among a huge amount of historical data. Therefore, read secondary sources with these questions in mind: What is the author's point or argument? What sort of evidence does he or she use to support the argument? Does the author's argument make sense to you? What political or ideological biases are revealed in the author's interpretation? How might somebody argue against the interpretation presented by the author?

All historical sources—whether primary, visual, or secondary—can only be so "objective." In fact, most evidence from the past omits important information about ordinary people's lives, children's lives, or particular ethnic groups. But good sources do reveal valuable information when you know what to look for and analyze them critically. In the hands of careful historians, they can offer a provocative glimpse into the hopes, dreams, and the thoughts and actions of people from the past.

5. **What Connections and Comparisons Can Be Made?** In considering a source, ask yourself: Does this source relate in any way to another source in the chapter, to a broader topic covered in the chapter, or to any themes or developments covered in a textbook or classroom? Looking for connections and comparisons helps you stand back from the source and identify larger historical trends—perhaps even about yourself and your own society—beyond just the immediate message in the source.

To spot these links, read the chapter introductions. These list some of the broad questions and themes around which the sources are organized. Sometimes the headnotes or "consider" points also suggest comparisons. In addition, the questions at the end of each chapter can help you make connections and comparisons. To answer these questions, you'll need to engage in analytical thought, look at several selections in the chapter together, and sometimes consider sources from several chapters.

6. **Employ the Models Presented in the "Using Primary Sources," "Using Visual Sources," and "Using Secondary Sources" Sections.** These provide examples of how a primary, a visual, and a secondary source might be read and studied.

Six-Point Checklist for Using this Book

- **Context**
- **Kind of source** (primary, visual, secondary)
- **Message** (what does the source seem to be saying?)
- **Critical analysis** (who created the source, and why?)
- **Connections and comparisons**
- **Models** (in the first chapter's "Using Primary Sources," "Using Visual Sources," and "Using Secondary Sources" sections)

Schematic of Evolution of Western Civilization

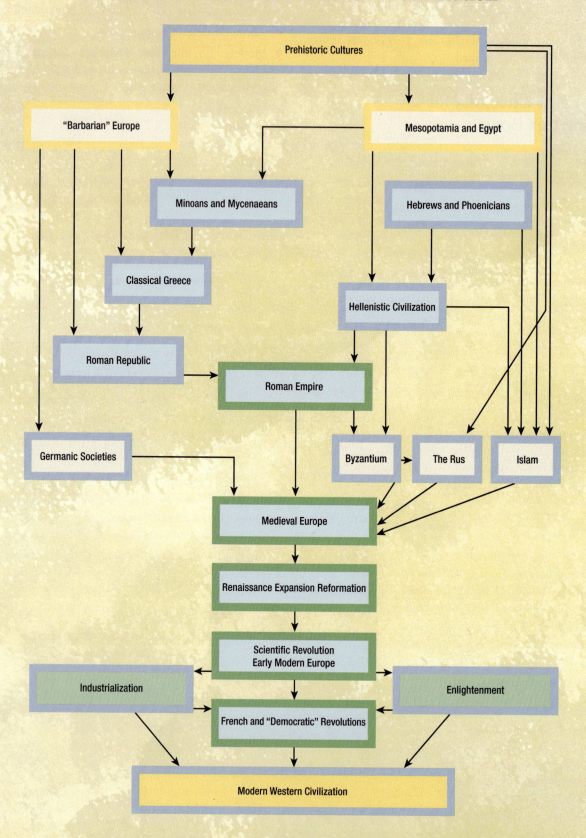

The Evolution of Western Civilization

This chart is a schematic illustration of the development of Western civilization up to modern times. Caution should be exercised when reading such a chart. The connections made are a matter more of judgment than of fact. Moreover, what is missing—the how and why of the connections—is of great importance. Nevertheless, the chart can make it easier to see some of the broadest connections between societies and civilizations, connections that are often lost when a single period or society is examined in detail.

CONSIDER: *Possible reasons for the various connections within the chart; what might be added to this chart to make it more useful.*

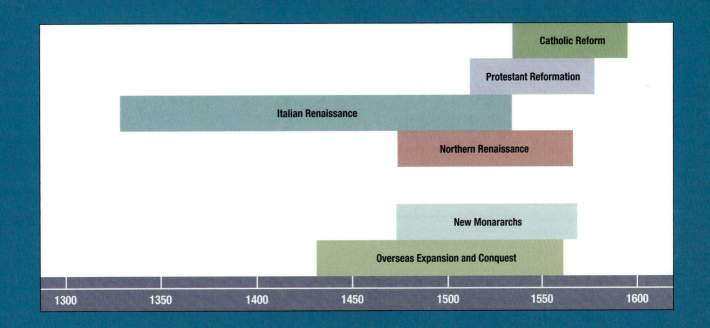

Renaissance, Reformation, and Expansion

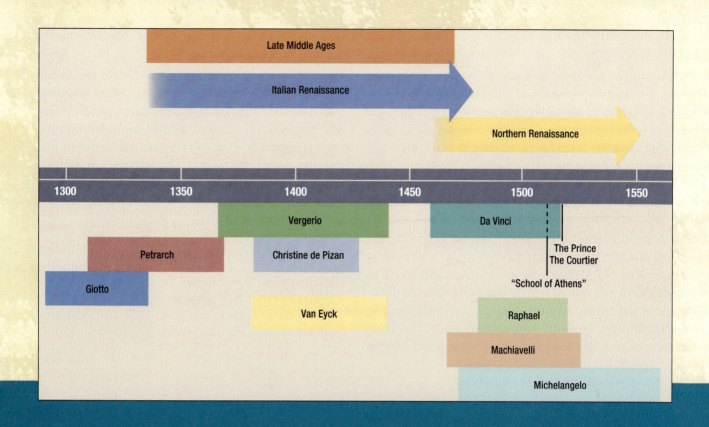

1 The Renaissance

Although in many ways a period of decline and dis-integration, the Late Middle Ages also witnessed an extraordinary outburst of cultural and intellectual creativity known as the Renaissance. The Renaissance started in the fourteenth century in the cities of northern Italy, where scholars and a social elite became more interested in the literature and ideas of ancient Greece and Rome. As interest in Classical civilization grew, so did a tendency to reject many of the ideas and practices of medieval civilization. While remaining deeply religious, people of the Renaissance concerned themselves more with the secular, physical world than medieval people did. The term that best encompasses the meaning of the Renaissance is *humanism*: a new concern with people as powerful, creative individuals in a dynamic secular world. All this was reflected in the literature, art, and societies of northern Italian cities from the fourteenth century through the beginning of the sixteenth century, when invasions and other problems led to a decline of the Renaissance in Italy.

In Northern Europe the Renaissance started during the fifteenth century and lasted through most of the sixteenth century. This Renaissance was heavily influenced by the earlier Italian Renaissance; indeed, it was common for people to travel south across the Alps and return north with the ideas and styles they were exposed to in northern Italy. Nevertheless, the Northern Renaissance had some roots and characteristics that distinguished it from the Italian Renaissance. Above all, it was more integrated with Christian concerns. For example, more emphasis was placed on learning Classical languages to improve translations of the Bible, studying Classical literature for its relation to Christian ideals and life, and producing artistic creations with predominantly religious themes.

This chapter concentrates on one broad issue: the Renaissance. Examined here are traits historians define as typical of the Renaissance, such as literary humanism, humanistic education, and humanism in general. What was literary humanism? How was the development of humanism reflected in educational changes such as the new emphasis on the liberal arts? What problems were faced by those involved in humanism? Artistic and political trends that reflect this humanism are also explored. In what ways did Renaissance art differ from medieval art? How are some of the main elements of the Renaissance reflected in the art of the period? How did political theory mirror characteristics of the Renaissance? What was the nature of the Renaissance in the North? How were some of the connections between medieval concerns and Renaissance style reflected in the art of the Northern Renaissance? Above all, the materials concern efforts by people of that time as well as modern scholars to distinguish the Renaissance as a whole from the preceding Middle Ages. How did important figures of the Italian Renaissance view the Middle Ages? How sharp was the break, if any, with the Middle Ages? How should the Renaissance be interpreted as a whole? Efforts to answer questions such as these have caused considerable scholarly disagreement, most notably over the interpretation by Jacob Burckhardt, which emphasizes the modernity and distinctness of the Italian Renaissance. Secondary sources exemplify this tradition of controversy over the meaning of the Renaissance.

❧ For Classroom Discussion

What was the Renaissance? Draw from the primary sources by Petrarch, Vergerio, de Pizan, Castiglione, and the paintings to answer this question. Several secondary sources deal with this question as well.

Primary Sources

Using Primary Sources: A *Letter to Boccaccio: Literary Humanism*

Primary sources are briefly defined and discussed in the Preface. What follows is a more specific guide to the use of primary sources, focusing on our first primary source, *A Letter to Boccaccio: Literary Humanism*, which immediately follows as an example.

1. When reading a written primary source such as the following selection from *A Letter to Boccaccio*, try to think of every line as evidence. Assume that you are a historian who knows very little about the Renaissance and that this document falls into your hands. Your job is to use this document as evidence to support some conclusions about the Renaissance.

   Actually, before you read this source you already know something about the Renaissance from the chapter introduction, the time line, and the headnote preceding this source. You can use this information to place the document in a historical context better, to gain a sense of how the evidence in the source can be used.

2. Think of questions as you read a primary source. This can keep you alert to how words and lines and sections of the source can be used as evidence. A general question to keep in mind might be, "What does this tell me about this civilization, about how people behaved, how they thought, what they believed?" Try reading each line as a piece of evidence to answer part of this general question. More specific questions can be derived from the headnote and the "consider" points just before the beginning of a source. Here the headnote and the "consider" points indicate that the source might be particularly useful for providing evidence about literary humanism, opposition to literary humanism, and connections between literary humanism and religion.

3. There are several ways you might use the material in this source as evidence. Read the first sentence. It might be argued that this line is evidence that some opposed literary humanism on religious grounds. ("Neither exhortations to virtue nor the argument of approaching death should divert us from literature.") The same line may provide evidence for how literary humanism was defended and even what helped account for its appeal ("in a good mind it excites the love of virtue, and dissipates . . . the fear of death").

   Read the second sentence. It may provide additional evidence that there was opposition to the study of literature on religious grounds ("To desert our studies . . .") and that for the elite, educated members of society ("the properly constituted mind") humanistic literature ("letters") is beneficial ("facilitate our life").

Read the rest of the paragraph. Here Petrarch adds to his argument that for the right people (those with "an acute and healthy intellect"), literary humanism is good, and in the process of making this argument, he provides evidence that central to literary humanism was an admiration of Classical literature and the values expressed in Classical writings. Petrarch cites with admiration Roman figures (Cato, Varro, and Livius Drusus), Roman literature ("Latin literature"), Greek literature, and secular literature (Livius Drusus' "interpretation of the civil law").

Read the second paragraph. Here there may be evidence that literary humanism ("literature" and "secular learning") was not in opposition to Christianity ("our own religion").

Read the third paragraph. What does this paragraph tell us about how different people perceived the relationship between literary humanism and Christianity ("no one . . . has been prevented by literature from following the path of holiness")? For whom might literary humanism have the most appeal ("one takes a lower, another a higher path")?

4. After working on various parts of the source, pull back and consider the source as a whole. Among other things, this aggressive defense of literary humanism provides evidence for what literary humanism was (a movement to revive Classical literature), what it was not (it did not reject Christian virtue or piety), and to whom it appealed (the educated elite). Further, consider the author. Here, the headnote tells us that the letter was written by Francesco Petrarch, who was important in spreading literary humanism; consider whether this colors the source or gives it greater weight as evidence.

A Letter to Boccaccio: Literary Humanism

Francesco Petrarch

Literary humanism, a movement to revive Classical literature and the values expressed in Classical writings, was central to the early Renaissance. This trend, which originated in northern Italy during the fourteenth century, represented a broadening in focus from otherworldly concerns and people as religious beings, which was typical of the Middle Ages, to include the problems of people and nature in this world. The individual most commonly associated with it and perhaps most responsible for its spread was the Florentine Francesco Petrarch (1304–1374). Best known for his love sonnets to Laura, he also collected and translated many Classical works and wrote numerous letters—often extolling the Classical authors and even writing in their style. In the following selection from a 1362 letter to his friend Boccaccio, Petrarch offered reassurance and responded to charges typically made against humanistic learning.

CONSIDER: *The nature of the charges Petrarch is refuting; how Petrarch related humanism to religion; Petrarch's perception of the benefits of literary humanism.*

Neither exhortations to virtue nor the argument of approaching death should divert us from literature; for in a good mind it excites the love of virtue, and dissipates, or at least diminishes, the fear of death. To desert our studies shows want of self-confidence rather than wisdom, for letters do not hinder but aid the properly constituted mind which possesses them; they facilitate our life, they do not retard it. Just as many kinds of food which lie heavy on an enfeebled and nauseated stomach furnish excellent nourishment for one who is well but famishing, so in our studies many things which are deadly to the weak mind may prove most salutary to an acute and healthy intellect, especially if in our use of both food and learning we exercise proper discretion. If it were otherwise, surely the zeal of certain persons who persevered to the end could not have roused such admiration. Cato, I never forget, acquainted himself with Latin literature as he was growing old, and Greek when he had really become an old man. Varro, who reached his hundredth year still reading and writing, parted from life sooner than from his love of study. Livius Drusus, although weakened by age and afflicted with blindness, did not give up his interpretation of the civil law, which he carried on to the great advantage of the state. . . .

Besides these and innumerable others like them, have not all those of our own religion whom we should wish most to imitate devoted their whole lives to literature, and grown old and died in the same pursuit? Some, indeed, were overtaken by death while still at work reading or writing. To none of them, so far as I know, did it prove a disadvantage to be noted for secular learning. . . .

While I know that many have become famous for piety without learning, at the same time I know of no one who has been prevented by literature from following the path of holiness. The apostle Paul was, to be sure,

SOURCE: James Harvey Robinson and Henry Winchester Rolfe, *Petrarch: The First Modern Scholar and Man of Letters* (New York: Haskell House, 1898), pp. 391–395.

accused of having his head turned by study, but the world has long ago passed its verdict upon this accusation. If I may be allowed to speak for myself, it seems to me that, although the path to virtue by the way of ignorance may be plain, it fosters sloth. The goal of all good people is the same, but the ways of reaching it are many and various. Some advance slowly, others with more spirit; some obscurely, others again conspicuously. One takes a lower, another a higher path. Although all alike are on the road to happiness, certainly the more elevated path is the more glorious. Hence ignorance, however devout, is by no means to be put on a plane with the enlightened devoutness of one familiar with literature. Nor can you pick me out from the whole array of unlettered saints, an example so holy that I cannot match it with a still holier one from the other group.

On the Liberal Arts
Peter Paul Vergerio

Closely associated with the rise of literary humanism was a new emphasis on the more broadly defined "liberal arts." This emphasis was manifested in a new concern with education; a change in educational curriculum constituted an institutional development that was enduring and that had wide-ranging effects. The first to express this emphasis systematically in an educational program was Peter Paul Vergerio (1370–1444). He taught in several Italian universities, and in his main treatise, On the Liberal Arts, he rejected much of the content and methods of medieval education. Vergerio presents his views on the growing importance of the liberal arts in the following selection from a letter written to Ubertinus of Carrara.

CONSIDER: *What is particularly humanistic rather than scholastic or medieval about this view; how Vergerio justifies his choice of the three subjects in this proposed curriculum; what Petrarch might think of this letter.*

Your grandfather, Francesco I, a man distinguished for his capacity in affairs and for his sound judgment, was in the habit of saying that a parent owes three duties to his children. The first of these is to bestow upon them names of which they need not feel ashamed. For not seldom, out of caprice, or even indifference, or perhaps from a wish to perpetuate a family name, a father in naming his child inflicts upon him a misfortune which clings to him for life. The second obligation is this: to provide that his child be brought up in a city of distinction, for this not only concerns his future self-respect, but is closely connected with

SOURCE: From William Harrison Woodward, *Vittorino da Feltre and Other Humanist Educators* (Cambridge, England: Cambridge University Press; New York: Bureau of Publications, Teachers College, Columbia University, 1963), pp. 96–97, 106–107. Reprinted by permission.

the third and most important care which is due from father to son. This is the duty of seeing that he be trained in sound learning. For no wealth, no possible security against the future, can be compared with the gift of an education in grave and liberal studies. By them a man may win distinction for the most modest name, and bring honour to the city of his birth however obscure it may be. But we must remember that whilst a man may escape from the burden of an unlucky name, or from the contempt attaching to a city of no repute, by changing the one or quitting the other, he can never remedy the neglect of early education. The foundation, therefore, of this last must be laid in the first years of life, the disposition moulded whilst it is susceptible and the mind trained whilst it is retentive.

This duty, common indeed to all parents, is specially incumbent upon such as hold high station. For the lives of men of position are passed, as it were, in public view; and are fairly expected to serve as witness to personal merit and capacity on the part of those who occupy such exceptional place amongst their fellow men. . . .

We come now to the consideration of the various subjects which may rightly be included under the name of "Liberal Studies." Amongst these I accord the first place to History, on grounds both of its attractiveness and of its utility, qualities which appeal equally to the scholar and to the statesman. Next in importance ranks Moral Philosophy, which indeed is, in a peculiar sense, a "Liberal Art," in that its purpose is to teach men the secret of true freedom. History, then, gives us the concrete examples of the precepts inculcated by philosophy. The one shews what men should do, the other what men have said and done in the past, and what practical lessons we may draw therefrom for the present day. I would indicate as the third main branch of study, Eloquence, which indeed holds a place of distinction amongst the refined Arts. By philosophy we learn the essential truth of things, which by eloquence we so exhibit in orderly adornment as to bring conviction to differing minds. And history provides the light of experience—cumulative wisdom fit to supplement the force of reason and the persuasion of eloquence. For we allow that soundness of judgment, wisdom of speech, integrity of conduct are the marks of a truly liberal temper.

The City of Ladies
Christine de Pizan

Most of the great cultural figures of the Renaissance were men. Nevertheless, some women were able to produce works, achieve recognition, and defend women against male detractors. The most famous of these was Christine de Pizan

SOURCE: Excerpts from *The Book of the City of Ladies* by Christine de Pizan, translated by Rosalind Brown-Grant (New York: Penguin Putnam, Inc., 1999) pp. 29, 30, 139–141.

(c.1363–c.1431). Born in Venice, she moved with her family to Paris, where her father became a physician and astrologer at the French royal court. Unusually well educated, she wrote several poems and books, the most widely read of which was The City of Ladies *(1405). In the following excerpt Christine de Pizan questions an allegorical figure representing Lady Reason about women's political and educational abilities and about men's low opinions of women.*

CONSIDER: *What the common assumptions and arguments about women are; how Christine de Pizan attacks those assumptions and arguments; ways in which her writing embodies traits of the Renaissance.*

35. Against those who claim that women aren't intelligent enough to learn the law.

Even though God has often endowed many women with great intelligence, it would not be right for them to abandon their customary modesty and to go about bringing cases before a court, as there are already enough men to do so. Why send three men to carry a burden which two can manage quite comfortably?

"However, if there are those who maintain that women aren't *intelligent* enough to learn the law, I would contradict them by citing numerous examples of women of both the past and the present who were great philosophers and who excelled in many disciplines which are much more difficult than simply learning the laws and the statutes of men. I'll tell you more about these women in a moment. Moreover, in reply to those who think that women are lacking in the ability to govern wisely or to establish good customs, I'll give you examples from history of several worthy ladies who mastered these arts. To give you a better idea of what I'm saying, I'll even cite you a few women from your own time who were widowed and whose competence in organizing and managing their households after their husbands' deaths attests to the fact that an intelligent woman can succeed in any domain."

✤

36. Against those men who claim it is not good for women to be educated.

After hearing these words, I, Christine, said, "My lady, I can clearly see that much good has been brought into the world by women. Even if some wicked women have done evil things, it still seems to me that this is far outweighed by all the good that other women have done and continue to do. This is particularly true of those who are wise and well educated in either the arts or the sciences, whom we mentioned before. That's why I'm all the more amazed at the opinion of some men who state that they are completely opposed to their daughters, wives or other female relatives engaging in study, for fear that their morals will be corrupted."

Rectitude replied, "This should prove to you that not all men's arguments are based on reason, and that these men in particular are wrong. There are absolutely no grounds for assuming that knowledge of moral disciplines, which actually inculcate virtue, would have a morally corrupting effect. Indeed, there's no doubt whatsoever that such forms of knowledge correct one's vices and improve one's morals. How could anyone possibly think that by studying good lessons and advice one will be any the worse for it? This view is completely unthinkable and untenable. I'm not saying that it's a good idea for men or women to study sorcery or any other type of forbidden science, since the Holy Church did not ban people from practising them for nothing. However, it's just that it's not true to say that women will be corrupted by knowing what's right and proper. . . .

"Therefore, it is not all men, especially not the most intelligent, who agree with the view that it is a bad idea to educate women. However, it's true that those who are not very clever come out with this opinion because they don't want women to know more than they do. Your own father, who was a great astrologer and philosopher, did not believe that knowledge of the sciences reduced a woman's worth. Indeed, as you know, it gave him great pleasure to see you take so readily to studying the arts. Rather, it was because your mother, as a woman, held the view that you should spend your time spinning like the other girls, that you did not receive a more advanced or detailed initiation into the sciences. But, as that proverb which we've already had occasion to quote says, 'What is in our nature cannot be taken away.' Despite your mother's opposition, you did manage to glean some grains of knowledge from your studies, thanks to your own natural inclination for learning. It's obvious to me that you do not esteem yourself any less for having this knowledge: in fact, you seem to treasure it, and quite rightly so."

The Prince
Niccolò Machiavelli

The Italian Renaissance developed in an environment in which politics took on an increasingly competitive, secular tone. Within each Italian state, parties fought for power while at the same time the states fought each other for dominance or advantage. After 1492, Italy was invaded numerous times by Spain, France, and the Holy Roman Empire. These developments are reflected in the life and work of the great Renaissance political theorist Niccolò Machiavelli (1469–1527).

SOURCE: From *The Prince and the Discourses* by Niccolò Machiavelli, translated by Luigi Ricci and revised by E. R. P. Vincent (1935), pp. 56, 65–66, by permission of Oxford University Press.

Born in Florence when it was under the rule of the Medicis, Machiavelli initiated his career in the Florentine civil service in 1498 during the period when the Medicis were out of power, replaced by a republican government. He rose to important diplomatic posts within the government, but was forced into retirement when the Medici family came back to power in 1512. He never gave up hope of returning to favor, and he wrote his most famous work, The Prince *(1513), in part as an application to the Medici rulers for a job in the Florentine government. The book has since become a classic treatise in political theory, above all for the way that it divorces politics from theology and metaphysics. The following selections from* The Prince *illustrate its style and some of its main themes.*

CONSIDER: *The ways in which this work reflects values or practices typical of the Renaissance; how these same principles might be applied to twentieth-century politics.*

It now remains to be seen what are the methods and rules for a prince as regards to his subjects and friends. And as I know that many have written of this, I fear that my writing about it may be deemed presumptuous, differing as I do, especially in this matter, from the opinions of others. But my intention being to write something of use to those who understand, it appears to me more proper to go to the real truth of the matter than to its imagination; and many have imagined republics and principalities which have never been seen or known to exist in reality; for how we live is so far removed from how we ought to live, that he who abandons what is done for what ought to be done, will rather learn to bring about his own ruin than his preservation. A man who wishes to make a profession of goodness in everything must necessarily come to grief among so many who are not good. Therefore it is necessary for a prince, who wishes to maintain himself, to learn how not to be good, and to use this knowledge and not use it, according to the necessity of the case. . . .

It is not, therefore, necessary for a prince to have all the above-named qualities, but it is very necessary to seem to have them. I would even be bold to say that to possess them and always to observe them is dangerous, but to appear to possess them is useful. Thus it is well to seem merciful, faithful, humane, sincere, religious, and also to be so; but you must have the mind so disposed that when it is needful to be otherwise you may be able to change to the opposite qualities. And it must be understood that a prince, and especially a new prince, cannot observe all those things which are considered good in men, being often obliged, in order to maintain the state, to act against faith, against charity, against humanity, and against religion. And, therefore, he must have a mind disposed to adapt itself according to the wind, and as the variations of fortune dictate, and, as I said before, not deviate from what is good, if possible, but be able to do evil if constrained.

A prince must take great care that nothing goes out of his mouth which is not full of the above-named five qualities, and, to see and hear him, he should seem to be all mercy, faith, integrity, humanity, and religion. And nothing is more necessary than to seem to have this last quality, for men in general judge more by the eyes than by the hands, for every one can see, but very few have to feel. Everybody sees what you appear to be, few feel what you are, and those few will not dare to oppose themselves to the many, who have the majesty of the state to defend them; and in the actions of men, and especially of princes, from which there is no appeal, the end justifies the means. Let a prince therefore aim at conquering and maintaining the state, and the means will always be judged honourable and praised by every one, for the vulgar is always taken by appearances and the issue of the event; and the world consists only of the vulgar, and the few who are not vulgar are isolated when the many have a rallying point in the prince.

The Book of the Courtier
Baldesar Castiglione

In the Italian states, the most prestigious life took place in the courts of rulers. While Machiavelli wrote about methods and rules for the successful prince, others described the qualities necessary for men or women hoping to rise or maintain their position in court life. The most famous of these writers was the Italian diplomat Baldesar Castiglione (1478–1529), who wrote The Book of the Courtier *while a member of the Duke of Urbino's court. In the following excerpt, Castiglione describes first, the best qualities of the courtier—the ideal "Renaissance man"—and second, the virtues and actions best suited to women of the court.*

CONSIDER: *Why Castiglione considers noble birth important; what talents Castiglione thinks are most important for the courtier's success; how a woman's path to success at court differs from a man's.*

"Thus, I would have our Courtier born of a noble and genteel family; because it is far less becoming for one of low birth to fail to do virtuous things than for one of noble birth, who, should he stray from the path of his forebears, stains the family name, and not only fails to achieve anything but loses what has been achieved already. For noble birth is like a bright lamp that makes manifest and visible deeds both good and bad, kindling and spurring on to virtue as much for fear of dishonor as for hope of praise. . . .

SOURCE: Baldesar Castiglione, *The Book of the Courtier,* trans. by Charles S. Singleton (New York: Doubleday, 1959), pp. 28–30, 32–34, 70, 206.

Besides his noble birth, I would wish the Courtier favored in this other respect, and endowed by nature not only with talent and with beauty of countenance and person, but with that certain grace which we call an 'air,' which shall make him at first sight pleasing and lovable to all who see him; and let this be an adornment informing and attending all his actions, giving the promise outwardly that such a one is worthy of the company and the favor of every great lord." . . .

"But to come to some particulars: I hold that the principal and true profession of the Courtier must be that of arms . . . which I wish him to exercise with vigor; and let him be known among the others as bold, energetic, and faithful to whomever he serves. . . . The more our Courtier excels in this art, the more will he merit praise; although I do not deem it necessary that he have the perfect knowledge of things and other qualities that befit a commander, for since this would launch us on too great a sea, we shall be satisfied, as we have said, if he have complete loyalty and an undaunted spirit, and be always seen to have them. . . .

Therefore, let the man we are seeking be exceedingly fierce, harsh, and always among the first, wherever the enemy is; and in every other place, humane, modest, reserved, avoiding ostentation above all things as well as that impudent praise of himself by which a man always arouses hatred and disgust in all who hear him."

"I would have him more than passably learned in letters, at least in those studies which we call the humanities. Let him be conversant not only with the Latin language, but with Greek as well, because of the abundance and variety of things that are so divinely written therein. Let him be versed in the poets, as well as in the orators and historians, and let him be practiced also in writing verse and prose, especially in our own vernacular; for, besides the personal satisfaction he will take in this, in this way he will never want for pleasant entertainment with the ladies, who are usually fond of such

things. . . . These studies, moreover, will make him fluent, and (as Aristippus said to the tyrant) bold and self-confident in speaking with everyone. However, I would have our Courtier keep one precept firmly in mind, namely, in this as in everything else, to be cautious and reserved rather than forward, and take care not to get the mistaken notion that he knows something he does not know."

I think that in her ways, manners, words, gestures, and bearing, a woman ought to be very unlike a man; for just as he must show a certain solid and sturdy manliness, so it is seemly for a woman to have a soft and delicate tenderness, with an air of womanly sweetness in her every movement, which, in her going and staying, and in whatever she says, shall always make her appear the woman without any resemblance to a man.

"Now, if this precept be added to the rules which these gentlemen have taught the Courtier, then I think she ought to be able to follow many such and adorn herself with the best accomplishments, as signor Gasparo says. For I hold that many virtues of the mind are as necessary to a woman as to a man; also, gentle birth; to avoid affectation, to be naturally graceful in all her actions, to be mannerly, clever, prudent, not arrogant, not envious, not slanderous, not vain, not contentious, not inept, to know how to gain and hold the favor of her mistress and of all others, to perform well and gracefully the exercises that are suitable for women. And I do think that beauty is more necessary to her than to the Courtier, for truly that woman lacks much who lacks beauty. Also she must be more circumspect, and more careful not to give occasion for evil being said of her, and conduct herself so that she may not only escape being sullied by guilt but even by the suspicion of it, for a woman has not so many ways of defending herself against false calumnies as a man has."

Visual Sources

Using Visual Sources:
The School of Athens:
Art and Classical Culture

Visual sources are briefly defined and discussed in the Preface. What follows is a more specific guide to the use of visual sources, focusing on our first visual source, *The School of Athens*, which immediately follows as an example.

1. Try to look at visual sources as if they were written, primary documents. As with primary documents, assume that you are a historian who knows very little about the Renaissance and who discovers this visual source, *The School of Athens* by Raphael. Your goal is to try to "read" it as evidence to support some conclusions about the Renaissance.

Without some guidance, "reading" a visual source as historical evidence is more difficult than using a written source. The reproduction makes the details harder to see and most people are not used to looking at a picture in this analytical way. Therefore in the first paragraph of the headnote to *The School of Athens* there is a written description that puts into words some of what appears in the visual source; in the second paragraph there is an analysis of the evidence drawn from the photo. Here, as with most visual sources, it is useful to go back and forth between the photo and the written description and analysis that accompany the photo.

2. As with primary documents, think of questions as you look at the visual source and as you read the written guide to it. The general question to keep in mind is, "What does this tell me about this civilization, about how people behaved, how they thought, or what they believed?" Here this general question might be rephrased to "What does this tell me about the civilization of the Renaissance, about the art and culture of the Renaissance, and about the main figures of the Renaissance?" Other questions are suggested in the "consider" points, such as how the society and culture of the Renaissance differed from those of the Middle Ages.

3. Here the first paragraph of the headnote alerts us to what can be seen and recognized in the fresco by the sixteenth-century viewers for whom it was intended. The painting admiringly shows Classical (Greek) philosophers like Plato, Aristotle, Socrates, Diogenes, and Pythagoras. At the same time, the fresco admiringly shows leading figures of the Italian Renaissance like Leonardo da Vinci, Michelangelo, and Bramante. It also shows the artist himself as a person proud of his work and position.

The second paragraph of the headnote suggests some of the ways the information derived from Raphael's *The School of Athens* can be used as historical evidence about the Renaissance. The title of the fresco and its grand content suggest that it was a tribute to Greek philosophy, and the headnote confirms this. The use of contemporary artists, architects, philosophers, and writers as models for the figures in the painting is evidence for how interconnected the cultural elite in northern Italy was. The nature of the fresco itself can be used as evidence that one trait of Renaissance art and perhaps culture in general was realism, as is suggested in the final sentence of the headnote. The headnote also provides information about where this fresco was placed—across from a fresco of Christian theologians—which suggests that the Renaissance valued Classical culture without rejecting Christianity.

4. Now pull back and consider the source as a whole. What might it mean that such a large fresco with this subject matter was commissioned, painted, and placed in such a place of prominence? What might be made of the individualized differences in the figures? In what ways might a similar sort of painting or fresco be created today and what might such a scene depict?

The School of Athens: Art and Classical Culture

Raphael

Raphael's famous fresco in the Vatican, The School of Athens, painted between 1508 and 1511, is one of the most revealing masterpieces of Renaissance art (figure 1.1). It shows the major Greek philosophers arranged in different positions and groups according to their philosophical inclinations. In the center stands Plato, pointing upward to confirm his commitment to his theory of ideas and holding a copy of his Timaeus in his left hand, and Aristotle, pointing downward to indicate his empirical orientation. Correspondingly, the left side of the painting is filled with metaphysical philosophers with a statue of Apollo (patron of poetry) overhead, while the right side shows physical scientists under a statue of Athena (goddess of reason). Socrates is on the left, counting out points on his fingers to a group of younger men. Sprawled on the steps in the center is Diogenes. At the lower left Phythagoras demonstrates his mathematics on a tablet. The figures of Classical authors and gods are actually portraits of Raphael's contemporaries as well. The figure of Plato is probably Leonardo da Vinci. Writing in the center foreground is the brooding, pessimistic philosopher Heraclitus, a portrait of Michelangelo. On the right bending over a geometric diagram is Euclid, a portrait of the architect Bramante. Behind him Ptolemy holds a globe, while on the far right the artist, Raphael, looks out of the picture.

In content, then, this painting is a tribute to Greek philosophy, which played such an important role in the Italian Renaissance. However, it goes further. Raphael belonged to a group of thinkers and artists who met to discuss philosophy, much as in this picture, but as implied in the picture, both the Platonic and Aristotelian points of view were respected in the Renaissance. Moreover, the artists, architects, sculptors, philosophers, and writers who served as models for the figures in this painting knew and communicated with each other; thus this fresco displays the many interconnections of the cultural elite in northern Italy, particularly in Florence. Even this

FIGURE 1.1 (© Scala/Art Resource, NY)

fresco's specific location in the Vatican is revealing. On the opposing wall is another fresco, Raphael's Disputa, *which depicts the great Christian theologians of various eras. The placement of these two frescos symbolizes values characteristic of the Renaissance: glorification of pagan culture without rejecting Christianity. Finally, the use of perspective and the newness of the architectural design exemplify the Renaissance traits of realism and bold innovation.*

CONSIDER: *The way in which this reflects a society and attitudes different from those of the Middle Ages.*

Giovanni Arnolfini and His Bride: Symbolism and the Northern Renaissance

Jan van Eyck

It should not be concluded even in art that the Renaissance constituted a sudden and complete break with the past. Even when in style and subject matter paintings reflect the realism, humanism, and individualism of the Renaissance, they also reflect medieval assumptions and concerns that remained.

This can be seen in a Northern Renaissance masterpiece, Giovanni Arnolfini and His Bride, *painted in 1434 by the Flemish artist Jan van Eyck (figure 1.2). The scene appears to be quite secular: Giovanni Arnolfini, an Italian businessman residing in Bruges, is standing with his bride in a private bridal chamber taking marriage vows (at this time two people could contract a legitimate marriage outside the Church). Around them various objects that might typically be found in such a room are quite realistically depicted. To the medieval eye these objects have well-known symbolic meaning that give this scene considerable religious and cultural significance. The single lighted candle was the traditional nuptial candle, symbolizing Christ and implying divine light. The convex mirror reflected the chamber, testifying to the presence of two witnesses (one of whom was the artist, van Eyck, who tells us just above the mirror that "Jan van Eyck was here"), and represented the all-seeing eye of God. The shoes (to the left), so appropriate for the muddy streets of Bruges, are off, indicating that this couple is standing on holy ground. The dog in the foreground symbolizes fidelity. The ripening peaches to the left on the chest and windowsill represent fertility and perhaps paradise lost. On the post of a chair near the bed is a carved Margaret, patron saint of childbirth. The pose of the couple suggests relationships*

FIGURE 1.2 (Erich Lessing/Art Resource, NY)

FIGURE 1.3 (Erich Lessing/Art Resource, NY)

between husband and wife: He is dominating by his frontal pose; she is deferentially turned toward him.

Thus this painting is both a realistic depiction of two individuals with distinct personalities (as revealed particularly in their faces) in a natural setting and a symbolic representation of the meanings of marriage in the fifteenth century, with all its religious implications. And that this is a portrait of an Italian merchant and his bride in a room furnished with items coming from all areas of Europe, in Bruges, a northern center of banking and commerce, reflects the growing importance and wealth of the middle class and international trade during this period.

CONSIDER: *The ways this reflects a society and attitudes similar to those of the Middle Ages.*

Wealth, Culture, and Diplomacy

Hans Holbein

Hans Holbein's 1533 painting, The Ambassadors *(figure 1.3), reveals the mixture of wealth, culture, and power that were key elements of the Renaissance. It depicts two sumptuously dressed French ambassadors at the Court of King Henry VII of England. Their clothes and stance stress the growing prestige and importance of diplomats in furthering the interests of states. Part of their mission was to broker an accord between*

SOURCE: Hans Holbein, *The Ambassadors* (London, The National Gallery).

the Catholic church and the Lutheran-sympathizing English monarchy, and the failure of that accord is indicated by the lute (representing the hoped-for harmony) resting on the lower shelf of the table between the two men and its broken string that lies next to the open Lutheran hymnbook. Next to the lute is a terrestrial globe, a surveyor's square, a pair of compasses, and a merchant's arithmetic book, all stressing the themes of intellectual, commercial, and territorial discovery as well as the conflict for lands and wealth among the European powers that were so important during the Renaissance. On the top shelf are instruments and a celestial globe representing the growing interest in understanding the heavens, time, place, and navigation. As a whole, the painting testifies to the cosmopolitan and competitive qualities of Renaissance life and politics among Europe's elites.

CONSIDER: *How this painting might fit with the themes of Renaissance humanism and individualism; the significance of Holbein, a German artist, painting this canvas of (and for) French diplomats who were stationed in England.*

 # Secondary Sources

Using Secondary Sources: *The Civilization of the Renaissance in Italy*

Secondary sources are briefly defined and discussed in the Preface. What follows is a more specific guide to the use of secondary sources, focusing on our first secondary source, *The Civilization of the Renaissance in Italy*, which immediately follows as an example.

1. Try to read a secondary source like *The Civilization of the Renaissance in Italy* by Jacob Burckhardt not as historical evidence (as you would read a primary source), but as a set of conclusions—an interpretation of the evidence from primary sources—by a scholar (usually a historian). Your job is to try to understand what the writer's interpretation is, to evaluate whether any arguments or evidence the writer presents seems to support it adequately, and to decide in what ways you agree or disagree with that interpretation.

2. Try to think of questions as you read a secondary source. This can keep you alert to why the author selects and presents only certain information and what conclusions the author is trying to convey to the reader. Perhaps the two most important questions to keep in mind are, What question is this author trying to answer? and What does all of what the author has written add up to? For each secondary source, the headnote to the source and the "consider" points provide some guidance for these two questions and related questions.

Here the headnote to this secondary source tells us that the author, Jacob Burckhardt, is trying to interpret the Renaissance, particularly as something distinct from the preceding Middle Ages and superior to it. The "consider" points and the headnote alert us to the fact that many historians, particularly medievalists, do not agree with Burckhardt's interpretation.

3. Try reading and summarizing in a few words what the author is trying to say or argue in each paragraph. What conclusions is he making?

One could summarize the first paragraph by saying that Burckhardt is trying to convince us that the Middle Ages was strikingly different from the Italian Renaissance. To convince us, first he argues that people in the Middle Ages were relatively unaware ("lay dreaming . . . beneath a common veil"), immature ("the veil was woven of faith, illusion, and childish prepossession"), unrealistic ("the world and history were seen" through this veil as "clad in strange hues"), and unindividualistic ("Man was conscious of himself only as a member of a race, people, party . . ."). Second, he argues that all this dramatically changed in Italy ("In Italy this veil first melted into air"), where people gained the ability to become rationalistic ("*objective* treatment . . . of all the things of this world became possible"), individualistic ("man became a spiritual *individual*"), and self-conscious ("recognised himself as such").

In the second paragraph, Burckhardt concludes that the Renaissance began in the fourteenth century in Italy ("the close of the thirteenth century"), was uniquely Italian ("would have been impossible in any other country"), and was admirably individualistic (these Italians "knew little of false modesty or of hypocrisy" and were "not . . . afraid of singularity").

4. Pull back and consider a secondary source as a whole. Try to formulate the author's arguments and conclusions in a nutshell.

Here you might say that Burckhardt concludes that the Italian Renaissance was a definitive break from the Middle Ages and the beginning of modernity characterized by rationalism and individualism.

Finally, do you agree with the author? From the headnote and "consider" points, you might keep in mind how controversial this interpretation has become. Indeed this controversy is the subject of the next secondary source, *The Myth of the Renaissance*.

The Civilization of the Renaissance in Italy

Jacob Burckhardt

Modern interpretations of the Renaissance almost uniformly start with the Swiss historian Jacob Burckhardt's The Civilization of the Renaissance in Italy, first published in 1860. Burckhardt rejected a chronological approach and pictured the Italian Renaissance of the fourteenth and fifteenth centuries as a whole, strikingly distinct from the preceding Middle Ages and clearly a superior civilization. Until the 1920s, historians almost unanimously accepted his interpretation. After that time various aspects of his thesis were attacked, particularly by medievalists. In recent decades, however, Burckhardt's work has gained new respectability, at least as an idealized cultural history of the Italian Renaissance. In any case, all historians who approach this topic must deal with Burckhardt's argument, some of the central points of which appear in the following excerpt.

CONSIDER: *What most distinguishes the Italian Renaissance from the preceding Middle Ages according to Burckhardt; any support the primary documents might provide for this argument; how a proud medievalist might respond to this argument.*

In the Middle Ages both sides of human consciousness—that which was turned within as that which was turned without—lay dreaming or half awake beneath a common veil. The veil was woven of faith, illusion, and childish prepossession, through which the world and history were seen clad in strange hues. Man was conscious of himself only as a member of a race, people, party, family, or corporation—only through some general category. In Italy this veil first melted into air; an *objective* treatment and consideration of the state and of all the things of this world became possible. The *subjective* side at the same time asserted itself with corresponding emphasis; man became a spiritual *individual*, and recognised himself as such. In the same way the Greek had once distinguished himself from the barbarian, and the Arabian had felt himself an individual at a time when other Asiatics knew themselves only as members of a race. . . .

In far earlier times we can here and there detect a development of free personality which in Northern Europe either did not occur at all, or could not display itself in the same manner. . . . But at the close of the thirteenth century Italy began to swarm with individuality; the charm laid upon human personality was dissolved; and a thousand figures meet us each in its own special shape and dress. Dante's great poem would have been impossible in any other country of Europe, if only for the reason that they all still lay under the spell of race. For Italy the august poet, through the wealth of individuality which he set forth, was the most national herald of his time. But this unfolding of the treasures of human nature in literature and art—this many-sided representation and criticism—will be discussed in separate chapters; here we have to deal only with the psychological fact itself. This fact appears in the most decisive and unmistakable form. The Italians of the fourteenth century knew little of false modesty or of hypocrisy in any shape; not one of them was afraid of singularity, of being and seeming unlike his neighbours.

The Myth of the Renaissance

Peter Burke

Many historians attacked Burckhardt's interpretation and the legacy built up around it. These historians argued that Burckhardt overemphasized how modern the Renaissance was. They stressed how much the Renaissance, even in Italy, was still part of the medieval world. Other historians have responded that criticisms of Burckhardt go too far. In the following selection Peter Burke criticizes Burckhardt's idea of the Renaissance as a myth and describes the main objections to it.

CONSIDER: *Why, according to Burke, Burckhardt's idea of the Renaissance is a myth; how a supporter of Burckhardt might respond; whether the sources give greater support to Burckhardt's or Burke's interpretation.*

SOURCE: Jacob Burckhardt, *The Civilization of the Renaissance in Italy,* trans. S. G. C. Middlemore (London: George Allen and Unwin, Ltd.; New York: The Macmillan Co., 1890), p. 129.

SOURCE: From Peter Burke, *The Renaissance,* pp. 1, 3–5. Reprinted with permission by Humanities Press International, Inc., Atlantic Highlands, NJ, 07716; and The Macmillan Press, Ltd.

Jacob Burckhardt defined the period in terms of two concepts, "individualism" and "modernity." "In the Middle Ages," according to Burckhardt, "human consciousness . . . lay dreaming or half awake beneath a common veil. . . . Man was conscious of himself only as a member of a race, people, party, family, or corporation—only through some general category." In Renaissance Italy, however, "this veil first melted into air . . . man became a spiritual *individual*, and recognised himself as such." Renaissance meant modernity. The Italian was, Burckhardt wrote, "the first-born among the sons of modern Europe." The fourteenth-century poet Petrarch was "one of the first truly modern men." The great renewal of art and ideas began in Italy, and at a later stage the new attitudes and the new artistic forms spread to the rest of Europe.

This idea of the Renaissance is a myth. . . .

Burckhardt's mistake was to accept the scholars and artists of the period at their own valuation, to take this story of rebirth at its face value and to elaborate it into a book. To the old formulae of the restoration of the arts and the revival of classical antiquity, he added new ones such as individualism, realism, and modernity. . . .

This nineteenth-century myth of the Renaissance is still taken seriously by many people. Television companies and organisers of package tours still make money out of it. However, professional historians have become dissatisfied with this version of the Renaissance, even if they continue to find the period and the movement attractive. The point is that the grand edifice erected by Burckhardt and his contemporaries has not stood the test of time. More exactly, it has been undermined by the researchers of the medievalists in particular. Their arguments depend on innumerable points of detail, but they are of two main kinds.

In the first place, there are arguments to the effect that so-called "Renaissance men" were really rather medieval. They were more traditional in their behaviour, assumptions and ideals than we tend to think—and also more traditional than they saw themselves. Hindsight suggests that even Petrarch, "one of the first truly modern men," according to Burckhardt, had many attitudes in common with the centuries he described as "dark". . . .

In the second place, the medievalists have accumulated arguments to the effect that the Renaissance was not such a singular event as Burckhardt and his contemporaries once thought and that the term should really be used in the plural. There were various "renascences" in the Middle Ages, notably in the twelfth century and in the age of Charlemagne. In both cases there was a combination of literary and artistic achievements with a revival of interest in classical learning, and in both cases contemporaries described their age as one of restoration, rebirth or "renovation."

Machiavelli and the Renaissance
Federico Chabod

Reactions to and appreciations of Machiavelli's thought in The Prince *form an apparently contradictory history in themselves. On the one hand, few thinkers in the history of political theory rank more highly than Machiavelli; he is recognized as being the first modern political theorist. On the other hand, there is a more popular tradition of rejecting his ideas as immoral; the term* Machiavellian *is pejorative, referring to political opportunism and ruthlessness. In the following selection Federico Chabod, an Italian historian who has written extensively on Machiavelli, analyzes Machiavelli and the significance of his ideas.*

CONSIDER: *Why Machiavelli's ideas are so appropriate to the historical realities of his time; how the selections from* The Prince *support this interpretation of Machiavelli.*

The *leitmotiv* of Machiavelli's posthumous life was his great assertion as a thinker, representing his true and essential contribution to the history of human thought, namely, the clear recognition of the autonomy and the necessity of politics, "which lies outside the realm of what is morally good or evil." Machiavelli thereby rejected the medieval concept of "unity" and became one of the pioneers of modern spirit. . . .

For Machiavelli accepted the political challenge in its entirety; he swept aside every criterion of action not suggested by the concept of *raison d'état*, i.e., by the exact evaluation of the historical moment and the constructive forces which *The Prince* must employ in order to achieve his aim; and he held that the activities of rulers were limited only by their capacity and energy. Hence, he paved the way for absolute governments, which theoretically were completely untrammelled, both in their home and in their foreign policies.

If this was made possible by the Florentine Secretary's recognition of the autonomy of politics, it depended, conversely, on his own peculiar conception of the State, which he identified with the government, or rather with its personal Head. Accordingly, in *The Prince* all his attention was riveted on the human figure of the man who held the reins of government and so epitomized in his person the whole of public life. Such a conception, determined directly by the historical experience which Machiavelli possessed in such outstanding measure and presupposing a sustained effort on the part of the central government, was essential to the success and preeminence of his doctrine.

SOURCE: Federico Chabod, *Machiavelli and the Renaissance,* trans. David Moore (Cambridge, MA: Harvard University Press, 1960), pp. 116–118. Copyright © 1958 by Federico Chabod. Reprinted by permission.

This was a turning-point in the history of the Christian world. The minds of political theorists were no longer trammelled by Catholic dogma. The structure of the State was not yet threatened in other directions by any revolt of the individual conscience. An entire moral world, if it was not eclipsed, had at any rate receded into the shadows, nor was any other at once forthcoming to take its place and to inspire a new fervour of religious belief; hence, political thought could express itself without being confused by considerations of a different character. It was an era in which unitarian States were being created amid the ruins of the social and political order of the Middle Ages, an era in which it was necessary to place all the weapons of resistance in the hands of those who had still to combat the forces of feudalism and particularism. It was, in short, an era in which it was essential that the freedom and grandeur of political action and the strength and authority of central government should be clearly affirmed. Only thus was it possible to obliterate once and for all the traces of the past and to offer to the society of the future, in the guise of a precept, the weapons which would preserve the life of the united nation in the face of disruptive elements old and new.

This was the great achievement of Niccolò Machiavelli, who accordingly became the legitimate representative of politics and government, the man who was at once admired and hated, followed and opposed, throughout two centuries of European history; and it was on him that the eyes of men were to be fixed, because only he, a poor, weary citizen of a city divided against itself, had proclaimed with an eloquence that was now muted the nature of the arms which the sovereign authority must employ in order to achieve victory.

Northern Sources of the Renaissance

Charles G. Nauert

Most modern scholars argue that there were some differences between the Italian and Northern European Renaissances. Perhaps most obviously, the Northern Renaissance came later. More importantly, while heavily influenced by Italian humanism, humanism in Northern Europe was more tied to Christian culture and concerns. In the following selection Charles Nauert explains differences between the Italian and Northern Renaissance and argues that the North accepted Renaissance culture only when that culture came to suit the particular historical needs of the North.

SOURCE: From Charles G. Nauert, *The Age of Renaissance and Reformation,* pp. 116–117. Reprinted by permission of Charles G. Nauert, Jr. © 1981.

CONSIDER: *The ways the Northern Renaissance differed from the Italian Renaissance; how Nauert explains these differences.*

The North itself would never have accepted Renaissance culture if that culture had not suited its needs. The reorganized, powerful monarchies of the late fifteenth and early sixteenth centuries needed a new ideal for their servants and courtiers, and the emphasis on public service, on personal merit, and on learning provided an attractive substitute for the traditional manners of the unlettered, unruly, and discredited feudal classes. The new ideal contained enough emphasis on social class and military prowess to make it credible to a society where the hereditary nobility still counted for much. For the kings, it offered the added advantage of servants who were refined and cultivated, and who would wield the pen as well as the sword for their master.

In addition to the monarchs and their courts, other important groups in the North also found humanistic culture attractive. The powerful, self-confident merchant oligarchies that governed the important towns, especially the prospering towns of the Rhine Valley and of south Germany, found in humanism a cultural ideal far more suited to the needs and prejudices of urban magnates than were the chivalric and scholastic traditions of the Middle Ages. The large group of would-be Church reformers found the characteristic Renaissance repudiation of the recent past and the desire to return to the original sources quite attractive, for the Roman past included the apostolic and early patristic age, when the Church was still pure and uncorrupted. . . .

The humanism that grew up in the North was not a mere copy of the Italian culture, but a grafting of Italian elements into a cultural tradition that varied from country to country. Obviously, for example, Germans or even Frenchmen could not revere the ancient Romans as their ancestors in quite the same sense that Italians could.

What did develop everywhere was a revulsion against the heritage of the immediate past (often more open and violent than in Italy because scholastic traditions and a clerical spirit had much greater strength in the North), and the conscious adoption of an idealized Greek and Roman Antiquity as the model for reforming literature, education, and the whole ideal of the educated man. Even more than in Italy, Northern humanists enthusiastically looked to the apostolic and patristic age of the Church as a valuable part of the ancient heritage they sought to restore. This emphasis on ancient Christianity, combined with the widespread movements of lay piety that flourished in the lower Rhine Valley and other parts of Northern Europe, explains why humanism north of the Alps directed much of its reformist activity toward reform of the Church and deepening of personal religious experience.

CHAPTER QUESTIONS

1. In what ways was the Renaissance a new development, strikingly different from the preceding Middle Ages? How might the "newness" of these developments be minimized or reinterpreted as an evolutionary continuation of the Middle Ages?

2. According to the sources in this chapter, what was particularly humanistic about the cultural productions and the attitudes of the Renaissance?

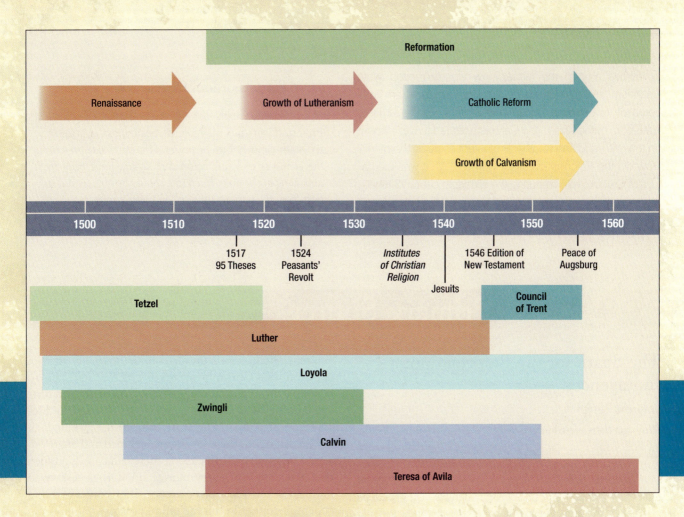

2 The Reformation

The Roman Catholic Church managed to hold together throughout the Middle Ages despite internal discord, heretical movements, and conflicts with secular authorities. In the sixteenth century the Protestant Reformation split it apart. The Reformation was initiated in 1517 by Martin Luther's challenges to official Church doctrine and papal authority. The movement spread in Germany, Northern Europe, and other parts of Europe. By mid-century a related but different form of Protestantism initiated in Geneva by John Calvin had become more dynamic, dominating the struggle against Catholicism in Central Europe and parts of France, Scotland, and England. Meanwhile, Catholic forces fought back politically and militarily under the leadership of the Holy Roman Emperor and Spain, and religiously through the Council of Trent and the Jesuits.

The importance of religious beliefs, the passion involved in the Reformation, and the historical significance of this division in the Western Christian Church have made the Reformation the object of intensive study. Moreover, a relatively large number of Reformation documents have been preserved.

Although representing a broad sampling of Reformation themes, the selections in this chapter center on three related topics. The first involves the much debated question of causes. Clearly, there was a combination of social, religious, political, and economic causes, but which predominated? What were some of the connections among these causes? The second also deals with causes of the Reformation, but from a somewhat different perspective. What moved Luther to reject Catholicism and develop new doctrines? What was the appeal of Lutheranism and Calvinism? In what ways were Catholic organizations such as the Jesuits and Carmelites able to attract members and play such an important role in Catholic reform? The third takes a more comparative perspective, concentrating on the differences and similarities among the faiths. How closely related were Calvinism and Lutheranism? Why did Lutheranism lose some of its dynamic force while Calvinism spread? How were both Lutheranism and Calvinism related to Catholicism on the one hand and to other Protestant sects on the other? How did the Reformation affect women? What was the nature of Catholic reform during the sixteenth century? Finally, the sources should shed light on the overall significance of the Reformation, one of the most profound revolutions in European history.

∾ **For Classroom Discussion**

Hold a debate, with one side presenting the features of Protestantism that might have been most appealing to sixteenth-century Europeans, and the other side presenting the elements of Catholicism that would have been most appealing at the time. Each side should be able to find support from the various primary and visual sources.

 Primary Sources

The Spark for the Reformation: Indulgences

Johann Tetzel

Although there were many causes of the Reformation, the immediate issue that sparked Luther into the position of a reformer was the sale of indulgences. Indulgences were remissions or exemptions for penance in purgatory due to an individual for the sins he had committed in life. They could be granted by the papacy because of the doctrine that it could draw on the treasury of merit or pool of spiritual wealth left by Christ and extraordinarily good Christians over time. As with some other practices of the Church, what was once used primarily for spiritual purposes, such as rewarding acts of penitence, was by the early sixteenth century being "abused" for secular purposes, such as providing money for Church officers. This was apparently the case with the sale of indulgences by Johann Tetzel (c. 1465–1519), a persuasive, popular Dominican friar who was appointed by Archbishop Albert of Mainz in 1517 to sell indulgences in Germany. Proceeds of the sale were to be split between Albert and the papacy. The following is an excerpt from a sermon on indulgences by Tetzel.

CONSIDER: *The most convincing "selling points" made by Tetzel; the requirements for obtaining effective indulgences; how Tetzel might have defended himself against attacks on this sale of indulgences as an abuse.*

You may obtain letters of safe conduct from the vicar of our Lord Jesus Christ, by means of which you are able to liberate your soul from the hands of the enemy, and convey it by means of contrition and confession, safe and secure from all pains of Purgatory, into the happy kingdom. For know, that in these letters are stamped and engraven all the merits of Christ's passion there laid bare. Consider, that for each and every mortal sin it is necessary to undergo seven years of penitence after confession and contrition, either in this life or in Purgatory.

How many mortal sins are committed in a day, how many in a week, how many in a month, how many in a year, how many in the whole extent of life! They are well-nigh numberless, and those that commit them must needs suffer endless punishment in the burning pains of Purgatory.

But with these confessional letters you will be able at any time in life to obtain full indulgence for all penalties imposed upon you, in all cases except the four reserved to the Apostolic See. Thence throughout your whole life, whenever you wish to make confession, you may receive the same remission, except in cases reserved to the Pope, and afterwards, at the hour of death, a full indulgence as to all penalties and sins, and your share of all spiritual blessings that exist in the church militant and all its members.

Do you not know that when it is necessary for anyone to go to Rome, or undertake any other dangerous journey, he takes his money to a broker and gives a certain per cent—five or six or ten—in order that at Rome or elsewhere he may receive again his funds intact, by means of the letters of this same broker? Are you not willing, then, for the fourth part of a florin, to obtain these letters, by virtue of which you may bring, not your money, but your divine and immortal soul, safe and sound into the land of Paradise?

SOURCE: From James Harvey Robinson and Merrick Whitcomb, eds., "Period of the Early Reformation in Germany," in *Translations and Reprints from the Original Sources of European History*, vol. II, no. 6, ed. Department of History of the University of Pennsylvania (Philadelphia: University of Pennsylvania Press, 1898), pp. 4–5.

Justification by Faith
Martin Luther

The early leader of the Reformation was Martin Luther (1483–1546). Born in Germany to a wealthy peasant family, Luther became an Augustinian monk and a professor of theology at the University of Wittenberg. While at this post in 1517, he became involved in the indulgence problem with Tetzel and issued rather academic challenges in his ninety-five theses. News of this act quickly spread, and a major controversy developed. Although originally intending to stimulate only modest reforms within the Catholic Church, Luther soon found himself espousing doctrines markedly differing from those authorized by the Church and taking actions that eventually resulted in his expulsion from the Church.

Luther himself attributed his spiritual evolution to certain crucial experiences. The most important of these was his first formulation of the doctrine of "justification by faith," which constituted the core of his beliefs and much of the basis for Protestantism. In the following excerpts from his autobiographical writings, Luther describes this experience.

CONSIDER: *What Luther meant by "justification by faith"; why this doctrine might have been so appealing to many Catholics; why this doctrine might have been threatening to the Catholic Church.*

I greatly longed to understand Paul's Epistle to the Romans and nothing stood in the way but that one expression, "the justice of God," because I took it to mean that justice whereby God is just and deals justly in punishing the unjust. My situation was that, although an impeccable monk, I stood before God as a sinner troubled in conscience, and I had no confidence that my merit would assuage him. Therefore I did not love a just and angry God, but rather hated and murmured against Him. Yet I clung to the dear Paul and had a great yearning to know what he meant.

Night and day I pondered until I saw the connection between the justice of God and the statement that "the just shall live by his faith." Then I grasped that the justice of God is that righteousness by which through grace and sheer mercy God justifies us through faith. There-upon I felt myself to be reborn and to have gone through open doors into paradise. The whole of Scripture took on a new meaning, and whereas before the "justice of God" had filled me with hate, now it became to be inexpressibly sweet in greater love. This passage of Paul became to me a gate to heaven. . . .

SOURCE: From Roland H. Bainton, *The Age of Reformation* (New York: D. Van Nostrand Co., Inc., 1956), pp. 97–98. Reprinted by permission.

If you have a true faith that Christ is your Saviour, then at once you have a gracious God, for faith leads you in and opens up God's heart and will, that you should see pure grace and overflowing love. This it is to behold God in faith that you should look upon His fatherly, friendly heart, in which there is no anger nor ungraciousness. He who sees God as angry does not see Him rightly but looks only on a curtain, as if a dark cloud had been drawn across his face.

On the Bondage of the Will
Martin Luther

A central distinction between Luther's views and those of Catholicism concerned the power of free will and good works to effect salvation. According to Catholicism, people had the ability to contribute to their own salvation by choosing to engage in good deeds, pious acts, approved behavior, and so forth. Luther rejected this, arguing that people were powerless to effect their own salvation, that salvation was granted only by God out of his mercy. The following is an excerpt from Luther's On the Bondage of the Will, written in 1520 in response to a defense of free will and good works by the famous Christian humanist Erasmus.

CONSIDER: *How Luther's arguments here follow from his ideas about justification by faith; the characteristics of God in Luther's eyes.*

I frankly confess that, for myself, even if it could be, I should not want "free-will" to be given me, nor anything to be left in my own hands to enable me to endeavour after salvation; not merely because in face of so many dangers, and adversities, and assaults of devils, I could not stand my ground and hold fast my "free-will" (for one devil is stronger than all men, and on these terms no man could be saved); but because, even were there no dangers, adversities, or devils, I should still be forced to labour with no guarantee of success, and to beat my fists at the air. If I lived and worked to all eternity, my conscience would never reach comfortable certainty as to how much it must do to satisfy God. Whatever work I had done, there would still be a nagging doubt as to whether it pleased God, or whether He required something more. The experience of all who seek righteousness by works proves that; and I learned it well enough myself over a period of many years, to my own great hurt. But now that God has taken my salvation out of the control of my own will, and put it

SOURCE: Luther, Martin & Packer, J. I. *Martin Luther on the bondage of the will*, trans. J. I. Packer and O. R. Jahnston (London: James Clarke & Co., 1957), pp. 313–314. Reprinted by Permission.

predestination. There is no need of refuting objections which the moment they are produced abundantly betray their hollowness. I will dwell only on those points which either form the subject of dispute among the learned, or may occasion any difficulty to the simple, or may be employed by impiety as specious pretexts for assailing the justice of God.

Constitution of the Society of Jesus

The Catholic Church was not passive in the face of the challenges from Protestant reformers. In a variety of ways the Church reformed itself from within and took the offensive against Protestants in doctrine and deed. Probably the most effective weapon of Catholic reform was the Society of Jesus (the Jesuits) founded by Ignatius Loyola (1491–1556). Loyola, a soldier who had turned to the religious life while recovering from wounds, attracted a group of highly disciplined followers who offered their services to the pope. In 1540, the pope formally accepted their offer. The Jesuits became an arm of the Church in combating Protestantism, spreading Catholicism to foreign lands and gaining influence within Catholic areas of Europe. The following is an excerpt from the Constitution of the Society of Jesus, approved by Pope Paul III in 1540.

CONSIDER: *The characteristics of this organization that help explain its success; how, in tone and content, this document differs from Lutheran and Calvinist documents.*

He who desires to fight for God under the banner of the cross in our society,—which we wish to distinguish by the name of Jesus,—and to serve God alone and the Roman pontiff, his vicar on earth, after a solemn vow of perpetual chastity, shall set this thought before his mind, that he is a part of a society founded for the especial purpose of providing for the advancement of souls in Christian life and doctrine and for the propagation of faith through public preaching and the ministry of the word of God, spiritual exercises and deeds of charity, and in particular through the training of the young and ignorant in Christianity and through the spiritual consolation of the faithful of Christ in hearing confessions; and he shall take care to keep first God and next the purpose of this organization always before his eyes. . . .

   All the members shall realize, and shall recall daily, as long as they live, that this society as a whole and in every part is fighting for God under faithful obedience to one most holy lord, the pope, and to the other Roman pontiffs who succeed him. And although we are taught in the gospel and through the orthodox faith to recognize and steadfastly profess that all the faithful of Christ are subject to the Roman pontiff as their head and as the vicar of Jesus Christ, yet we have adjudged that, for the special promotion of greater humility in our society and the perfect mortification of every individual and the sacrifice of our own wills, we should each be bound by a peculiar vow, in addition to the general obligation, that whatever the present Roman pontiff, or any future one, may from time to time decree regarding the welfare of souls and the propagation of the faith, we are pledged to obey without evasion or excuse, instantly, so far as in us lies, whether he send us to the Turks or any other infidels, even to those who inhabit the regions men call the Indies; whether to heretics or schismatics, or, on the other hand, to certain of the faithful.

The Way of Perfection
Teresa of Avila

While the Society of Jesus was the best-known Catholic religious order founded during the Reformation, other orders were founded or reformed and played roles in reasserting the strength of Catholicism. Many of these were women's orders that emphasized meditation, prayer, and mystical religious experiences. The most famous leader of these women's orders was Saint Teresa of Avila (1515–1582), a Spanish saint and founder of the reformed order of Carmelites. The following excerpt is from her book The Way of Perfection.

CONSIDER: *How she reacted to the Lutheran Reformation; ways this religious order and Catholicism might be appealing to women.*

When this convent was originally founded, for the reasons set down in the book which, as I say, I have already written, and also because of certain wonderful revelations by which the Lord showed me how well He would be served in this house, it was not my intention that there should be so much austerity in external matters, nor that it should have no regular income: on the contrary, I should have liked there to be no possibility of want. I acted, in short, like the weak and wretched woman that I am, although I did so with good intentions and not out of consideration for my own comfort.

SOURCE: James Harvey Robinson, ed., *Readings in European History*, vol. II (Boston: Ginn, 1904), pp. 162–163.

SOURCE: E. Allison Peers, ed. and trans., *The Complete Works of Saint Teresa of Jesus*, vol. II (London and New York: Sheed and Ward, 1950), pp. 3, 13.

At about this time there came to my notice the harm and havoc that were being wrought in France by these Lutherans and the way in which their unhappy sect was increasing. This troubled me very much, and, as though I could do anything, or be of any help in the matter, I wept before the Lord and entreated Him to remedy this great evil. I felt that I would have laid down a thousand lives to save a single one of all the souls that were being lost there. And, seeing that I was a woman, and a sinner, and incapable of doing all I should like in the Lord's service, and as my whole yearning was, and still is, that, as He has so many enemies and so few friends, these last should be trusty ones, I determined to do the little that was in me—namely, to follow the evangelical counsels as perfectly as I could, and to see that these few nuns who are here should do the same, confiding in the great goodness of God, Who never fails to help those who resolve to forsake everything for His sake. . . .

It seems over-bold of me to think that I can do anything towards obtaining this. But I have confidence, my Lord, in these servants of Thine who are here, knowing that they neither desire nor strive after anything but to please Thee. For Thy sake they have left the little they possessed, wishing they had more so that they might serve Thee with it. Since Thou, my Creator, art not ungrateful, I do not think Thou wilt fail to do what they beseech of Thee, for when Thou wert in the world, Lord, Thou didst not despise women, but didst always help them and show them great compassion. *Thou didst find more faith and no less love in them than in men, and one of them was Thy most sacred Mother, from whose merits we derive merit, and whose habit we wear, though our sins make us unworthy to do so. We can do nothing in public that is of any use to Thee, nor dare we speak of some of the truths over which we weep in secret, lest Thou shouldst not hear this our just petition. Yet, Lord, I cannot believe this of Thy goodness and righteousness, for Thou art a righteous Judge, not like judges in the world, who, being, after all, men and sons of Adam, refuse to consider any woman's virtue as above suspicion. Yes, my King, but the day will come when all will be known. I am not speaking on my own account, for the whole world is already aware of my wickedness, and I am glad that it should become known; but, when I see what the times are like, I feel it is not right to repel spirits which are virtuous and brave, even though they be the spirits of women.*

Visual Sources

Luther and the New Testament

The frontispiece of Luther's 1546 edition of the New Testament (figure 2.1) reveals much about the Protestant Reformation. First, most words are written in German, not Latin, thus reflecting the Protestant view that the Bible should be read by everyone. The place is Wittenberg, where Luther initiated the Reformation by posting his ninety-five theses in 1517. The year, 1546, was that of Luther's death. In the picture Christ on the cross is flanked by the praying Luther on the right and his patron, the elector of Saxony, on the left. This symbolizes the two unified in the central Protestant belief of justification by faith, the actual political-religious alliance of the two that was so important for the spread of Lutheranism in Germany, and the compatibility of Church and state according to Lutheranism. The general simplicity and lack of ornamentation of this work reflect Lutheranism and part of what it rejected about Catholicism. The book itself, produced mechanically, indicates the importance of the recently invented printing press for the Reformation.

CONSIDER: *How this frontispiece might explain or symbolize the causes of the Reformation.*

Luther and the Catholic Clergy Debate
Sebald Beham

Both Catholics and Protestants often used art to propagate their views in the Reformation debate. Nuremberg artist Sebald Beham's 1525 woodcut (figure 2.2) appeared in a broadsheet with a text by Hans Sachs entitled Luther and the Artisans. *On the left are the "godless"—members of trades, including a painter holding a stick and brush, a bell caster, and a fisherman with his net—all relying on religious commissions from the Catholic church. They complain that Luther has unjustly attacked the clergy for practices such as the sale of indulgences and rental of church lands. They are led by a nun and a priest, who points an accusing finger at Luther. On the right is a group of humble peasants—representing the "common man"—led by Martin Luther, who uses the Bible to answer charges against him and instruct his accusers to seek the kingdom of God. Christ, above in a circle of clouds and holding orb and scepter as Lord of the world, casts his judgment against the clergy by including his scepter to Luther's side.*

CONSIDER: *What this painting reveals about the Reformation; how this painting compares to the previous illustration.*

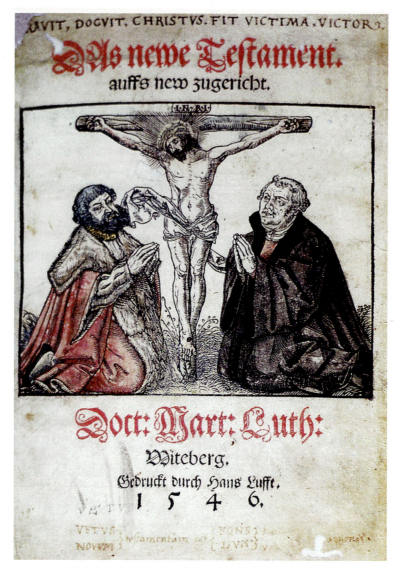

FIGURE 2.1 (Siftung Luthergedenkstatten in Sachsen-Anhalt)

FIGURE 2.2 (© Bildarchiv Preussischer Kulturbesitz/Art Resource, NY)

Loyola and Catholic Reform

Peter Paul Rubens

In this painting by Peter Paul Rubens (figure 2.3), commissioned by the Jesuits in 1619, Ignatius Loyola is shown preaching and casting out demons from the Church. In the center Loyola, with a halo and backed on his right by the clergy, preaches. He is supported above by angels. To the upper left the demons flee from their victims below, who are both overwhelmed and newly hopeful from the experience.

A comparison with (figure 2.1), the frontispiece of the 1546 edition of Luther's German translation of the New Testament, reveals part of the nature of Catholic reform.

Here, the emphasis is on the Church's intervening between God and man, on the importance of the sacraments, and on the need for an ordained priesthood. The Catholic Church was willing to utilize the wealth and splendor available to it in its cause, as demonstrated not only by Loyola's robes and the grandeur of this Church interior, but in the commissioning of a leading artist like Rubens to paint in the new, elaborate, rich baroque style.

CONSIDER: *If you view this picture and the previous two as propaganda pieces, in what ways might they be appealing, and to whom?*

FIGURE 2.3 (© Erich Lessing/Art Resource, NY)

Secondary Sources

What Was the Reformation?

Euan Cameron

Historians usually agree that the Reformation comprised the general religious transformations in Europe during the sixteenth century. However, they often disagree on what exactly was at the core of the Reformation. In the following selection Euan Cameron argues that the essence of the Reformation was a combination of religious reformers' protests and laymen's political ambitions.

CONSIDER: *How the protests by churchmen and scholars combined with the ambitions of politically active laymen to become the essence of the Reformation; what this interpretation implies about the causes for the Reformation.*

The Reformation, the movement which divided European Christianity into catholic and protestant traditions, is unique. No other movement of religious protest or reform since antiquity has been so widespread or lasting in its effects, so deep and searching in its criticism of received wisdom, so destructive in what it abolished or so fertile in what it created. . . .

The European Reformation was not a simple revolution, a protest movement with a single leader, a defined set of objectives, or a coherent organization. Yet neither was it a floppy or fragmented mess of anarchic or contradictory ambitions. It was a series of *parallel* movements; within *each* of which various sorts of people with differing perspectives for a crucial period in history combined forces to pursue objectives which they only partly understood.

First of all, the Reformation was a protest by churchmen and scholars, privileged classes in medieval society, against their own superiors. Those superiors, the Roman papacy and its agents, had attacked the teachings of a few sincere, respected academic churchmen which had seemed to threaten the prestige and privilege of clergy and papacy. Martin Luther, the first of those protesting clerics, had attacked "the Pope's crown and the monks' bellies," and they had fought back, to defend their status. The protesting churchmen—the "reformers"—responded to the Roman counter-attack not by silence or furtive opposition, but by publicly denouncing their accusers in print. Not only that: they developed their teachings to make their protest more coherent, and to justify their disobedience.

Then the most surprising thing of all, in the context of medieval lay people's usual response to religious dissent, took place. Politically active laymen, not (at first) political rulers with axes to grind, but rather ordinary, moderately prosperous householders, took up the reformers' protests, identified them (perhaps mistakenly) as their own, and pressed them upon their governors. This blending and coalition—of reformers' protests and laymen's political ambitions—is the essence of the Reformation. It turned the reformers' movement into a new form of religious dissent: it became not a "schism," in which a section of the catholic Church rose in political revolt against authority, without altering beliefs or practices; nor yet a "heresy," whereby a few people deviated from official belief or worship, but without respect, power, or authority. Rather it promoted a new pattern of worship and belief, publicly preached and acknowledged, which *also* formed the basis of new religious *institutions* for all of society, within the whole community, region, or nation concerned.

A Political Interpretation of the Reformation

G. R. Elton

In more recent times the religious interpretation of the Reformation has been challenged by political historians. This view is illustrated by the following selection from the highly authoritative New Cambridge Modern History. *Here, G. R. Elton of Cambridge argues that while spiritual and other factors are relevant, primary importance for explaining why the Reformation did or did not take hold rests with political history.*

CONSIDER: *How Elton supports his argument; the ways in which Cameron might refute this interpretation.*

The desire for spiritual nourishment was great in many parts of Europe, and movements of thought which gave intellectual content to what in so many ways was an inchoate search for God have their own dignity. Neither of these, however, comes first in explaining why the Reformation took root here and vanished there—why, in fact, this complex of antipapal "heresies" led to a permanent division within the Church that had looked to Rome. This particular place is occupied by politics and

SOURCE: From Euan Cameron, *The European Reformation*, pp. 1–2, © 1991. Reprinted by permission of Oxford University Press.

SOURCE: From G. R. Elton, ed., *The New Cambridge Modern History*, vol. II, *The Reformation* (Cambridge, England: Cambridge University Press, 1958), p. 5. Reprinted by permission.

the play of secular ambitions. In short, the Reformation maintained itself wherever the lay power (prince or magistrates) favoured it; it could not survive where the authorities decided to suppress it. Scandinavia, the German principalities, Geneva, in its own peculiar way also England, demonstrate the first; Spain, Italy, the Habsburg lands in the east, and also (though not as yet conclusively) France, the second. The famous phrase behind the settlement of 1555—*cuius regio eius religio*—was a practical commonplace long before anyone put it into words. For this was the age of uniformity, an age which held at all times and everywhere that one political unit could not comprehend within itself two forms of belief or worship.

The tenet rested on simple fact: as long as membership of a secular polity involved membership of an ecclesiastical organisation, religious dissent stood equal to political disaffection and even treason. Hence governments enforced uniformity, and hence the religion of the ruler was that of his country. England provided the extreme example of this doctrine in action, with its rapid official switches from Henrician Catholicism without the pope, through Edwardian Protestantism on the Swiss model and Marian papalism, to Elizabethan Protestantism of a more specifically English brand. But other countries fared similarly. Nor need this cause distress or annoyed disbelief. Princes and governments, no more than the governed, do not act from unmixed motives, and to ignore the spiritual factor in the conversion of at least some princes is as false as to see nothing but purity in the desires of the populace. The Reformation was successful beyond the dreams of earlier, potentially similar, movements not so much because (as the phrase goes) the time was ripe for it, but rather because it found favour with the secular arm. Desire for Church lands, resistance to imperial and papal claims, the ambition to create self-contained and independent states, all played their part in this, but so quite often did a genuine attachment to the teachings of the reformers.

The Catholic Reformation

John C. Olin

The history of the Catholic Church during the sixteenth century is almost as controversial as the history of the Protestant Reformation. Indeed, variations on the terminology used, from "Catholic reform," "Catholic Reformation," and "Catholic revival" to "Counter Reformation" reflect important differences in historians' interpretations of that history. The hub of the controversy is the extent to which reform and revival in the Catholic

SOURCE: John C. Olin, "The Catholic Reformation," in *The Meaning of the Renaissance and Reformation*, ed. Richard L. DeMolen (Boston: Houghton Mifflin Co., 1974), pp. 268, 289–290.

Church was a reaction to the Protestant Reformation or a product of forces independent of the Protestant Reformation. In the following selection John C. Olin, a historian specializing in Reformation studies, addresses this issue and analyzes the nature of Catholic reform during the sixteenth century.

CONSIDER: *For Olin, the problems in labeling Catholic reform the Counter Reformation; what the inner unity and coherence of the Catholic reform movement was.*

Catholic reform in all its manifestations, potential and actual, was profoundly influenced by the crisis and subsequent schism that developed after 1517. It did not suddenly arise then, but it was given new urgency, as well as a new setting and a new dimension, by the problems that Protestantism posed. What had been, and probably would have remained, a matter of renewal and reform within the confines of religious and ecclesiastical tradition became also a defense of that tradition and a struggle to maintain and restore it. A very complex pattern of Catholic activity unfolded under the shock of religious revolt and disruption. It cannot satisfactorily be labeled the Counter Reformation, for the term is too narrow and misleading. There was indeed a reaction to Protestantism, but this factor, as important as it is, neither subsumes every facet of Catholic life in the sixteenth century nor adequately explains the source and character of the Catholic revival.

Our initial task, then, is to break through the conventional stereotype of Protestant Reformation and Catholic Counter Reformation to view Catholic reform in a more comprehensive and objective way. This will entail consideration of the reaction to schism and the advance of Protestantism, but this subject can neither serve as a point of departure nor be allowed to usurp the stage. The survival of Catholicism and its continued growth suggest another perspective, as do the lives and devotion of so many of the most important Catholic figures of this time. Indeed, if the real significance of the Catholic Reformation must be found in its saints, as has recently been remarked, then emphasis on schism, controversy, and the more secular reflexes of ecclesiastical man may be slightly misplaced.

❧

Certain basic lineaments stand out in the Catholic reform movement, from the days of Savonarola and Ximenes to the close of the Council of Trent. The first and the most obvious was the widespread awareness of the need for reform and the serious efforts made to achieve it. This movement was in the beginning scattered and disparate, a matter of individual initiative and endeavor rather than a coordinated program affecting the church as a whole. Ximenes is the major example of an ecclesiastical or institutional reformer prior to 1517.

Erasmus and the Christian humanists, however widespread and deep their influence, worked in a private capacity, so to speak, and sought essentially personal reorientation and renewal, though they did envision a broader reform of Christian life and society. With the pontificate of Paul III, Catholic reform became more concerted and official, and reached out to encompass the entire church. The arrival of Contarini in Rome in 1535 ushered in the new era. New blood was infused into the papal administration, the early Jesuits were organized and began their extensive activities, and the General Council was finally convened at Trent. Despite its diversity, the movement had an inner unity and coherence and followed an identifiable and continuous course.

Of what did this inner unity and coherence consist? It was manifested in the first place in the desire for religious reform. . . . [W]hat features distinguish the Catholic reformers and link them in a common endeavor[?] As we see it, two characteristics run like a double rhythm through the Catholic Reformation: the preoccupation of the Catholic reformers with individual or personal reformation, and their concern for the restoration and renewal of the Church's pastoral mission. In short, Catholic reform had a marked personal and pastoral orientation.

The Catholic reformers focused on the individual Christian and his spiritual and moral life. They sought essentially a *reformatio in membris* rather than dogmatic or structural change. The members of Christ's church must lead better Christian lives and be instructed and guided along that path. This is the burden of Savonarola's prophetic preaching, the goal of Erasmus and the Christian humanists, the objective of Ignatius Loyola and his *Spiritual Exercises*. The Theatines, Capuchins, and Jesuits emphasized this in terms of the greater commitment and sanctification of their members. The reforms of Ximenes in Spain, Giberti in Verona, and the Council of Trent for the universal church had this as an underlying purpose in their concern for the instruction and spiritual advancement of the faithful. . . .

Such a focus presupposes concern for the reform of the institutional church as well, for if men are to be changed by religion, then religion itself must be correctly represented and faithfully imparted. Thus the church's pastoral mission—the work of teaching, guiding, and sanctifying its members—must be given primacy and rendered effective. Hence the stress on training priests, selecting good men as bishops and insisting that they reside in their dioceses, instructing the young and preaching the gospel, restoring discipline in the church, and rooting out venality and unworthiness in the service of Christ and the salvation of souls. The Bark of Peter was not to be scuttled or rebuilt, but to be steered back to its original course with its crew at their posts and responsive to their tasks. The state of the clergy loomed large in Catholic reform. If their ignorance, corruption, or neglect had been responsible for the troubles that befell the church, as nearly everyone affirmed, then their reform required urgent attention and was the foundation and root of all renewal. This involved personal reform, that of the priests and bishops who are the instruments of the church's mission, and its purpose and consequence were a matter of the personal reform of the faithful entrusted to their care. The immediate objective, however, was institutional and pastoral. The church itself was to be restored so that its true apostolate might be realized.

The Legacy of the Reformation
Steven E. Ozment

Various historians have identified widespread changes stemming from the Reformation. The most obvious of these were the changes in religious affiliation and the conflicts between Protestants and Catholics that developed. However, there were other cultural and social changes stemming from the Reformation that directly affected daily life. In the following selection Steven Ozment analyzes the legacy of the Reformation, emphasizing how it displaced many of the beliefs, practices, and institutions of daily life.

CONSIDER: *How the changes emphasized by Ozment might have affected daily life; what connections there might be between the Reformation and witchcraft according to Ozment.*

Viewed in these terms, the Reformation was an unprecedented revolution in religion at a time when religion penetrated almost the whole of life. The Reformation constituted for the great majority of people, whose social status and economic condition did not change dramatically over a lifetime, an upheaval in the world as they knew it, regardless of whether they were pious Christians or joined the movement. In the first half of the sixteenth century cities and territories passed laws and ordinances that progressively ended or severely limited a host of traditional beliefs, practices, and institutions that touched directly the daily life of large numbers of people: mandatory fasting; auricular confession; the veneration of saints, relics, and images; the buying and selling of indulgences; pilgrimages and shrines; wakes and processions for the dead and dying; endowed masses in memory of the dead; the doctrine of purgatory; Latin Mass and liturgy; traditional ceremonies, festivals, and holidays; monasteries, nunneries, and mendicant orders; the sacramental status of marriage; extreme unction, confirmation, holy orders, and penance; clerical celibacy; clerical

SOURCE: From Steven E. Ozment, *The Age of Reformation*, pp. 435–436. © 1980. Reprinted by permission of the Yale University Press.

immunity from civil taxation and criminal jurisdiction; nonresident benefices; papal excommunication and interdict; canon law; papal and episcopal territorial government; and the traditional scholastic education of clergy. Modern scholars may argue over the degree to which such changes in the official framework of religion connoted actual changes in personal beliefs and habits. Few, however, can doubt that the likelihood of personal change increased with the incorporation of Protestant reforms in the laws and institutions of the sixteenth century. As historians write the social history of the Reformation, I suspect they will discover that such transformations in the religious landscape had a profound, if often indirect, cultural impact.

While the Reformation influenced the balance of political power both locally and internationally, it was not a political revolution in the accepted sense of the term; a major reordering of traditional social and political groups did not result, although traditional enemies often ended up in different religious camps and the higher clergy was displaced as a political elite. The larger social impact of the Reformation lay rather in its effectively displacing so many of the beliefs, practices, and institutions that had organized daily life and given it security and meaning for the greater part of a millennium. Here the reformers continued late medieval efforts to simplify religious, and enhance secular, life. If scholars of popular religion in Reformation England are correct, Protestant success against medieval religion actually brought new and more terrible superstitions to the surface. By destroying the traditional ritual framework for dealing with daily misfortune and worry, the Reformation left those who could not find solace in its message—and there were many—more anxious than before, and especially after its leaders sought by coercion what they discovered could not be gained by persuasion alone. Protestant "disenchantment" of the world in this way encouraged new interest in witchcraft and the occult, as the religious heart and mind, denied an outlet in traditional sacramental magic and pilgrimage piety, compensated for new Protestant sobriety and simplicity by embracing superstitions even more socially disruptive than the religious practices set aside by the Reformation.

Women in the Reformation

Marilyn J. Boxer and Jean H. Quataert

The great figures of the Reformation were men, and traditionally focus has been on their struggles and their doctrines. In recent years scholars have questioned what role women played in the Reformation and whether the Reformation benefited women socially or in any aspect of public life. These questions are addressed by Marilyn J. Boxer and Jean H. Quataert, both specializing in women's studies, in the following excerpt from their book Connecting Spheres.

CONSIDER: *Ways women helped spread the Reformation; why the Reformation did not greatly change women's place in society.*

Defying stereotypes, women in good measure also were instrumental in spreading the ideas of the religious Reformation to the communities, towns, and provinces of Europe after 1517. In their roles as spouses and mothers they were often the ones to bring the early reform ideas to the families of Europe's aristocracy and to those of the common people in urban centers as well. The British theologian Richard Hooker (c. 1553–1600) typically explained the prominence of women in reform movements by reference to their "nature," to the "eagerness of their affection," not to their intelligence or ability to make conscious choices. Similarly, Catholic polemicists used notions about women's immature and frail "nature" to discredit Protestantism.

The important role played by women in the sixteenth-century Reformation should not surprise us, for they had been equally significant in supporting earlier heresies that challenged the established order and at times the gender hierarchy, too. Many medieval anticlerical movements that extolled the virtues of lay men praised lay women as well. . . .

Since the message of the Reformation, like that of the earlier religious movements, meant a loosening of hierarchies, it had a particular appeal to women. By stressing the individual's personal relationship with God and his or her own responsibility for behavior, it affirmed the ability of each to find truth by reading the original Scriptures. Thus, it offered a greater role for lay participation by women, as well as men, than was possible in Roman Catholicism. . . .

[Nevertheless,] the Reformation did not markedly transform women's place in society, and the reformers had never intended to do so. To be sure, they called on men and women to read the Bible and participate in religious ceremonies together. But Bible-reading reinforced the Pauline view of woman as weak-minded and sinful. When such practice took a more radical turn in the direction of lay prophesy, as occurred in some Reform churches southwest of Paris, or in the coming together of women to discuss "unchristian pieces" as was recorded in Zwickau, reformers—Lutheran and Calvin alike—pulled back in horror. The radical or Anabaptist brand of reform generally offered women a more active role in religious life than did Lutheranism, even allowing them to preach.

SOURCE: Excerpted from *Connecting Spheres: Women in the Western World, 1500 to the Present,* edited by Marilyn J. Boxer and Jean H. Quataert. © 1987 by Oxford University Press, Inc.

"Admonished to Christian righteousness" by more conservative Protestants, Anabaptists were charged with holding that "marriage and whoredom are one and the same thing." The women were even accused of having "dared to deny their husbands' marital rights." During an interrogation one woman explained that "she was wed to Christ and must therefore be chaste, for which she cited the saying, that no one can serve two masters."

The response of the magisterial Reformers was unequivocal. The equality of the Gospel was not to overturn the inequalities of social rank or the hierarchies of the sexual order. As the Frenchman Pierre Viret explained it in 1560, appealing to the old polarities again, the Protestant elect were equal as Christians and believers—as man and woman, master and servant, free and serf. Further, while the Reformation thus failed to elevate women's status, it deprived them of the emotionally sustaining presence of female imagery, of saints and protectors who long had played a significant role at crucial points in their life cycles. The Reformers rejected the special powers of the saints and downplayed, for example, Saints Margaret and Ann, who had been faithful and succoring companions for women in childbirth and in widowhood. With the rejection of Mary as well as the saints, nuns, and abbesses, God the Father was more firmly in place.

CHAPTER QUESTIONS

1. What were the most important differences between Catholicism and Protestantism in the sixteenth century? In what ways do these differences explain the appeal of each faith and the causes of the Reformation?

2. Considering the information in the preceding chapter, how might the Reformation be related to some of the intellectual and cultural developments of the Renaissance?

3. In what ways would it be accurate to describe Luther and his doctrines—and indeed the Reformation in general—as more medieval and conservative than humanistic and modern?

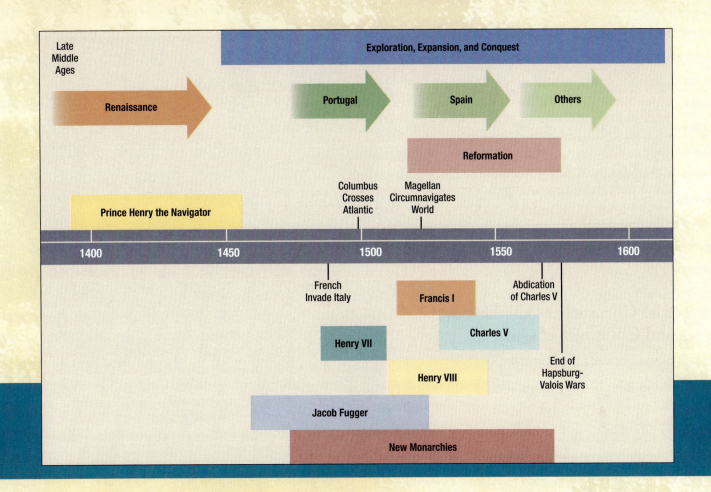

3 Overseas Expansion and New Politics

Between the mid-fifteenth and mid-sixteenth centuries much of Europe gained a new political and economic strength, which had been missing during the Late Middle Ages. This was manifested in a number of ways. First, central governments acquired new authority and power under a series of talented monarchs, often referred to by historians as the "new monarchs." This was particularly so in England, France, and Spain, but even in the Holy Roman Empire, where the emperor was often relatively weak, Emperor Charles V rose in stature and power. Second, European states supported a new wave of expansion into the rest of the world. Led by Portugal and then Spain, these states sent explorers, missionaries, merchants, colonists, and armed forces throughout the world, quickly establishing vast empires. Third, modern diplomacy was developed, enabling states to have recognized representatives with authority and expertise in foreign countries. This reflected and facilitated the new political strength and competitiveness of European states.

Sources in this chapter deal with each of these aspects of the new political and economic strength of fifteenth- and sixteenth-century Europe. In particular, questions related to exploration and expansion are addressed. What were the motives for expansion? Why did the expansion occur at this time? What connections were there between expansion and nationalism? What were the consequences of expansion? Some documents concern political developments of the period, particularly the reign of Charles V, the most renowned ruler of the time. What were his role and position? How were they affected by expansion? What were some of the connections between his position and the new commercial and financial prosperity?

In short, the sources in this chapter reveal a new political and economic strength that relates to the religious, cultural, and intellectual developments covered in the two preceding chapters. While this Renaissance civilization did not represent a complete break with the civilization of the Middle Ages, the selections emphasize what is different and more recognizably "modern" about this period. Historical patterns were being established that would characterize Europe for several succeeding generations, as will be seen in the following chapters.

❧ For Classroom Discussion

What were the reasons for Europe's overseas expansion? Use the selections by Azurara, Columbus, and Diaz del Castillo, as well as the analysis by Richard Reed.

Primary Sources

The Chronicle of the Discovery and Conquest of Guinea

Gomes Eannes de Azurara

The great geographic expansion and conquests of the fifteenth and sixteenth centuries were initiated by Prince Henry (the Navigator) of Portugal (1394–1460). Although he did not personally participate in the explorations, he established a naval school and base of operations on the southwestern tip of Portugal from which he sent expeditions down the west coast of Africa. One of the clearest explanations of the motives for this effort has been provided by Gomes Eannes de Azurara, a friend of Prince Henry (referred to as "the Lord Infant"), who chronicled the voyages of 1452–1453 at the request of King Alfonso V.

CONSIDER: *The explanations that sound more like rationalizations than reasons for explorations; whether economic, military, and religious motives are complementary or contradictory; ways this document reflects the history of a country engaged with Islam.*

We imagine that we know a matter when we are acquainted with the doer of it and the end for which he did it. And since in former chapters we have set forth the Lord Infant as the chief actor in these things, giving as clear an understanding of him as we could, it is meet that in this present chapter we should know his purpose in doing them. And you should note well that the noble spirit of this Prince, by a sort of natural constraint, was ever urging him both to begin and to carry out very great deeds. For which reason, after the taking of Ceuta he always kept ships well armed against the Infidel, both for war, and because he had also a wish to know the land that lay beyond the isles of Canary and that Cape called

Bojador, for that up to his time, neither by writings, nor by the memory of man, was known with any certainty the nature of the land beyond that Cape. Some said indeed that Saint Brandan had passed that way; and there was another tale of two galleys rounding the Cape, which never returned. But this doth not appear at all likely to be true, for it is not to be presumed that if the said galleys went there, some other ships would not have endeavoured to learn what voyage they had made. And because the said Lord Infant wished to know the truth of this,—since it seemed to him that if he or some other lord did not endeavour to gain that knowledge, no mariners or merchants would ever dare to attempt it—(for it is clear that none of them ever trouble themselves to sail to a place where there is not a sure and certain hope of profit)—and seeing also that no other prince took any pains in this matter, he sent out his own ships against those parts, to have manifest certainty of them all. And to this he was stirred up by his zeal for the service of God and of the King Edward his Lord and brother, who then reigned. And this was the first reason of his action.

The second reason was that if there chanced to be in those lands some population of Christians, or some havens, into which it would be possible to sail without peril, many kinds of merchandise might be brought to this realm, which would find a ready market, and reasonably so, because no other people of these parts traded with them, nor yet people of any other that were known; and also the products of this realm might be taken there, which traffic would bring great profit to our countrymen.

The third reason was that, as it was said that the power of the Moors in that land of Africa was very much greater than was commonly supposed, and that there were no Christians among them, nor any other race of men; and because every wise man is obliged by natural prudence to wish for a knowledge of the power of his enemy; therefore the said Lord Infant exerted himself to cause this to be fully discovered, and to make it known determinately how far the power of those infidels extended.

SOURCE: Gomes Eannes de Azurara, *The Chronicle of the Discovery and Conquest of Guinea*, vol. I, trans. Charles Raymond Beazley and Adgar Prestage (London: The Hakluyt Society, 1896), pp. 27–29.

The fourth reason was because during the one and thirty years that he had warred against the Moors, he had never found a Christian king, nor a lord outside this land, who for the love of our Lord Jesus Christ would aid him in the said war. Therefore he sought to know if there were in those parts any Christian princes, in whom the charity and the love of Christ was so ingrained that they would aid him against those enemies of the faith.

The fifth reason was his great desire to make increase in the faith of our Lord Jesus Christ and to bring to him all the souls that should be saved,—understanding that all the mystery of the Incarnation, Death, and Passion of our Lord Jesus Christ was for this sole end—namely the salvation of lost souls—whom the said Lord Infant by his travail and spending would fain bring into the true path. For he perceived that no better offering could be made unto the Lord than this; for if God promised to return one hundred goods for one, we may justly believe that for such great benefits, that is to say for so many souls as were saved by the efforts of this Lord, he will have so many hundreds of guerdons in the kingdom of God, by which his spirit may be glorified after this life in the celestial realm. For I that wrote this history saw so many men and women of those parts turned to the holy faith, that even if the Infant had been a heathen, their prayers would have been enough to have obtained his salvation. And not only did I see the first captives, but their children and grandchildren as true Christians as if the Divine grace breathed in them and imparted to them a clear knowledge of itself.

Letter to Lord Sanchez, 1493

Christopher Columbus

The voyages of Christopher Columbus (1451–1506) opened the New World to Europe and marked the entry of Spain into the process of exploration, expansion, and conquest initiated by Portugal. Columbus was a Genoese explorer who, after great difficulties, convinced the Spanish monarchs, Queen Isabella and King Ferdinand, to support his voyages across the Atlantic. He expected to discover a western route to Asia and its riches. Instead, he landed on several islands of the Caribbean, which he assumed were part of Asia. The following letter to Lord Raphael Sanchez, treasurer to the Spanish monarchs, was written by Columbus in Lisbon on March 14, 1493, shortly after returning from his first voyage across the Atlantic. In this excerpt, he describes the native people he encountered.

Source: *Select Letters of Christopher Columbus,* trans. and ed. R. H. Hajor (London: The Hakluyt Society, 1847), pp. 6–10.

Consider: *How Columbus viewed the natives; what Columbus was most concerned with; how this letter reflects Columbus' motives.*

The inhabitants of both sexes in this island, and in all the others which I have seen, or of which I have received information, go always naked as they were born, with the exception of some of the women, who use the covering of leaf, or small bough, or an apron of cotton which they prepare for that purpose. None of them, as I have already said, are possessed of any iron, neither have they weapons, being unacquainted with, and indeed incompetent to use them, not from any deformity of body (for they are well-formed), but because they are timid and full of fear. They carry however in lieu of arms, canes dried in the sun, on the ends of which they fix heads of dried wood sharpened to a point, and even these they dare not use habitually; for it has often occurred when I have sent two or three of my men to any of the villages to speak with the natives, that they have come out in a disorderly troop, and have fled in such haste at the approach of our men, that the fathers forsook their children and the children their fathers. This timidity did not arise from any loss or injury that they had received from us; for, on the contrary, I gave to all I approached whatever articles I had about me, such as cloth and many other things, taking nothing of theirs in return: but they are naturally timid and fearful. As soon however as they see that they are safe, and have laid aside all fear, they are very simple and honest, and exceedingly liberal with all they have; none of them refusing any thing he may possess when he is asked for it, but on the contrary inviting us to ask them. They exhibit great love towards all others in preference to themselves: they also give objects of great value for trifles, and content themselves with very little or nothing in return. I however forbad that these trifles and articles of no value (such as pieces of dishes, plates, and glass, keys, and leather straps) should be given to them, although if they could obtain them, they imagined themselves to be possessed of the most beautiful trinkets in the world. It even happened that a sailor received for a leather strap as much gold as was worth three golden nobles, and for things of more trifling value offered by our men, especially newly coined blancas, or any gold coins, the Indians would give whatever the seller required; as, for instance, an ounce and a half or two ounces of gold, or thirty or forty pounds of cotton, with which commodity they were already acquainted. Thus they bartered, like idiots, cotton and gold for fragments of bows, glasses, bottles, and jars; which I forbad as being unjust, and myself gave them many beautiful and acceptable articles which I had brought with me, taking nothing from them in return; I did this in order that I might the more easily conciliate them, that they might be led to become

Christians, and be inclined to entertain a regard for the King and Queen, our Princes and all Spaniards, and that I might induce them to take an interest in seeking out, and collecting, and delivering to us such things as they possessed in abundance, but which we greatly needed. They practise no kind of idolatry, but have a firm belief that all strength and power, and indeed all good things, are in heaven, and that I had descended from thence with these ships and sailors, and under this impression was I received after they had thrown aside their fears. Nor are they slow or stupid, but of very clear understanding; and those men who have crossed to the neighbouring islands give an admirable description of everything they observed; but they never saw any people clothed, nor any ships like ours. On my arrival at that sea, I had taken some Indians by force from the first island that I came to, in order that they might learn our language, and communicate to us what they knew respecting the country; which plan succeeded excellently, and was a great advantage to us, for in a short time, either by gestures and signs, or by words, we were enabled to understand each other. These men are still travelling with me, and although they have been with us now a long time, they continue to entertain the idea that I have descended from heaven; and on our arrival at any new place they published this, crying out immediately with a loud voice to the other Indians, "Come, come and look upon beings of a celestial race": upon which both women and men, children and adults, young men and old, when they got rid of the fear they at first entertained, would come out in throngs, crowding the roads to see us, some bringing food, others drink, with astonishing affection and kindness. . . . In all these islands there is no difference of physiognomy, of manners, or of language, but they all clearly understand each other, a circumstance very propitious for the realization of what I conceive to be the principal wish of our most serene King, namely, the conversion of these people to the holy faith of Christ, to which indeed, as far as I can judge, they are very favourable and well-disposed.

Memoirs: The Aztecs

Bernal Diaz del Castillo

While many Europeans who first came into contact with non-Western peoples viewed them with arrogance, others were quite impressed with what they saw. This was particularly true of some Spanish observers in Mexico. Before Cortez's conquest of Mexico in 1519, the Aztecs dominated much of the "middle American" world. This selection, written a half-century later by Bernal Diaz (1492–1581), a member of Cortez's conquering army, gives a sense of the Aztec's highly developed civilization and the splendor of their capital.

CONSIDER: *What most impressed Diaz; why Diaz was astonished at the wealth of this civilization; how this account compares with that of Columbus.*

When we gazed upon all this splendour . . . we scarcely knew what to think, and we doubted whether all that we beheld was real. A series of large towns stretched themselves along the banks of the lake, out of which still larger ones rose magnificently above the waters. Innumerable crowds of canoes were plying everywhere around us; at regular distances we continually passed over new bridges, and before us lay the great city of Mexico in all its splendour. . . .

Motecusuma himself, according to his custom, was sumptuously attired, had on a species of half boot, richly set with jewels, and whose soles were made of solid gold. The four grandees who supported him were also richly attired, which they must have put on somewhere on the road, in order to wait upon Motecusuma; they were not so sumptuously dressed when they first came out to meet us. Besides these distinguished caziques, there were many other grandees around the monarch, some of whom held the canopy over his head, while others again occupied the road before him, and spread cotton cloths on the ground that his feet might not touch the bare earth. No one of his suite ever looked at him full in the face; every one in his presence stood with eyes downcast, and it was only his four nephews and cousins who supported him that durst look up. . . .

Our commander, attended by the greater part of our cavalry and foot, all well armed, as, indeed, we were at all times, had proceeded to the Tlatelulco. . . . The moment we arrived in this immense market, we were perfectly astonished at the vast numbers of people, the profusion of merchandise which was there exposed for sale, and at the good police and order that reigned throughout. The grandees who accompanied us drew our attention to the smallest circumstance, and gave us full explanation of all we saw. Every species of merchandise had a separate spot for its sale. We first of all visited those divisions of the market appropriated for the sale of gold and silver wares, of jewels, of cloths interwoven with feathers, and of other manufactured goods; besides slaves of both sexes. . . . Next to these

SOURCE: I. I. Lockhart, trans., *The Memoirs of the Conquistador Bernal de Castillo* (London: J. Hatchard and Son, 1844), pp. 220–221, 235–238.

came the dealers in coarser wares—cotton, twisted thread, and cacao. . . . In one place were sold the stuffs manufactured of nequen; ropes, and sandals; in another place, the sweet maguey root, ready cooked, and various other things made from this plant. In another division of the market were exposed the skins of tigers, lions, jackals, otters, red deer, wild cats, and of other beasts of prey, some of which were tanned. In another place were sold beans and sage, with other herbs and vegetables. A particular market was assigned for the merchants in fowls, turkeys, ducks, rabbits, hares, deer, and dogs; also for fruit-sellers, pastry-cooks, and tripe-sellers. Not far from these were exposed all manner of earthenware, from the large earthen cauldron to the smaller pitchers. Then came the dealers in honey and honey-cakes, and other sweetmeats. Next to these, the timber-merchants, furniture-dealers, with their stores of tables, benches, cradles, and all sorts of wooden implements, all separately arranged. . . .

In this market-place there were also courts of justice, to which three judges and several constables were appointed, who inspected the goods exposed for sale. . . . I wish I had completed the enumeration of all this profusion of merchandise. The variety was so great that it would occupy more space than I can well spare to note them down in; besides which, the market was so crowded with people, and the thronging so excessive in the porticoes, that it was quite impossible to see all in one day. . . .

Indeed, this infernal temple, from its great height, commanded a view of the whole surrounding neighbourhood. From this place we could likewise see the three causeways which led into Mexico. . . . We also observed the aqueduct which ran from Chapultepec, and provided the whole town with sweet water. We could also distinctly see the bridges across the openings, by which these causeways were intersected, and through which the waters of the lake ebbed and flowed. The lake itself was crowded with canoes, which were bringing provisions, manufactures, and other merchandise to the city. From here we also discovered that the only communication of the houses in this city, and of all the other towns built in the lake, was by means of drawbridge or canoes. In all these towns the beautiful white plastered temples rose above the smaller ones, . . . and this, it may be imagined, was a splendid sight.

After we had sufficiently gazed upon this magnificent picture, we again turned our eyes toward the great market, and beheld the vast numbers of buyers and sellers who thronged them. The bustle and noise occasioned by this multitude of human beings was so great that it could be heard at a distance of more than four miles.

Letter to Charles V: Finance and Politics

Jacob Fugger

The explorations and conquests of the fifteenth and sixteenth centuries were connected with the commercial expansion occurring in Europe at the same time. Central to this expansion was the rise of great international financial houses, such as the House of Fugger. The House of Fugger originated in Augsburg, Germany, and the Fuggers established branches throughout Europe and became directly tied not only to the growth of commerce but also to political developments as financiers to royal families. The extent of the Fuggers' political influence is suggested by the tone and content of the following letter, written in 1523, by Jacob Fugger, head of the firm, to Charles V, head of the House of Hapsburg, Holy Roman Emperor, King of Spain, and the most powerful ruler in Europe. The letter refers to the financial support provided by the Fuggers that enabled Charles, rather than his competitor Francis I of France, to be elected Holy Roman Emperor in 1519 by the electoral princes of Germany.

CONSIDER: *The tone of this letter; the interests the Fuggers might have in establishing a relationship with Charles V; Jacob Fugger's options had Charles rejected this request for repayment of the loan.*

Your Imperial Majesty doubtless knows how I and my kinsmen have ever hitherto been disposed to serve the House of Austria in all loyalty to the furtherance of its well-being and prosperity; wherefore, in order to be pleasing to Your Majesty's Grandsire, the late Emperor Maximilian, and to gain for Your Majesty the Roman Crown, we have held ourselves bounden to engage ourselves towards divers princes who placed their Trust and Reliance upon myself and perchance on No Man besides. We have, moreover, advanced to Your Majesty's Agents for the same end a Great Sum of Money, of which we ourselves have had to raise a large part from our Friends. It is well known that Your Imperial Majesty could not have gained the Roman Crown save with mine aid, and I can prove the same by the writings of Your Majesty's Agents given by their own hands. In this matter I have not studied mine own Profit. For had I left the House of Austria and had been minded to further France, I had obtained much money and property, such as was then offered to me. How grave a Disadvantage had in this case accrued to Your Majesty and the House of Austria, Your Majesty's Royal Mind well knoweth.

SOURCE: From Richard Ehrenberg, *Capital and Finance in the Age of the Renaissance: A Study of the Fuggers and Their Connections,* trans. H. M. Lucas (New York: Augustus M. Kelley, 1963), p. 80. Reprinted by permission.

Visual Sources

Portrait of the Merchant Georg Gisze

Hans Holbein the Younger

German artist Hans Holbein the Younger (1497–1543) painted this portrait of Georg Gisze in 1532 (figure 3.1). The note in his hand reveals that the merchant is standing in a corner of the London office of his trading firm, which was based in Danzig—an important German-Polish commercial center on the Baltic coast. The London location indicates the international nature of commerce during this period, and the silk clothing, signet rings, pewter box of gold coins, and the oriental carpet suggest that this is a lucrative business. Another note near a pair of scales hanging from a shelf contains a personal statement from Gisze: "No joy without sorrow." The vase and flowers, perhaps symbols of love and religious beliefs, suggest that business is not all important to this merchant.

SOURCE: Berlin, Gemäldegalerie der Staatlichen, Museen Preusischer Kulturbesitz.

CONSIDER: *How merchants like Gisze, who paid to have their portraits painted by artists such as Hans Holbein the*

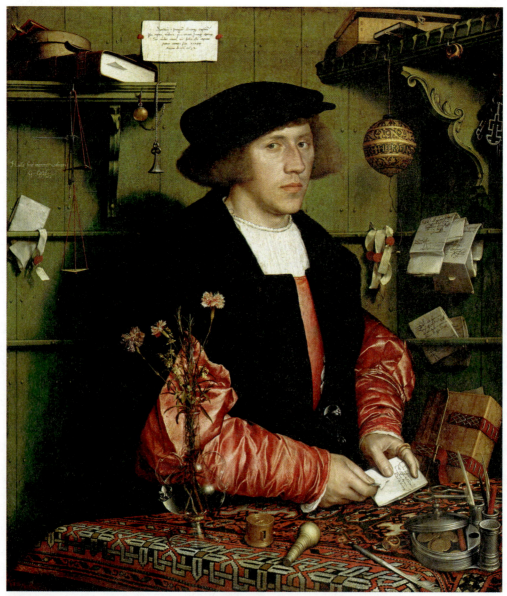

FIGURE 3.1 (© Bildarchiv Preussischer Kulturbesitz/Art Resource, NY)

Younger, wanted to be perceived; evidence for the rise of international commerce in this painting.

The Assets and Liabilities of Empire

Frans Fracken II

This painting by Frans Fracken II (figure 3.2) represents the abdication of Emperor Charles V in 1555. In the center sits Charles V with outstretched hands, symbolically giving Spain and the Netherlands to his son Philip on his left and the Empire to his brother Ferdinand on his right. Next to Philip stand various political figures, and below them are banners representing the provinces. In the foreground is an allegorical scene representing Spain's dominance of the sea and the New World. On the left is the bearded Neptune with a globe and his court; on the right is an Indian and other exotic figures and animals offering homage (in the form of gold treasure). The event occurred in Brussels on October 25, 1555, shortly after Charles assented to the Peace of Augsburg, which has been in-

terpreted as a double defeat for him: a recognition of Lutheranism and a political victory for German princes over imperial authority. There Charles made a speech, which included the following statements:

> I had no inordinate ambition to rule a multitude of kingdoms, but merely sought to secure the welfare of Germany, to provide for the defense of Flanders, to consecrate my forces to the safety of Christianity against the Turk, and to labor for the extension of the Christian religion. But although such zeal was mine, I was unable to show so much of it as I might have wished, on account of the troubles raised by the heresies of Luther and other innovators of Germany, and on account of serious war into which the hostility and envy of neighboring princes had driven men, and from which I have safely emerged, thanks to the favor of God. . . . I am determined then to retire to Spain, to yield to my son Philip the

FIGURE 3.2   (© Rijksmuseum, Amsterdam)

possession of all my states, and to my brother, the king of the Romans, the Empire. . . . Above all, beware of infection from the sects of neighboring lands. Extirpate at once the germs, if they appear in your midst, for fear lest they may spread abroad and utterly overthrow your state, and lest you may fall into the direst calamities.

CONSIDER: *How this picture and speech reflect the position and predicament of the Hapsburgs during this period.*

The Conquest of Mexico as Seen by the Aztecs

With the exception of a few written documents, most accounts of Aztec culture, like that of Incan and Mayan cultures, come from pictographs, sculptures, and other artifacts. Historical events are often depicted from the point of view of the conqueror rather than the vanquished. Here we see one of the few depictions of the Spanish conquest of the Aztec from the perspective of the conquered people (figure 3.3). In this Aztec manuscript from about 1519 to 1522, shortly after Cortez entered Mexico in 1519, the bloody and brutal suppression of the Aztec is shown in all its hor-

ror. Notice the Aztec offering what appears to be a wreath to Cortez, holding a sword about to be swung.

CONSIDER: *The symbols of conquest and destruction shown in the illustration.*

Exploration, Expansion, and Politics

Aside from the various motivations for the voyages of discovery during the fifteenth and sixteenth centuries, a number of factors combined to make those voyages physically possible when earlier they were not. Technological discoveries significantly improved shipbuilding and navigation. But also important was the understanding and mapping of prevailing ocean currents and winds in relation to land masses. It was much easier to sail with, rather than against, currents and winds, and sailors counted on finding land masses for supplies along the way.

The early voyages tended to take advantage of currents and winds as shown in this map. Thus, for example, early voyages to North America usually took a more southerly route westward across the Atlantic and returned on a more northerly route, while Portuguese ships headed east to the Indian Ocean by following winds and currents to Brazil and

FIGURE 3.3   (© Biblioteca Apostolica Vaticana)

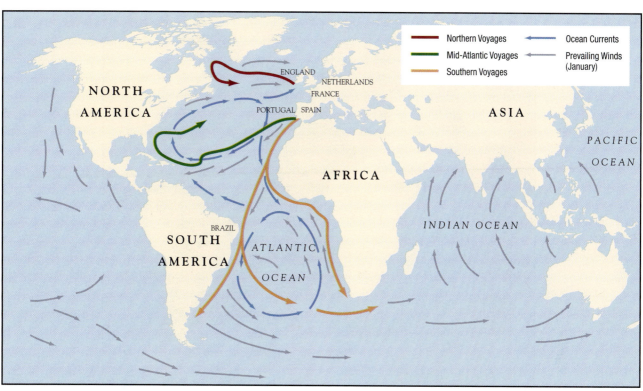

MAP 3.1   Overseas Explorations

then crossed the Atlantic farther south. Prevailing currents and winds also explain the difficulty of westward voyages around the tip of South America. These patterns of voyages also shed light on some of the geopolitical results of expansion. For example, even though Portugal's efforts were directed toward an eastern route to the Far East, she acquired Brazil (her only territory in the New World) to the west since it was on a route favored by winds and currents.

CONSIDER: *How map 3.1 helps explain the pattern of exploration and colonization by the various European powers.*

Map 3.2 shows some of the geopolitical connections of international finance during the sixteenth century. First, it shows the extent of Fugger agencies throughout Europe, thus indicating how much international finance had grown by this time. Second, it reveals some of the direct connections between industry and finance, for the Fuggers were involved in both and often took mineral concessions or rights in mines as security or repayment for loans. Third, it suggests some of the political connections between the Fuggers and the House of Hapsburg; most of the firm's branches and mines were within Hapsburg lands, and not surprisingly the Fuggers became tied to the Hapsburgs by a series of loans.

CONSIDER: *How map 3.2 relates to the letter of Jacob Fugger to Charles V.*

Secondary Sources

The Expansion of Europe

Richard B. Reed

In analyzing the overseas expansion of the fifteenth and sixteenth centuries, historians typically emphasize a combination of economic and religious factors to explain the motivation

SOURCE: Richard B. Reed, "The Expansion of Europe," in *The Meaning of the Renaissance and Reformation,* ed. Richard L. DeMolen (Boston: Houghton Mifflin, 1974), p. 299. Reprinted by permission.

behind expansion while focusing on the establishment of adequate knowledge and technology as key conditions for its occurrence. In the following selection Richard B. Reed argues that European expansion was a nationalistic phenomenon, and because of this Portugal was able to become the early leader.

CONSIDER: *Why Italy and Germany did not participate in overseas expansion; how one might attack Reed's argument that Portugal was in a better position to initiate expansion than any other country; other factors that might help explain why Portugal led in overseas expansion.*

MAP 3.2   Commercial Expansion and Politics

The expansion of Europe was an intensely nationalistic phenomenon. It was an aspect of the trend, most evident in the late fifteenth and early sixteenth centuries, toward the establishment of strong centralized authority in the "new monarchies," as they have been called, and the emergence of the nation-state. A policy of overseas expansion required a degree of internal stability and national consciousness that only a powerful central government could command. Portugal achieved this position long before her eventual competitors, and under the leadership of the dynamic house of Avis became a consolidated kingdom comparatively free from feudal divisions before the end of the fifteenth century. While Spain was still divided into a number of conflicting political jurisdictions, England and France were preoccupied with their own and each other's affairs, and the Dutch were still an appendage of the Empire, the Portuguese combined the advantages of their natural geographic situation with their political and economic stability to initiate the age of discovery. Spain in the sixteenth century, and England, France, and the Netherlands in the seventeenth century, became active colonial powers only after each had matured into strong national entities, independent of feudal political and economic restrictions. . . .

The importance of the nation-state in Renaissance expansion is particularly apparent when the Italian city-states are considered. Venice and Genoa, cities that had contributed so many of the medieval travelers and early Renaissance geographers and mapmakers, did not participate directly in Europe's overseas expansion. Yet Italian names dominated the rolls of the early voyagers. Prince Henry employed Venetians and Florentines in his naval establishment, while Columbus, Vespucci, Verrazano, the Cabots, and many others sailed for Spain, France, and England. Italian cartography was the best in Europe until the second half of the sixteenth century, and a high proportion of the books and pamphlets that chronicled new discoveries emanated from the presses of Vicenza, Venice, Rome, and Florence. Italian bankers and merchants were also very active in the commercial life of the principal Iberian cities. A divided Italy was instrumental in making Renaissance expansion possible, but it could not take full advantage of its own endowments. Germans, too, figured prominently in the expansion of the sixteenth century, as the names of Federmann, Staden, Welser, and Fugger attest. But Germany, like Italy, was not united, and the emergence of these two nations as colonial powers had to wait until their respective consolidations in the nineteenth century.

While every nationality in Western Europe was represented in Renaissance expansion, it was by no means an international venture. On the contrary, it was very much an expression of that nationalistic fervor that characterized political developments in the fifteenth and sixteenth centuries. It was primarily a state enterprise, often financed privately but controlled and protected by the governments of the concerned powers. There was no co-operation between nations, and even after the upheaval of the Protestant Reformation, when political loyalties and alignments were conditioned by religious sympathies, there were no colonial alliances that provided for mutual Protestant or Catholic overseas policies.

The Effects of Expansion on the Non-European World

M. L. Bush

While the expansion of Europe was of great significance for European history, it was of even greater consequence for the non-European world touched by the explorers. However, its effects differed greatly in the New World, where the Spanish dominated, and the East, where the Portuguese were the leaders. In the following selection M. L. Bush analyzes these differences.

CONSIDER: *Internal factors in non-Western societies that help explain these differences; contrasts between Portugal and Spain that help explain the different consequences for non-Western societies.*

The Castilian Empire in the West and the Portuguese Empire in the East had very different effects upon the world outside of Europe. In the first place, the Castilian expansion westwards precipitated a series of overseas migrations which were unparalleled in earlier times. For most of the sixteenth century, 1,000 or 2,000 Spaniards settled in the New World each year. Later this was followed by a large wave of emigrants from northwestern Europe, fleeing from persecution at home to the Atlantic sea-board of North America and the Caribbean, and a final wave of Africans forced into slavery in the West Indies and in Brazil. On the other hand, in the East, there was virtually no settlement in the sixteenth century. Europe impressed itself only by fort, factory and church, by colonial official, trader and missionary.

In the second place, the settlement of the New World had a severe effect upon native peoples, whereas in the East, European influence was very slight until much later times.

In the early 1520s, the conquistadors brought with them smallpox and typhoid. Between them these European diseases soon decimated the Indian population, particularly in the great epidemics of the 1520s, 1540s and 1570s. In central Mexico, for example, an Indian population which numbered 11,000,000 in 1519 numbered no more than 2,500,000 by the end of the century. In addition, the Indian was beset by enormous grazing herds of horned cattle which the white settler introduced. He escaped the herds by working for the white settler, but if this led him to the crowded labour settlements, as it quite often did, he stood less chance of escaping infection. Either through falling hopelessly in debt as a result of desiring the goods of the white man, or through entering the labour settlements on a permanent basis to avoid the herds and also the system of obligatory labour introduced by the Spaniard,[1] there was a strong tendency for the Indian to become europeanised. He became a wage-earner, a debtor and a Christian. The Indian was exploited. But in the law he remained free. Enslavement was practised, but it was not officially tolerated. Moreover, the Franciscan order, a powerful missionary force in the New World, did its best to save the Indian from the evil ways of the white man. In Bartholomew de Las Casas and Francisco de Vitoria, the Indian found influential defenders; and through their schemes for separate Indian Christian communities, he found a partial escape from the white man. But the Indian mission towns, which were permitted by Charles V, were objected to by his successor, Philip II, and they only survived in remote areas.

With few exceptions, the way of life of the surviving Indians was basically changed by the coming of the white man. The outstanding exception was in Portuguese Brazil where the more primitive, nomadic Indians had a greater opportunity to retreat into the bush. There was also less settlement in Brazil, and generally less impression was made because of Portuguese preoccupations elsewhere,

SOURCE: M. L. Bush, *Renaissance, Reformation and the Outer World* (New York: Harper & Row, 1967), pp. 143–145.

[1]This system depended upon every Indian village offering a proportion of its menfolk or labour service for a limited amount of time throughout the year.

and also because of their lack of resources for empire-building on the Spanish scale. Furthermore, within the Spanish Empire, the European impressed himself less on the Incas in Peru than upon the Aztecs in Mexico. Because of the slow subjection of Peru, several Inca risings, the nature of the terrain, the smallness of the Spanish community, the process of europeanisation was much slower, and in the long run much less complete. The remnants of the Inca aristocracy became Spanish in their habits and Catholic in their religion, but the peasantry tended to remain pagan. In contrast to these developments, the westernisation of the East was a development of more modern times.

The West impinged upon the East in the sixteenth century mainly through the missionary. With the arrival of St. Francis Xavier in 1542 in India, an impressive process of conversion was begun. Concentrating upon the poor fishermen of the Cape Comorin coast, within ten years he had secured, it was said, 60,000 converts. The Jesuits fixed their attention on the East, choosing Goa as their main headquarters outside of Rome. Little was accomplished in Malaya, Sumatra and China in the sixteenth century, and Christianity soon suffered setbacks in the Moluccas after a promising start; but in Ceylon the conversion of the young king of Kotte in 1557 was a signal triumph, and so were the conversions in Japan. In the 1580s Jesuit missionaries in Japan claimed to have converted 150,000, most of whom, however, were inhabitants of the island of Kyushu.

Christianity was not a new religion in the East. There were extensive communities of Nestorian Christians, but they were regarded as alien as the Muslim by the Europeans. The new Christians by 1583 were supposed to number 600,000. But compared with the expansion of Islam in the East—a process which was taking place at the same time—the expansion of Christianity was a minute achievement.

Finally, the Portuguese sea empire did little to transport Portuguese habits abroad. Their empire was essentially formed in response to local conditions. On the other hand, the Spanish land empire was to a much greater extent reflective of Castilian ways.

In the New World a carefully developed and regulated system of government was established in which it was seen that the care taken to limit the independent power of feudal aristocrats in the Old World should also be applied to the New. There was a firm insistence upon government officials being royal servants. However, the government of the New World became much more regulated from the centre than that of the old. There was less respect for aristocratic privilege. Less power was unreservedly placed in the hands of the nobility. In the New World, in fact, the weaknesses of government, at first, did not lie in the powers and privileges of the nobility but

rather in the cumbersome nature of the government machinery. Nevertheless, in spite of these precautions, the New World, by the early seventeenth century, had become a land of great feudal magnates enjoying, in practice, untrammelled power.

Red, White, and Black: The Peoples of Early America

Gary Nash

Europeans often came into conflict with the peoples they encountered overseas. In the Americas, diverging understanding of the meaning of land ownership and, more broadly, private property, would lead to continual conflict. Europeans took for granted that people had the right to buy and sell land. Yet, this was not the case for Native Americans. In North America, European settlers would fence in land and hunt for private profit. This would undermine the entire livelihood of nomadic tribes that depended on freedom to move, hunt, and establish temporary communities. In the following selection, Gary Nash, a historian of early American history at UCLA, describes the clash of cultures and economic systems between white settlers and the native inhabitants of North America.

CONSIDER: *The differences between the Native American and European world views concerning land and personal identity; in light of what we now know regarding ecological destruction, how you might evaluate the Native American view of the symmetry of nature.*

While Native American and European cultures were not nearly so different as the concepts of "savagery" and "civilization" imply, societies on the eastern and western sides of the Atlantic had developed different systems of values in the centuries that preceded contact. Underlying the physical confrontations that would take place when European and Native American met were incompatible ways of looking at the world. These latent conflicts can be seen in contrasting European and Indian views of man's relationship to his environment, the concept of property, and personal identity.

In the European view the natural world was a resource for man to use. "Subdue the earth," it was said in Genesis, "and have dominion over every living thing that moves on the earth." The cosmos was still ruled by God, of course, and supernatural forces, manifesting themselves in earthquakes, hurricanes, drought, and flood, could not be controlled by man. But a scientific revolution was under way in the early modern period, which

SOURCE: Gary B. Nash, *Red, White and Black: The Peoples of Early America,* 3d ed. (Englewood Cliffs, NJ: Prentice-Hall, 1982), pp. 25–27. Copyright © 1982, 1992. Reprinted by permission of Prentice-Hall.

gave humans more confidence that they could comprehend the natural world—and thus eventually control it. For Europeans the secular and the sacred were distinct, and man's relationship to his natural environment fell into the secular sphere.

In the Indian ethos no such separation of secular and sacred existed. Every part of the natural world was sacred, for Native Americans believed the world was inhabited by a great variety of "beings," each possessing spiritual power and all linked together to form a sacred whole. "Plants, animals, rocks, and stars," explains Murray Wax, "are thus seen not as objects governed by laws of nature but as 'fellows' with whom the individual or band may have a more or less advantageous relationship." Consequently, if one offended the land by stripping it of its cover, the spiritual power in the land—called *manitou* by some woodlands tribes—would strike back. If one overfished or destroyed game beyond one's needs, the spiritual power inhering in fish and animals would take revenge because humans had broken the mutual trust and reciprocity that governed relations between all beings—human and nonhuman. To exploit the land or to treat with disrespect any part of the natural world was to cut oneself off from the spiritual power dwelling in all things and "was thus equivalent to repudiating the vital force in Nature."

Because Europeans regarded the land as a resource to be exploited for man's gain it was easier to regard it as a commodity to be privately held. Private ownership of property became one of the fundamental bases upon which European culture rested. Fences became the symbols of exclusively held property, inheritance became the mechanism for transmitting these "assets" from one generation to another within the same family, and courts provided the institutional apparatus for settling property disputes. In a largely agricultural society property became the basis of political power. In fact, political rights in England derived from the ownership of a specified quantity of land. In addition, the social structure was largely defined by the distribution of property, with those possessing great quantities of it standing at the apex of the social pyramid and the mass of propertyless individuals forming the broad base.

In the Indian world this view of land as a privately held asset was incomprehensible. Tribes recognized territorial boundaries, but within these limits the land was held in common. Land was not a commodity but a part of nature that was entrusted to the living by the Creator. . . . Thus, land was a gift of the Creator, to be used with care, and was not for the exclusive possession of particular human beings.

In the area of personal identity Indian and European values also differed sharply. Europeans were acquisitive, competitive, and over a long period of time had been enhancing the role of the individual. Wider choices and greater opportunities for the individual to improve his status—by industriousness, valor, or even personal sacrifice leading to martyrdom—were regarded as desirable. Personal ambition, in fact, played a large role in the migration of Europeans across the Atlantic in the sixteenth and seventeenth centuries. In contrast, the cultural traditions of Native Americans emphasized the collectivity rather than the individual. Because land and other natural resources were held in common and society was far less hierarchical than in Europe, the accumulative spirit and personal ambition were inappropriate. . . . Hence, individualism was more likely to lead to ostracism than admiration in Indian communities.

🙠 CHAPTER QUESTIONS

1. What factors best explain the West's overseas expansion?

2. In what ways was overseas expansion tied to the political and economic developments of the fifteenth and sixteenth centuries?

3. What consequences flowed from this interaction of Western and non-Western civilizations?

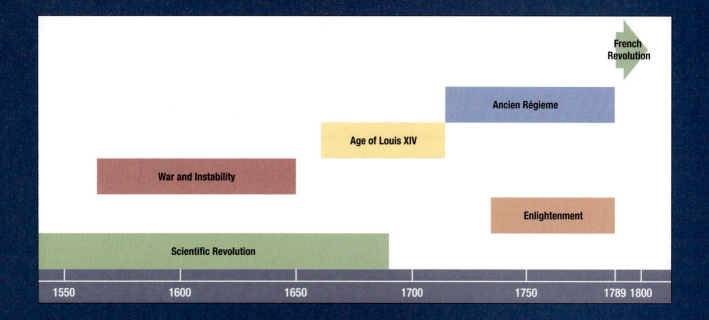

II

The Early Modern Period

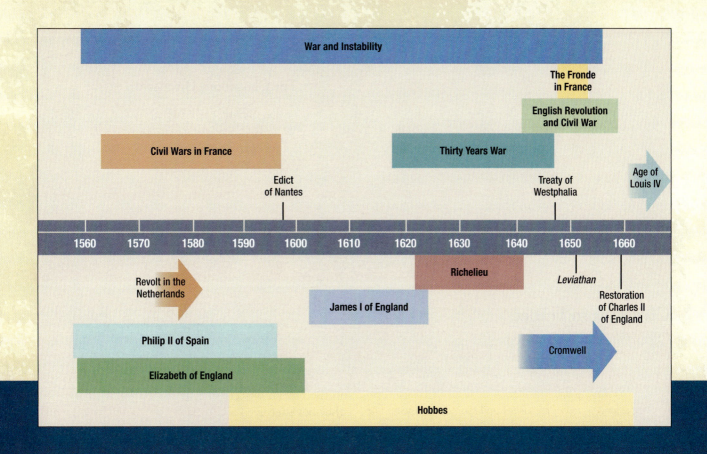

4 War and Revolution: 1560–1660

Between 1560 and 1660 war and revolution broke out throughout Europe. In France different political and religious factions struggled under a weak monarchy in what amounted at times to an extended civil war during the second half of the sixteenth century. Although stronger kings and ministers brought more stability during the seventeenth century, the nobility again rose at mid-century before the final assertion of French absolutism under Louis XIV. In Germany political and religious divisions contributed to the outbreak of a local war in 1618, which quickly turned into a bloody international war lasting thirty years, until it was ended by the Treaty of Westphalia in 1648. Few wars in history have been as devastating to Germany as this; perhaps a third of the people lost their lives. In England the growing conflict between king and Parliament, further fueled by religious and social divisions, led to a revolution and civil war during the 1640s and the extraordinary rule of Oliver Cromwell during the 1650s. In

1660 relative stability was restored under Charles II. Finally, in the Netherlands extended bloodshed marked the long effort by Spain to retain control over the Dutch, who finally succeeded in gaining complete independence in 1648.

The documents in this chapter deal with three of the upheavals—in France, in Central Europe, and in England—during the period from the mid-sixteenth to mid-seventeenth centuries. What was the nature of the civil wars in sixteenth-century France? In what ways was monarchical absolutism an answer to the political and religious struggles in France? Was the Thirty Years' War in Central Europe primarily a German conflict or a struggle against the predominance of Spain? How important were religious as compared with political causes of this war? Beyond the death and destruction involved, how decisive or significant was this war? What was the nature of the conflict between royal and parliamentary authority in England? How did political theory in England reflect these

49

conflicts? What were some of several consequences of all these struggles?

The materials in this chapter characterize this century as one of extraordinary violence—sometimes directed at women in particular—and struggle for political and religious control. The violence diminishes and a new sense of stability is gained in the second half of the seventeenth century, as will be seen in the next chapter.

 For Classroom Discussion

How do you explain the Thirty Years' War? Compare the interpretations of Friedrich and Holborn as well as Anderson's analysis of peace and war.

 # Primary Sources

Civil War in France
Ogier Ghiselin de Busbecq

France was one of the first areas in which the turmoil, instability, and war characteristic of the period between 1560 and 1660 occurred. There, political and religious divisions combined to produce a long period of bloodshed and sporadic civil war. The nature and effects of this turmoil are described in the following selection from a letter written in 1575 by Ogier Ghiselin de Busbecq, the Holy Roman Emperor's ambassador to France.

CONSIDER: *Busbecq's perception of the forces and grievances that were threatening to worsen the civil wars that had already broken out; the consequences of the civil wars for various segments of society.*

Ever since the commencement of the civil wars which are distracting the country, there has been a terrible change for the worse. So complete is the alteration, that those who knew France before would not recognise her again. Everywhere are to be seen shattered buildings, fallen churches, and towns in ruins; while the traveller gazes horror-stricken on spots which have but lately been the scenes of murderous deeds and inhuman cruelties. The fields are left untilled: the farmer's stock and tools have been carried off by the soldier as his booty, he is plundered alike by Frenchman and by foreigner. Commerce is crippled; the towns lately thronged with merchants and customers are now mourning their desolation in the midst of closed shops and silent manufactories. Meanwhile, the inhabitants, ground down by ceaseless exactions, are crying out at the immense sums which are being squandered for nought, or applied to purposes for which they were never intended. They demand a reckoning in tones which breathe a spirit of rebellion. Men of experience, members of the oldest families in France, are in many cases regarded with suspicion, and either not

allowed to come to Court, or left to vegetate at home. Besides the two parties into which Frenchmen are divided by their religious differences, there are also feuds and quarrels which affect every grade of society.

In the first place, the feeling against the Italians who are in the French service is very strong; the high promotion they have received and the important duties with which they have been intrusted, arouse the jealousy of men who consider them ignorant of French business, and hold that they have neither merit, services, nor birth to justify their appointment. . . .

The feuds which separate the leading families of France are more bitter than those described in ancient tragedy; this is the state of feeling which exists between the Houses of Guise, Vendôme and Bourbon, not to mention that of Montmorency, which, through its alliances and connections, has a considerable party of its own.

Political Will and Testament
Richelieu

The civil wars in France were ended under the rule of Henry IV at the end of the sixteenth century. This strong king prevailed over rival factions and strengthened the French monarchy. But religious conflict and the competition with the nobility for authority were not over in France. Rather, the monarchy was built up toward a position of absolutism under a series of powerful figures, including Cardinal Richelieu (1585–1642), who served as principal adviser to the king between 1624 and 1642 and virtual ruler for most of that period. In the following selection from his Political Will and Testament, *Richelieu presents his view of monarchical power.*

CONSIDER: *How Richelieu justifies monarchical power; how Machiavelli might have responded to this view.*

SOURCE: From Charles Thornton Forster and F. H. Blackburne Daniell, *The Life and Letters of Ogier Ghiselin de Busbecq,* vol. II (London, 1881), pp. 38–40.

SOURCE: Armand Jean du Plessis, Duc de Richelieu, *Political Will and Testament,* vol. II (London, 1695), pp. 45–46.

Power being one of the most necessary ingredients towards the grandeur of kings, and the prosperity of their governments; those who have the chief management of affairs are particularly obliged not to omit anything which may contribute to authorize their master so far as to make all the world reject him.

As goodness is the object of love, power is the cause of dread: and it is most certain, that among all the princes who are capable to stir a state, fear grounded upon esteem and reverence has so much force, that it engages everyone to perform his duty.

If this principle is of great efficacy in respect to the internal part of states, it is to the full as prevailing abroad: subjects and strangers looking with the same eyes upon a formidable power, both the one and the other abstain from offending a prince, whom they are sensible is in a condition to hurt them, if he were so inclined.

I have observed by the by, that the ground of the power I am speaking of must be esteem and respect; . . . that when it is grounded upon any other principle, it is very dangerous; in the case instead of creating a reasonable fear, it inclines men to hate princes, who are never in a worse condition than when it turns to public aversion.

The power which induces men to respect and fear princes with love . . . is a tree which has five divers branches, which all draw their nutriment and substance from one and the same root.

The Prince must be powerful by his reputation.

By a reasonable army always kept on foot.

And by a notable sum of money in his coffers, to supply unexpected exigencies, which often come to pass when they are least expected.

Finally, by the possession of his subjects' hearts. . . .

The Powers of the Monarch in England

James I

In England friction between the monarchy and Parliament increased under the Stuart kings, starting with James I. Already the Scottish monarch, James became King of England on the death of Elizabeth in 1603. James had a scholarly background and a reputation for his strong views about the monarchy. One of his clearest presentations of these views was in a speech to Parliament made in 1610. In it, he comments on the nature of the king's power, not simply in England but everywhere.

Source: From J. R. Tanner, *Constitutional Documents of the Reign of James I, c.e. 1603–1625* (Cambridge, England: Cambridge University Press, 1930), pp. 15–16. Reprinted by permission.

Consider: *How James justifies the high position and vast powers he feels should rightly belong to kings; the limits to monarchical powers.*

The state of Monarchy is the supremest thing upon earth; for kings are not only God's lieutenants upon earth and sit upon God's throne, but even by God himself they are called gods. There be three principal similitudes that illustrate the state of Monarchy: one taken out of the Word of God and the two other out of the grounds of policy and philosophy. In the Scriptures kings are called gods, and so their power after a certain relation compared to the Divine power. Kings are also compared to the fathers of families, for a king is truly *parens patriae*, the politic father of his people. And lastly, kings are compared to the head of his microcosm of the body of man.

Kings are justly called gods for that they exercise a manner or resemblance of Divine power upon earth; for if you will consider the attributes to God you shall see how they agree in the person of a king. God hath power to create or destroy, make or unmake, at his pleasure; to give life or send death; to judge all, and to be judged nor accomptable to none; to raise low things and to make high things low at his pleasure; and to God are both soul and body due. And the like power have kings; they make and unmake their subjects; they have power of raising and casting down; of life and of death; judges over all their subjects and in all causes, and yet accomptable to none but God only. They have power to exalt low things and abase high things, and make of their subjects like men at the chess, a pawn to take a bishop or a knight, and to cry up or down any of their subjects as they do their money. And to the King is due both the affection of the soul and the service of the body of his subjects. . . .

As for the father of a family, they had of old under the Law of Nature *patriam potestatem*, which was *potestatem vitae et necis*, over their children or family, (I mean such fathers of families as were the lineal heirs of those families whereof kings did originally come), for kings had their first original from them who planted and spread themselves in colonies through the world. Now a father may dispose of his inheritance to his children at his pleasure, yea, even disinherit the eldest upon just occasions and prefer the youngest, according to his liking; make them beggars or rich at his pleasure; restrain or banish out of his presence, as he finds them give cause of offence, or restore them in favour again with the penitent sinner. So may the King deal with his subjects.

And lastly, as for the head of the natural body, the head hath the power of directing all the members of the body to that use which the judgment in the head thinks most convenient.

The Powers of Parliament in England

The House of Commons

James' views on monarchical powers were not accepted by members of Parliament. Indeed, from the beginning of his reign through the reign of his son Charles I, king and Parliament struggled over their relative powers. Along with other problems, this struggle culminated in the 1640s with the outbreak of civil war and the eventual beheading of Charles I. The nature of this struggle is partially revealed in the following statements issued by the House of Commons in 1604 to the new king, James I.

CONSIDER: *The powers over which the House of Commons and the king differed; the justifications used by James I and the House of Commons for their claims; any ways in which compromise was possible between these two positions.*

Now concerning the ancient rights of the subjects of this realm, chiefly consisting in the privileges of this House of Parliament, the misinformation openly delivered to your Majesty hath been in three things:

First, That we held not privileges of right, but of grace only, renewed every Parliament by way of donature upon petition, and so to be limited.

Secondly, That we are no Court of Record, nor yet a Court that can command view of records, but that our proceedings here are only to acts and memorials, and that the attendance with the records is courtesy, not duty.

Thirdly and lastly, That the examination of the return of writs for knights and burgesses is without our compass, and due to the Chancery.

Against which assertions, most gracious Sovereign, tending directly and apparently to the utter overthrow of the very fundamental privileges of our House, and therein of the rights and liberties of the whole Commons of your realm of England which they and their ancestors from time immemorable have undoubtedly enjoyed under your Majesty's most noble progenitors, we, the knights, citizens, and burgesses of the House of Commons assembled in Parliament, and in the name of the whole commons of the realm of England, with uniform consent for ourselves and our posterity, do expressly protest, as being derogatory in the highest degree to the true dignity, liberty, and authority of your Majesty's High Court of Parliament, and consequently to the rights of all your Majesty's said subjects and the whole body of this your kingdom: And desire that this our protestation may be recorded to all posterity.

And contrariwise, with all humble and due respect to your Majesty our Sovereign Lord and Head, against those misinformations we most truly avouch,

First, That our privileges and liberties are our right and due inheritance, no less than our very lands and goods.

Secondly, That they cannot be withheld from us, denied, or impaired, but with apparent wrong to the whole state of the realm.

Thirdly, And that our making of request in the entrance of Parliament to enjoy our privilege is an act only of manners, and doth weaken our right no more than our suing to the King for our lands by petition. . . .

Fourthly, We avouch also, That our House is a Court of Record, and so ever esteemed.

Fifthly, That there is not the highest standing Court in this land that ought to enter into competency, either for dignity or authority, with this High Court of Parliament, which with your Majesty's royal assent gives laws to other Courts but from other Courts receives neither laws nor orders.

Sixthly and lastly, We avouch that the House of Commons is the sole proper judge of return of all such writs and of the election of all such members as belong to it, without which the freedom of election were not entire: And that the Chancery, though a standing Court under your Majesty, be to send out those writs and receive the returns and to preserve them, yet the same is done only for the use of the Parliament, over which neither the Chancery nor any other Court ever had or ought to have any manner of jurisdiction.

From these misinformed positions, most gracious Sovereign, the greatest part of our troubles, distrusts, and jealousies have risen.

The Hammer of Witches

Heinrich Krämer and Jacob Sprenger

The upheavals of the period between 1560 and 1660 included growing violence against women in the form of persecuting women as witches. While witch hunting was widespread, it was particularly prevalent in Germany, where both Catholics and Protestants took part in the hunts and prosecutions. Authorities often used witch-hunters' manuals as guides to beliefs about witches. The most influential of these manuals, the Malleus Maleficarum (The Hammer of Witches), was written in 1486 by two Dominican Inquisitors. The following excerpt focuses on why most witches were women.

CONSIDER: *Exactly why, according to these authors, women are more likely than men to be witches; what this reveals about attitudes toward women.*

SOURCE: From J. R. Tanner, *Constitutional Documents of the Reign of James I, C.E. 1603–1625* (Cambridge, England: Cambridge University Press, 1930), pp. 220–222. Reprinted by permission.

SOURCE: Alan C. Kors and Edward Peters, eds. *Witchcraft in Europe, 1100–1700, A Documentary History.* (Philadelphia: University of Pennsylvania Press, 1972), pp. 114, 119, 121, 123.

As for the first question, why a greater number of witches is found in the fragile feminine sex than among men . . . the first reason is, that they are more credulous, and since the chief aim of the devil is to corrupt faith, therefore he rather attacks them . . . the second reason is, that women are naturally more impressionable, and . . . the third reason is that they have slippery tongues, and are unable to conceal from their fellow-women those things which by evil arts they know. . . . But the natural reason is that she is more carnal than a man, as is clear from her many carnal abominations. And it should be noted that there was a defect in the formation of the first woman, since she was formed from a bent rib, that is, a rib of the breast, which is bent as it were in a contrary direction to a man. And since through this defect she is an imperfect animal, she always deceives. . . . And this is indicated by the etymology of the world; for Femina comes from Fe and Minus, since she is ever weaker to hold and preserve the faith. . . . To conclude. All witchcraft comes from carnal lust, which is in women insatiable.

Visual Sources

The Surrender of Breda

Diego Valázquez

The long, draining Thirty Years' War (1618–1648) marked the first half of the seventeenth century. A major component of that complex set of conflicts was the effort of Protestants in Holland to free themselves from their Catholic Spanish overlords.

In this canvass (figure 4.1) commissioned by his monarch, Spanish artist Diego Valázquez celebrates the 1625 victory of Spain's Catholic forces over Protestant

FIGURE 4.1   (© Erich Lessing/Art Resource, NY)

Breda in Holland. The long war between the rebellious Dutch and their Spanish overlords had begun six years earlier. The painting centers on the moment when, after a year-long siege, Breda's commander Justin of Nassau handed over the keys of the city to his graceful counterpart, General Ambrogio Spinola. As indicated by his posture, the Spanish general greets the Dutch commander consolingly and with praise for the brave defense he and his soldiers have mounted. The magnanimity of the victorious Spanish reflects the sense that during the sixteenth and first decades of the seventeenth centuries, Spain's monarchs thought of themselves as the most powerful rulers in Europe, thanks to their glorious history of military conquest. The many long pikes held up vertically symbolize the order and strength of the Spanish forces, although in fact—as was typically the case on all sides of the Thirty Years' War—many of these soldiers were foreign mercenaries. Spinola's grace also suggests the Spanish belief in the ultimate justice of their Catholic cause.

Despite this Spanish victory, General Spinola's overly generous chivalric gesture and terms of surrender allowed the Dutch forces to keep their weapons and remain intact as they exited the town. The Dutch would again turn those forces against the declining armies of Spain and ultimately gain victory in the war.

CONSIDER: *How the vision of "honorable" battle is depicted in this painting; the nature of seventeenth-century warfare suggested by Valázquez's painting.*

War and Violence

Jan Brueghel and Sebastien Vrancx

This painting (figure 4.2), by the Flemish artists Jan Brueghel (1568–1625) and Sebastien Vrancx (1573–1647), is of marauding armies during the Thirty Years' War. This war was a disaster for Germany not only because of its length and viciousness, but because of the common use of mercenary soldiers. In this picture mercenaries, without common uniforms or banners, attack what appears to be a wagon train of civilians probably fleeing on hearing rumors of their approach. Women and children are being attacked by the mercenaries, as are men, whether armed or not. Johann Jakob Christoffel von Grimmelshausen, a contemporary observer of such mercenaries, described them as inflicting "nothing but hurting and harming and being in their turn hurt and harmed, this was their whole purpose and existence. From this nothing could divert them—not winter or summer, snow or ice, heat or cold, wind or rain, mountain or valley, . . . or the very fear of eternal damnation itself. At this task they laboured until at last, in battles,

FIGURE 4.2 (© Erich Lessing/Art Resource, NY)

sieges, assaults, campaigns, or even in their winter quarters, which is the soldiers' paradise, one by one they died, perished and rotted." The picture conveys the sense of almost random, out-of-control violence that was so typical of this period.

CONSIDER: The ways in which this painting and this observation might be used to describe how the Thirty Years' War was experienced by those involved.

Leviathan: Political Order and Political Theory

Thomas Hobbes

Although England avoided the Thirty Years' War, it had its own experiences with passionate war and disruption of authority. Between 1640 and 1660 England endured the civil war, the trial and execution of its king, Charles I, the rise to power of Oliver Cromwell, and the return to power of the Stuart king, Charles II. These events stimulated Thomas Hobbes (1588–1679) to formulate one of the most important statements of political theory in history.

Hobbes supported the royalist cause during the civil war and served as tutor to the future Charles II. Applying some of the new philosophical and scientific concepts being developed during the seventeenth century, he presented a theory for the origins and proper functioning of the state and political authority. His main ideas appear in Leviathan (1651), the title page of which appears here (figure 4.3). It shows a giant monarchical figure, with symbols of power and authority, presiding over a well-ordered city and surrounding lands. On close examination one can see that the monarch's body is com-

FIGURE 4.3 (© HIP/Art Resource, NY)

posed of the citizens of this commonwealth who, according to Hobbes' theory, have mutually agreed to give up their independence to an all-powerful sovereign who will keep order. This is explained in the following selection from Hobbes' book, in which he relates the reasons for the formation of a commonwealth to the nature of authority in that commonwealth.

SOURCE: Thomas Hobbes, *Leviathan*, vol. III of *The English Works of Thomas Hobbes,* ed. Sir William Molesworth (London: John Bohn, 1889), pp. 113, 151–153, 157, 159.

CONSIDER: Why men form such a commonwealth and why they give such power to the sovereign; how Hobbes' argument compares with that of James I; why both those *favoring more power for the House of Commons and those favoring increased monarchical power might criticize this argument.*

Whatsoever therefore is consequent to a time of war, where every man is enemy to every man; the same is consequent to the time, wherein men live without other security, than what their own strength, and their own invention shall furnish them withal. In such condition, there is no place for industry; because the fruit thereof is uncertain: and consequently no culture of the earth; no navigation, nor use of the commodities that may be imported by sea; no commodious building; no instruments of moving, and removing, such things as require much force; no knowledge of the face of the earth; no account of time; no arts; no letters; no society; and which is worst of all, continual fear, and danger of violent death; and the life of man, solitary, poor, nasty, brutish, and short. . . .

The final cause, end, or design of men who naturally love liberty, and dominion over others, in the introduction of that restraint upon themselves, in which we see them live in commonwealths, is the foresight of their own preservation, and of a more contented life thereby; that is to say, of getting themselves out from that miserable condition of war, which is necessarily consequent, as hath been shown in chapter XIII, to the natural passions of men, when there is no visible power to keep them in awe, and tie them by fear of punishment to the performance of their covenants, and observation of those laws of nature set down. . . .

For the laws of nature, as *justice, equity, modesty, mercy,* and, in sum, *doing to others, as we would be done to,* of themselves, without the terror of some power, to cause them to be observed, are contrary to our natural passions, that carry us to partiality, pride, revenge, and the like. And covenants, without the sword, are but words, and of no strength to secure a man at all. . . .

The only way to erect such a common power, as may be able to defend them from the invasion of foreigners, and the injuries of one another, and thereby to secure them in such

sort, as that by their own industry, and by the fruits of the earth, they may nourish themselves and live contentedly; is, to confer all their power and strength upon one man, or upon one assembly of men, that may reduce all their wills, by plurality of voices, unto one will: which is as much as to say, to appoint one man, or assembly of men, to bear their person; and every one to own, and acknowledge himself to be author of whatsoever he that so beareth their person, shall act, or cause to be acted, in those things which concern the common peace and safety; and therein to submit their wills, every one to his will, and their judgments, to his judgment. This is more than consent, or concord; it is a real unity of them all, in one and the same person, made by covenant of every man with every man, in such manner, as if every man should say to every man, *I authorise and give up my right of governing myself, to this man, or to this assembly of men, on this condition, that thou give up thy right to him, and authorise all his actions in like manner.* This done, the multitude so united in one person, is called a COMMONWEALTH, . . . This is the generation of that great LEVIATHAN, or rather, to speak more reverently, of that *mortal god,* to which we owe under the *immortal God,* our peace and defence. For by this authority, given him by every particular man in the

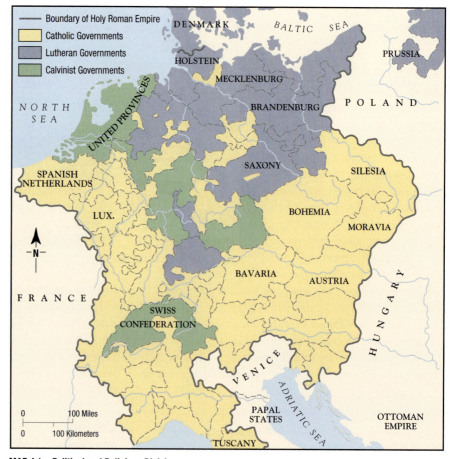

MAP 4.1   Political and Religious Divisions

commonwealth, he hath the use of so much power and strength conferred on him, that by terror thereof, he is enabled to perform the wills of them all, to peace at home, and mutual aid against their enemies abroad. And in him consisteth the essence of the commonwealth; which to define it, is *one person, of whose acts a great multitude, by mutual covenants one with another, have made themselves every one the author, to the end he may use the strength and means of them all, as he shall think expedient, for their peace and common defence.*

And he that carrieth this person, is called SOVEREIGN, and said to have *sovereign power;* and every one besides, his *subject.*

Germany and the Thirty Years' War

These maps center on circumstances in Germany during the Thirty Years' War. The first (map 4.1) shows the approximate political and religious divisions at the beginning of the war. This map is simplified for clarity in a number of ways. It does not show areas of minority religious allegiance or areas where Protestant sects other than Calvinists or Lutherans made up substantial proportions of the population. It denotes only some of the political divisions, which numbered close to three hundred in this area. The second map (map 4.2) shows the main areas of battle during the Thirty Years' War. Map 4.3 indicates the changes in population, primarily due to war and plague, between 1618 and 1648.

Together, these maps reveal some of the political and religious problems facing Germany. Despite the theoretical existence of the Holy Roman Empire, Germany was in reality the most politically and religiously divided area in seventeenth-century Europe. It is thus not surprising that historians find it difficult to determine the political and religious factors causing this war and the responsibility for its long continuation. Some of the demographic effects are indicated

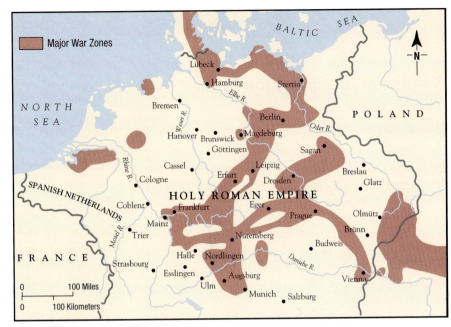

MAP 4.2   Main War Zones

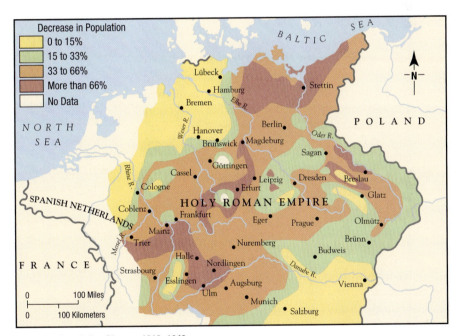

MAP 4.3   Population Change: 1618–1648

through a comparison of the main areas of battle and changes in population. Indeed, the continued political and religious division of Germany after this war, along with such massive destruction of the area and the population, helps explain Germany's weakness and inability to unify for the following two centuries.

CONSIDER: *In what ways the geopolitical and religious divisions of Germany explain the duration and extent of damages of the Thirty Years' War; how historians might use these maps to support their interpretations of the causes and significance of the Thirty Years' War.*

Secondary Sources

A Political Interpretation of the Thirty Years' War

Hajo Holborn

Historians have long disagreed about the essential causes of the Thirty Years' War. Some focus on a particular area, such as Germany or Spain; others emphasize a particular set of causes, such as religion or politics; and still others argue that it was only part of a general seventeenth-century crisis affecting all aspects of society. In the following selection Hajo Holborn, a historian known for his work on German history, argues that the war was primarily a political struggle in the German states of the Hapsburgs. He accepts the religious issue as at most a contributing cause.

CONSIDER: *The role religion played in the conflict even though it may not have been primary in causing the war; other factors that might have caused the war.*

It was not a conflict among European powers, not even an acute controversy between the emperor and the princes of the Empire or among these princes themselves that led to the outbreak of the long war that lived on in the memory of the German people as the "Great War" and in the books of the historians as the Thirty Years' War. Rather, it was a struggle between the estates and the monarchy in the territories of the Habsburg dynasty which set fire to all of Germany and to the European continent. Without the grave crisis in the constitutional life of the Empire, the weakness of the German states, and the ambitions of the great powers of Europe, the events that occurred in Bohemia could not have developed into a disaster from which Germany was to emerge crippled and mutilated.

It is difficult to determine to what extent differences in the interpretation of Christian faith were a direct cause of the catastrophe. There is no doubt but that religious motivation was strong in the lives of individuals and societies, and even in the relations among states and nations, in this age. But the confessional war started at a time when enthusiasm for the religious revivals, both Protestant and Catholic, had lost much of its original force and religious ideas had again become conventionalized. Frank skepticism was rare in Germany, but ever larger groups of people had ceased to find in religious ideals the full satisfaction of their human aspirations.

Nevertheless, the reality of heaven and hell was nowhere questioned, nor was the necessity of basing the political and social order on principles that would keep Satan from undoing the work of God. Religious zeal found expression not only in the ghastly fury of witch trials, which reached its climax during these years, but also in the care with which all governments attended to the direction of church life in their dominions. Yet while on the one hand religion deteriorated into superstition, on the other it tended to become formalized and to lose genuineness. Every political action was publicly cloaked in religious terms, but religion seemed to be used more and more to rationalize actions motivated by secular interests.

A Religious Interpretation of the Thirty Years' War

Carl J. Friedrich

An older scholarly tradition attributes primary importance to religion in explaining the causes of the Thirty Years' War. This tradition has been revived by Carl J. Friedrich, a highly respected historian from Harvard. In The Age of the Baroque, 1610–1660, Friedrich places the war in the context of the still strong religious assumptions of the time, arguing that historians who emphasize political causes overlook the importance of this religious context. The following is an excerpt from that work.

CONSIDER: *The evidence Friedrich uses to support his argument; why, according to Friedrich, many historians have rejected the religious interpretation of the war; how Holborn might criticize this argument.*

It has been the fashion to minimize the religious aspect of the great wars which raged in the heart of Europe, over the territory of the Holy Roman Empire of the German Nation. Not only the calculating statecraft of Richelieu and Mazarin, but even Pope Urban VIII's own insistence lent support to such a view in a later age which had come to look upon religion and politics as fairly well separated fields of thought and action. Liberal historians found it difficult to perceive that for baroque man religion and politics were cut from the same cloth, indeed that the most intensely political issues were precisely the religious ones. Gone was the neopaganism of the renaissance, with

SOURCE: Hajo Holborn, *A History of Modern Germany: The Reformation* (New York: Alfred A. Knopf, 1959), pp. 305–306.

SOURCE: Excerpts from *The Age of the Baroque* by Carl J. Friedrich. Copyright 1952 by Harper & Row, Publishers, Inc. Reprinted by permission of HarperCollins Publishers, Inc.

its preoccupation with self-fulfillment here and now. Once again, and for the last time, life was seen as meaningful in religious, even theological, terms, and the greater insight into power which the renaissance had brought served merely to deepen the political passion brought to the struggle over religious faiths.

Without a full appreciation of the close links between secular and religious issues, it becomes impossible to comprehend the Thirty Years' War. Frederick, the unlucky Palatine, as well as Ferdinand, Tilly and Gustavus Adolphus, Maximilian of Bavaria and John George of Saxony, they all must be considered fools unless their religious motivation is understood as the quintessential core of their politics. Time and again, they appear to have done the "wrong thing," if their actions are viewed in a strictly secular perspective. To be sure, men became increasingly sophisticated as the war dragged on; but even after peace was finally concluded in 1648, the religious controversies continued. Ever since the Diet of Augsburg (1555) had adopted the callous position that a man must confess the religion of those who had authority over the territory he lived in—a view which came to be known under the slogan of "*cujus regio, ejus religio*"— the intimate tie of religion and government had been the basis of the Holy Empire's tenuous peace. Born of the spirit of its time—Lutheran otherworldliness combining with Humanistic indifferentism—this doctrine was no more than an unstable compromise between Catholics and Lutherans, the Calvinists being entirely outside its protective sphere. But in the seventeenth century not only the Calvinists, who by 1618 had become the fighting protagonists of Protestantism, but likewise the more ardent Catholics, inspired by the Council of Trent, by the Jesuits and Capuchins, backed by the power of Spain and filled with the ardor of the Counter Reformation, had come to look upon this doctrine as wicked and contrary to their deepest convictions.

When Ferdinand, after claiming the crown of Bohemia by heredity, proceeded to push the work of counter reformation, his strongest motivation was religious; so was the resistance offered by the Bohemian people, as well as Frederick's acceptance of the crown of Bohemia on the basis of an election. Dynastic and national sentiments played their part, surely, but they reinforced the basic religious urge. The same concurrence of religious with dynastic, political, even economic motives persisted throughout the protracted struggle, but the religious did not cease to be the all-pervasive feeling; baroque man, far from being bothered by the contradictions, experienced these polarities as inescapable.

If religion played a vital role in persuading Ferdinand II to dismiss his victorious general, it was even more decisive in inspiring Gustavus Adolphus to enter the war against both the emperor and the League. The

nineteenth century, incapable of feeling the religious passions which stirred baroque humanity and much impressed with the solidified national states which the seventeenth century bequeathed to posterity, was prone to magnify the dynastic and often Machiavellian policies adopted by rulers who professed to be deeply religious, and the twentieth century has largely followed suit in denying the religious character of these wars. But it is precisely this capacity to regard the statesman as the champion of religion, to live and act the drama of man's dual dependence upon faith and power that constituted the quintessence of the baroque.

War and Peace in the Old Regime
M. S. Anderson

Western societies rarely went for long periods of time without becoming involved in wars. However, war was particularly prevalent and destructive in the period between 1618 and 1660. Historians have long debated the causes for these wars. In the following selection, M. S. Anderson, who has written extensively on the Early Modern period, analyzes what war meant to Europeans and the broader significance of war during the seventeenth century.

CONSIDER: *How Europeans perceived the causes, nature, and consequences of war; the distinctions between war and peace; the connections between war and politics.*

In early modern Europe almost everyone regarded war as a normal, perhaps even a necessary, part of human life. Events seemed to bear out this view; in the period 1618–60 every year saw serious armed conflict between states somewhere in Europe, and during a large proportion of it destructive struggles were being waged simultaneously in several parts of the continent. The ubiquity and apparent inevitability of war meant that serious discussion of its causes was rare. As an integral and unavoidable aspect of existence it was received like bad weather or epidemics, as something clearly beyond the power of the ordinary man to avert, something demanding acceptance rather than analysis. Luther's dictum that "war is as necessary as eating, drinking or any other business" reflects in typically blunt terms this matter-of-fact and fatalistic attitude. Nor was there much grasp of the deeper and more lasting effects it might sometimes have. It was only too obvious that in the short term it meant for many death, destruction and loss. But against this was put the venerable and well-established argument that

SOURCE: M. S. Anderson. *War and Society in Europe of the Old Regime, 1618–1789.* (New York: St. Martin's Press, 1988), pp. 13–15.

prolonged peace weakened the moral fibre of a society, making it lax, slothful, even corrupt, whereas war focused and mobilized energies, called forth many of the better qualities of man, and had a generally tonic and purifying effect. It was clear also that a successful war could heighten the personal prestige of a ruler; the vindication of claims put forward by monarchs to disputed territories, to alleged hereditary rights, even merely to precedence over rivals or to specific symbols of such precedence, were by far the most common ostensible causes of conflict. Occasionally it was realized that war might have important long-term economic results, that it might foster the trade of a victorious state against that of its defeated enemies and that economic rivalry might be one of its causes. Struggles inspired simply or even mainly by this kind of material rivalry were not frequent in this period but they did take place. . . . However the idea that war might, through the demands it made on societies and the impetus it gave to the growth of powerful central governments, help fundamentally to change these societies, was still a strange one. . . .

Finally, a clear-cut distinction between war and peace, a dividing line whose crossing was instantly recognizable, was something which was only beginning to emerge. The position of neutrals was still ambiguous, their status poorly guaranteed by embryonic international law and liable to frequent infringements. There was a general belief that a belligerent had some right to march its forces across neutral territory if it made good any damage they caused in the process (the right of *transitus innoxius*). Frontiers were still poorly defined, zones of contact between neighbouring powers rather than lines clearly demarcated. The hold of central governments over officials and commanders in border areas was often still incomplete, so that in these areas locally inspired acts of oppression and outright violence could frequently occur, though usually without involving the states concerned in formal conflict. In this violent age incidents of this kind formed a sort of grumbling undertone to international relations, seldom actively menacing peace between states but always a potential threat. . . .

Armed conflict in early seventeenth-century Europe, therefore, ramified into every aspect of life and was able to do this because it was still in many ways badly defined, because the boundary between peace and war was still fuzzy. But lack of clear definition did nothing to reduce its importance. Most of the governments of Europe were first and foremost, as they had been for generations, machines for waging war. Both the scale on which they fought and the effective control they could exert over their fighting forces were to increase markedly during the seventeenth and early eighteenth centuries.

The Causes of the English Civil War
Conrad Russell

The civil war in England, which broke out in the middle of the seventeenth century, is even more controversial among historians than the Thirty Years' War. At the heart of the controversy are two related issues: first, what the balance of religious, political, economic, and social forces was in causing the civil war; second, what groups or classes can be said to have supported each side. In the following selection Conrad Russell argues that the civil war resulted from a conjunction of three causes of instability: the problem of multiple kingdoms (England and Scotland), the problem of religious division, and the financial pressures on the crown.

CONSIDER: *How Russell's three causes worked together; why Charles' attempt to enforce English religion on Scotland in 1637 was so important.*

[The English Civil War] was the result of three long-term causes of instability, all of them well established before Charles came to the throne, and all of them ones which can be observed to have troubled European, as well as British, monarchies. There is nothing peculiarly British (still less English) about any of them: they were not even exceptionally acute in England. What is peculiar to the two cases of England and the Netherlands is that all of them came to a head at the same time. These three long-term causes were the problem of multiple kingdoms, the problem of religious division, and the breakdown of a financial and political system in the face of inflation and the rising cost of war.

The problem of multiple kingdoms was always a likely cause of instability from 1603 onwards. The temptation to press for greater harmonization was always there, and was always likely to produce serious troubles. In 1603 England encountered . . . the shock of subjection to a supranational authority. . . . [T]he English . . . wished to treat both James and Charles as if they were only kings of a single nation-state called England. Since this was patently not the case, and the kings could not help knowing it, the English were always likely to misread royal actions, and in particular to press their kings to do things which, in British terms, they could not do. When, as in 1637, a British king fell victim to a similar misapprehension, and attempted to govern all Britain as king of England, he found this was something he could not do. . . .

England's basic error in 1603 was the failure to absorb that what had taken place was the union of two sovereign, and therefore legally equal, states. Not even James

SOURCE: From Conrad Russell, *The Causes of the English Civil War,* pp. 213–217. © Conrad Russell 1990. Reprinted by permission of Oxford University Press.

could really turn Scotland into "North Britain." It was a state with institutions, law, and culture of its own, and one determined to insist that any resulting relationship must be a legally equal partnership. . . .

[T]he problem of religious division . . . derived its explosive force from the belief that religion ought to be enforced. It was a problem of a society which had carried on the assumptions appropriate to a society with a single church into one which had many churches. . . .

But August 1640, when the Scottish army, by entering England, merged the religious problem with the British problem, was too early for it to have cooled enough. One might say of the English Calvinists what Machiavelli said of the Pope in Italy: they were too weak to unite the country, but too strong to allow anyone else to do so. When the Scots entered England, they were able to join forces with a large group of people who preferred Scottish religion to what was coming to be taken for their own.

The strains caused for monarchies by the combination of inflation with the massive increases in the cost of war known collectively as "the military revolution" is also a European theme. The financial difficulties faced, after the conclusion of the long wars of the 1590s, by James VI and I, Philip III of Spain, and Henri IV of France have too much in common to be entirely coincidental. The changes following the regular use of gunpowder, especially the trend to larger-scale fortifications and to larger armies, much increased the economic drain of war. The resulting financial pressures put strain on the principle of consent to taxation everywhere in Europe, and perhaps only the Netherlands, with the advantage of a visible enemy at the gate, were able to combine consent with the levying of taxes on the scale needed. England, because the principle of consent to taxation was so particularly well entrenched, was perhaps put under more constitutional strain by this process than some other powers. . . .

No one, or even two, of these forces was in the event enough: it took the conjunction of all three to drive England into civil war. . . . Both the religious and the financial problem had been plainly visible by the 1550s, and they had not created civil war in ninety years since then. England in 1637 was, no doubt, a country with plenty of discontents, some of them potentially serious, but it was also still a very stable and peaceful one, and one which does not show many visible signs of being on the edge of a major upheaval. . . . The attempt which Charles made in 1637 to enforce English religion on Scotland, was thus by far the likeliest reason for a merging of these three long-term causes of instability. It is difficult to argue that Charles took this risk with his eyes open. It is equally difficult to see what action a king could have taken which would have been better designed to precipitate an English civil war.

The Devil's Handmaid: Women in the Age of Reformations

William Monter

As indicated by the document The Hammer of Witches, *beliefs in witchcraft were widespread during the sixteenth and seventeenth centuries, and authoritative sources supported the belief that most witches were women. Many people were also accused of killing their children (infanticide). For both witchcraft and infanticide, the vast majority of those accused were women. In this selection, William Monter, a historian specializing in the Reformation era, analyzes why witchcraft and infanticide seemed to grow in sixteenth- and seventeenth-century Europe.*

CONSIDER: *Which three developments best explain the growing prosecutions for witchcraft and infanticide during this period; which groups of women were most affected and why.*

Three key developments combined and interacted to shape the male hysteria about witchcraft and infanticide in Reformation Europe. First and foremost, public institutions—state and church alike—were increasingly interfering in daily life. Throughout Protestant and Catholic Europe, the state enforced attendance at church; church officials preached obedience to the state; and both increasingly tried to regulate everyone's behavior. Ecclesiastical courts such as Catholic inquisitions or Calvinist consistories depended heavily on state enforcement of their policies; states like England or France relied on clergymen to provide records of baptisms or to proclaim government edicts from the pulpit.

Secondly, these increasingly active public authorities inhabited a fear-ridden world. Most Protestant and Catholic Europeans still peered at their neighbors from walled towns and fortified castles; Luther's greatest hymn begins, "A Mighty Fortress is our God." We cannot find many material reasons for such pervasive fears at this time; bubonic plague, the great killer of pre-industrial Europe, did most of its damage either before or after the age of reformations. The reformers of Protestant and Catholic Europe, determined to attack all forms of "superstition" (including, of course, witchcraft), reduced the influence of benevolent magic, like exorcisms or special prayers, but provided nothing to replace them. Modern science did not yet exist; official medicine often had no

SOURCE: William Monter, "Protestant Wives, Catholic Saints, and the Devil's Handmaid: Women in the Age of Reformations," in Renate Bridenthal, Claudia Koonz, and Susan Stuard, eds., *Becoming Visible: Women in European History,* First and Second Editions, copyright © 1977 & 1987 by Houghton Mifflin Company. Used with permission.

explanations (and worse, no effective remedies) for many illnesses. Under such conditions, Protestant and Catholic reformers imposed the "Triumph of Lent" on unwed mothers of stillborns, and made old women with deviant dreams into scapegoats for sixteenth-century Christianity's obsession with the Devil.

Finally, the patriarchal theories of late-Renaissance Europe played an important role in determining which groups of women became victims of these obsessions. Accused witches were disproportionately widows, while infanticide defendants were single women; both groups lived outside direct male supervision in this age of reinforced patriarchal nuclear families. Their "unnatural" position aroused suspicion and sometimes fear; neighborhood enmities did the rest.

☙ CHAPTER QUESTIONS

1. Clearly, there were both political and religious aspects to the turmoil between 1560 and 1660. On balance, which do you think were most important? On what evidence have you based your answer? What argument can be formulated that admits the importance of both aspects?

2. How might the themes in this chapter be related to the political and religious developments from the mid-fifteenth to the mid-sixteenth centuries that were the focus of the two preceding chapters?

3. How might the rise of monarchical absolutism be related to the turmoil of this period?

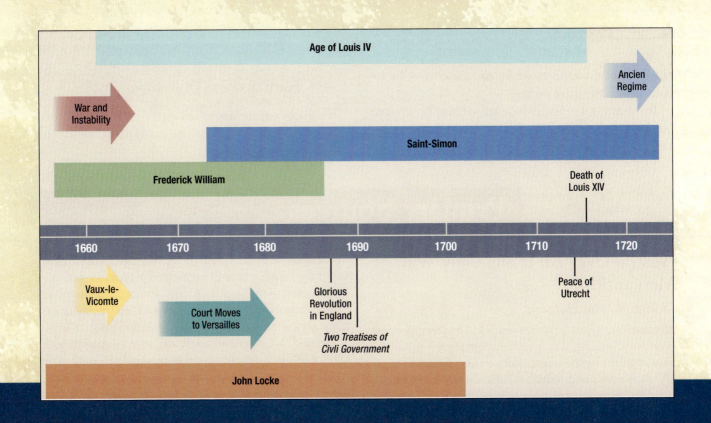

5 Aristocracy and Absolutism in the Seventeenth Century

The second half of the seventeenth century was a period of relative political stability in Europe. Although wars still occurred, they lacked the intensity of the preceding period. In the ascendant states, such as France, Prussia, Austria, Russia, and England, central governments were gaining authority. The primary power, and for many states the model of political authority, was France. There, Louis XIV, supported by a strong standing army, a policy of mercantilism, and a growing bureaucracy, wielded absolute power. There were similar situations in Prussia, Austria, and Russia. A different pattern occurred in England, where the central government remained strong while the monarchy itself weakened. There, after the return to power of the Stuart kings between 1660 and 1688, a revolution furthered the authority of Parliament.

During this period, important social, political, and economic changes occurred unevenly and generally benefited those who were already prominent and well to do. Aristocrats lost some of their independence to kings in countries like France and Prussia, but they continued to staff most of the important government offices, to maintain their elevated prestige, and to influence cultural styles and tastes. For most people, the structure of society, the way of life, and the relevant institutions changed little throughout this period.

This chapter concentrates on two broad topics: the growth of central government and Early Modern society. The selections address a number of questions. For the first topic, what was the nature of monarchical absolutism in France? How did it differ from Prussian monarchical absolutism? How did the pattern of monarchical absolutism compare with the growth of parliamentary power in England? What institutions and policies were developed to facilitate the growth of central governments? For the second topic, what was the nature of the family in Early Modern Europe? What were typical attitudes toward childhood?

What were the traditional values and patterns of life for commoners during this period?

This dual focus should provide some broad insights into Europe during the seventeenth century and help establish a background for eighteenth-century developments.

❧ **For Classroom Discussion**

What was monarchical absolution? Use the analysis of Durand and the documents by von Hornick, Frederick William, and Saint-Simon.

 Primary Sources

Austria Over All If She Only Will: Mercantilism

Philipp W. von Hornick

Mercantilism, a loose set of economic ideas and corresponding government policies, was a common component of political absolutism during the seventeenth century. Typical mercantilist goals were the acquisition of bullion, a positive balance of trade, and economic self-sufficiency. An unusually clear and influential statement of mercantilist policies was published in 1684 by Philipp Wilhelm von Hornick. A lawyer and later a government official, Hornick set down what he considered to be the nine principal rules for a proper economic policy. These are excerpted here.

CONSIDER: *The political and military purposes served by encouraging mercantilist policies; the foreign policy decisions such economic policies would support; the political and economic circumstances that would make it easiest for a country to adhere to and benefit from mercantilist policies.*

NINE PRINCIPAL RULES OF NATIONAL ECONOMY

If the might and eminence of a country consist in its surplus of gold, silver, and all other things necessary or convenient for its *subsistence*, derived, so far as possible, from its own resources, without *dependence* upon other countries, and in the proper fostering, use, and application of these, then it follows that a general national *economy* (*Landes-Oeconomie*) should consider how such a surplus, fostering, and enjoyment can be brought about, without *dependence* upon others, or where this is not feasible in every respect, with as little *dependence* as possible upon foreign countries, and sparing use of the country's own cash. For this purpose the following nine rules are especially serviceable.

First, to inspect the country's soil with the greatest care, and not to leave the agricultural possibilities or a single cor-

ner or clod of earth unconsidered. Every useful form of *plant* under the sun should be experimented with, to see whether it is adapted to the country, for the distance or nearness of the sun is not all that counts. Above all, no trouble or expense should be spared to discover gold and silver.

Second, all commodities found in a country, which cannot be used in their natural state, should be worked up within the country; since the payment for *manufacturing* generally exceeds the value of the raw material by two, three, ten, twenty, and even a hundred fold, and the neglect of this is an abomination to prudent managers.

Third, for carrying out the above two rules, there will be need of people, both for producing and cultivating the raw materials and for working them up. Therefore, attention should be given to the population, that it may be as large as the country can support, this being a well-ordered state's most important concern, but, unfortunately, one that is often neglected. And the people should be turned by all possible means from idleness to remunerative *professions*; instructed and encouraged in all kinds of *inventions*, arts, and trades; and, if necessary, instructors should be brought in from foreign countries for this.

Fourth, gold and silver once in the country, whether from its own mines or obtained by *industry* from foreign countries, are under no circumstances to be taken out for any purpose, so far as possible, or allowed to be buried in chests or coffers, but must always remain in *circulation*; nor should much be permitted in uses where they are at once *destroyed* and cannot be utilized again. For under these conditions, it will be impossible for a country that has once acquired a considerable supply of cash, especially one that possesses gold and silver mines, ever to sink into poverty; indeed, it is impossible that it should not continually increase in wealth and property. Therefore,

Fifth, the inhabitants of the country should make every effort to get along with their domestic products, to confine their luxury to these alone, and to do without foreign products as far as possible (except where great need leaves no alternative, or if not need, wide-spread, unavoidable abuse, of which Indian spices are an example). And so on.

Sixth, in case the said purchases were indispensable because of necessity or *irremediable* abuse, they should be obtained from these foreigners at first hand, so far as possible, and not for gold or silver, but in exchange for other domestic wares.

Seventh, such foreign commodities should in this case be imported in unfinished form, and worked up within the country, thus earning the wages of *manufacture* there.

Eighth, opportunities should be sought night and day for selling the country's superfluous goods to these foreigners in manufactured form, so far as this is necessary, and for gold and silver; and to this end, *consumption*, so to speak, must be sought in the farthest ends of the earth, and developed in every possible way.

Ninth, except for important considerations, no importation should be allowed under any circumstances of commodities of which there is sufficient supply of suitable quality at home; and in this matter neither sympathy nor compassion should be shown foreigners, be they friends, kinsfolk, *allies*, or enemies. For all friendship ceases, when it involves my own weakness and ruin. And this holds good, even if the domestic commodities are of poorer quality, or even higher priced. For it would be better to pay for an article two dollars which remain in the country than only one which goes out, however strange this may seem to the ill-informed.

A Secret Letter: Monarchical Authority in Prussia

Frederick William, The Great Elector

Seventeenth-century monarchs attained unprecedented authority within their realms, often through the skillful use of policies designed to enhance their power. The most dramatic consolidation of power was made by the head of the Hohenzollerns, Frederick William (1640–1688), known as the "great elector" of Brandenburg-Prussia. He instituted new taxes, developed a trained bureaucracy staffed by members of the nobility, modernized his army, and asserted his own authority over competing claims from the nobility and representative institutions. In 1667 he wrote a secret letter of advice to his son, who was in line to inherit the throne. An excerpt of this letter appears here.

CONSIDER: *The greatest threats to monarchical authority according to Frederick William; the policies Frederick William thought were most important for maintaining power; which of Frederick William's recommendations echo the attitudes expressed in mercantilist doctrines.*

It is necessary that you conduct yourself as a good father to your people, that you love your subjects regardless of their religious convictions, and that you try to promote their welfare at all times. Work to stimulate trade everywhere, and keep in mind the population increase of the Mark of Brandenburg. Take advantage of the advice of the clergy and nobility as much as you can; listen to them and be gracious to them all, as befits one of your position; recognize ability where you find it, so that you will increase the love and affection of your subjects toward you. But, it is essential that you always be moderate in your attitudes, in order not to endanger your position and lose respect. With those of your own station in life, be careful never to give way in matters of precedence and in all to which you are entitled; on the contrary, hold fast to the eminence of your superior position. Remember that one can lose one's superior position if one allows too great pomposity and too great a show upon the part of members of the court.

Be keenly interested in the administration of justice throughout your land. See to it that justice is maintained for the poor as well as for the rich without discrimination of any kind. See to it that lawsuits are carried out without delay, without procrastination, for in doing this, you will solidify your own position. . . .

Seek to maintain friendly relations with the princes and the nobility of the Empire. Correspond with them frequently and maintain your friendship with them. Be certain not to give them cause for ill-will; try not to arouse emotions of jealousy or enmity, but be sure that you are always in a strong position to maintain your weight in disputes that may arise. . . .

It is wise to have alliances, if necessary, but it is better to rely on your own strength. You are in a weak position if you do not have the means and do not possess the confidence of the people. These are the things, God be praised, which have made me powerful since the time I began to have them. I only regret that, in the beginning of my reign, I forsook these policies and followed the advice of others against my will.

Mémoires: The Aristocracy Undermined in France

Saint-Simon

Louis XIV of France was the most powerful ruler of his time. He had inherited the throne as a child in 1643. He took personal command by 1661, ruling France until his death in 1715. Contemporary rulers viewed him as a model ruler. One of the ways in which he reinforced his position was by conducting a magnificent court life at his palace of Versailles. There, nobles hoping for favors or appointments competed for his attention and increasingly became dependent upon royal whim. One of

SOURCE: From *Documents of German History,* edited by Louis Snyder. Copyright © 1958 by Rutgers, The State University.

SOURCE: Orest Ranum and Patricia Ranum, eds. and trans., *The Century of Louis XIV.* Reprinted by permission of Harper & Row (New York, 1972), pp. 81, 83, 87–88.

those nobles, the Duke of Saint-Simon (1675–1755), felt slighted and grew to resent the king. Saint-Simon chronicled life at Versailles in his Mémoires. In the following excerpt, he shows how Louis XIV used this court life to his own ends.

CONSIDER: *How the king's activities undermined the position of the nobility; the options available to a noble who wanted to maintain or increase his own power; how the king's activities compare with the great elector's recommendations to his son.*

Frequent fetes, private walks at Versailles, and excursions were means which the King seized upon in order to single out or to mortify [individuals] by naming the persons who should be there each time, and in order to keep each person assiduous and attentive to pleasing him. He sensed that he lacked by far enough favors to distribute in order to create a continuous effect. Therefore he substituted imaginary favors for real ones, through jealousy—little preferences which were shown daily, and one might say at each moment—[and] through his artfulness. The hopes to which these little preferences and these honors gave birth, and the deference which resulted from them—no one was more ingenious than he in unceasingly inventing these sorts of things. Marly, eventually, was of great use to him in this respect; and Trianon, where everyone, as a matter of fact, could go pay court to him, but where ladies had the honor of eating with him and where they were chosen at each meal; the candlestick which he had held for him each evening at bedtime by a courtier whom he wished to honor, and always from among the most worthy of those present, whom he named aloud upon coming out from saying his prayers.

Louis XIV carefully trained himself to be well informed about what was happening everywhere, in public places, in private homes, in public encounters, in the secrecy of families or of [amorous] liaisons. Spies and tell tales were countless. They existed in all forms: some who were unaware that their denunciations went as far as [the King], others who knew it; some who wrote him directly by having their letters delivered by routes which he had established for them, and those letters were seen only by him, and always before all other things; and lastly, some others who sometimes spoke to him secretly in his cabinets, by the back passageways. These secret communications broke the necks of an infinity of persons of all social positions, without their ever having been able to discover the cause, often very unjustly, and the King, once warned, never reconsidered, or so rarely that nothing was more [determined]. . . .

In everything he loved splendor, magnificence, profusion. He turned this taste into a maxim for political reasons, and instilled it into his court on all matters. One could please him by throwing oneself into fine food, clothes, retinue, buildings, gambling. These were occasions which enabled him to talk to people. The essence of it

was that by this he attempted and succeeded in exhausting everyone by making luxury a virtue, and for certain persons a necessity, and thus he gradually reduced everyone to depending entirely upon his generosity in order to subsist. In this he also found satisfaction for his pride through a court which was superb in all respects, and through a greater confusion which increasingly destroyed natural distinctions. This is an evil which, once introduced, became the internal cancer which is devouring all individuals—because from the court it promptly spread to Paris and into the provinces and the armies, where persons, whatever their position, are considered important only in proportion to the table they lay and their magnificence ever since this unfortunate innovation—which is devouring all individuals, which forces those who are in a position to steal not to restrain themselves from doing so for the most part, in their need to keep up with their expenditures; [a cancer] which is nourished by the confusion of social positions, pride, and even decency, and which by a mad desire to grow keeps constantly increasing, whose consequences are infinite and lead to nothing less than ruin and general upheaval.

Second Treatise of Civil Government: Legislative Power

John Locke

In England royal absolutism had been under attack throughout the seventeenth century and finally was defeated by the Glorious Revolution of 1688–1689. At that point there was a definitive shift in power to Parliament, which was controlled by the upper classes. John Locke (1632–1704), in his Two Treatises of Civil Government (1690), justified the revolution and the new political constitution of England and expounded political ideas that became influential during the eighteenth and nineteenth centuries. This work and other writings established Locke as a first-rate empirical philosopher and political theorist. In the following selection from his Second Treatise of Civil Government, Locke analyzes legislative power.

CONSIDER: *The purposes for entering into society; the extent of and limitations on legislative power; how Locke justifies his argument; how these ideas are contrary to monarchical absolutism.*

134. The great end of men's entering into society being the enjoyment of their properties in peace and safety, and the great instrument and means of that being the laws established in that society, the first and fundamental positive law of all commonwealths is the establishing of the

---

SOURCE: John Locke, *Two Treatises of Civil Government* (London: J. M. Dent, Everyman, 1924), pp. 183–184, 189–190.

legislative power, as the first and fundamental natural law which is to govern even the legislative. Itself is the preservation of the society and (as far as will consist with the public good) of every person in it. This legislative is not only the supreme power of the commonwealth, but sacred and unalterable in the hands where the community have once placed it. Nor can any edict of anybody else, in what form soever conceived, or by what power soever backed, have the force and obligation of a law which has not its sanction from that legislative which the public has chosen and appointed; for without this the law could not have that which is absolutely necessary to its being a law, the consent of the society, over whom nobody can have a power to make laws but by their own consent and by authority received from them; and therefore all the obedience, which by the most solemn ties any one can be obliged to pay, ultimately terminates in this supreme power, and is directed by those laws which it enacts. Nor can any oaths to any foreign power whatsoever, or any domestic subordinate power, discharge any member of the society from his obedience to the legislative, acting pursuant to their trust, nor oblige him to any obedience contrary to the laws so enacted or farther than

they do allow, it being ridiculous to imagine one can be tied ultimately to obey any power in the society which is not the supreme.

❧

142. These are the bounds which the trust that is put in them by the society and the law of God and Nature have set to the legislative power of every commonwealth, in all forms of government. First: They are to govern by promulgated established laws, not to be varied in particular cases, but to have one rule for rich and poor, for the favourite at Court, and the countryman at plough. Secondly: These laws also ought to be designed for no other end ultimately but the good of the people. Thirdly: They must not raise taxes on the property of the people without the consent of the people given by themselves or their deputies. And this properly concerns only such governments where the legislative is always in being, or at least where the people have not reserved any part of the legislative to deputies, to be from time to time chosen by themselves. Fourthly: Legislative neither must nor can transfer the power of making laws to anybody else, or place it anywhere but where the people have.

 Visual Sources

The Early Modern Château

The following picture of the château, grounds, and park of Vaux-le-Vicomte in France (figure 5.1) reveals both the wealth of France and certain trends of the seventeenth

century. The château was built between 1657 and 1660 on the orders of France's superintendent of finance, Fouquet, and according to the plans of the architect Le Vau, the painter Lebrun, and the landscape gardener Le Nôtre. With its

FIGURE 5.1 (© Richard Kalvar/Magnum Photos)

geometric orderliness and balance, it exemplifies the Classical style. In its conquest and manipulation of nature according to the rational plans of humans, it reflects the growing scientific spirit of the age. It also reflects a fundamentally stable society that was still dominated politically, socially, and economically by a small elite. It and buildings like it do not call out for military defense as did medieval castles. It later served as a model for Versailles, which itself became the model of monarchical splendor in seventeenth- and eighteenth-century Europe.

CONSIDER: *Why such buildings and parks might have been built and how Saint-Simon might have viewed such projects.*

Maternal Care
Pieter de Hooch

This scene of domestic life (figure 5.2) is painted by the seventeenth-century Dutch artist Pieter de Hooch. Entitled Maternal Care, it shows a girl kneeling while her mother examines and delouses her head. The scene takes place in Holland, the most urban and commercial European country. The moderate wealth of the rooms, revealed particularly by the paintings and the quality of the drapes, and the emphasis on cleanliness, privacy, and relative austerity, indicate that this is a middle-class home.

CONSIDER: *What the painter intended to communicate to the viewer of this painting.*

FIGURE 5.2 (© Rijksmuseum, Amsterdam)

Secondary Sources

Absolutism: Myth and Reality

G. Durand

During the seventeenth century, several monarchs attained such unprecedented power and authority that historians have used the term "absolutism" to describe these political systems. Other historians have argued that the term is misleading, that neither the ambitions of the monarchs nor the results constituted political absolutism. In the following selection G. Durand analyzes the myth and the reality of absolutism.

CONSIDER: *Why Durand prefers to view absolutism as a tendency; how Durand evaluates the goals and attitudes of the monarchs; whether the primary sources by Frederick William and Saint-Simon support Durand's analysis.*

Viewed as a tendency rather than as a political system, absolutism is an undeniable reality. In every state the sovereign sought to free himself from pressure and control. The means were everywhere the same; the monarch tried to rule through councillors whom he chose rather than nobles who claimed such positions as their right. He also tried to recover control of the administration of justice which had been taken over by the feudal nobility and the church. These tendencies produced two institutions common to every state.

First a small, inner or secret council, a cabinet ("Conseil des Affaires"), distinct from the traditional councils which had grown from the division of the functions of the old *Curia Regis*. There is great similarity between, for instance, the *Consejo de Estado* in Castile, the inner circle of the privy council in England, the Austrian Council of State of 1748 and the Imperial council set up by Catherine the Great in 1769.

Second, a system of unifying and centralising judicial institutions. In France the drafting of customary law in the sixteenth century and the publication of the Codes and Great Ordinances in the seventeenth, formed the basis for royal intervention in the judicial process. The procedures of *évocation* to a higher court, or judgement by special commissioners named by the king, were specifically French; but an institution like the *conseil des parties* had its counterpart in the Royal Council of Castile, the English Star Chamber, or the Austrian *Hofrat*.

From this we may infer the existence of a general climate of absolutism, more or less pervasive, which offered the monarch no more than the opportunity to deliberate on matters of state without being affected by intrigue and pressure, and to ensure that the judicial process followed his wishes and directives.

As an actual political system, absolutism is a myth. The monarchs themselves never regarded themselves as absolute, except in the case of the autocrats of Russia, where the lack of fundamental laws, of established customs and corporate orders within the state allowed the growth of a dictatorial form of government. In France, however, even Louis XIV never planned to abolish the Parlement, but merely curbed its pretensions and in December 1655 limited its right of remonstrance; nor did he try to abolish the estates. Monarchs did not try to create a system of institutions which would destroy any possibility of resistance through inertia. They merely sought to restrict the activities of persons who might cause trouble and to set up a new administrative structure parallel to the old; a handful of commissioners directed, urged on and controlled the system inherited from a time when counsel, remonstrance and shared power were the rule. Sovereigns also continued to delegate their administrative powers through the sale of offices, or to farm them out to financial potentates who became virtual states within the state. The kings of Spain suffered the tyranny of their own councils. In practice absolutism seems much more the result of circumstances and personalities than of a deliberate intention to revolutionise the whole structure of the state.

The English Revolution, 1688–1689

George Macaulay Trevelyan

In England two blows to monarchical authority proved to be turning points. The first was the civil war and the execution of Charles I in the 1640s. But although this was a victory for Parliament, the Cromwellian period that followed and the return from exile of Charles II in 1660 cast doubt on the permanence of Parliament's victory. The second was the "Glorious Revolution" of 1688, which removed James II from power without the turmoil of the first revolution. In the following selection Cambridge historian George Macaulay Trevelyan compares the two revolutions and analyzes the significance of the second one. Following the Whig tradition,

SOURCE: From George Durand, "What Is Absolutism?" in *Louis XIV and Absolutism*, pp. 23–24, ed. by Ragnhild Hatton, copyright © 1976 The Macmillan Press, Ltd. Reprinted by permission of the publisher.

SOURCE: George Macaulay Trevelyan, *The English Revolution, 1688–1689*. Reprinted by permission of Oxford University Press (Oxford, England, 1938), pp. 164–166.

❧ CHAPTER QUESTIONS

1. What conditions facilitated the development of monarchical absolutism in the seventeenth century? What policies were used by kings to this end?

2. Why might mercantilist doctrines be particularly appealing to seventeenth-century monarchs?

3. How does family life reflect broader social, economic, and political aspects of the seventeenth century?

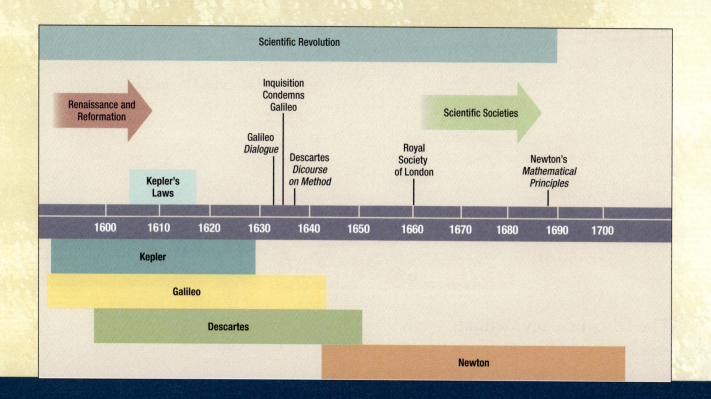

6 The Scientific Revolution

One of the most important intellectual revolutions in Western civilization occurred in the seventeenth century. Building on some sixteenth-century breakthroughs and a more deeply rooted interest in the workings of the natural world, a small elite of thinkers and scientists—Descartes, Galileo, Newton, Kepler, Bacon, and Boyle—established the foundations for the modern sciences of astronomy, mathematics, physics, and chemistry. Although at first their work was known to only a few, their ideas spread widely during the eighteenth century.

In the process of developing the modern sciences, these thinkers challenged the established conception of the universe as well as previous assumptions about knowledge. This ultimately successful challenge, now known as the Scientific Revolution, had a number of key elements. First, the view of the universe as being stable, fixed, and finite, with the earth at its center, gave way to a view of the universe as moving and almost infinite, with the earth merely one of millions of bodies, all subject to the laws of nature.

Second, earlier methods for ascertaining the truth, which primarily involved referring to traditional authorities such as Aristotle, Ptolemy, and the Church, were replaced by methods that emphasized scepticism, rationalism, and rigorous reasoning based on observed facts and mathematical laws. Third, although these thinkers remained concerned with their own deeply held religious beliefs, the general scientific orientation shifted from theological questions to secular questions that focused on how things worked.

The primary documents in this chapter emphasize two broad questions that faced these seventeenth-century scientists. First, how can one ascertain the truth? The answers of Descartes, Galileo, and Newton are examined. Second, what is the proper line between science and scriptural authority? Galileo, who came most directly into conflict with Church authorities, provides us with clues.

The secondary documents concentrate on the nature and causes of the Scientific Revolution. In what ways was seventeenth-century science different from the science of earlier centuries? What explains these differences? What were the motives of seventeenth-century scientists?

Most of these intellectual developments were known to only a few throughout Europe. In the eighteenth century these scientific ideas and methods became popularized as part of the intellectual ferment of the Enlightenment.

❧ **For Classroom Discussion**

What is the core of the Scientific Revolution? Use the sources by Descartes, Galileo, and Newton, as well as the analysis by Shapin.

 Primary Sources

The Discourse on Method

René Descartes

Seventeenth-century science needed new philosophical and methodological standards for truth to replace those traditionally used to support scientific assumptions. These were forcefully provided by René Descartes (1596–1650) in his Discourse on Method *(1637). Born and educated in France, but spending his most productive years in Holland, Descartes gained fame as a mathematician, physicist, and metaphysical philosopher. The following excerpt from his* Discourse *contains the best-known statement of his approach to discovering truth.*

CONSIDER: *The ways in which Descartes' approach constitutes a break with traditional ways of ascertaining the truth; the weaknesses of this approach and how a modern scientist might criticize this method; how this approach reflects Descartes' background as a mathematician.*

In place of the multitude of precepts of which logic is composed, I believed I should find the four following rules quite sufficient, provided I should firmly and steadfastly resolve not to fail of observing them in a single instance.

The first rule was never to receive anything as a truth which I did not clearly know to be such; that is, to avoid haste and prejudice, and not to comprehend anything more in my judgments than that which should present itself so clearly and so distinctly to my mind that I should have no occasion to entertain a doubt of it.

The second rule was to divide every difficulty which I should examine into as many parts as possible, or as might be required for resolving it.

The third rule was to conduct my thoughts in an orderly manner, beginning with objects the most simple and the easiest to understand, in order to ascend as it were by

steps to the knowledge of the most composite, assuming some order to exist even in things which did not appear to be naturally connected.

The last rule was to make enumerations so complete, and reviews so comprehensive, that I should be certain of omitting nothing.

Those long chains of reasoning, quite simple and easy, which geometers are wont to employ in the accomplishment of their most difficult demonstrations, led me to think that everything which might fall under the cognizance of the human mind might be connected together in a similar manner, and that, provided only one should take care not to receive anything as true which was not so, and if one were always careful to preserve the order necessary for deducing one truth from another, there would be none so remote at which he might not at last arrive, nor so concealed which he might not discover. And I had no great difficulty in finding those with which to make a beginning, for I knew already that these must be the simplest and easiest to apprehend; and considering that, among all those who had up to this time made discoveries in the sciences, it was the mathematicians alone who had been able to arrive at demonstrations—that is to say, at proofs certain and evident—I did not doubt that I should begin with the same truths which they investigated.

Letter to Christina of Tuscany: Science and Scripture

Galileo Galilei

The most renowned scientist at the beginning of the seventeenth century was the Italian astronomer, mathematician, and physicist Galileo Galilei (1564–1642). His discoveries

SOURCE: René Descartes, *The Discourse on Method,* in *The Philosophy of Descartes,* ed. and trans. Henry A. P. Torrey (New York: Henry Holt, 1982), pp. 46–48.

SOURCE: From Galileo Galilei, *Discoveries and Opinions of Galileo,* Stillman Drake, ed. and trans. Reprinted by permission of Doubleday & Company, Inc. (New York, 1957), pp. 182–183. Copyright © 1957 by Stillman Drake.

about gravity, velocity, and the movement of astronomical bodies were grounded in a scientific method that ran contrary to the accepted standards for truth and authority. In the following excerpt from a letter to the Grand Duchess Christina of Tuscany (1615), Galileo defends his ideas and delineates his view of the correct line between science and scriptural authority.

CONSIDER: According to Galileo's view, the kinds of topics or questions that are appropriately scientific and those that are appropriately theological; how Galileo's views compare with those of Descartes; why Galileo's views are so crucial to the Scientific Revolution.

I think that in discussions of physical problems we ought to begin not from the authority of scriptural passages, but from sense-experiences and necessary demonstrations; for the holy Bible and the phenomena of nature proceed alike from the divine Word, the former as the dictate of the Holy Ghost and the latter as the observant executrix of God's commands. It is necessary for the Bible, in order to be accommodated to the understanding of every man, to speak many things which appear to differ from the absolute truth so far as the bare meaning of the words is concerned. But Nature, on the other hand, is inexorable and immutable; she never transgresses the laws imposed upon her, or cares a whit whether her abstruse reasons and methods of operation are understandable to men. For that reason it appears that nothing physical which sense-experience sets before our eyes, or which necessary demonstrations prove to us, ought to be called in question (much less condemned) upon the testimony of biblical passages which may have some different meaning beneath their words. For the Bible is not chained in every expression to conditions as strict as those which govern all physical effects; nor is God any less excellently revealed in Nature's actions than in the sacred statements of the Bible. . . .

From this I do not mean to infer that we need not have an extraordinary esteem for the passages of holy Scripture. On the contrary, having arrived at any certainties in physics, we ought to utilize these as the most appropriate aids in the true exposition of the Bible and in the investigation of those meanings which are necessarily contained therein, for these must be concordant with demonstrated truths. I should judge that the authority of the Bible was designed to persuade men of those articles and propositions which, surpassing all human reasoning, could not be made credible by science, or by any other means than through the very mouth of the Holy Spirit.

Yet even in those propositions which are not matters of faith, this authority ought to be preferred over that of all human writings which are supported only by bare assertions or probable arguments, and not set forth in a demonstrative way. This I hold to be necessary and proper to the same extent that divine wisdom surpasses all human judgment and conjecture.

But I do not feel obliged to believe that that same God who has endowed us with senses, reason, and intellect has intended to forgo their use and by some other means to give us knowledge which we can attain by them.

The Papal Inquisition of 1633: Galileo Condemned

Not surprisingly, Galileo found his views under attack from a variety of corners, including important groups within the Church. Ultimately his defense of Copernicanism, which held that the earth was not the center of the universe, was formally condemned by the Church. When he argumentatively summarized these ideas again in his Dialogue Concerning the Two Chief World Systems (1632), he was brought before the Papal Inquisition, forced to recant his views, and confined to a villa on the outskirts of Florence. The following are some of the main charges against Galileo during his trial for heresy before the Inquisition in 1633.

CONSIDER: Why Galileo's views were so threatening to the Church; some of the long-range consequences of such a stance by the Church toward these views.

We say, pronounce, sentence, and declare that you, the said Galileo, by reason of the matters adduced in trial, and by you confessed as above, have rendered yourself in the judgment of this Holy Office vehemently suspected of heresy, namely, of having believed and held the doctrine—which is false and contrary to the sacred and divine Scriptures—that the Sun is the center of the world and does not move from east to west and that the Earth moves and is not the center of the world; and that an opinion may be held and defended as probable after it has been declared and defined to be contrary to the Holy Scripture; and that consequently you have incurred all the censures and penalties imposed and promulgated in the sacred canons and other constitutions, general and particular, against such delinquents. From which we are content that you be absolved, provided that, first, with a sincere heart and unfeigned faith, you abjure, curse, and detest before us the aforesaid errors and heresies and every other error and heresy contrary to the Catholic and Apostolic Roman Church in the form to be prescribed by us for you.

SOURCE: Excerpt from George Santillana, *The Crime of Galileo,* p. 310. Reprinted by permission of The University of Chicago Press (Chicago, 1955). Copyright © 1955.

Mathematical Principles of Natural Philosophy

Sir Isaac Newton

The greatest scientific synthesis of the seventeenth century was made by Isaac Newton (1642–1727), who was born in England and attained a post as professor of mathematics at Cambridge University. Newton made his most important discoveries early in life. By the beginning of the eighteenth century he was the most admired scientific figure in Europe. He made fundamental discoveries concerning gravity, light, and differential calculus. Most important, he synthesized various scientific findings and methods into a description of the universe as working according to measurable, predictable mechanical laws. Newton's most famous work, Mathematical Principles of Natural Philosophy *(1687), contains his theory of universal gravitation. In the following selection from that work, Newton describes his four rules for arriving at knowledge.*

CONSIDER: *Why Newton's rules might be particularly useful for the experimental sciences; ways these rules differ from those of Descartes.*

RULE I

We are to admit no more causes of natural things than such as are both true and sufficient to explain their appearances.

SOURCE: Sir Isaac Newton, *Mathematical Principles of Natural Philosophy,* trans. Andrew Motte, rev. Florian Cajori (Berkeley, CA: University of California Press, 1947), pp. 398, 400. Reprinted by permission of the University of California Press.

To this purpose the philosophers say that Nature does nothing in vain, and more is in vain when less will serve; for Nature is pleased with simplicity, and affects not the pomp of superfluous causes.

RULE II

Therefore to the same natural effects we must, as far as possible, assign the same causes.

As to respiration in a man and in a beast; the descent of stones in *Europe* and in *America*; the light of our culinary fire and of the sun; the reflection of light in the earth, and in the planets.

RULE III

The qualities of bodies, which admit neither intensification nor remission of degrees, and which are found to belong to all bodies within the reach of our experiments, are to be esteemed the universal qualities of all bodies whatsoever.

For since the qualities of bodies are only known to us by experiments, we are to hold for universal all such as universally agree with experiments; and such as are not liable to diminution can never be quite taken away.

RULE IV

In experimental philosophy we are to look upon propositions inferred by general induction from phenomena as accurately or very nearly true, notwithstanding any contrary hypotheses that may be imagined, till such time as other phenomena occur, by which they may either be made more accurate, or liable to exceptions.

This rule we must follow, that the argument of induction may not be evaded by hypotheses.

 Visual Sources

The Alchemist

Cornelis Bega

This 1663 painting (figure 6.1) by Dutch artist Cornelis Bega (c. 1631–1664) shows an alchemist at work. Here he is about to place a red, powdery material on scales he is holding—apparently part of a typical alchemist's experiment, perhaps to create new substances or transmute material into gold. The books, papers, jars, bottles, and hidden substances in this room are other tools of his trade. This crowded, shabby interior and the alchemist's unkempt clothing suggest the questionable or futile results of his efforts, but during the seventeenth century some scientists still took alchemy quite seriously.

CONSIDER: *The ways this painting presents a contradictory image of alchemy; how this scene might fit with our understanding of the Scientific Revolution.*

A Vision of the New Science

One of the most important figures of the Scientific Revolution was the astronomer and mathematician Johannes Kepler (1571–1630). Figure 6.2 shows a page from the front of one

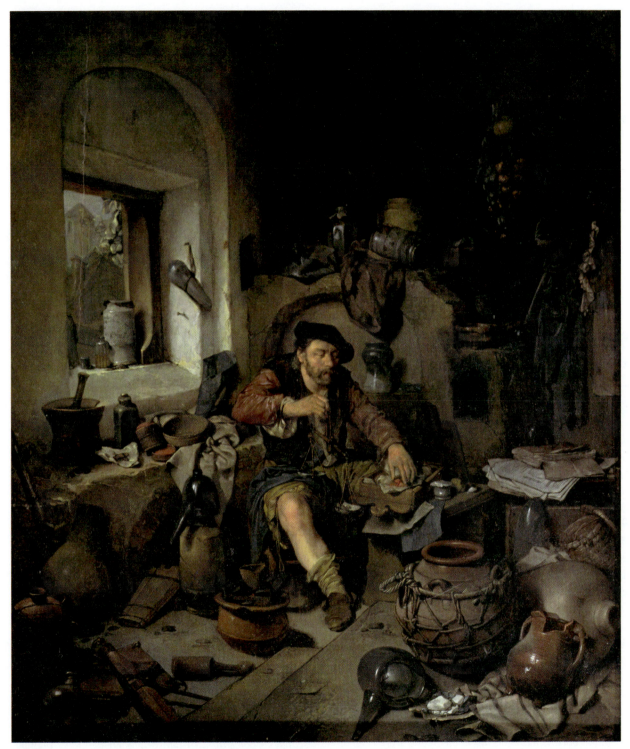

FIGURE 6.1 (© H. Shickman Gallery, New York, USA /The Bridgeman Art Library International)

of his works, first printed in Nuremberg in 1627, in which the "edifice" of astronomy is presented allegorically. The older but still respectable pillars of astronomy of Hipparchus and Ptolemy give way to the new, sturdy pillars of Kepler's immediate predecessors, Copernicus and Tycho Brahe. In the lower left panel Kepler is pictured in his study; in the center panel is a map of the island where Brahe's observatory was located; in the right-hand panel is a picture of two people working on a printing press. Throughout are various instruments used in astronomy.

The picture reveals much about the Scientific Revolution. The instruments emphasize how important measurement and observation were to the new science. The depiction of the old and new pillars suggests that the new scientists were replacing if not necessarily challenging the old, accepted scientific authorities by building on the work of their immediate predecessors—here Brahe on Copernicus, and Kepler on Brahe and Copernicus. The importance of communication among scientists is indicated by tribute to the printing press.

CONSIDER: *How this picture illustrates the ways in which seventeenth-century scientists were breaking with earlier scientific assumptions.*

The Anatomy Lesson of Dr. Tulp

Rembrandt van Rijn

This 1632 painting by Dutch artist Rembrandt van Rijn (1606–1669; figure 6.3) shows Dr. Nicholass Tulp using the body of a hanged criminal to give an anatomy lesson. Public autopsies such as this took place in The Netherlands as well as other areas in seventeenth-century Europe. Typically they were attended by students, colleagues, and ordinary citizens and were held in anatomy theatres such as this one in Amsterdam. The dress of the seven men—all surgeons—observing Dr. Tulp's work suggests that they are taking part in an important official occasion. Their attentive presence—especially of the two surgeons closest to Dr. Tulp—reveals the growing interest in understanding the human body, the effort to associate surgery with science, and the rising prestige of their profession. However, only Dr. Tulp had attended university. In addition to holding a doctorate in medicine and serving here as a teacher, Dr. Tulp was an important public official in Amsterdam: only he wears his hat in the indoor scene.

On the far right stands an open book, suggesting the learning that has gone into this lecture and the growing connections between academic writings about medicine and the facts of the human body. However, during the seventeenth century surgeons did not enjoy high reputations, and confidence in the medical profession in general was, with some good reason,

FIGURE 6.2 (Private Collection/© The Bridgeman Art Library International)

low. Moreover anatomy lessons such as this were held not only for "scientific" purposes. They had to be justified as research to confirm Christian beliefs about God's omnipotence. There were also less solemn aspects to these events: Observers typically paid a fee, and a banquet often followed the autopsy.

CONSIDER: *The changing views toward science and medicine suggested by this painting.*

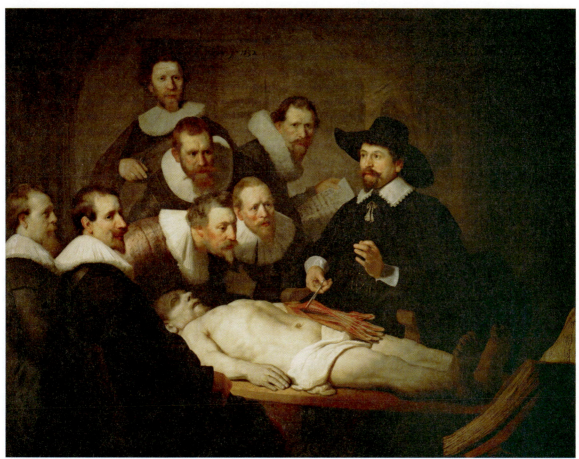

FIGURE 6.3 (© Erich Lessing/Art Resource, NY)

 ## Secondary Sources

Early Modern Europe: Motives for the Scientific Revolution

Sir George Clark

By the seventeenth century, certain broad historical developments had set the stage for individuals to make the discoveries we associate with the Scientific Revolution. In addition, these individuals were motivated in ways that medieval people were not and used the new and growing body of techniques, materials, and knowledge to make their discoveries. In the following selection, British historian Sir George Clark, a recognized authority on the seventeenth century, examines some of the motives that led people to engage in scientific work.

SOURCE: Sir George Clark, *Early Modern Europe*. Reprinted by permission of The Oxford University Press (Oxford, England, 1957), pp. 164–165.

CONSIDER: *The distinctions Clark makes among different people engaged in scientific work; why, more than thirteenth- or fourteenth-century people, these seventeenth-century people had a "disinterested desire to know."*

There were an infinite number of motives which led men to engage in scientific work and to clear the scientific point of view from encumbrances; but we may group together some of the most important under general headings, always remembering that in actual life each of them was compounded with the others. There were economic motives. The Portuguese explorers wanted their new instrument for navigation; the German mineowners asked questions about metallurgy and about machines for lifting and carrying heavy loads; Italian engineers improved their canals and locks and harbours by applying the principles of hydrostatics; English trading companies employed experts who used new methods of drawing charts. Not far removed from the economic motives were those of the physicians and surgeons, who revolutionized anatomy and physiology, and did much more good than harm with their new medicines and new operations, though some of them now seem absurd. Like the doctors, the soldiers called science to their aid in designing and aiming artillery or in planning fortifications. But there were other motives far removed from the economic sphere. Jewellers learnt much about precious and semi-precious stones, but so did magicians. Musicians learnt the mathematics of harmony; painters and architects studied light and colour, substances and proportions, not only as craftsmen but as artists. For a number of reasons religion impelled men to scientific study. The most definite and old-established was the desire to reach absolute correctness in calculating the dates for the annual fixed and movable festivals of the Church: it was a pope who presided over the astronomical researchers by which the calendar was reformed in the sixteenth century. Deeper and stronger was the desire to study the wonders of science, and the order which it unravelled in the universe, as manifestations of the Creator's will. This was closer than any of the other motives to the central impulse which actuated them all, the disinterested desire to know.

Nature as a Machine: The Clock

Steven Shapin

A new way of thinking about nature became central to the Scientific Revolution. During the seventeenth century, natural philosophers increasingly used the model of a machine to describe the workings of the natural world. In the following selection, Steven Shapin argues that the mechanical clock served as the most appealing metaphor for understanding nature.

CONSIDER: *Why natural philosophers wanted to model nature on the characteristics of a machine; why, of all machines, the clock became the preferred metaphor.*

The framework that modern natural philosophers preferred to Aristotelian teleology was one that explicitly modeled nature on the characteristics of a *machine*. So central was the machine metaphor to important strands of new science that many exponents liked to refer to their practice as the *mechanical philosophy*. Modern practitioners disputed the nature and the limits of mechanical explanation, but *proper* mechanical accounts of nature were widely recognized as the goal and the prize. . . .

Of all the mechanical constructions whose characteristics might serve as a model for the natural world, it was the

clock more than any other that appealed to many early modern natural philosophers. Indeed, to follow the *clock metaphor* for nature through the culture of early modern Europe is to trace the main contours of the mechanical philosophy, and therefore of much of what has been traditionally construed as central to the Scientific Revolution. . . .

For those sectors of European society for whom the clock and its regulatory functions were important aspects of daily experience, this machine came to offer a metaphor of enormous power, comprehensibility, and consequence. The allure of the machine, and especially the mechanical clock, as a uniquely intelligible and proper metaphor for explaining natural processes not only broadly follows the contours of daily experience with such devices but also recognizes their potency and legitimacy in ordering human affairs. . . .

In 1605 the German astronomer Johannes Kepler (1571–1630) announced his conversion from his former belief that "the motor cause" of planetary motion "was a soul": "I am much occupied with the investigation of the physical causes. My aim in this is to show that the machine of the universe is not similar to a divine animated being, but similar to a clock." In the 1630s Descartes elaborated a set of extended causal analogies between the movements of mechanical clocks and those of all natural bodies, not excepting even the movements of the human body: "We see that clocks . . . and other machines of this kind, although they have been built by men, do not for this reason lack the power to move by themselves in diverse ways." Why shouldn't human respiration, digestion, locomotion, and sensation be accounted for in just the way we explain the motions of a clock, an artificial fountain, or a mill? In the 1660s the English mechanical philosopher Robert Boyle (1627–91) wrote that the natural world was "as it were, a great piece of clock-work." Just as the spectacular late sixteenth-century clock in the cathedral at Strasbourg (fig. 6) used mechanical parts and movements to mimic the complex motions of the (geocentric) cosmos, so Boyle, Descartes, and other mechanical philosophers recommended the clock metaphor as a philosophically legitimate way of understanding how the natural world was put together and how it functioned.

No Scientific Revolution for Women

Bonnie S. Anderson and Judith P. Zinsser

The Scientific Revolution was generally carried out by men. A few women participated directly in the Scientific Revolution, but they were the exception rather than the rule. The Scien-

SOURCE: Steven Shapin, *The Scientific Revolution* (Chicago: University of Chicago Press, 1996), pp. 30, 32–34.

SOURCE: Excerpts from *A History of Their Own*, vol. II, by Bonnie Anderson and Judith Zinsser. Copyright © 1988 by Bonnie Anderson and Judith Zinsser. Reprinted by permission of HarperCollins Publishers, Inc.

tific Revolution was based on principles such as observing, measuring, experimenting, and coming to reasoned conclusions. Were these principles applied by men to change assumptions about women, particularly about female physiology? Bonnie S. Anderson and Judith P. Zinsser address this question in their interpretive survey of women in European history, A History of Their Own.

CONSIDER: *According to Anderson and Zinsser, why there was no Scientific Revolution for women; how perceptions of female physiology relate to broader assumptions about women and men.*

In the sixteenth and seventeenth centuries Europe's learned men questioned, altered, and dismissed some of the most hallowed precepts of Europe's inherited wisdom. The intellectual upheaval of the Scientific Revolution caused them to examine and describe anew the nature of the universe and its forces, the nature of the human body and its functions. Men used telescopes and rejected the traditional insistence on the smooth surface of the moon. Galileo, Leibnitz, and Newton studied and charted the movement of the planets, discovered gravity and the true relationship between the earth and the sun. Fallopio dissected the human body, Harvey discovered the circulation of the blood, and Leeuwenhoek found spermatozoa with his microscope.

For women, however, there was no Scientific Revolution. When men studied female anatomy, when they spoke of female physiology, of women's reproductive organs, of the female role in procreation, they ceased to be scientific. They suspended reason and did not accept the evidence of their senses. Tradition, prejudice, and imagination, not scientific observation, governed their conclusions about women. The writings of the classical authors like Aristotle and Galen continued to carry the same authority as they had when first written, long after they had been discarded in other areas. Men spoke in the name of the new "science" but mouthed words and phrases from the old misogyny. In the name of "science" they gave a supposed physiological basis to the traditional views of women's nature, function, and role. Science affirmed what men had always known, what custom, law, and religion had postulated and justified. With the authority of their "objective," "rational" inquiry they restated ancient premises and arrived at the same traditional conclusions: the innate superiority of the male and the justifiable subordination of the female.

✖ CHAPTER QUESTIONS

1. What were the main ways in which the science of the seventeenth century constituted a break from the past? What were some of the main problems facing seventeenth-century scientists in making this break? How did they handle these problems?

2. How would you explain the occurrence of the Scientific Revolution in the seventeenth century rather than in the sixteenth or eighteenth century?

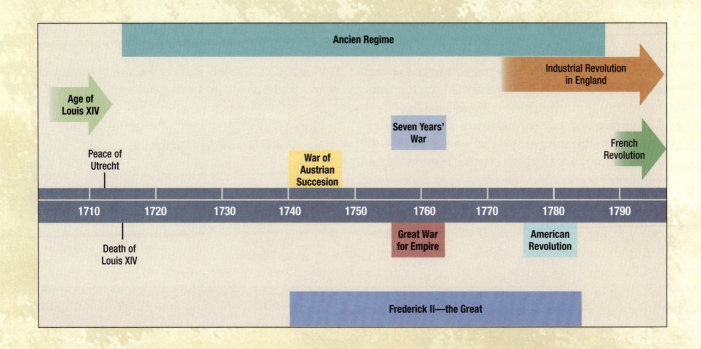

7 Politics and Society in the Ancien Régime

By the time of the death of Louis XIV in 1715, France no longer threatened to overwhelm the rest of Europe. Indeed, during most of the eighteenth century a rough balance of power developed amid the shifting diplomatic alliances and wars. There were two major sets of rivalries among states between 1715 and 1789. In Central Europe, the older Hapsburg Empire was pitted against the newer, assertive Prussia. Although Prussia acquired the status of a major power as a result of this competition, the Hapsburg Empire managed to hold on to most of its lands and to expand at the cost of weaker states like Poland and the Ottoman Empire. Outside of Europe, England and France struggled for supremacy over colonial territories in the Great War for Empire.

During this period preceding the French Revolution, referred to as the "Ancien Régime," most of the same political and social trends that had characterized the second half of the seventeenth century continued, namely, aristocratic dominance, strong monarchies, expanding central governments, and traditional ways of life. Important changes that were initiated—such as agricultural, commercial, and industrial developments that strengthened the middle classes and led to urban growth—were limited in scope and area.

The sources in this chapter center on four aspects of the Ancien Régime between 1715 and 1789. First, the nature and position of the still-dominant aristocracy are examined. What were its responsibilities? What was the position of women within the aristocracy and outside of the aristocracy? Is it true that the aristocracy was frivolous? How did the aristocracy react to pressures from the monarchy on the one side and the middle classes on the other? What were the attitudes of the aristocracy toward the peasantry? Second, the development of the eighteenth-century state is analyzed. What role did Prussia's monarchs play in making her a major power? How did wars contribute to and reflect the growing importance of the state? Third, the importance of commerce and the middle class in

England is explored. What were the connections among commerce, the middle classes, and the English aristocracy? What was the relationship between the development of commerce and industry and England's colonial concerns and growing nationalism? What were some of the effects of the commerce in slaves engaged in by the English and others? Fourth, the assumptions most people held during the Ancien Régime are examined.

The sources in this chapter stress the relative political stability that characterized much of the period between 1715 and 1789. Stability was not the rule in intellectual matters, as will be seen in the next chapter.

❧ For Classroom Discussion

Were politics and society in the Ancien Régime dominated by the aristocracy? Use the analyses by Krieger and Roberts, the source by Frederick the Great, and the paintings by Fragonard and Lawson.

Primary Sources

Political Testament

Frederick the Great

From a distance it may seem that eighteenth-century monarchs were much like those of the seventeenth century, similar in powers, position, and prestige. On closer examination, however, some differences are evident. Frederick II (the Great) of Prussia (1712–1786) was one of the most admired eighteenth-century monarchs. He ascended the throne in 1740 and ruled actively until his death in 1786. Frederick II continued the Prussian tradition of relying on a strong army to maintain and increase his holdings and prestige. At the same time he reorganized the army and the bureaucracy and introduced new ideas into both the theory and the practice of government. In the following excerpts from his Political Testament *(1752), he sets out his conception of politics and the proper role of the sovereign.*

CONSIDER: *How this conception of the monarch differs from that expressed by seventeenth-century monarchs; why Frederick emphasized the need to protect and support the nobility; who the crown's greatest political rivals for power were; the advantages and disadvantages to the monarch of religious toleration.*

Politics is the science of always using the most convenient means in accord with one's own interests. In order to act in conformity with one's interests one must know what these interests are, and in order to gain this knowledge one must study their history and application. . . . One must attempt, above all, to know the special genius of the people which one wants to govern in order to

know if one must treat them leniently or severely, if they are inclined to revolt . . . to intrigue. . . .

[The Prussian nobility] has sacrificed its life and goods for the service of the state, its loyalty and merit have earned it the protection of all its rulers, and it is one of the duties [of the ruler] to aid those [noble] families which have become impoverished in order to keep them in possession of their lands: for they are to be regarded as the pedestals and the pillars of the state. In such a state no factions or rebellions need be feared . . . it is one goal of the policy of this state to preserve the nobility.

A well conducted government must have an underlying concept so well integrated that it could be likened to a system of philosophy. All actions taken must be well reasoned, and all financial, political and military matters must flow towards one goal: which is the strengthening of the state and the furthering of its power. However, such a system can flow but from a single brain, and this must be that of the sovereign. Laziness, hedonism and imbecility, these are the causes which restrain princes in working at the noble task of bringing happiness to their subjects . . . a sovereign is not elevated to his high position, supreme power has not been confined to him in order that he may live in lazy luxury, enriching himself by the labor of the people, being happy while everyone else suffers. The sovereign is the first servant of the state. He is well paid in order that he may sustain the dignity of his office, but one demands that he work efficiently for the good of the state, and that he, at the very least, pay personal attention to the most important problems. . . .

You can see, without doubt, how important it is that the King of Prussia govern personally. Just as it would have been impossible for Newton to arrive at his system of attractions if he had worked in harness with Leibnitz and Descartes, so a system of politics cannot be arrived at and continued if it has not sprung from a single brain. . . . All parts of the government are inexorably linked with

SOURCE: Frederick II, *Political Testament,* in *Europe in Review,* eds. George L. Mosse et al. (Chicago: Rand McNally, 1957), pp. 110–112. Reprinted by permission of George L. Mosse.

each other. Finance, politics and military affairs are inseparable; it does not suffice that one will be well administered; they must all be . . . a Prince who governs personally, who has formed his [own] political system, will not be handicapped when occasions arise where he has to act swiftly: for he can guide all matters towards the end which he has set for himself. . . .

Catholics, Lutherans, Reformed, Jews and other Christian sects live in this state, and live together in peace: if the sovereign, actuated by a mistaken zeal, declares himself for one religion or another, parties will spring up, heated disputes ensue, little by little persecutions will commence and, in the end, the religion persecuted will leave the fatherland and millions of subjects will enrich our neighbors by their skill and industry.

It is of no concern in politics whether the ruler has a religion or whether he has none. All religions, if one examines them, are founded on superstitious systems, more or less absurd. It is impossible for a man of good sense, who dissects their contents, not to see their error; but these prejudices, these errors and mysteries were made for men, and one must know enough to respect the public and not to outrage its faith, whatever religion be involved.

The Complete English Tradesman

Daniel Defoe

During the eighteenth century England was growing in strength and prosperity, particularly in the areas of commerce and manufacturing. A primary beneficiary of these economic developments was the rising commercial middle class. This class was becoming more assertive as the English were becoming more nationalistic. Daniel Defoe (1659c.–1731) speaks about these trends in the following selection from The Complete English Tradesman *(1726). Although best known for* Robinson Crusoe, *Defoe wrote many works and followed a commercial career for some time.*

CONSIDER: *The support Defoe offers for his view that commerce rightly dominates the country economically; how the economic policies that Defoe would recommend compare with policies typical of mercantilism; the connections between commerce and social class in England; the apparent advantages of having colonies and the colonial policies that Defoe's views imply.*

I . . . advance these three points in honour of our country —1. That we are the greatest trading country in the world, because we have the greatest exportation of the

growth and product of our land, and of the manufacture and labour of our people; and the greatest importation and consumption of the growth, product, and manufactures of other countries from abroad, of any nation in the world.

2. That our climate is the best and most agreeable to live in, because a man can be more out of doors in England than in other countries.

3. That our men are the stoutest and best, because, strip them naked from the waist upwards, and give them no weapons at all but their hands and heels, and turn them into a room or stage, and lock them in with the like number of other men of any nation, man for man, and they shall beat the best men you shall find in the world.

And so many of our noble and wealthy families, as we have shown, are raised by and derived from trade, so it is true, and indeed it cannot well be otherwise, that many of the younger branches of our gentry, and even of the nobility itself, have descended again into the spring from whence they flowed, and have become tradesmen; and thence it is that, as I said above, our tradesmen in England are not, as it generally is in other countries, always of the meanest of our people. Nor is trade itself in England, as it generally is in other countries, the meanest thing that men can turn their hand to; but, on the contrary, trade is the readiest way for men to raise their fortunes and families; and therefore it is a field for men of figure and of good families to enter upon. . . .

As to the wealth of the nation, that undoubtedly lies chiefly among the trading part of the people; and though there are a great many families raised within few years, in the late war, by great employments and by great actions abroad, to the honour of the English gentry, yet how many more families among the tradesmen have been raised to immense estates, even during the same time, by the attending circumstances of the war; such as the clothing, the paying, the victualling and furnishing, &c., both army and navy. And by whom have the prodigious taxes been paid, the loans supplied, and money advanced upon all occasions? By whom are the banks and companies carried on, and on whom are the customs and excises levied? Have not the trade and tradesmen borne the burden of the war? And do they not still pay four million a year interest for the public debts? On whom are the funds levied, and by whom the public credit supported? Is not trade the inexhausted fund of all funds, and upon which all the rest depend?

Again; in how superior a port or figure (as we now call it) do our tradesmen live, to what the middling gentry either do or can support! An ordinary tradesman now, not in the city only, but in the country, shall spend more money by the year, than a gentleman of four or five hundred pounds a year can do, and shall increase and lay up every year too; whereas the gentleman shall at the

SOURCE: Daniel Defoe, *The Complete English Tradesman*, vols. 17–18 of *The Novels and Miscellaneous Works of Daniel Defoe* (London: Thomas Tegg, 1840–1841), chap. 25.

best stand stock still just where he began, nay, perhaps, decline: and as for the lower gentry, from a hundred pounds a year to three hundred, or thereabouts, though they are often as proud and high in their appearance as the other; as to them, I say, a shoemaker in London shall keep a better house, spend more money, clothe his family better, and yet grow rich too. It is evident where the difference lies; an estate's a pond, but trade's a spring: the first, if it keeps full, and the water wholesome, by the ordinary supplies and drains from the neighbouring grounds, it is well, and it is all that is expected; but the other is an inexhausted current, which not only fills the pond, and keeps it full, but is continually running over, and fills all the lower ponds and places about it.

This being the case in England, and our trade being so vastly great, it is no wonder that the tradesmen in England fill the lists of our nobility and gentry; no wonder that the gentlemen of the best families marry tradesmen's daughters, and put their younger sons apprentices to tradesmen; and how often do these younger sons come to buy the elder sons' estates, and restore the family, when the elder and head of the house, proving rakish and extravagant, has wasted his patrimony, and is obliged to make out the blessing of Israel's family, where the younger son bought the birthright, and the elder was doomed to serve him!

Trade is so far here from being inconsistent with a gentleman, that, in short, trade in England makes gentlemen, and has peopled this nation with gentlemen; for, after a generation or two, the tradesman's children, or at least their grandchildren, come to be as good gentlemen, statesmen, parliamentarian, privy-counsellors, judges, bishops, and noblemen, as those of the highest birth and the most ancient families; as we have shown. . . .

All this confirms what I have said before, viz., that trade in England neither is or ought to be levelled with what it is in other countries; or the tradesmen depreciated as they are abroad, and as some of our gentry would pretend to do in England; but that as many of our best families rose from trade, so many branches of the best families in England, under the nobility, have stooped so low as to be put apprentices to tradesmen in London, and to set up and follow those trades when they have come out of their times, and have thought it no dishonour to their blood. . . .

The greatness of the British nation is not owing to war and conquests, to enlarging its dominions by the sword, or subjecting the people of other countries to our power; but it is all owing to trade, to the increase of our commerce at home, and the extending it abroad.

It is owing to trade, that new discoveries have been made in lands unknown, and new settlements and plantations made, new colonies planted, and new governments formed, in the uninhabited islands, and the uncultivated continent of America; and those plantings and settlements have again enlarged and increased the trade, and thereby the wealth and power of the nation by whom they were discovered and planted; we have not increased our power, or the number of our subjects, by subduing the nations which possess those countries, and incorporating them into our own; but have entirely planted our colonies, and peopled the countries with our own subjects, natives of this island; and, excepting the negroes, which we transport from Africa to America, as slaves to work in the sugar and tobacco plantations, all our colonies, as well in the islands, as on the continent of America, are entirely peopled from Great Britain and Ireland, and chiefly the former; the natives having either removed further up into the country, or, by their own folly and treachery raising war against us, been destroyed and cut off. . . .

The Slave Trade

Anonymous

Part of the commercial prosperity enjoyed by several Western nations was built on the slave trade, which flourished in the seventeenth and eighteenth centuries. Slaves were generally shipped in British vessels, but the French and others engaged in this trade as well. Most slaves were taken across the Atlantic to Europe's colonial holdings, which in turn shipped goods such as sugar, metals, and wood products to the home country. Although there was little widespread opposition to slavery in Europe during the seventeenth and early eighteenth centuries, by the middle of the eighteenth century antislavery sentiments were growing. The following is an account of what was involved in the slave trade, written in 1771 by an anonymous Frenchman who argued for its abolition.

CONSIDER: *The attitudes that permitted and supported the slave trade; the effects of this experience on the blacks; the legacy of this trade for the colonies.*

As soon as the ships have lowered their anchors off the coast of Guinea, the price at which the captains have decided to buy the captives is announced to the Negroes who buy prisoners from various princes and sell them to the Europeans. Presents are sent to the sovereign who rules over that particular part of the coast, and permission to trade is given. Immediately the slaves are brought by inhuman brokers like so many victims dragged to a sacrifice. White men who covet that portion of the human race receive them in a little house they have erected on the shore, where they have entrenched themselves

SOURCE: Leon Apt and Robert E. Herzstein, eds., *The Evolution of Western Society,* vol. II (Hinsdale, IL: The Dryden Press, 1978), pp. 279–280.

with two pieces of cannon and twenty guards. As soon as the bargain is concluded, the Negro is put in chains and led aboard the vessel, where he meets his fellow sufferers. Here sinister reflections come to his mind; everything shocks and frightens him and his uncertain destiny gives rise to the greatest anxiety. At first he is convinced that he is to serve as a repast to the white men, and the wine which the sailors drink confirms him in this cruel thought, for he imagines that this liquid is the blood of his fellows.

The vessel sets sail for the Antilles, and the Negroes are chained in a hold of the ship, a kind of lugubrious prison where the light of day does not penetrate, but into which air is introduced by means of a pump. Twice a day some disgusting food is distributed to them. Their consuming sorrow and the sad state to which they are reduced would make them commit suicide if they were not deprived of all the means for an attempt upon their lives. Without any kind of clothing it would be difficult to conceal from the watchful eyes of the sailors in charge of any instrument apt to alleviate their despair. The fear of a revolt, such as sometimes happens on the voyage from Guinea, is the basis of a common concern and produces as many guards as there are men in the crew. The slightest noise or a secret conversation among two Negroes is punished with utmost severity. All in all, the voyage is made in a continuous state of alarm on the part of the white men, who fear a revolt, and in a cruel state of uncertainty on the part of the Negroes, who do not know the fate awaiting them.

When the vessel arrives at a port in the Antilles, they are taken to a warehouse where they are displayed, like any merchandise, to the eyes of buyers. The plantation owner pays according to the age, strength and health of the Negro he is buying. He has him taken to his plantation, and there he is delivered to an overseer who then and there becomes his tormentor. In order to domesticate him, the Negro is granted a few days of rest in his new place, but soon he is given a hoe and a sickle and made to join a work gang. Then he ceases to wonder about his fate; he understands that only labor is demanded of him. But he does not know yet how excessive this labor will be. As a matter of fact, his work begins at dawn and does not end before nightfall; it is interrupted for only two hours at dinnertime. The food a full-grown Negro is given each week consists of two pounds of salt beef or cod and two pots of tapioca meal, amounting to about two pints of Paris. A Negro of twelve or thirteen years or under is given only one pot of meal and one pound of beef or cod. In place of food some planters give their Negroes the liberty of working for themselves every Saturday; others are even less generous and grant them this liberty only on Sundays and holidays. Therefore, since the nourishment of the Negroes is insufficient, their tendency to cheat must be attributed to the necessity of finding the food they lack.

Letter to Lady R., 1716: Women and the Aristocracy
Lady Mary Wortley Montagu

During the eighteenth century women continued to remain limited in the economic and political roles they could play, but it was possible for aristocratic women to take up influential social and cultural roles. In particular, many women used letter writing as an art, and from these letters much insight about the position and attitudes of women can be gained. Lady Mary Wortley Montagu (1689–1762) was a well-known British literary figure, writing essays and poetry in addition to her volumes of letters. The following is a selection from a letter written in 1716 to Lady R.

CONSIDER: *The assumptions about marriage among the aristocracy; connections among marriage, love, and economic interests; the position of aristocratic women reflected by this letter.*

No woman dares appear coquette enough to encourage two lovers at a time. And I have not seen any such prudes as to pretend fidelity to their husbands, who are certainly the best natured set of people in the world, and look upon their wives' gallants as favourably as men do upon their deputies, that take the troublesome part of their business off their hands. They have not however the less to do on that account; for they are generally deputies in another place themselves; in one word, 'tis the established custom for every lady to have two husbands, one that bears the name, and another that performs the duties. And these engagements are so well known, that it would be a downright affront, and publicly resented, if you invited a woman of quality to dinner, without, at the same time, inviting her two attendants of lover and husband, between whom she sits in state with great gravity. The submarriages generally last twenty years together, and the lady often commands the poor lover's estate, even to the utter ruin of his family.

These connections, indeed, are as seldom begun by any real passion as other matches; for a man makes but an ill figure that is not in some commerce of this nature; and a woman looks out for a lover as soon as she's married, as part of her equipage, without which she could not be genteel; and the first article of the treaty is establishing the pension, which remains to the lady, in case the gallant should prove inconstant. This chargeable point of honour I look upon as the real foundation of so many

SOURCE: Mary Wortley Montagu, *Works,* vol. II (London: Richard Phillips, 1803), pp. 57–59.

wonderful instances of constancy. I really know some women of the first quality, whose pensions are as well known as their annual rents, and yet nobody esteems them the less; on the contrary, their discretion would be called in question, if they should be suspected to be mistresses for nothing. A great part of their emulation consists in trying who shall get most.

Women of the Third Estate

The vast majority of eighteenth-century Europeans were not members of the aristocracy. More than 90 percent were peasants, artisans, domestics, and laborers—often referred to in France as members of the Third Estate. While both men and women of the Third Estate shared much, women's positions and grievances often differed from those of men. Articulate records of these women's grievances are difficult to find, but the flood of formal petitions preceding the French Revolution of 1789 provides us with some rich sources. The following is a "Petition of the Women of the Third Estate to the King," dated several months prior to the outbreak of the French Revolution.

CONSIDER: *What options seem available to women; the problems identified and solutions proposed; ways in which men's interests and women's interests might clash.*

1 January 1789. Almost all women of the Third Estate are born poor. Their education is either neglected or misconceived, for it consists in sending them to learn from

---

SOURCE: Excerpts from *Not in God's Image* by Julia O'Faolain and Lauro Martines. Copyright © 1973 by Julia O'Faolain and Lauro Martines. Reprinted by permission of Harper & Row, Publishers, Inc.

teachers who do not themselves know the first word of the language they are supposed to be teaching. . . . At the age of fifteen or sixteen, girls can earn five or six sous a day. If nature has not granted them good looks, they get married, without a dowry, to unfortunate artisans and drag out a grueling existence in the depths of the provinces, producing children whom they are unable to bring up. If, on the other hand, they are born pretty, being without culture, principles, or any notion of morality, they fall prey to the first seducer, make one slip, come to Paris to conceal it, go totally to the bad here, and end up dying as victims of debauchery.

Today, when the difficulty of earning a living forces thousands of women to offer themselves to the highest bidder and men prefer buying them for a spell to winning them for good, any woman drawn to virtue, eager to educate herself, and with natural taste . . . is faced with the choice either of casting herself into a cloister which will accept a modest dowry or of going into domestic service. . . .

If old age overtakes unmarried women, they spend it in tears and as objects of contempt for their nearest relatives.

To counter such misfortunes, Sire, we ask that men be excluded from practicing those crafts that are women's prerogative, such as dressmaking, embroidery, millinery, etc. Let them leave us the needle and the spindle and we pledge our word never to handle the compass or the set-square.

We ask, Sire . . . to be instructed and given jobs, not that we may usurp men's authority but so that we may have a means of livelihood, and so that the weaker among us who are dazzled by luxury and led astray by example should not be forced to join the ranks of the wretched who encumber the streets and whose lewd audacity disgraces both our sex and the men who frequent them.

 Visual Sources

Happy Accidents of the Swing

Jean-Honoré Fragonard

The aristocracy remained dominant culturally during the Ancien Régime, commissioning most of the art of the period. It is not surprising, then, that the art reflected aristocratic values and tastes. The Swing by Jean-Honoré Fragonard (figure 7.1) exemplifies a type of painting quite popular among France's eighteenth-century aristocracy.

Fragonard was commissioned by Baron de Saint-Julien in 1767 to paint a picture of his mistress on a swing being pushed by a bishop who did not know that the woman was the baron's mistress, with the baron himself watching from a strategic place of hiding. In the picture the woman on the swing seems well aware of what is happening, flinging off her shoe toward

a statue of the god of discretion in such a way as to cause her gown to billow out revealingly.

This painting reflects a certain religious irreverence on the part of the eighteenth-century aristocracy, for the joke is on the unknowing bishop. The significance of this irreverence is magnified by the fact that Saint-Julien had numerous dealings with the clergy, since he was at this time a government official responsible for overseeing clerical wealth.

The lush setting of the painting and the tenor of the scene suggest the love of romantic luxury and concern for sensual indulgence by this most privileged but soon to be declining part of society.

CONSIDER: *The evidence in this picture of the attitudes of lifestyle of the eighteenth-century French aristocracy.*

FIGURE 7.1 (© Wallace Collection, London, UK/Bridgeman Art Library)

Act of Humanity

Jean Defraine

In Act of Humanity (c. 1783), painter Jean Defraine shows that the old tradition of aristocratic responsibility for social welfare is still upheld in the eighteenth century (figure 7.2). Here, an aristocrat is visiting a family stricken by both illness and poverty. The realistic depiction of poverty is accompanied by the comforting suggestion that its effects can be alleviated through charitable gestures. Such humanitarian acts on the part of the aristocracy were considered one of the few appropriate cures for social problems of the poor.

CONSIDER: How this picture compares with Happy Accidents of the Swing.

The Battle of Fontenoy

C. C. P. Lawson

War, though still common in the eighteenth century, was more controlled and orderly and less vicious than during the first half of the seventeenth century. This is suggested in this painting by C. C. P. Lawson (figure 7.3) of a typical eighteenth-century land battle, The Battle of Fontenoy. Aristocratic traditions are maintained by the commanders, who calmly salute each other before the battle begins. The troops are uniformed and orderly, *apparently under the firm control of officers. The characteristics of eighteenth-century battles depicted here reflect the realities of military tactics and economics. As argued by the modern historian R. J. White in* Europe in the Eighteenth Century *(New York: St. Martin's Press, 1965),*

a supposedly wholesome mixture of aristocrats and scum was the principal substance of the armed forces everywhere in the eighteenth century. Warfare was predominantly defensive, dogged by caution and conducted according to strict rules of procedure. The almost baroque movements of armed forces in the stately game of siege warfare, the rigid adherence to the rules of the game as laid down in *Fighting Instructions* [a standard military manual], which often appear so ludicrous to modern observers, were not invented to charm later generations, but were the offspring of the peculiar necessities of a world of limited material resources and rationally conceived purposes.

CONSIDER: *How the arrangement of the troops in this picture reflects the social structure of the eighteenth century.*

FIGURE 7.2

FIGURE 7.3 © Victoria & Albert Museum, London/Art Resource, NY

The Atlantic Slave Trade

Many societies were familiar with slavery well before the fifteenth century. Moreover, slave trading from Africa took place to the east and north before it turned west across the Atlantic. However, after the sixteenth century the Atlantic slave trade increased dramatically. Chart 7.1 traces the volume of slave exports from Africa across the Atlantic between the fifteenth and nineteenth centuries.

CONSIDER: *Which periods had the largest volumes of slave exports; how the differences in the slave trade over the centuries might be explained.*

Chart 7.1	
Period	*Volume*
1450–1600	367,000
1601–1700	1,868,000
1701–1800	6,133,000
1801–1900	3,330,000
Total	11,698,000

Secondary Sources

Slavery—White, Black, Muslim, Christian

David Brion Davis

From the Western perspective, the focus of African slavery is usually the triangular trade across the Atlantic between Europe, Africa, and the Americas that flourished during the seventeenth and eighteenth centuries. However, the roots of that slave trade go deeper and broader. In the following selection, the American historian David Brion Davis emphasizes the importance of the long history of warfare between Christians and Muslims and the piracy, kidnapping, and enslavement of people from both groups that took place.

CONSIDER: *The significance of the Muslim enslavement of Christians; why the story of the Muslim enslavement of Christians is less well known in the West.*

The origins of African slavery in the New World cannot be understood without some knowledge of the millennium of warfare between Christians and Muslims that took place in the Mediterranean and Atlantic and the piracy and kidnapping that went along with it. In 1627 pirates from the Barbary Coast of North Africa raided distant Iceland and enslaved nearly four hundred astonished residents. In 1617 Muslim pirates, having long enslaved Christians along the coasts of Spain, France, Italy, and even Ireland, captured 1,200 men and women in Portuguese Madeira. Down to the 1640s, there were many more English slaves in Muslim North Africa than African slaves under English control in the Caribbean. Indeed, a 1624 parliamentary proclamation estimated that the Barbary states held at least 1,500 English slaves, mostly sailors captured in the Mediterranean or Atlantic.

The historian Robert C. Davis concludes that between 1580 and 1680 some 850,000 Christian slaves were taken in chains to the Maghreb. The number of enslavements would surely exceed a million if we move down a century to the late eighteenth and early nineteenth centuries, when the question of enslaved white American sailors became a central issue of foreign policy for the administrations of Washington, Adams, and Jefferson. Only a tiny percentage of Christian slaves were ransomed or converted to Islam; the few who were fortunate enough to get away complained of being fed "nothing but bread and water," of being treated "like dogs," and of being whipped while working as galley slaves or as carriers of heavy rocks in building or repairing public works. Their rate of mortality equaled that of African slaves on the infamous Middle Passage.

This large-scale enslavement of Europeans in the sixteenth and seventeenth centuries did not lead to movements against slavery as an institution. In fact, some of the ransomed European slaves engaged in their own slaving raids against Muslims as a form of revenge. Daniel Defoe's fictional Robinson Crusoe (published in 1719) is on a mid-seventeenth-century slavetrading vessel bound for Guinea when he himself is captured and enslaved by a "Turkish rover of Sallee [Salé]" off the northwest coast of Africa. After two years of enslavement, Crusoe escapes, shoots and kills one naked black "savage," and is then rescued by a humane and charitable Portuguese slave-trading captain, who takes Crusoe to Brazil, where for four years he makes a small fortune as a slaveholding planter.

I do not mean to suggest that the Muslim enslavement of Christians evoked no opposition whatever to slavery. Benjamin Franklin was not the first but simply the most famous man to turn the enslavement of whites by Barbary pirates into a strong and clever antislavery argument; he mocked a proslavery speech in Congress by comparing it to a fictional 1687 speech of the Divan of Algiers defending the "plundering and enslaving" of Christians. But that was in 1790, in the last month of Franklin's life, well after cultural and intellectual changes had already launched antislavery movements in England, America, and France. It is most unlikely that Franklin would have dreamed of writing such a piece in his young manhood, when he in fact owned and sold Negro slaves.

In the preceding centuries, before the rise of humanitarian reform, including the antislavery movement, the continuing enslavement of Christians by Muslims and of Muslims by Christians actually conditioned both groups to accept the institution of slavery on a wider scale and thus prepared the way for the vast Atlantic slave system. In the fifteenth century, for example, Portuguese leaders saw the enslavement and baptism of black Africans as a continuation of the centuries-old reconquest of Iberia and crusade against the Moors.

SOURCE: *The New York Review of Books,* July 5, 2001, p. 51.

The Ancien Régime: Ideals and Realities

John Roberts

It is difficult to look back at past societies with other than our own assumptions. However, people in the Ancien Régime— eighteenth-century Europe—had their own beliefs, values, and perceptions about the world and their place in it. In the following selection John Roberts describes what most eighteenth-century Europeans would take for granted, emphasizing their mental conservatism.

CONSIDER: *The ways in which their assumptions differ from our own; the ways in which they are the same as ours; why their view of innovation and the past is so important.*

What would be taken for granted by most continental Europeans in the eighteenth century and, to some extent, by Englishmen and English settlers abroad, would be assumptions which can be sketched briefly in such propositions as these: God made the world and gave it a moral and social structure; His revelation in Jesus Christ imposes a duty upon society to protect the Church, Christian truth and moral principles in a positive way by promoting sound behaviour and belief and harrying bad; Christianity teaches that the existing structure of society is in principle good and should be upheld; this structure is organized hierarchically and for the most part its hierarchies are hereditary, their apex usually being found in a monarch; privileges and duties are distributed in a manner which can be justified by reference to this hierarchy. It is also true (our list of assumptions could continue) that while the organization of society around hereditary units was a fundamental datum of society under the *ancien régime*, it took for granted respect for other groups in which men came together for religious, professional, economic or social purposes; corporations with these ends were thought the proper regulators of much of daily life—the practice of trade or the enjoyment of legal rights, for example—and the interests of individuals belonging to them came emphatically second to those of these legal persons. . . .

It was also then assumed that much more of personal behaviour should be regulated by law and traditional practice than today. . . .

Social restraint reflected the pervasive anti-individualism of the *ancien régime*. Moreover, moral and ideological truth were thought indivisible and this left little room in theory for the vagaries of the individual. . . .

Across all these assumptions ran an overriding mental conservatism. One of the deepest differences between our own age and the *ancien régime* is the pervading conviction of those times that it was innovation which needed to be justified, not the past. A huge inertia generated by usage, tradition, prescription and the brutal fact of simple ignorance, lay heavily upon the institutions of the eighteenth century. As there had been for centuries, there was a self-evident justification for the ways of our fathers, for the forms and laws they had evolved and set down. One way in which this expressed itself was in an intense legalism, a fascination with old documents, judgments, lineage and inheritance. The higher classes were preoccupied with questions of blood, ancestry and family honour. Yet none of this preoccupation with the past was true historical-mindedness. Men were obsessed with the past as guidance, as precedent, even as spectacle, but not for its own sake. Few men had much sense that they were not looking at the same world as their ancestors.

The Resurgent Aristocracy

Leonard Krieger

Historians have at times exaggerated the importance of the rise of the middle class and the decline of the aristocracy in the eighteenth century. Recently, historians have begun to emphasize the middle of the eighteenth century as a period during which the aristocracy was actually resurgent, making efforts to regain its position and increase its influence—often with considerable success. This view is illustrated in the following selection by Leonard Krieger of the University of Chicago.

CONSIDER: *The evidence Krieger offers for a resurgence of the aristocracy; the ways in which the aristocracy adapted to eighteenth-century political needs.*

In the eighteenth century, surprisingly, aristocracies—or at least important parts of them—were resurgent. Appreciating the principle of what would later become a proverbial prescription for men to join what they could not beat, nobles in the several countries of Europe picked themselves up and began to appropriate commanding positions in the governmental structures of the new states and even in the network of commercial relations. The Whig oligarchy that ruled Britain without serious challenge between the accession of the Hanoverian dynasty in 1714 and George III's assertion of royal influence after 1760 represented a landowning aristocracy that was sponsoring a capitalized and scientific agriculture in response to demands of the market and that had economic ties with merchants and bankers of the City. The French peers, refueled by Louis XIV's calculated infusion of subsidies, made a serious bid to refashion the monarchy in their own image after the death of the Sun King in 1715, and when this attempt failed, a more economically progressive and modern-minded judicial and administrative aristocracy (*no-blesse de robe* and *noblesse d'office*) rose to continue the counteroffensive on behalf of the privileged. In Russia various sections of the military and landed nobility dictated the succession to the throne—in general they preferred tsarinas in the expectation that they would behave consistently as members of the "weaker sex"—and dominated the social policy of the government from the death of Peter the Great in 1725 through the accession of Catherine the Great in 1762. The long period from 1718 to 1772 that the Swedes euphemistically called their "era of liberty" was actually an age of aristocratic sovereignty, exercised constitutionally in a nominal monarchy through the nobles' oligarchic control over both the *Riksdag*, or parliament, and the bureaucracy. The Dutch gave the same high-flown label to the period from 1702 to 1747, when the small but influential class of Regents, an oligarchy comprised of urban patricians, resumed its sway after the death of William III and kept the office of *stadholder* vacant. The seven provinces that made up the Dutch "Republic" were, in this respect, expanded versions of the independent city-states in Europe. Concentrated mainly in Switzerland and Germany, they too were stabilized during the first half of the eighteenth century under the rule of exclusive patrician oligarchies. . . .

The aristocracies' new lease on life for the eighteenth century was thus predicated upon the modernization of their premises, and they thereby shifted the arena of social conflict from outside to inside the structure of the state. Where they had formerly defended their privileged rights to landownership, manorial lordship, judicial immunities, and tax exemptions by denying the jurisdiction of the central governments, they now defended these privileges by occupying and controlling the governmental agencies which exercised the jurisdiction. This aristocratic penetration of the state ran counter to the standards of general law, equal citizenship, and uniform administration which had served and continued to serve bureaucrats as guides in extending the scope of central government. But the hierarchical tendency was no mere atavism. Despite the obvious and reciprocal hostility between it and the leveling tendency with which it shared the state, the coexistence of the two tendencies, however mismatched in logic, was a faithful response to a fundamental social demand of the age. European society required, for the military security of its inhabitants, for the direction and subsidization of its economy, and for the prevention of religious turbulence and popular disorder, the imposition of unified control over a larger area and more people than the contemporary instruments of government could manage. Hence the employment of the traditional social and corporate hierarchies by the government as extensions of the governing arm into the mass of inhabitants. All people were subject, but some were more subject than others.

Lords and Peasants

Jerome Blum

The aristocracy made up a small percentage of Europe's population. Some 80 to 90 percent of the people were still peasants. While peasants lived in a variety of different circumstances, most lived at not much more than a subsistence level. They were usually thought of as at the bottom of society. In the following selection Jerome Blum analyzes attitudes held toward the peasants by seigniors (lords) and by peasants themselves.

CONSIDER: *How lords viewed peasants in relation to themselves; how the lords' attitudes reflected actual social conditions; possible consequences of the negative attitudes held about peasants.*

With the ownership of land went power and authority over the peasants who lived on the land. There were a multitude of variations in the nature of that authority and in the nature of the peasants' subservience to their seigniors, in the compass of the seigniors' supervision and control, and in the obligations that the peasants had to pay their lords. The peasants themselves were known by many different names, and so, too, were the obligations they owed the seigniors. But, whatever the differences, the status of the peasant everywhere in the servile lands was associated with unfreedom and constraint. In the hierarchical ladder of the traditional order he stood on the bottom rung. He was "the stepchild of the age, the broad, patient back who bore the weight of the entire social pyramid . . . the clumsy lout who was deprived and mocked by court, noble and city." . . .

The subservience of the peasant and his dependence upon his lord were mirrored in the attitudes and opinions of the seigniors of east and west alike. They believed that the natural order of things had divided humankind into masters and servants, those who commanded and those who obeyed. They believed themselves to be naturally superior beings and looked upon those who they believed were destined to serve them as their natural inferiors. At

SOURCE: From Blum, Jerome, *The End of the Old Order in Rural Europe*, pp. 29–31, 44–49. Copyright 1978 by Princeton University Press. Reprinted by permission of Princeton University Press.

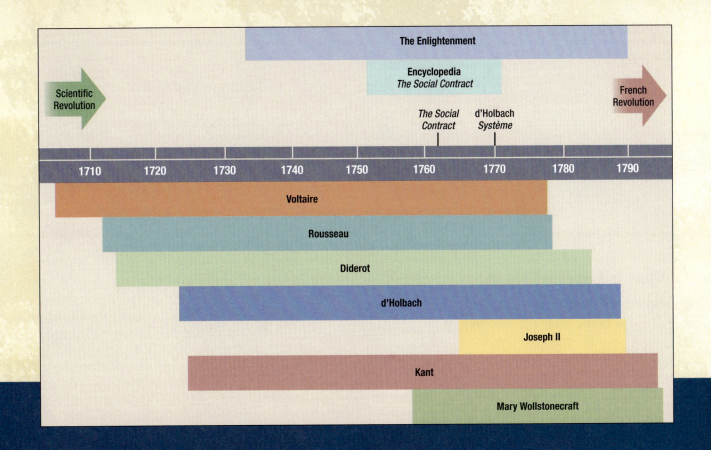

8 The Enlightenment

As a period of intellectual history in Western civilization, the eighteenth century is known quite appropriately as the Enlightenment. At that time a group of thinkers, called the *philosophes*, developed and popularized related sets of ideas that formed a basis for modern thought. Their methods emphasized scepticism, empirical reasoning, and satire. They spread their ideas through works ranging from pamphlets to the great *Encyclopedia* and numerous meetings in aristocratic "salons." Although centered in France, this intellectual movement took place throughout Europe.

Most of the *philosophes* believed that Western civilization was on the verge of enlightenment, that reasoning and education could quickly dispel the darkness of the past that had kept people in a state of immaturity. The main objects of their criticism were institutions, such as governments and the Church, and irrational customs that perpetuated old ways of thinking and thus hindered progress. While critical

and combative, the *philosophes* were not political or social revolutionaries. Their ideas were revolutionary in many ways, but in practice these thinkers hoped for rather painless change—often through reform from above by enlightened monarchs. Enlightenment thinkers usually admired England, where liberal ideas and practices were most developed.

The sources in this chapter concern three issues. First, what was the nature of Enlightenment thought? What was the professed spirit of the Enlightenment? What patterns of morality were embodied in Enlightenment ideas? In what ways was authority rejected and nature elevated to great importance? Second, how should we characterize the *philosophes?* Who were they? What were their common psychological traits, their religious beliefs, and their interactions? Finally, how did Enlightenment thought affect eighteenth-century politics before the French Revolution? Was there such a phenomenon as "enlightened despotism," and if so, what did it mean?

Together, the sources should reveal an intellectual movement still tied to the traditional society of the Ancien Régime but with strikingly modern characteristics. Toward the end of the eighteenth century, many of the ideas of the Enlightenment played an important role in the French Revolution—the subject of the next chapter.

❧ **For Classroom Discussion**

What was the Enlightenment? Use the selections by Porter and Becker as well as the documents by Kant, d'Holbach, and Diderot.

Primary Sources

What Is Enlightenment?

Immanuel Kant

One of the most pervasive themes among Enlightenment thinkers was a self-conscious sense of a spirit of enlightenment. This is illustrated in the following excerpt from a short essay by Immanuel Kant (1724–1804) of Köigsberg in East Prussia. Kant, one of the world's most profound philosophers, is particularly known for his analysis of the human mind and how it relates to nature, as set forth in his Critique of Pure Reason *(1781). In the following essay, written in 1784, Kant defines the spirit of the Enlightenment and describes some of its implications.*

CONSIDER: *What Kant means by "freedom" and why he feels freedom is so central to the Enlightenment; how people can become enlightened and the appropriate environment to facilitate this enlightenment; what Kant would consider "mature"; how Kant relates enlightenment and politics.*

Enlightenment is man's leaving his self-caused immaturity. Immaturity is the incapacity to use one's intelligence without the guidance of another. Such immaturity is self-caused if it is not caused by lack of intelligence, but by lack of determination and courage to use one's intelligence without being guided by another. *Sapere Aude!* Have the courage to use your own intelligence! is therefore the motto of the enlightenment.

Through laziness and cowardice a large part of mankind, even after nature has freed them from alien guidance, gladly remain immature. It is because of laziness and cowardice that it is so easy for others to usurp the role of guardians. It is so comfortable to be a minor! If I have a book which provides meaning for me, a pastor who has conscience for me, a doctor who will judge my diet for me and so on, then I do not need to exert myself. I do not have any need to think; if I can pay, others will

SOURCE: Immanuel Kant, "What Is Enlightenment?" in *The Philosophy of Kant,* Carl J. Friedrich, ed. Reprinted by permission of Random House, Inc. (New York, 1949), pp. 132–134, 138–139. Copyright © 1949 by Random House, Inc.

take over the tedious job for me. The guardians who have kindly undertaken the supervision will see to it that by far the largest part of mankind, including the entire "beautiful sex," should consider the step into maturity, not only as difficult but as very dangerous. . . .

But it is more nearly possible for a public to enlighten itself: this is even inescapable if only the public is given its freedom. . . .

All that is required for this enlightenment is *freedom;* and particularly the least harmful of all that may be called freedom, namely, the freedom for man to make *public* use of his reason in all matters. . . .

The question may now be put: Do we live at present in an enlightened age? The answer is: No, but in an age of enlightenment. Much still prevents men from being placed in a position or even being placed into position to use their own minds securely and well in matters of religion. But we do have very definite indications that this field of endeavor is being opened up for men to work freely and reduce gradually the hindrances preventing a general enlightenment and an escape from self-caused immaturity. In this sense, this age is the age of enlightenment and the age of Frederick (The Great). . . .

I have emphasized the main point of enlightenment, that is of man's release from his self-caused immaturity, primarily *in matters of religion.* I have done this because our rulers have no interest in playing the guardian of their subjects in matters of arts and sciences. Furthermore immaturity in matters of religion is not only most noxious but also most dishonorable. But the point of view of a head of state who favors freedom in the arts and sciences goes even farther; for he understands that there is no danger in legislation permitting his subjects to make *public* use of their own reason and to submit *publicly* their thoughts regarding a better framing of such laws together with a frank criticism of existing *legislation.* We have a shining example of this; no prince excels him whom we admire. Only he who is himself enlightened does not fear spectres when he at the same time has a well-disciplined army at his disposal as a guarantee of public peace. Only he can say what (the ruler of a) free state dare not say: *Argue as much as you want and about whatever you want but obey!*

The System of Nature

Baron d'Holbach

Most Enlightenment thinkers rejected traditional sources of authority such as the Church or custom. Instead, they argued that people should rely on reason, experience, and nature as their guides. Baron d'Holbach (1723–1789) exemplifies this in his varied writings. A German aristocrat and scientist who assumed French citizenship, d'Holbach is best known for his attacks on organized religion and his contributions to Diderot's Encyclopedia. *In the following selection from his* System of Nature *(1770), d'Holbach focuses on the meaning of enlightenment and what should be done to obtain this enlightenment.*

CONSIDER: *Why enlightenment is so important; whether "nature" has a meaning similar to God for d'Holbach; the views about the nature of enlightenment that Kant and d'Holbach share.*

The source of man's unhappiness is his ignorance of Nature. The pertinacity with which he clings to blind opinions imbibed in his infancy, which interweave themselves with his existence, the consequent prejudice that warps his mind, that prevents its expansion, that renders him the slave of fiction, appears to doom him to continual errour. He resembles a child destitute of experience, full of idle notions: a dangerous leaven mixes itself with all his knowledge: it is of necessity obscure, it is vacillating and false:—He takes the tone of his ideas on the authority of others, who are themselves in errour, or else have an interest in deceiving him. To remove this Cimmerian darkness, these barriers to the improvement of his condition; to disentangle him from the clouds of errour that envelop him, that obscure the path he ought to tread; to guide him out of this Cretan labyrinth, requires the clue of Ariadne, with all the love she could bestow on Theseus. It exacts more than common exertion; it needs a most determined, a most undaunted courage—it is never effected but by a persevering resolution to act, to think for himself; to examine with rigour and impartiality the opinions he has adopted. . . .

The most important of our duties, then, is to seek means by which we may destroy delusions that can never do more than mislead us. The remedies for these evils must be sought for in Nature herself; it is only in the abundance of her resources, that we can rationally expect to find antidotes to the mischiefs brought upon us by an ill-directed, by an overpowering enthusiasm. It is time these remedies were sought; it is time to look the

evil boldly in the face, to examine its foundations, to scrutinize its super-structure: reason, with its faithful guide experience, must attack in their entrenchments those prejudices to which the human race has but too long been the victim. For this purpose reason must be restored to its proper rank,—it must be rescued from the evil company with which it is associated. . . .

Truth speaks not to these perverse beings:—her voice can only be heard by generous minds accustomed to reflection, whose sensibilities make them lament the numberless calamities showered on the earth by political and religious tyranny—whose enlightened minds contemplate with horrour the immensity, the ponderosity of that series of misfortunes with which errour has in all ages overwhelmed mankind.

The *civilized man,* is he whom experience and social life have enabled to draw from nature the means of his own happiness; because he has learned to oppose resistance to those impulses he receives from exterior beings, when experience has taught him they would be injurious to his welfare.

The *enlightened man,* is man in his maturity, in his perfection; who is capable of pursuing his own happiness; because he has learned to examine, to think for himself, and not to take that for truth upon the authority of others, which experience has taught him examination will frequently prove erroneous. . . .

It necessarily results, that man in his researches ought always to fall back on experience, and natural philosophy: These are what he should consult in his religion—in his morals—in his legislation—in his political government—in the arts—in the sciences—in his pleasures—in his misfortunes. Experience teaches that Nature acts by simple, uniform, and invariable laws. It is by his senses man is bound to this universal Nature; it is by his senses he must penetrate her secrets; it is from his senses he must draw experience of her laws. Whenever, therefore, he either fails to acquire experience or quits its path, he stumbles into an abyss, his imagination leads him astray.

Prospectus for the Encyclopedia of Arts and Sciences

Denis Diderot

More than any other work, the Encyclopedia of Arts and Sciences, *edited by Denis Diderot (1713–1784) and Jean-le-Rond d'Alembert (1717–1783), epitomizes the Enlightenment.*

SOURCE: Baron d'Holbach, *The System of Nature,* trans. H. D. Robinson (Boston: J. P. Mendum, 1853), pp. viii–ix, 12–13, 15.

SOURCE: "The Encyclopedia Announced" from *Major Crises in Western Civilization, Volume II, 1745 to the Nuclear Age* by Richard W. Lyman and Lewis W. Spitz, copyright © 1965 by Harcourt Brace & Company and renewed 1993 by Richard W. Lyman and Lewis W. Spitz, reprinted by permission of the publisher.

Written between 1745 and 1780, it presented to the public the sum of knowledge considered important by Enlightenment thinkers. The critical Enlightenment spirit underlying the Encyclopedia *led traditional authorities to condemn it and to suppress it more than once. The following is an excerpt from the* Prospectus *that appeared in 1750, announcing the forthcoming* Encyclopedia. *The* Prospectus *was written by Diderot, a philosopher, novelist, and playwright who had already been in trouble with the authorities for his writings. The* Prospectus *apparently aroused widespread expectations; even before the first volume of the* Encyclopedia *appeared, more than a thousand orders for it had been received.*

CONSIDER: *What a reader could hope to gain by purchasing the* Encyclopedia *and how these hopes themselves reflect the spirit of the Enlightenment; how this selection from the* Prospectus *reflects the same ideas expressed by Kant and d'Holbach; how the Enlightenment as described here related to the scientific revolution of the seventeenth century.*

It cannot be denied that, since the revival of letters among us, we owe partly to dictionaries the general enlightenment that has spread in society and the germ of science that is gradually preparing men's minds for more profound knowledge. How valuable would it not be, then, to have a book of this kind that one could consult on all subjects and that would serve as much to guide those who have the courage to work at the instruction of others as to enlighten those who only instruct themselves!

This is one advantage we thought of, but it is not the only one. In condensing to dictionary form all that concerns the arts and sciences, it remained necessary to make people aware of the assistance they lend each other; to make use of this assistance to render principles more certain and their consequences clearer; to indicate the distant and close relationships of the beings that make up nature, which have occupied men; to show, by showing the interlacing both of roots and of branches, the impossibility of understanding thoroughly some parts of the whole without exploring many others; to produce a general picture of the efforts of the human spirit in all areas and in all centuries; to present these matters with clarity; to give to each the proper scope, and to prove, if possible, our epigraph by our success: . . .

The majority of these works appeared during the last century and were not completely scorned. It was found that if they did not show much talent, they at least bore the marks of labor and of knowledge. But what would these encyclopedias mean to us? What progress have we not made since then in the arts and sciences? How many truths discovered today, which were not foreseen then? True philosophy was in its cradle; the geometry of infinity

did not yet exist; experimental physics was just appearing; there was no dialectic at all; the laws of sound criticism were entirely unknown. Descartes, Boyle, Huyghens, Newton, Leibnitz, the Bernoullis, Locke, Bayle, Pascal, Corneille, Racine, Bourdaloue, Bossuet, etc., either had not yet been born or had not yet written. The spirit of research and competition did not motivate the scholars: another spirit, less fecund perhaps, but rarer, that of precision and method, had not yet conquered the various divisions of literature; and the academies, whose efforts have advanced the arts and sciences to such an extent, were not yet established. . . . At the end of this project you will find the tree of human knowledge, indicating the connection of ideas, which has directed us in this vast operation.

The Philosophe

Enlightenment thinkers often referred to themselves as "philosophes," which is technically the French word for philosophers. The term had a special meaning bound up with the spirit of the Enlightenment. This is dealt with directly in the following selection, "The Philosopher," from the Encyclopedia. *It has traditionally been assumed that Diderot is the author of "The Philosopher," but it may have been written by another person, perhaps Du Marsais. In any case, it is an authoritative treatment of the topic according to Enlightenment precepts.*

CONSIDER: *The characteristics of the philosopher; how this compares to Kant's definition of enlightenment and d'Holbach's definition of a civilized or enlightened man; how a twentieth-century philosopher might differ with this definition of a philosopher.*

Other men make up their minds to act without thinking, nor are they conscious of the causes which move them, not even knowing that such exist. The philosopher, on the contrary, distinguishes the causes to what extent he may, often anticipates them, and knowingly surrenders himself to them. In this manner he avoids objects that may cause him sensations that are not conducive to his well being or his rational existence, and seeks those which may excite in him affections agreeable with the state in which he finds himself. Reason is in the estimation of the philosopher what grace is to the Christian. Grace determines the Christian's action; reason the philosopher's.

SOURCE: Merrick Whitcomb, ed., "French Philosophers of the Eighteenth Century," in *Translations and Reprints from the Original Sources of European History,* vol. VI, no. 1, ed. Department of History of the University of Pennsylvania (Philadelphia: University of Pennsylvania Press, 1898), pp. 21–23.

Other men are carried away by their passions, so that the acts which they produce do not proceed from reflection. These are the men who move in darkness; while the philosopher, even in his passions, moves only after reflection. He marches at night, but a torch goes on ahead.

The philosopher forms his principles upon an infinity of individual observations. The people adopt the principle without a thought of the observations which have produced it, believing that the maxim exists, so to speak, of itself; but the philosopher takes the maxim at its source, he examines its origin, he knows its real value, and only makes use of it, if it seems to him satisfactory.

Truth is not for the philosopher a mistress who vitiates his imagination, and whom he believes to find everywhere. He contents himself with being able to discover it wherever he may chance to find it. He does not confound it with its semblance; but takes for true that which is true, for false that which is false, for doubtful that which is doubtful, and for probable that which is only probable. He does more—and this is the great perfection of philosophy; that when he has no real grounds for passing judgment, he knows how to remain undetermined.

The world is full of persons of understanding, even of much understanding, who always pass judgment. They are guessing always, because it is guessing to pass judgment without knowing when one has proper grounds for judgment. They misjudge of the capacity of the human mind; they believe it is possible to know everything, and so they are ashamed not to be prepared to pass judgment, and they imagine that understanding consists in passing judgment. The philosopher believes that it consists in judging well: he is better pleased with himself when he has suspended the faculty of determining, than if he had determined before having acquired proper grounds for his decision.

❧

The philosophic spirit is then a spirit of observation and of exactness, which refers everything to its true principles; but it is not the understanding alone which the philosopher cultivates; he carries further his attention and his labors.

Man is not a monster, made to live only at the bottom of the sea or in the depths of the forest; the very necessities of his life render intercourse with others necessary; and in whatsoever state we find him, his needs and his well-being lead him to live in society. To that reason demands of him that he should know, that he should study and that he should labor to acquire social qualities.

Our philosopher does not believe himself an exile in the world; he does not believe himself in the enemy's country; he wishes to enjoy, like a wise economist, the goods that nature offers him; he wishes to find his pleasure with others; and in order to find it, it is necessary to assist in producing it; so he seeks to harmonize with those with whom chance or his choice has determined he shall live; and he finds at the same time that which suits him: he is an honest man who wishes to please and render himself useful.

❧

The philosopher is then an honest man, actuated in everything by reason, one who joins to the spirit of reflection and of accuracy the manners and qualities of society.

Philosophical Dictionary: The English Model

Voltaire

François Marie Arouet, who later adopted the name Voltaire (1694–1778), was certainly the most famous of the philosophes. Writing almost every type of literature, from drama and satire to history and essays, he exhibited most of the main elements of the Enlightenment. One of these was the philosophes' admiration for and idealization of England's political system. Voltaire gained familiarity with England during a three-year visit, from 1726 to 1729, and played an important role in popularizing the ideas of English scientists and the principles of the English political system. The following is an excerpt from his Philosophical Dictionary, *first published in 1764.*

CONSIDER: *What Voltaire admires about the English constitution; the implied criticism of the French political system; whether Voltaire idealizes the English system.*

The English constitution has, in fact, arrived at that point of excellence, in consequence of which all men are restored to those natural rights, which, in nearly all monarchies, they are deprived of. These rights are, entire liberty of person and property; freedom of the press; the right of being tried in all criminal cases by a jury of independent men—the right of being tried only according to the strict letter of the law; and the right of every man to profess, unmolested, what religion he chooses, while he renounces offices, which the members of the Anglican or established church alone can hold. These are denominated privileges. And, in truth, invaluable privileges they are in comparison with the usages of most other nations of the world! To be secure on lying down that you shall rise in possession of the same property with which you retired to rest; that you shall not be torn from the arms of your wife, and from your children, in the dead of night,

SOURCE: Voltaire, *Philosophical Dictionary,* in Voltaire, *Works,* trans. W. F. Fleming (New York: E. R. Dumont, 1901), vol. 5, pp. 293–294.

to be thrown into a dungeon, or buried in exile in a desert; that, when rising from the bed of sleep, you will have the power of publishing all your thoughts; and that, if you are accused of having either acted, spoken, or written wrongly, you can be tried only according to law. These privileges attach to every one who sets his foot on English ground. A foreigner enjoys perfect liberty to dispose of his property and person; and, if accused of any offence, he can demand that half the jury shall be composed of foreigners.

I will venture to assert, that, were the human race solemnly assembled for the purpose of making laws, such are the laws they would make for their security.

A Vindication of the Rights of Woman

Mary Wollstonecraft

While the Enlightenment was dominated by men, there were possibilities for active involvement by women. Several women played particularly important roles as patrons and intellectual contributors to the gatherings of philosophes and members of the upper-middle-class and aristocratic elite held in the salons of Paris and elsewhere. It was, however, far more difficult for a woman to publish serious essays in the Enlightenment tradition. Indeed, Enlightenment thinkers did little to change basic attitudes about the inferiority of women. One person who managed to do both was Mary Wollstonecraft (1759–1797), a British author who in 1792 published A Vindication of the Rights of Woman. *The book was a sharply reasoned attack against the oppression of women and an argument for educational change. In the following excerpt Wollstonecraft addresses the author of a proposed new constitution for France that, in her opinion, does not adequately deal with the rights of women.*

CONSIDER: *Why education is so central to her argument; the ways in which this argument reflects the methods and ideals of the Enlightenment.*

Contending for the rights of woman, my main argument is built on this simple principle, that if she be not prepared by education to become the companion of man, she will stop the progress of knowledge and virtue; for truth must be common to all, or it will be inefficacious with respect to its influence on general practice. And how can woman be expected to co-operate unless she knows why she ought to be virtuous? unless freedom strengthens her reason till she comprehends her duty, and sees in what manner it is connected with her real

good. If children are to be educated to understand the true principle of patriotism, their mother must be a patriot; and the love of mankind, from which an orderly train of virtues spring, can only be produced by considering the moral and civil interest of mankind; but the education and situation of woman at present shuts her out from such investigations.

In this work I have produced many arguments, which to me were conclusive, to prove that the prevailing notion respecting a sexual character was subversive of morality, and I have contended, that to render the human body and mind more perfect, chastity must more universally prevail, and that chastity will never be respected in the male world till the person of a woman is not, as it were, idolised, when little virtue or sense embellish it with the grand traces of mental beauty, or the interesting simplicity of affection.

Consider, sir, dispassionately these observations, for a glimpse of this truth seemed to open before you when you observed, "that to see one-half of the human race excluded by the other from all participation of government was a political phenomenon, that, according to abstract principles, it was impossible to explain." If so, on what does your constitution rest? If the abstract rights of man will bear discussion and explanation, those of woman, by a parity of reasoning, will not shrink from the same test; though a different opinion prevails in this country, built on the very arguments which you use to justify the oppression of woman—prescription.

Consider—I address you as a legislator—whether, when men contend for their freedom, and to be allowed to judge for themselves respecting their own happiness, it be not inconsistent and unjust to subjugate women, even though you firmly believe that you are acting in the manner best calculated to promote their happiness? Who made man the exclusive judge, if woman partake with him of the gift of reason?

The Age of Reason: Deism

Thomas Paine

Many Enlightenment thinkers were strongly opposed to traditional religious institutions and ideas. Yet only a few went so far as to profess atheism. More typical was some form of deism, a belief in a God who created a rational universe with natural laws but who no longer intervened in the course of events. A good example of this belief is found in the following excerpt from Thomas Paine's Age of Reason *(1794). Paine (1737–1809) was an unusually international person. Born in England, he became an American patriot and later a*

SOURCE: Mary Wollstonecraft, *The Rights of Woman* (London: J. M. Dent and Sons, Ltd., 1929), pp. 10–11.

SOURCE: Moncure Daniel Conway, ed., *The Writings of Thomas Paine*, vol. IV (New York: G. P. Putnam's Sons, 1896), pp. 21–23.

member of the French Convention (1792–1793). His most famous works are Common Sense *and* The Rights of Man, *in both of which he justifies revolution. In* The Age of Reason *Paine places himself within the tradition of Enlightenment thought and summarizes his religious views.*

CONSIDER: *Why Paine is so opposed to traditional religious institutions; how this opposition is consistent with other Enlightenment thought; how a sincere, sophisticated member of the Catholic Church might have responded to this.*

As several of my colleagues, and others of my fellow-citizens of France, have given me the example of making their voluntary and individual profession of faith, I also will make mine; and I do this with all that sincerity and frankness with which the mind of man communicates with itself.

I believe in one God, and no more; and I hope for happiness beyond this life.

I believe the equality of man, and I believe that religious duties consist in doing justice, loving mercy, and endeavouring to make our fellow-creatures happy.

But, lest it should be supposed that I believe many other things in addition to these, I shall, in the progress of this work, declare the things I do not believe, and my reasons for not believing them.

I do not believe in the creed professed by the Jewish church, by the Roman church, by the Greek church, by the Turkish church, by the Protestant church, nor by any church that I know of. My own mind is my own church.

All national institutions of churches, whether Jewish, Christian, or Turkish, appear to me no other than human inventions set up to terrify and enslave mankind, and monopolize power and profit.

I do not mean by this declaration to condemn those who believe otherwise; they have the same right to their belief as I have to mine. But it is necessary to the happiness of man, that he be mentally faithful to himself. Infidelity does not consist in believing, or in disbelieving; it consists in professing to believe what he does not believe.

It is impossible to calculate the moral mischief, if I may so express it, that mental lying has produced in society. When a man has so far corrupted and prostituted the chastity of his mind, as to subscribe his professional belief to things he does not believe, he has prepared himself for the commission of every other crime. He takes up the trade of a priest for the sake of gain, and, in order to qualify himself for that trade, he begins with a perjury. Can we conceive anything more destructive to morality than this?

Soon after I had published the pamphlet *Common Sense,* in America, I saw the exceeding probability that a revolution in the system of government would be followed by a revolution in the system of religion. The adulterous connection of church and state, wherever it had taken place, whether Jewish, Christian, or Turkish, had so effectually prohibited, by pains and penalties, every discussion upon established creeds, and upon first principles of religion, that until the system of government should be changed, those subjects could not be brought fairly and openly before the world; but that whenever this should be done, a revolution in the system of religion would follow. Human inventions and priest-craft would be detected; and man would return to the pure, unmixed, and unadulterated belief of one God, and no more.

The Social Contract

Jean Jacques Rousseau

More than anyone else, Jean Jacques Rousseau (1712–1778) tested the outer limits of Enlightenment thought and went on to criticize its very foundations. Born in Geneva, he spent much of his life in France (mainly in Paris), where he became one of the philosophes who contributed to the Encyclopedia. *Yet he also undermined Enlightenment thought by holding that social institutions had corrupted people and that human beings in the state of nature were purer, freer, and happier than they were in modern civilization. This line of thought provided a foundation for the growth of Romanticism in the late eighteenth and early nineteenth centuries. Rousseau's most important political work was* The Social Contract *(1762), in which he argued for popular sovereignty. In the following selection from that work, Rousseau focuses on what he considers the fundamental argument of the book—the passage from the state of nature to the civil state by means of the social contract.*

CONSIDER: *Rousseau's solution to the main problem of* The Social Contract; *the advantages and disadvantages of the social contract; what characteristics of Enlightenment thought are reflected in this selection.*

"The problem is to find a form of association which will defend and protect with the whole common force the person and goods of each associate, and in which each, while uniting himself with all, may still obey himself alone, and remain as free as before." This is the fundamental problem of which *The Social Contract* provides the solution.

The clauses of this contract are so determined by the nature of the act that the slightest modification would make them vain and ineffective; so that, although they have perhaps never been formally set forth, they are everywhere the same and everywhere tacitly admitted

SOURCE: Jean Jacques Rousseau, *The Social Contract and Discourses* (London: J. M. Dent, Everyman Library, 1913), pp. 14–15, 18–19.

and recognised, until, on the violation of the social compact, each regains his original rights and resumes his natural liberty, while losing the conventional liberty in favour of which he renounced it.

These clauses, properly understood, may be reduced to one—the total alienation of each associate, together with all his rights, to the whole community; for, in the first place, as each gives himself absolutely, the conditions are the same for all; and, this being so, no one has any interest in making them burdensome to others.

Moreover, the alienation being without reserve, the union is as perfect as it can be, and no associate has anything more to demand: for, if the individuals retained certain rights, as there would be no common superior to decide between them and the public, each, being on one point his own judge, would ask to be so on all; the state of nature would thus continue, and the association would necessarily become inoperative or tyrannical.

Finally, each man, in giving himself to all, gives himself to nobody; and as there is no associate over whom he does not acquire the same right as he yields others over himself, he gains on equivalent for everything he loses, and an increase of force for the preservation of what he has.

If then we discard from the social compact what is not of its essence, we shall find that it reduces itself to the following terms—

Each of us puts his person and all his power in common under the supreme direction of the general will, and, in our corporate capacity, we receive each member as an indivisible part of the whole.

❧

The passage from the state of nature to the civil state produces a very remarkable change in man, by substituting justice for instinct in his conduct, and giving his actions the morality they had formerly lacked. Then only, when the voice of duty takes the place of physical impulses and right of appetite, does man, who so far had considered only himself, find that he is forced to act on different principles, and to consult his reason before listening to his inclinations. Although, in this state, he deprives himself of some advantages which he got from nature, he gains in return others so great, his faculties are so stimulated and developed, his ideas so extended, his feelings so ennobled, and his whole soul so uplifted, that, did not the abuses of this new condition often degrade him below that which he left, he would be bound to bless continually the happy moment which took him from it for ever, and, instead of a stupid and unimaginative animal, made him an intelligent being and a man.

Let us draw up the whole account in terms easily commensurable. What man loses by the social contract is his natural liberty and an unlimited right to everything he tries to get and succeeds in getting; what he gains is civil liberty and the proprietorship of all he possesses. If we are to avoid mistake in weighing one against the other, we must clearly distinguish natural liberty, which is bounded only by the strength of the individual, from civil liberty, which is limited by the general will; and possession, which is merely the effect of force or the right of the first occupier, from property, which can be founded only on a positive title.

We might, over and above all this, add, to what man acquires in the civil state, moral liberty, which alone makes him truly master of himself; for the mere impulse of appetite is slavery, while obedience to a law which we prescribe to ourselves is liberty. But I have already said too much on this head, and the philosophical meaning of the word liberty does not now concern us.

Visual Sources

Frontispiece of the *Encyclopédie*

This illustration (figure 8.1) appeared at the beginning of the 1751 edition to the Encyclopédie. *A description guided the reader to its allegorical meanings. In the center and above all other figures stands Truth, "wrapped in a veil, radiant with a light which parts the clouds and disperses them." Close on her left is Reason, who lifts a veil from Truth; below her, Philosophy pulls the veil away. Theology, holding a Bible, kneels at the feet of Truth. On Truth's right is Imagination, "preparing to adorn and crown Truth." Below them are figures representing Geometry, Physics, Astronomy, Optics, Botany, Chemistry, Agriculture, History, and the arts. At the bottom are practitioners who will use the guides above them to make progress. As a whole and in its allegorical detail, this illustration represented the optimistic spirit of the* Encyclopédie *and the Enlightenment.*

CONSIDER: *The meaning of the Enlightenment as represented by this illustration; the connections between first, the ideals of truth, reason, and imagination, second, the sciences and arts, and third, the practitioners depicted in this illustration.*

Experiment with an Air Pump
Joseph Wright

Few paintings provide a better image of the Enlightenment than Experiment with an Air Pump *(1768) by the British artist Joseph Wright (figure 8.2). The experiment takes place in the* center of the picture; its apparent success is evidenced by the dead bird inside a closed glass bowl from which the air has been pumped out. The informally dressed experimenter is carefully observing his work. Around him are members of his family and some well-dressed friends.

The form and content of this picture symbolize the Enlightenment. A small source of light is sufficient to enlighten humanity and reveal the laws of nature. Science is not just for specialists but something amateurs can understand and practice to obtain practical results. That it is a British painting is particularly significant, for the English led in developing useful machines and were identified as having a more pragmatic approach to science and ideas than other peoples. The painting also reveals customary images of the sexes: the experimenter boldly forging on while to his left a friend or associate calmly explains what is happening to a woman and her daughter, whose sensibilities are as appropriately fragile as the dying bird—the main object of their concern.

CONSIDER: Any common themes in this painting and the documents by Kant, d'Holbach, and Diderot.

Propaganda and the Enlightened Monarch

Joseph II of Austria

Emperor Joseph II of Austria (1765–1790) is generally thought to have been one of the most enlightened eighteenth-century kings and indeed considered himself to be an enlightened monarch. Some of what this meant is indicated by this picture Joseph II had painted of himself (figure 8.3). It shows him plowing a field with a farmer and members of his court. To make sure he and his office were recognizable to viewers, Joseph remained appropriately dressed, including

FIGURE 8.1 (© The Granger Collection, New York)

wearing his powdered wig. This scene also affirms the growing interest in agricultural improvements during the eighteenth century, particularly among aristocratic innovators. Joseph II tells of some of his hopes in a number of letters excerpted here.

CONSIDER: What there was about this scene and these letters that could be considered enlightened; any inconsistencies with these statements and the reality of being a monarch; how Kant might have viewed Joseph II.

SOURCE: "Letters of Joseph II," in *The Pamphleteer,* vol. XIX (London, 1882), pp. 282, 288–290.

FIGURE 8.2   (© Art Resource, NY)

FIGURE 8.3   (© Erich Lessing/Art Resource, NY)

Mr. Vice-Chancellor—The present system of taxation in my dominions, and the inequality of the taxes which are imposed on the nation, form a subject too important to escape my attention. I have discovered that the principles on which it is founded are unsound, and have become injurious to the industry of the peasant; that there is neither equality, nor equity, between the hereditary provinces with each other, nor between individual proprietors, and therefore it can no longer continue.

With this view I give you the necessary orders to introduce a new system of taxation, by which the contribution, requisite for the wants of the state, may be effected without augmenting the present taxes, and the industry of the peasant, at the same time, be freed from all impediments.

❧

Since my accession to the throne, I have ever been anxious to conquer the prejudices against my station, and have taken pains to gain the confidence of my people; I have several times since given proof, that the welfare of my subjects is my passion; that to satisfy it, I shun neither labor, nor trouble, nor even vexations, and reflect well on the means which are likely to promote my views; and yet in my reforms, I everywhere find opposition from people, of whom I least expect it.

❧

Sir,—Till now the Protestant religion has been opposed in my states; its adherents have been treated like foreigners; civil rights, possession of estates, titles, and appointments, all were refused them.

I determined from the very commencement of my reign to adorn my diadem with the love of my people, to act in the administration of affairs according to just, impartial, and liberal principles; consequently, I granted toleration, and removed the yoke which had oppressed the protestants for centuries.

Fanaticism shall in future be known in my states only by the contempt I have for it; nobody shall any longer be exposed to hardships on account of his creed; no man shall be compelled in future to profess the religion of the state, if it be contrary to his persuasion, and if he have other ideas of the right way of insuring blessedness.

In future my Empire shall not be the scene of abominable intolerance. Fortunately no sacrifices like those of Calas and Sirven have ever disgraced any reign in this country.

If, in former times, the will of the monarch furnished opportunities for injustice, if the limits of executive power were exceeded, and private hatred acted her part, I can only pity those monarchs who were nothing but kings.

Tolerance is an effect of that beneficent increase of knowledge which now enlightens Europe, and which is owing to philosophy and the efforts of great men; it is a convincing proof of the improvement of the human mind, which has boldly reopened a road through the dominions of superstition, which was trodden centuries ago by Zoroaster and Confucius, and which, fortunately for mankind, has now become the highway of monarchs. Adieu!

Secondary Sources

The Secularization of European Thought

Roy Porter

The Enlightenment owes its substance and popularity to a relatively small group of eighteenth-century philosophes *and a broader number of intellectuals who came from many countries but were centered in France. Although they often argued among themselves, there was a set of approaches and propositions upon which most of them agreed. In the following selection, Roy Porter argues that these people launched the secularization of European thought.*

CONSIDER: *How the primary sources support or contradict Porter's interpretation; the consequences of the Enlightenment for Christian religion; how the Enlightenment spread throughout societies.*

The Enlightenment thus decisively launched the secularization of European thought. To say this, is not to claim that the *philosophes* were all atheists or that people thereafter ceased to be religious. Both are manifestly untrue. After all, the reaction against the French Revolution produced powerful evangelical and ecclesiastical revivals all over Europe. But, after the Enlightenment, the Christian religion ceased, once and for all, to preoccupy public culture. The Enlightenment is what sets Dante and Erasmus, Bernini, Pascal, Racine and Milton – all great Christian writers and artists – on one side of the great cultural divide, and Delacroix, Schopenhauer, George Eliot and Darwin on the other. Romanticism, one might suggest, is what is left of the soul when the religion has been drained out of it.

As the Enlightenment gained ground, it spelt the end of public wars of faith, put a stop to witch-persecutions and heretic-burnings, and signalled the demise of magic and astrology, the erosion of the occult, the waning of belief in the literal, physical existence of Heaven and Hell, in the Devil and all his disciples. The supernatural disappeared from public life. To fill the gap, nineteenth-century sentimentality had to endow Nature with its own

SOURCE: Roy Porter, *The Enlightenment*, 2nd ed. (London: Palgrave, 2001), pp. 66–68.

holiness and invent new traditions, above all, a public show of patriotism. Religion remained, of course, but it gradually lost its props in learning, science, and in the well-stocked imagination. The Enlightenment sapped their credibility. . . .

The Enlightenment was the era which saw the emergence of a secular intelligentsia large and powerful enough for the first time to challenge the clergy. For centuries the priesthood had commanded the best broadcasting media (churches, pulpits), had monopolized posts in the leading educational establishments (schools, universities, seminaries), and had enjoyed legal privileges over the distribution of information.

This changed. It was during the eighteenth century that substantial bodies of *literati* outside the churches began to make a living out of knowledge and writing. Some earned a crust from Grub Street journalism; a few got very rich on the proceeds of their pens. Voltaire said that in his youth, society had been dominated by the well-born; later it had been taken over by men of letters. Such propagandists exploited such new channels of communication as newspapers and magazines (the *Spectator* might be called a kind of daily secular sermon) and utilized the opportunities offered by public opinion in what Habermas has dubbed the 'public sphere' [69].

They appealed to an ever-broadening reading public, eager for new forms of writing, such as essays and fiction and biography. In turn, their impact was reinforced by such secular institutions as the reading clubs, academies, and literary and scientific societies mentioned above. The First Estate, the 'Lords Spiritual', was thus challenged by a new body, the 'Fourth Estate' (roughly, the press), in a struggle to win the ear of the 'Second Estate' (the traditional political classes) and the emergent 'Third Estate' (the Commons).

The Heavenly City of the Eighteenth-Century Philosophers
Carl L. Becker

Another point of interpretive division among historians of the Enlightenment centers on how modern and secular the philosophes were. Nineteenth- and early-twentieth-century historians argued that the philosophes were more modern than medieval and indeed drew more from the Classical pagan world than from the medieval world. This view still predominates among historians of the period. A famous challenge to this view was made more than sixty years ago by Cornell historian Carl Becker. His book, The Heavenly City of the Eighteenth-Century Philosophers *(1932), be-*

came the most influential book on the subject, although today it is no longer as popular as it once was. In the following selection from this work, Becker presents the substance of his thesis.

CONSIDER: *The ways in which the philosophes were more medieval than modern; the support Becker offers for his argument that there was much Christian philosophy in the philosophes' writings; how Kant would react to Becker's interpretation.*

We are accustomed to think of the eighteenth century as essentially modern in its temper. Certainly, the *Philosophes* themselves made a great point of having renounced the superstition and hocus-pocus of medieval Christian thought, and we have usually been willing to take them at their word. Surely, we say, the eighteenth century was preëminently the age of reason, surely the *Philosophes* were a skeptical lot, atheists in effect if not by profession, addicted to science and the scientific method, always out to crush the infamous, valiant defenders of liberty, equality, fraternity, freedom of speech, and what you will. All very true. And yet I think the *Philosophes* were nearer the Middle Ages, less emancipated from the preconceptions of medieval Christian thought, than they quite realized or we have commonly supposed. . . .

But, if we examine the foundations of their faith, we find that at every turn the *Philosophes* betray their debt to medieval thought without being aware of it. They denounced Christian philosophy, but rather too much, after the manner of those who are but half emancipated from the "superstitions" they scorn. They had put off the fear of God, but maintained a respectful attitude toward the Deity. They ridiculed the idea that the universe had been created in six days, but still believed it to be a beautifully articulated machine designed by the Supreme Being according to a rational plan as an abiding place for mankind. The Garden of Eden was for them a myth, no doubt, but they looked enviously back to the golden age of Roman virtue, or across the waters to the unspoiled innocence of an Arcadian civilization that flourished in Pennsylvania. They renounced the authority of church and Bible, but exhibited a naïve faith in the authority of nature and reason. They scorned metaphysics, but were proud to be called philosophers. They dismantled heaven, somewhat prematurely it seems, since they retained their faith in the immortality of the soul. They courageously discussed atheism, but not before the servants. They defended toleration valiantly, but could with difficulty tolerate priests. They denied that miracles ever happened, but believed in the perfectibility of the human race. We feel that these Philosophers were at once too credulous and too skeptical. They were the victims of common sense. In spite of their rationalism and their humane sympathies, in spite of their aversion to hocus-pocus and enthusiasm and dim perspectives, in spite of their skepti-

SOURCE: Carl L. Becker, *The Heavenly City of the Eighteenth-Century Philosophers.* Reprinted by permission of Yale University Press (New Haven, CT, 1932), pp. 29–31, 102–103.

cism, their engaging cynicism, their brave youthful blasphemies and talk of hanging the last king in the entrails of the last priest—in spite of all of it, there is more of the Christian philosophy in the writings of the *Philosophes* than has yet been dreamt of in our histories.

Women in the Salons

Bonnie S. Anderson and Judith P. Zinsser

As with the Renaissance and Scientific Revolution, the central figures of the Enlightenment were men. However, some women did directly participate as writers, and perhaps even more importantly, they participated as saloniéres—organizers of gatherings in the salons of homes where Enlightenment figures mingled with women and men of the social and cultural elite. Did the men of the Enlightenment try to change traditional views of women in the same way they tried to change traditional views about men and human nature? In the following selection Bonnie S. Anderson and Judith P. Zinsser address this question.

CONSIDER: *Why, according to Anderson and Zinsser, there was no Enlightenment for women; ways in which the Enlightenment, in the long run, might have benefited women.*

. . . Parisian women established the institution of the salon by the last quarter of the seventeenth century. Aspiring hostesses competed to attract the talented, the witty, and the powerful to their homes. Outside the powerful French court and frequently in opposition to it, these new social circles offered women a new possibility: that of being a salonière, who by her graciousness and skill enabled conversation to flourish, artists to find patrons, and aristocrats to be amused. As a salonière, a woman brought the circles of power into her home. In the environment she created, she could help or hinder not only artistic and literary reputations, but political policies as well. The financial remedies for France's economy were debated in the salons; the king's choices of ministers were strongly influenced by the backing of powerful salonières. Salonières were privy to court secrets; salons were frequented by statesmen and ambassadors as well as intellectuals and artists. Salonières could make or break careers and often provided havens for new political philosophies and the new political opposition to the monarchy. . . .

In the salon, a woman could meet and marry a man of superior social rank or wealth. In the salon, a woman of enterprise could make her way by attracting the famous. The salon became the base of influential women who swayed kings, governments, political opinion, and literary and artistic taste. . . .

Rational conversation, sociability between women and men, delight in the pleasures of this world are the hallmarks of Enlightenment culture. The men who mingled with the Bluestockings and frequented the salons were the men who produced the Enlightenment. It is a tragedy for women that these men, who were aided, sponsored, and lionized by the salonières, produced— with very few exceptions—art and writing which either ignored women completely or upheld the most traditional views of womanhood. Just as there was no Renaissance or Scientific Revolution for women, in the sense that the goals and ideals of those movements were perceived as applicable only to men, so there was no Enlightenment for women. Enlightenment thinkers questioned all the traditional limits on men—and indeed challenged the validity of tradition itself. They championed the rights of commoners, the rights of citizens, the rights of slaves, Jews, Indians, and children, but not those of women. Instead, often at great cost to their own logic and rationality, they continued to reaffirm the most ancient inherited traditions about women: that they were inferior to men in the crucial faculties of reason and ethics and so should be subordinated to men. In philosophy and in art, men of the Enlightenment upheld the traditional ideal of woman: silent, obedient, subservient, modest, and chaste. The salonière—witty, independent, powerful, well-read, and sometimes libertine—was condemned and mocked. A few Enlightenment thinkers did question and even reject subordinating traditions about women. But those who argued for a larger role for women—like the English-woman Mary Wollstonecraft in her *Vindication of the Rights of Woman* (1792), the French Marquis de Condorcet in his *Admission of Women to Civic Rights* (1790), the German Theodor von Hippel in his *On the Civic Improvement of Women* (1792), the Spaniard Josefa Amar y Borbón in her *Discourse in Defense of Women's Talent and Their Capacity for Government and Other Positions Held by Men* (1786)—prompted outrage and then were forgotten. Instead, most philosophers and writers reiterated the most limiting traditions of European culture regarding women, often in works which condemned traditional behavior for men.

The Problem of Enlightened Absolutism

H. M. Scott

Historians have long debated exactly how much the Enlightenment influenced monarchs of the time. Traditionally, there has been considerable acceptance of the view that monarchs such as Joseph II of Austria and Frederick II of Prussia

SOURCE: Excerpts from *A History of Their Own*, vol. II, by Bonnie Anderson and Judith Zinsser. Copyright © 1988 by Harper & Row, Publishers, Inc. Reprinted by permission of Harper & Row, Publishers, Inc.

SOURCE: H. M. Scott, "The Problem of Enlightened Absolutism," in *Enlightened Absolutism: Reform and Reformers in Late Eighteenth-Century Europe,* ed. H. M. Scott. © 1990 H. M. Scott; published in the United States of America by the University of Michigan Press.

were enlightened. In recent decades this view was seriously narrowed and questioned to the point where many historians felt that enlightened despotism and enlightened absolutism were no longer terms that could usefully be applied to these eighteenth-century monarchs. More recently, other historians have come to the conclusion that the term is useful. In the following selection H. M. Scott surveys this controversy and concludes that enlightened absolutism was real.

CONSIDER: *The characteristics of enlightened absolutism; why Joseph II (see the visual sources in this chapter) and Frederick II (see the primary sources in the preceding chapter) might be considered enlightened monarchs; how enlightened absolutism differs from seventeenth-century absolutism (see sources in Chapter 16).*

Few historical concepts have had their obituaries written more frequently than enlightened absolutism, yet so obstinately refuse to die. In its classical form, the theory of enlightened absolutism asserted that during the second half of the eighteenth century the domestic policies of most European states were influenced and even dictated by the ideas of the Enlightenment and were therefore sharply distinguished from what had gone before. Government became a systematic and rational attempt to apply the best recent knowledge to the task of ruling, while the main aim of internal policy came to be the improvement of educational opportunities, social conditions and economic life. . . .

Together, rulers and their influential advisers carried through a wide-ranging series of reforms, the principal inspiration for which was the political philosophy of the Enlightenment. Administrations and legal and fiscal systems were modernised; commercial and economic development was encouraged; efforts were made to improve agriculture and even to abolish the institution of serfdom; state control over the Catholic Church was extended and a determined attempt was made to channel some of its wealth into increased and improved pastoral activity; teaching in universities was brought up to date; and the provision of secondary and primary education was vastly increased. These reforms, and the amount of success achieved, were remarkable in the context of the later eighteenth century, and the sense of social responsibility which lay behind many of these measures was also novel and striking. Though the precise policies adopted varied from country to country, a common explanation was found in the movement of ideas known as the European Enlightenment, which was at its peak exactly when the policies of enlightened absolutism were being pursued: the middle decades of the eighteenth century until the outbreak of the French Revolution in 1789.

During the past two generations, the historical reputation of enlightened absolutism has undergone remark-able vicissitudes, above all in Anglo-American historical writing about later eighteenth-century Europe. It first rose to prominence during the 1930s, and for a generation thereafter was widely accepted among historians. By the 1960s, however, the tide was beginning to turn and the sceptics, who saw only the conventional aims of state-building in these policies and regarded the enlightened professions which accompanied them as mere window-dressing, were gaining the ascendant. The critics of enlightened absolutism argued that few monarchs, and certainly none of the major rulers, could afford to adhere blindly to an enlightened blueprint and ignore, or even neglect, the demands of self-defence. The competitive states-system within which the great powers operated required large and powerful armies and administrative and fiscal systems to support them. These priorities pre-empted much of the scope for enlightened reform. Above all, critics of the notion of enlightened absolutism argued that the success of these initiatives was often incomplete and could, at times, be very limited indeed. . . .

During the 1970s, the widespread assumption that enlightened absolutism was a fiction came to be challenged by a growing number of monographic studies of particular countries which make clear that the reforms of this period were influenced by ideas and were not simply another stage in the growth of the absolutist state. This trend has increased during the 1980s. . . .

[I]t has become clear that enlightened absolutism is not an idea in the mind of historians. The remarkable extent and the considerable success of the reforming initiatives is now established beyond question.

❧ CHAPTER QUESTIONS

1. What core of ideas and attitudes most clearly connects Enlightenment thinkers as revealed in these sources? How do these ideas relate to eighteenth-century society and institutions?

2. What policies would an eighteenth-century ruler have to pursue to fit to the greatest degree the ideas and assumptions of Enlightenment thinkers? What hindrances were faced by monarchs who wanted to be more enlightened?

3. What ideas and attitudes of Enlightenment thinkers do you think remain valid for the problems facing today's world? What Enlightenment ideas and attitudes no longer seem valid or appropriate?

4. In what ways do the sources support the argument that together, the Scientific Revolution and the Enlightenment constitute a single intellectual revolution of great long-term significance?

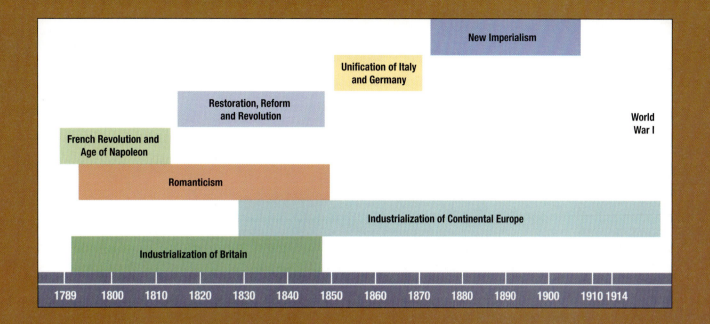

New Imperialism

Unification of Italy and Germany

Restoration, Reform and Revolution

French Revolution and Age of Napoleon

World War I

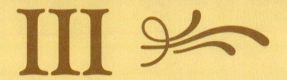

Romanticism

Industrialization of Continental Europe

Industrialization of Britain

| 1789 | 1800 | 1810 | 1820 | 1830 | 1840 | 1850 | 1860 | 1870 | 1880 | 1890 | 1900 | 1910 | 1914 |

III

The Nineteenth Century

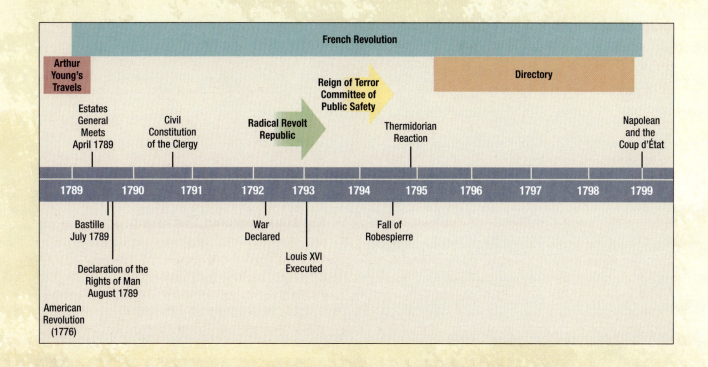

9 The French Revolution

In 1789 the French Revolution ended the relative political and social stability of the Ancien Régime. This, and the earlier American Revolution, led to political and social changes that swept through Western civilization in the nineteenth and twentieth centuries.

Although the causes of the French Revolution are deep and controversial, most agree it was precipitated by financial problems that led Louis XVI to call a meeting of an old representative institution, the Estates General, in 1789. A struggle for power soon developed between a resurgent aristocracy and a rising middle class, both demanding support from the king. In an environment where peasants were turning against the aristocracy in the countryside and crowds were resorting to violence in Paris, the king managed to alienate both sides. Revolutionary legislation soon followed. By 1792 France was a constitutional monarchy, feudalism was abolished, liberal principles echoing Enlightenment thought were formally recognized, Church lands were con-

fiscated, and government administration was reorganized. The country was at war internally with counter-revolutionary forces and externally with much of the rest of Europe.

A second revolution in 1792 set France on a more radical course. Louis XVI was executed, and the government was declared a republic. Real power rested in the hands of the small Committee of Public Safety, which attacked internal dissent through the Reign of Terror and external wars through national mobilization. The period ended with a return to a more moderate course in 1794 and 1795, known as the Thermidorian Reaction. With power in the hands of the well-to-do middle class, an uneasy balance was maintained between forces clamoring for more radical policies and those wishing to return the monarchy until 1799, when Napoleon Bonaparte rose to power by means of a *coup d'état*.

Historians are fascinated by revolutions, for change is unusually rapid and dramatic. They are particularly interested in the causes of revolutions. In this chapter several primary documents address questions related to the causes of the French Revolution. What were some early signs of revolutionary discontent? What complaints were voiced by the middle class and by the commoners—the Third Estate? How did leaders of this Third Estate see themselves? Related secondary documents explore some of the interpretive debates over the revolution: Was this mainly a social revolution? What was the influence of politics on the French Revolution? Other sources examine the course and effects of the French Revolution. What happened is of particular importance, since the French Revolution was seen as a model for other revolutions and hoped-for revolutions. What were the main changes enacted during the revolution? How can we explain the most radical phase—the Reign of Terror? What

role did women play in revolutionary events? What part did nationalism play in revolutionary developments?

In short, the selections should provide broad insights into the nature and significance of the French Revolution, which more than any other event marks a dividing line between the Early Modern and the Modern eras of Western civilization.

❧ For Classroom Discussion

What caused the French Revolution? Use evidence from three primary sources—Signs of Revolution, Discontents of the Third Estate, and Declaration of the Rights of Man and Citizen—as well as the arguments in the first two secondary sources by Georges Lefebvre and Donald M. G. Sutherland.

 # Primary Sources

Travels in France: Signs of Revolution

Arthur Young

In one sense, the French Revolution came as a great surprise. One of the last places people might have expected a revolution to occur was in a country so advanced and with such a stable monarchy as France. Yet to some sensitive observers of the time, the signs of revolution were at hand during the late 1780s. One of these observers was Arthur Young (1741–1820), a British farmer and diarist, best known for his writings on agricultural subjects. Between 1787 and 1789 he traveled extensively throughout France, keeping a diary of his experiences. In the following selection from that diary, Young notes deep dissatisfactions among the French.

CONSIDER: *The problems and dissatisfactions that gave the French a sense of impending revolution; the specific problems that seemed most likely to lead to a revolutionary crisis and the steps that might have been taken to avoid such a crisis; how Young felt about these problems and dissatisfactions.*

PARIS, OCTOBER 17, 1787

One opinion pervaded the whole company, that they are on the eve of some great revolution in the government: that every thing points to it: the confusion in the finances great; with a *deficit* impossible to provide for without the states-general of the kingdom, yet no ideas formed of

what would be the consequence of their meeting: no minister existing, or to be looked to in or out of power, with such decisive talents as to promise any other remedy than palliative ones: a prince on the throne, with excellent dispositions, but without the resources of a mind that could govern in such a moment without ministers: a court buried in pleasure and dissipation; and adding to the distress, instead of endeavouring to be placed in a more independent situation: a great ferment amongst all ranks of men, who are eager for some change, without knowing what to look to, or to hope for: and a strong leaven of liberty, increasing every hour since the American revolution; altogether form a combination of circumstances that promise e'er long to ferment into motion, if some master hand, of very superior talents, and inflexible courage, is not found at the helm to guide events, instead of being driven by them. It is very remarkable, that such conversation never occurs, but a bankruptcy is a topic: the curious question on which is, *would a bankruptcy occasion a civil war, and a total overthrow of the government?* These answers that I have received to this question, appear to be just: such a measure, conducted by a man of abilities, vigour, and firmness, would certainly not occasion either one or the other. But the same measure, attempted by a man of a different character, might possibly do both. All agree, that the states of the kingdom cannot assemble without more liberty being the consequence; but I meet with so few men that have any just ideas of freedom, that I question much the species of this new liberty that is to arise. They know not how to value the privileges of THE PEOPLE: as to the nobility and the clergy, if a revolution added any thing to their scale, I think it would do more mischief than good. . . .

SOURCE: Arthur Young, *Arthur Young's Travels in France During the Years 1787, 1788, 1789,* 4th ed., ed. Miss Betham-Edwards (London: Bell, 1892), pp. 97–98, 124, 134.

RENNES, SEPTEMBER 2, 1788

The discontents of the people have been double, first on account of the high price of bread, and secondly for the banishment of the parliament. The former cause is natural enough, but why the people should love their parliament was what I could not understand, since the members, as well as of the states, are all noble, and the distinction between the *noblesse* and *roturiers* no where stronger, more offensive, or more abominable than in Bretagne. They assured me, however, that the populace have been blown up to violence by every art of deception, and even by money distributed for that purpose. The commotions rose to such a height before the camp was established, that the troops here were utterly unable to keep the peace. . . .

NANTES, SEPTEMBER 22, 1788

Nantes is as *enflammé* in the cause of liberty, as any town in France can be; the conversations I witnessed here, prove how great a change is effected in the minds of the French, nor do I believe it will be possible for the present government to last half a century longer, unless the clearest and most decided talents are at the helm. The American revolution has laid the foundation of another in France, if government does not take care of itself.

The Cahiers: Discontents of the Third Estate

Pressured by discontent and financial problems, Louis XVI called for a meeting of the Estates General in 1789. This representative institution, which had not met for 175 years, reflected the traditional formal divisions in French society: the First Estate, the clergy; the Second Estate, the nobility; and the Third Estate, all the rest from banker and lawyer to peasant. In anticipation of the meeting of the Estates General, the king requested and received cahiers, lists of grievances drawn up by local groups of each of the three Estates. These cahiers have provided historians with an unusually rich source of materials revealing what was bothering people just before the outbreak of the revolution in 1789. The following is an excerpt from a cahier from the Third Estate in Carcassonne.

CONSIDER: *How these grievances of the Third Estate compare to the grievances noted by Young; why these grievances might be revolutionary; the ways in which these grievances are peculiar to the Third Estate and not shared by the First and Second Estates.*

SOURCE: "Cahier of the Grievances, Complaints, and Protests of the Electoral District of Carcassonne . . ." From James Harvey Robinson, ed., *Readings in European History,* vol. II (Boston: Ginn, 1904), pp. 399–400.

8. Among these rights the following should be especially noted: the nation should hereafter be subject only to such laws and taxes as it shall itself freely ratify.

9. The meetings of the Estates General of the kingdom should be fixed for definite periods, and the subsidies judged necessary for the support of the state and the public service should be noted for no longer a period than to the close of the year in which the next meeting of the Estates General is to occur.

10. In order to assure to the third estate the influence to which it is entitled in view of the number of its members, the amount of its contributions to the public treasury, and the manifold interests which it has to defend or promote in the national assemblies, its votes in the assembly should be taken and counted by head.

11. No order, corporation, or individual citizen may lay claim to any pecuniary exemptions. . . . All taxes should be assessed on the same system throughout the nation.

12. The due exacted from commoners holding fiefs should be abolished, and also the general or particular regulations which exclude members of the third estate from certain positions, offices, and ranks which have hitherto been bestowed on nobles either for life or hereditarily. A law should be passed declaring members of the third estate qualified to fill all such offices for which they are judged to be personally fitted.

13. Since individual liberty is intimately associated with national liberty, his Majesty is hereby petitioned not to permit that it be hereafter interfered with by arbitrary orders for imprisonment. . . .

14. Freedom should be granted also to the press, which should however be subjected, by means of strict regulations, to the principles of religion, morality, and public decency.

What Is the Third Estate?

Emmanuel Joseph Sieyès

Before the Estates General met, issues arose among the Estates, particularly over whether the combined First and Second Estates should be able to hold the preponderance of power when the Estates General met. One of the most wide-ranging attacks on the privileged orders and assertion of

SOURCE: From Merrick Whitcomb, ed., "French Philosophers of the Eighteenth Century," in *Translations and Reprints from the Original Sources of European History,* vol. VI, no. 1, ed. Department of History of the University of Pennsylvania (Philadelphia: University of Pennsylvania Press, 1898), pp. 34–35.

Third Estate rights came from Emmanuel Joseph Sieyès (1748–1836). A clergyman strongly influenced by Enlightenment ideas, Sieyès was eventually elected as a representative of the Third Estate and played an active role in events throughout the revolutionary and Napoleonic periods. The following is a selection from his pamphlet, What Is the Third Estate?, *which was published in January 1789 and gained quick popularity.*

CONSIDER: *The basis for the attack by Sieyès on the nobility; why members of the bourgeoisie might find this pamphlet very appealing; how the tone and content of this pamphlet compare with the cahier.*

It suffices here to have made it clear that the pretended utility of a privileged order for the public service is nothing more than a chimera; that with it all that which is burdensome in this service is performed by the Third Estate; that without it the superior places would be infinitely better filled; that they naturally ought to be the lot and the recompense of ability and recognized services, and that if privileged persons have come to usurp all the lucrative and honorable posts, it is a hateful injustice to the rank and file of citizens and at the same time a treason to the public weal.

Who then shall dare to say that the Third Estate has not within itself all that is necessary for the formation of a complete nation? It is the strong and robust man who has one arm still shackled. If the privileged order should be abolished, the nation would be nothing less, but something more. Therefore, what is the Third Estate? Everything; but an everything shackled and oppressed. What would it be without the privileged order? Everything, but an everything free and flourishing. Nothing can succeed without it, everything would be infinitely better without the others. . . .

What is a nation? A body of associates, living under a common law, and represented by the same legislature, etc.

Is it not evident that the noble order has privileges and expenditures which it dares to call its rights, but which are apart from the rights of the great body of citizens? It departs there from the common order, from the common law. So its civil rights make of it an isolated people in the midst of the great nation. This is truly *imperium in imperio.*

In regard to its political rights, these also it exercises apart. It has its special representatives, which are not charged with securing the interests of the people. The body of its deputies sit apart; and when it is assembled in the same hall with the deputies of simple citizens, it is none the less true that its representation is essentially distinct and separate; it is a stranger to the nation, in the first place, by its origin, since its commission is not derived from the people; then by its object, which consists of defending not the general, but the particular interest.

The Third Estate embraces then all that which belongs to the nation; and all that which is not the Third Estate, cannot be regarded as being of the nation. What is the Third Estate? It is the whole.

Revolutionary Legislation: Abolition of the Feudal System

During the summer of 1789, France was swept with a variety of revolutionary activities. The Third Estate had successfully formed the National Assembly. On July 14 a mob had stormed the Bastille, an act that symbolized a violent tearing down of the Ancien Régime and the beginning of the popular revolution. In the countryside the peasantry rose against the nobility. Faced with these pressures, elements of the nobility in the National Assembly moved on August 4 and 5 to abolish their own feudal rights and privileges. In sum, these laws constituted a formal repudiation of the feudal system and many of the institutions of the Ancien Régime. The following selection comes from that legislation.

CONSIDER: *The extent to which these measures satisfied the grievances of the Third Estate as expressed in the* cahier *and the pamphlet by Sieyès; why members of the nobility proposed and supported these measures themselves; whether these measures should be interpreted as a repudiation of the monarchy as an institution or specifically of Louis XVI as the king.*

ARTICLE I. The National Assembly hereby completely abolishes the feudal system. It decrees that, among the existing rights and dues, . . . all those originating in or representing real or personal serfdom or personal servitude, shall be abolished without indemnification.

🙠

IV. All manorial courts are hereby suppressed without indemnification. . . .

V. Tithes of every description, as well as the dues which have been substituted for them . . . are abolished, on condition, however, that some other method be devised to provide for the expenses of divine worship, the support of the officiating clergy, for the assistance of the poor, for repairs and rebuilding of churches and parsonages, and for the maintenance of all institutions, seminaries, schools, academies, asylums, and organizations to which the present funds are devoted.

🙠

SOURCE: From James Harvey Robinson, ed., "The French Revolution, 1789–1791," in *Translations and Reprints from the Original Sources of European History,* vol. I, no. 5, ed. Department of History of the University of Pennsylvania (Philadelphia: University of Pennsylvania Press, 1898), pp. 2–5.

VII. The sale of judicial and municipal offices shall be suppressed forthwith. Justice shall be dispensed *gratis*.

✎

IX. Pecuniary privileges, personal or real, in the payment of taxes are abolished forever. Taxes shall be collected from all the citizens, and from all property, in the same manner and in the same form. . . .

X. . . . All the peculiar privileges, pecuniary or otherwise, of the provinces, principalities, districts, cantons, cities and communes, are once for all abolished and are absorbed into the law common to all Frenchmen.

XI. All citizens, without distinction of birth, are eligible to any office or dignity, whether ecclesiastical, civil or military; and no profession shall imply any derogation.

✎

XVII. The National Assembly solemnly proclaims the King, Louis XVI, the *Restorer of French Liberty*.

XVIII. The National Assembly shall present itself in a body before the King, in order to submit to him the decrees which have just been passed, to tender to him the tokens of its most respectful gratitude. . . .

XIX. The National Assembly shall consider, immediately after the constitution, the drawing up of the laws necessary for the development of the principles which it has laid down in the present decree.

The Declaration of the Rights of Man and Citizen

No document better summarizes the ideals underlying the French Revolution than The Declaration of the Rights of Man and Citizen. *After an extended discussion, this document was passed by the National Assembly on August 27, 1789; later a revised version of it was incorporated into the Constitution of 1791. Its provisions are a combination of general statements about human rights and specific statements about what the government should and should not do. This document corresponds to the American Declaration of Independence. It is also viewed more broadly as containing the general principles for democratic revolutions in the eighteenth and nineteenth centuries.*

CONSIDER: *How this document reflects ideals of the Enlightenment; at which social groups this document was aimed; who would suffer most from or be most infuriated by its provisions; the ways in which this document is inconsistent with monarchical government; how a monarch might retain meaningful powers while still conforming to this document.*

The representatives of the French people, organized as a National Assembly, believing that the ignorance, neglect or contempt of the rights of man are the sole cause of public calamities and of the corruption of governments, have determined to set forth in a solemn declaration the natural, inalienable and sacred rights of man, in order that this declaration, being constantly before all the members of the social body, shall remind them continually of their rights and duties; in order that the acts of the legislative power, as well as those of the executive power, may be compared at any moment with the ends of all political institutions and may thus be more respected; and, lastly, in order that the grievances of the citizens, based hereafter upon simple and incontestable principles, shall tend to the maintenance of the constitution and redound to the happiness of all. Therefore the National Assembly recognizes and proclaims, in the presence and under the auspices of the Supreme Being, the following rights of man and of the citizen:—

ARTICLE 1. Men are born and remain free and equal in rights. Social distinctions may only be founded upon the general good.

2. The aim of all political association is the preservation of the natural and imprescriptible rights of man. These rights are liberty, property, security and resistance to oppression.

3. The principle of all sovereignty resides essentially in the nation. No body nor individual may exercise any authority which does not proceed directly from the nation.

4. Liberty consists in the freedom to do everything which injures no one else; hence the exercise of the natural rights of each man has no limits except those which assure to the other members of the society the enjoyment of the same rights. These limits can only be determined by law.

5. Law can only prohibit such actions as are hurtful to society. Nothing may be prevented which is not forbidden by law, and no one may be forced to do anything not provided for by law.

6. Law is the expression of the general will. Every citizen has a right to participate personally or through his representative in its formation. It must be the same for all, whether it protects or punishes. All citizens, being equal in the eyes of the law, are equally eligible to all dignities and to all public positions and occupations, according to their abilities, and without distinction except that of their virtues and talents.

SOURCE: James Harvey Robinson, ed., "The French Revolution, 1789–1791," in *Translations and Reprints from the Original Sources of European History,* vol. I, no. 5, ed. Department of History of the University of Pennsylvania (Philadelphia: University of Pennsylvania Press, 1898), pp. 6–8.

7. No person shall be accused, arrested or imprisoned except in the cases and according to the forms prescribed by law. Any one soliciting, transmitting, executing or causing to be executed any arbitrary order shall be punished. But any citizen summoned or arrested in virtue of the law shall submit without delay, as resistance constitutes an offence.

8. The law shall provide for such punishments only as are strictly and obviously necessary, and no one shall suffer punishment except it be legally inflicted in virtue of a law passed and promulgated before the commission of the offence.

9. As all persons are held innocent until they shall have been declared guilty, if arrest shall be deemed indispensable, all harshness not essential to the securing of the prisoner's person shall be severely repressed by law.

10. No one shall be disquieted on account of his opinions, including his religious views, provided their manifestation does not disturb the public order established by law.

11. The free communication of ideas and opinions is one of the most precious of the rights of man. Every citizen may, accordingly, speak, write and print with freedom, but shall be responsible for such abuses of this freedom as shall be defined by law.

12. The security of the rights of man and of the citizen requires public military force. These forces are, therefore, established for the good of all and not for the personal advantage of those to whom they shall be entrusted.

13. A common contribution is essential for the maintenance of the public forces and for the cost of administration. This should be equitably distributed among all the citizens in proportion to their means.

14. All the citizens have a right to decide, either personally or by their representatives, as to the necessity of the public contribution; to grant this freely; to know to what uses it is put; and to fix the proportion, the mode of assessment, and of collection, and the duration of the taxes.

15. Society has the right to require of every public agent an account of his administration.

16. A society in which the observance of the law is not assured, nor the separation of powers defined, has no constitution at all.

17. Since property is an inviolable and sacred right, no one shall be deprived thereof except where public necessity, legally determined, shall clearly demand it, and then only on condition that the owner shall have been previously and equitably indemnified.

Declaration of the Rights of Woman and the Female Citizen

Olympe de Gouges

While men of the French Revolution stood for principles of natural rights, equality before the law, and universal liberties, few favored applying those principles to women. However, several women and women's organizations struggled to win rights for women that corresponded to those gained by men. Olympe de Gouges (1743–1793), a self-educated daughter of a butcher and an author of several pamphlets and plays, was one of the most famous of these women. The following excerpts are from her September 1791 pamphlet, which she modeled on the National Assembly's Declaration of the Rights of Man and Citizen. Her critical writings would eventually bring her into conflict with Robespierre and the Jacobins. Charged for counterrevolutionary activities, she was arrested and executed in 1793.

CONSIDER: *What Gouges demands; the arguments and language she uses to support her demands.*

Mothers, daughters, sisters [and] representatives of the nation demand to be constituted into a national assembly. Believing that ignorance, omission, or scorn for the rights of woman are the only causes of public misfortunes and of the corruption of governments, [the women] have resolved to set forth in a solemn declaration the natural, inalienable, and sacred rights of woman. . . .

ARTICLE 1

Woman is born free and lives equal to man in her rights. Social distinctions can be based only on the common utility.

ARTICLE 4

Liberty and justice consist of restoring all that belongs to others; thus, the only limits on the exercise of the natural rights of woman are perpetual male tyranny; these limits are to be reformed by the laws of nature and reason.

ARTICLE 6

The laws must be the expression of the general will; all female and male citizens must contribute either personally or through their representatives to its formation; it must be the same for all: male and female citizens, being equal in the eyes of the law, must be equally admitted to all honors, positions, and public employment according to their capacity and without other distinctions besides those of their virtues and talents.

SOURCE: Olympe de Gouges, "The Declaration of the Rights of Women," in *Women in Revolutionary Paris, 1789–1795,* Darline Gay Levy, et al., eds. (Urbana, IL: University of Illinois Press, 1980), pp. 89–93.

ARTICLE 11

The free communication of thoughts and opinions is one of the most precious rights of woman, since the liberty assures the recognition of children by their fathers. Any female citizen thus may say freely, I am the mother of a child which belongs to you, without being forced by a barbarous prejudice to hide the truth; [an exception may be made] to respond to the abuse of this liberty in cases determined by the law.

ARTICLE 17

Property belongs to both sexes whether united or separate; for each it is an inviolable and sacred right; no one can be deprived of it, since it is the true patrimony of nature, unless the legally determined public need obviously dictates it, and then only with a just and prior indemnity.

POSTSCRIPT

Woman, wake up; the tocsin of reason is being heard throughout the whole universe; discover your rights. The powerful empire of nature is no longer surrounded by prejudice, fanaticism, superstition, and lies. The flame of truth has dispersed all the clouds of folly and usurpation. Enslaved man has multiplied his strength and needs recourse to yours to break his chains. Having become free, he has become unjust to his companion. Oh, women, women! When will you cease to be blind? What advantage have you received from the Revolution? A more pronounced scorn, a more marked disdain. In the centuries of corruption you ruled only over the weakness of men. The reclamation of your patrimony, based on the wise decrees of nature—what have you to dread from such a fine undertaking? The bon mot of the legislator of the marriage of Cana? Do you fear that our French legislators, correctors of that morality, long ensnared by political practices now out of date, will only say again to you: women, what is there in common between you and us? Everything, you will have to answer. If they persist in their weakness in putting this non sequitur in contradiction to their principles, courageously oppose the force of reason to the empty pretensions of superiority; unite yourselves beneath the standards of philosophy; deploy all the energy of your character, and you will soon see these haughty men, not groveling at your feet as servile adorers, but proud to share with you the treasures of the Supreme Being. Regardless of what barriers confront you, it is in your power to free yourselves; you have only to want to. Let us pass not to the shocking tableau of what you have been in society; and since national education is in question at this moment, let us see whether our wise legislators will think judiciously about the education of women.

The Declaration of Independence

The American Revolution preceded the French Revolution by a few years. Yet its priority in time does not give it priority in historical importance. At that time America was at the fringes of Western civilization while France was at its heart. Nevertheless, the American Revolution influenced the French Revolution in a variety of ways. One similarity between the two is their two great declarations: the American Declaration of Independence *(1776) and the French* Declaration of the Rights of Man and Citizen *(1789). Although it is uncertain whether the French were directly influenced by the American document, both are products of common ideas of the late eighteenth century and show evidence of a strong relationship between these ideas and revolutionary activities in Western civilization. The* Declaration of Independence *was written primarily by Thomas Jefferson. The following selection comes from the beginning of this document.*

CONSIDER: *The usefulness of this standard for evaluating the legitimacy of a revolution; similarities between the French and American declarations; how these two documents differ in purpose and substance.*

When in the Course of human events, it becomes necessary for one people to dissolve the political bonds which have connected them with another, and to assume among the powers of the earth, the separate and equal station to which the Laws of Nature and of Nature's God entitle them, a decent respect to the opinions of mankind requires that they should declare the causes which impel them to the separation.—We hold these truths to be self-evident, that all men are created equal, that they are endowed by their Creator with certain unalienable Rights, that among these are Life, Liberty and the pursuit of Happiness.—That to secure these rights, Governments are instituted among Men, deriving their just powers from the consent of the governed,—That whenever any Form of Government becomes destructive of these ends, it is the Right of the People to alter or to abolish it, and to institute new Government, laying its foundation on such principles and organizing its powers in such form, as to them shall seem most likely to effect their Safety and Happiness. Prudence, indeed, will dictate that Governments long established should not be changed for light and transient causes; and accordingly all experience hath shewn, that mankind are more disposed to suffer, while evils are sufferable, than to right themselves by abolishing the forms to which they are accustomed. But when a long train of abuses and usurpations, pursuing invariably the same Object evinces a design to reduce them under

SOURCE: *The Declaration of Independence, 1776* (Washington, D.C.: U.S. Department of State, 1911), pp. 3–8.

absolute Despotism, it is their right, it is their duty, to throw off such Government, and to provide new Guards for their future security.—Such has been the patient sufferance of these Colonies; and such is now the necessity which constrains them to alter their former Systems of Government.

Speech to the National Convention— February 5, 1794: The Terror Justified

Maximilien Robespierre

Between 1793 and 1794, France experienced the most radical phase of the revolution, known as the Reign of Terror. During this period France was essentially ruled by the twelve-member Committee of Public Safety elected by the National Convention every month. The outstanding member of this committee was Maximilien Robespierre (1758–1794), a provincial lawyer who rose within the Jacobin Club and gained a reputation for incorruptibility and superb oratory. Historians have argued over Robespierre, some singling him out as a bloodthirsty individual with the major responsibility for the executions during the Reign of Terror, others seeing him as a sincere, idealistic, effective revolutionary leader called to the fore by events of the time. In the following speech to the National Convention on February 5, 1794, Robespierre defines the revolution and justifies extreme actions, including terror, in its defense.

CONSIDER: *What Robespierre means when he argues that terror flows from virtue; how the use of terror relates to the essence of the revolution; how this speech might be interpreted as an Enlightenment attack on the Ancien Régime carried to its logical conclusion.*

It is time to mark clearly the aim of the Revolution and the end toward which we wish to move; it is time to take stock of ourselves, of the obstacles which we still face, and of the means which we ought to adopt to attain our objectives. . . .

What is the goal for which we strive? A peaceful enjoyment of liberty and equality, the rule of that eternal justice whose laws are engraved, not upon marble or stone, but in the hearts of all men.

We wish an order of things where all low and cruel passions are enchained by the laws, all beneficent and generous feelings aroused; where ambition is the desire to merit glory and to serve one's fatherland; where distinctions are born only of equality itself; where the citizen is subject to the magistrate, the magistrate to the people,

SOURCE: Raymond P. Stearns, ed., *Pageant of Europe.* Reprinted by permission of Harcourt Brace Jovanovich, Inc. (New York, 1947), pp. 404–405.

the people to justice; where the nation safeguards the welfare of each individual, and each individual proudly enjoys the prosperity and glory of his fatherland; where all spirits are enlarged by the constant exchange of republican sentiments and by the need of earning the respect of a great people; where the arts are the adornment of liberty, which ennobles them; and where commerce is the source of public wealth, not simply of monstrous opulence for a few families.

In our country we wish to substitute morality for egotism, probity for honor, principles for conventions, duties for etiquette, the empire of reason for the tyranny of customs, contempt for vice for contempt for misfortune, pride for insolence, the love of honor for the love of money . . . that is to say, all the virtues and miracles of the Republic for all the vices and snobbishness of the monarchy.

We wish in a word to fulfill the requirements of nature, to accomplish the destiny of mankind, to make good the promises of philosophy . . . that France, hitherto illustrious among slave states, may eclipse the glory of all free peoples that have existed, become the model of all nations. . . . That is our ambition; that is our aim.

What kind of government can realize these marvels? Only a democratic government. . . . But to found and to consolidate among us this democracy, to realize the peaceable rule of constitutional laws, it is necessary to conclude the war of liberty against tyranny and to pass successfully through the storms of revolution. Such is the aim of the revolutionary system which you have setup. . . .

Now what is the fundamental principle of democratic, or popular government—that is to say, the essential mainspring upon which it depends and which makes it function? It is virtue: I mean public virtue . . . that virtue which is nothing else but love of fatherland and its laws. . . .

The splendor of the goal of the French Revolution is simultaneously the source of our strength and of our weakness: our strength, because it gives us an ascendancy of truth over falsehood, and of public rights over private interests; our weakness, because it rallies against us all vicious men, all those who in their hearts seek to despoil the people. . . . It is necessary to stifle the domestic and foreign enemies of the Republic or perish with them. Now in these circumstances, the first maxim of our politics ought to be to lead the people by means of reason and the enemies of the people by terror.

If the basis of popular government in time of peace is virtue, the basis of popular government in time of revolution is both virtue and terror: virtue without which terror is murderous, terror without which virtue is powerless. Terror is nothing else than swift, severe, indomitable justice; it flows, then, from virtue.

A Soldier's Letters to His Mother: Revolutionary Nationalism

François-Xavier Joliclerc

Despite tremendous internal difficulties, including counter-revolutionary movements in a number of provinces, French armies held back foreign forces after war broke out in 1792, but by 1794 the French forces had made gains even beyond the 1789 borders. Part of the reason for this success was the nationalistic enthusiasm that developed along with the revolution. This nationalism is demonstrated by the following letters from François-Xavier Joliclerc, a conscript in the French army, to his mother.

CONSIDER: *The divisions within French society revealed in these letters; why such sentiments among soldiers are so important and how political leaders or military strategists might capitalize on them; whether the nationalism revealed in these letters is inherent in the nature of the French Revolution or in any particular phase of that revolution.*

13 December, 1793

My dear mother,

You continue to point out to me, in all your letters, that we must get out of the army, cost what it may. Here are the difficulties and the obstacles that I can see.

First of all, it is difficult to find replacements despite the enormous sums that are expended for this purpose. Secondly, we have just had a call-up of men eighteen to twenty-five; and the call-up of those from twenty-five to thirty-five is being prepared. As soon as we got home, we

SOURCE: From Ludwig F. Schaefer, Daniel P. Resnick, and George F. Netterville, eds., *The Shaping of Western Civilization,* vol. II, trans. Daniel P. Resnick (New York: Holt, Rinehart and Winston, Inc., 1970), p. 216. Reprinted by permission of the editors.

would have to get ready to go back, regretting the money we had spent. Thirdly, when *la patrie* calls us to her defense, we ought to fly there as if running to a good meal. Our life, our wealth, and our talents do not belong to us. It is to the nation, *la patrie,* that all that belongs.

I know well that you and all the others in our village do not share these sentiments. They are not aroused by the cries of an outraged fatherland, and all that they do results from being compelled to. But I have been brought up in conscience and thought, and have always been republican in spirit, although obliged to live in a monarchy. These principles of love for *la patrie, la liberté, la république,* are not only engraved in my heart, but are deeply etched and will remain there as long as it will please the Supreme Being to sustain in me the breath of life.

Even if it cost me three quarters of my possessions to have you share these sentiments with me, I would gladly part with them and consider it a very small sacrifice. Oh, if only one day you could know the price of liberty and lose your senseless attachment to material things.

30 May, 1794

What about my lot? I am at my post, where I ought to be, and every good man who knows what's what ought to fly to the aid of his country in danger. If I should perish there, you ought to rejoice. Can one make a finer sacrifice than to die for one's country? Can one die for a more just, glorious, and fairer cause? No! Would you rather see me die on a mattress of straw in my bed at Froidefontaine [his home village] working with wood or stone?

No, dear mother. Think that I am at my post and you will be consoled. If your conscience reproaches you in some way, sell even the last of your petticoats for *la patrie.* She is our only rudder, and it is she who guides us and gives us happiness. . . .

Your son, Joliclerc

Visual Sources

Allegory of the Revolution

Jeaurat de Bertray

Jeaurat de Bertray's Allegory of the Revolution (figure 9.1) is literally a jumble of historical and revolutionary symbols. At the top is a portrait of Jean Jacques Rousseau, at the time considered by many the spiritual and intellectual father of the French Revolution, even though he never advocated revolution and died eleven years before it began. Below him are the new flags of the French Republic, the one on the left with the nationalistic words "love of country." Further to the left is a triangular monument to Equality, below it two maidens representing Goodness and Good Faith, and in the center a bundle of rods and arms topped by a red liberty cap, all symbolizing a fair, forceful republican government. Just below is paper money, the assignats, that helped finance the revolution and pay off debts, and in the center right grows a liberty tree. To the right are two unfinished pillars, the first dedicated to the

FIGURE 9.1   (© Snark/Art Resource, NY)

regeneration of morals and The Declaration of the Rights of Man and Citizen, *the second to the French Revolution. Just below them and in the background are symbols of forceful determination to uphold and defend the revolution: a guillotine, a cannon, and a soldier. In the right foreground is a peasant wearing a liberty cap and sowing a field. This painting pulls together many symbols and elements of the revolutionary ideology. It was painted in 1794, the time of the most radical phase of the revolution.*

CONSIDER: *Connections between this picture,* The Declaration of the Rights of Man and Citizen, *and the Enlightenment; the ways in which the Ancien Régime is rejected symbolically in this picture.*

Henri de la Rochjacquelein
Pierre-Narcisse Guérin

As events developed during France's revolutionary years, the new republican government had to battle not only foreign troops, but also uprisings within France. The most serious of these erupted in the Vendée region of western France. Years later, Pierre-Narcisse Guérin (1774–1833) would celebrate the cause of the Vendée rebels.

As suggested by Guérin's painting of Henri Duverger (figure 9.2), comte de la Rochejacquelein (1772–1794), the Vendée peasants, led by local nobles and clergy, rebelled in the name of "our king, our priests, and the Old Regime." Guérin depicts the young aristocratic general Rochejacquelein amid

FIGURE 9.2   (© Réunion des Musées Nationaux/Art Resource, NY)

one of the close-quarter battles that defined the Vendée revolt. Standing firm in tall boots and yellow pants, a white sash around his waist and his wounded right arm in a sling, Rochejacquelein fires a gun point-blank at the enemy, whose bayonets we see just inches away. Behind Rochejacquelein stand his equally determined but more modestly dressed peasant guerrilla followers, one with a rifle, another with only a pitchfork to stress the popularity of this rebellion. Above flies the white flag of the rebel Royalist cause, echoed by the sacred heart pinned to the general's chest.

Rochejacquelein would survive this battle only to be killed in 1794. However, the uprising he helped lead spread until revolts broke out in some sixty of France's eighty-three depart-

ments. These all-too-real enemies outside and within France's borders threatened the fledgling Republic.

CONSIDER: How this painting portrays the rebel Royalist cause; how supporters of the French Revolution might have viewed this painting.

Internal Disturbances and the Reign of Terror

Understanding of the Reign of Terror has often been distorted by an image of random and purposeless brutality. One way to gain clearer insights into the Terror is through the use of

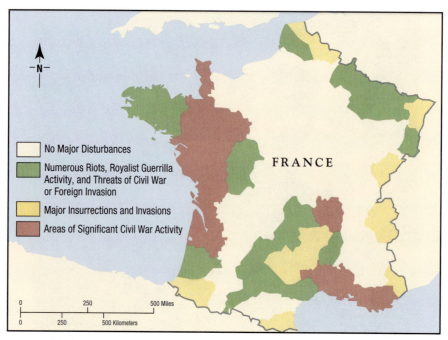

MAP 9.1   Internal Disturbances

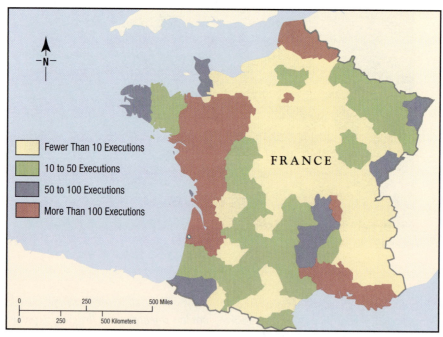

MAP 9.2   The Incidence of the Terror

maps and statistics, which reveal where the Terror occurred, how intensive it was, and who its victims were. Maps 9.1 and 9.2 compare the amount of civil disturbance facing government officials and the number of executions occurring in the various departments of France during the period of the Terror. The two pie charts (charts 9.1 and 9.2) compare the estimated percentages of France's population belonging to the

various classes in 1789 and during the Terror from March 1793 to August 1794.

CONSIDER: *How these maps and charts support an argument that the Reign of Terror was not random or purposeless; the hypotheses that might be drawn from these maps and charts about the causes or effects of the Terror.*

Chart 9.1 (left):

Peasants and Farmers: 86%

Working Class: 8%

Middle Class: 4%

Nobility: 1 1/2%
Clergy: 1/2%

CHART 9.1   Classes in France

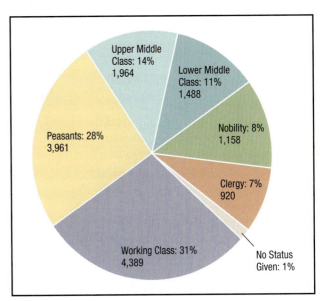

Upper Middle Class: 14% 1,964

Lower Middle Class: 11% 1,488

Nobility: 8% 1,158

Clergy: 7% 920

Peasants: 28% 3,961

Working Class: 31% 4,389

No Status Given: 1%

CHART 9.2   Executions During the Reign of Terror

Secondary Sources

The Coming of the French Revolution

Georges Lefebvre

Probably no event in modern history has been interpreted at greater length and with greater passion than the French Revolution. The historiographic tradition related to this event is so extensive that numerous books and articles have been written on this historiography itself. A central controversy involves the cause or causes of the revolution and is dealt with in the following selection from The Coming of the French Revolution *by Georges Lefebvre. Lefebvre held the prestigious chair of French revolutionary history at the Sorbonne until his death in 1959. His work on the French Revolution continues to be highly respected.*

CONSIDER: *The most important cause of the French Revolution, according to Lefebvre; how this interpretation relates the revolution in France to areas outside of France; how social, economic, and political factors are linked in this interpretation of the French Revolution; how this view is supported by the primary documents.*

The ultimate cause of the French Revolution of 1789 goes deep into the history of France and of the western world. At the end of the eighteenth century the social

SOURCE: From Georges Lefebvre, *The Coming of the French Revolution,* pp. 1–3. Copyright 1947 by Princeton University Press. Reprinted by permission of Princeton University Press.

structure of France was aristocratic. It showed the traces of having originated at a time when land was almost the only form of wealth, and when the possessors of land were the masters of those who needed it to work and to live. It is true that in the course of age-old struggles (of which the Fronde, the last revolt of the aristocracy, was as recent as the seventeenth century) the king had been able gradually to deprive the lords of their political power and subject nobles and clergy to his authority. But he had left them the first place in the social hierarchy. Still restless at being merely his "subjects," they remained privileged persons.

Meanwhile the growth of commerce and industry had created, step by step, a new form of wealth, mobile or commercial wealth, and a new class, called in France the bourgeoisie, which since the fourteenth century had taken its place as the Third Estate in the General Estates of the kingdom. This class had grown much stronger with the maritime discoveries of the fifteenth and sixteenth centuries and the ensuing exploitation of new worlds, and also because it proved highly useful to the monarchical state in supplying it with money and competent officials. In the eighteenth century commerce, industry and finance occupied an increasingly important place in the national economy. It was the bourgeoisie that rescued the royal treasury in moments of crisis. From its ranks were recruited most members of the liberal professions and most public employees. It had developed a new ideology which the "philosophers" and "economists" of the time had simply put into definite form. The role of the nobility had correspondingly declined; and the clergy, as the ideal which it proclaimed lost prestige, found its authority growing weaker. These groups preserved the highest rank in the legal structure of the country, but in reality economic power, personal abilities and confidence in the future had passed largely to the bourgeoisie. Such a discrepancy never lasts forever. The Revolution of 1789 restored the harmony between fact and law. This transformation spread in the nineteenth century throughout the west and then to the whole globe, and in this sense the ideas of 1789 toured the world.

The Revolution of the Notables
Donald M. G. Sutherland

Georges Lefebvre's interpretation for the causes of the French Revolution became part of what has been called the "classical view" of the origins of the revolution. In recent years this view has been strongly criticized by increasing numbers of historians, most of whom reject Lefebvre's social-economic view in favor of a more political analysis. In the following selection Donald M. G. Sutherland reviews this controversy.

CONSIDER: *The basis for the attack on the classical view; why "exclusivism" is so important for these interpretations; how a representative of the classical view might respond.*

There was a time when historians could be fairly confident in describing the origins of the French Revolution. The operative concept was "aristocratic reaction." It meant several things at once. Politically, it referred to the undermining of the absolutism of Louis XIV which was thought to have subverted the independence and privileges of the aristocracy. The parlements, the regional sovereign and appeal courts of which that of Paris was by far the most important, were the driving forces behind the noble offensive. They were able to transform their right of registering laws and edicts into a veto on progressive royal legislation. The Crown was consequently much weaker. This had implications in the social sphere as well. In the course of the eighteenth century, the aristocracy ended up monopolizing the highest offices in government, the military, the Church and judiciary. This in turn had its effects on the bourgeoisie. No longer able to advance to the top of the major social and political institutions of the day, the bourgeoisie became increasingly alienated from the state and from respectable society. Frustrated from achieving its highest ambitions, its loyalties

strained, ever open to suggestive criticisms of the system, it was well placed to take advantage of the political crisis of 1788–9 to overthrow the old order altogether. One of the many crises of the Old Regime was a crisis of social mobility.

The argument was irresistibly attractive, partly because of its internal elegance and partly because it explained so much. It made sense of the reign of Louis XIV, the eighteenth century and the Revolution too. The struggle between revolution and counterrevolution could be reduced to two actors, the bourgeoisie and the aristocracy, who had first come to blows in the closing years of the reign of Louis XIV. The aristocracy lost, of course, and specialists of the nineteenth century could move on to the next round, the struggle between the bourgeoisie and the working class.

Unfortunately, research and reflective criticism over the past twenty years have rendered the classical view of the origins of the Revolution utterly untenable. In the first place, it assumes rather than demonstrates the aristocracy's progressive monopoly of high posts. It assumes, too, that the society of the seventeenth century was more open than its successor but relies on incomplete evidence and a limited range of contemporary complaints. The Duc de Saint-Simon's famous observation that Louis XIV raised up the "vile bourgeoisie" turns out to be untrue in the case of the episcopate, partially true but grossly misleading of the ministry and unknown in the case of the officer corps of the army. . . .

Closer examination of some of the major signs of noble exclusivism shows that restrictions were often aimed at excluding the rich parvenu nobles, not a rising bourgeoisie. . . . The Old Regime aristocracy was thus comparatively young and was in a constant process of renewal.

The doors of the Second Estate were well oiled to men of talent but above all to those with money. Society was therefore capable of absorbing the most thrusting, entrepreneurial and ambitious men of the plutocracy. . . .

The effect of the revisionist critique of the classical interpretation has been to reassert the importance of the political origins of the Revolution. If the nobility had always been a dominant class, if whatever trends there were towards exclusivism are problematic to interpret, if opportunities for advancement were far greater than was ever suspected, and if nobles and bourgeois shared similar economic functions and interests, the notion that the Revolution originated in a struggle between two distinct classes has to be abandoned. Politics remains. Both groups could agree to unite to overthrow absolutism in favour of a liberal constitution but, according to which revisionist historian one follows, they fell out either over means or because of a failure of political leadership or the form the political crisis took, or even over something as amorphous as "style."

SOURCE: From Donald Sutherland, *France, 1789–1815,* pp. 15–18, © 1986 Oxford University Press. Reprinted by permission of HarperCollins Publishers, Ltd., and Oxford University Press.

Loaves and Liberty: Women in the French Revolution

Ruth Graham

Historians have long recognized that women played an important role in certain aspects of the French Revolution. But only in the last twenty years have extensive examinations been made of the significance of the French Revolution for women's history. The following selection by Ruth Graham is a good example of this work.

CONSIDER: *Any connections between sex and class lines in the French Revolution; the ways in which women became a "revolutionary force unprecedented in history" during the revolution; what Graham means by women's victories and defeats.*

It would be wrong to assume that because women had come into the Revolution in 1789 asking for bread and liberty and had come out in 1795 with starvation and restriction of their movements, they had gained nothing. They won laws protecting their rights in marriage, property, and education. True, women were denied political rights in the French Revolution (as were the majority of men when the Convention scrapped the democratic constitution of 1793) but nowhere else at the time did women share political rights with men.

Although women were a cohesive group during the Revolution, they responded mainly to the needs of their class and were never an autonomous force. The ideology of the revolutionary authorities who distrusted women's political movements derived seemingly from Rousseau, but actually from the facts of their lives: France's small-scale, home-based economy needed middle- and working-class women to contribute their special skills and labor to their families. Women were not yet a large, independent group in the working class.

In the early days of the French Revolution, women from the middle classes (as can be seen from cahiers written by them) welcomed the restoration of their natural rights as wives and mothers to participate in society as men's "natural companions." Women of the urban poor—wage earners, artisans of women's crafts, owners of small enterprises, such as the market women—agitated for bread rather than for women's rights. There is, however, evidence that "respectable" middle-class women joined them. Although these movements crossed class lines, which were perhaps not rigidly fixed, they did not

cross sex lines. When men participated, as they did in the October Days of 1789, they came as armed escorts or separate detachments.

As the Revolution entered its more radical phase, as economic crisis followed war and civil strife, the polarization between the rich and the poor sharpened the older struggle between aristocrat and patriot. During the last days of the National Convention, the women who surged into the hall crying "Bread and the Constitution of 1793!" truly represented the poor, whom the upper classes and their women now feared. The bread riots belonged to the women of the poor, who incited their men to insurrection, but the insurrection belonged to both of them, the sans-culottes and their women.

Yet, the Revolution had called upon women to make great sacrifices and they did; in consequence, women became a revolutionary force unprecedented in history. The men in power feared women who challenged the Revolution's failure to guarantee bread for the poor. So feared were the women of the French Revolution that they became legendary—they became Mme. Defarge later to those who feared revolution itself.

A new elite of the upper middle class, men of wealth and talent, rose to power in the four years of the Directory following the dissolution in 1795 of the National Convention. Their women had no political rights but emerged as influential ladies of the salon, such as the brilliant writer Mme. de Staë, and Mme. Tallien, former wife of an aristocrat and now derisively called "Our Lady of Thermidor," as a symbol of the reaction. One of these ladies, Josephine de Beauharnais, the widow of a general, became the mistress of one of the Directors before she married the young Napoleon Bonaparte, who soon afterward became general of the armies in Italy.

Outside of Paris, away from the glamour of these women, middle-class morality prevailed. Napoleon subscribed to this morality. When he became emperor in 1804, he wrote laws into his code to strengthen the authority of the husband and father of the family as a safeguard for private property. Women lost whatever rights they had gained in the Revolution, for now they had to obey their husbands unconditionally. Napoleon left women the right to divorce (for Napoleon to use against Josephine when she failed to provide him an heir), but this right was taken from them after 1815 by the restoration of the Bourbon monarchy.

What could not be taken from women was their memory of victories during the French Revolution: their march to Versailles in the October Days, their petitions to the legislature, their club meetings, their processions, their insurrections. Their defeats served as lessons for next time. "We are simple women," a woman was reported to have said at a club meeting in the days of the

SOURCE: Ruth Graham, "Loaves and Liberty: Women in the French Revolution," in *Becoming Visible: Women in European History,* ed. Renate Bridenthal and Claudia Koonz (Boston: Houghton Mifflin, 1977), pp. 251–253.

uprising of the Paris Commune in May 1871, nearly a century later, "but not made of weaker stuff than our grandmothers of '93. Let us not cause their shades to blush for us, but be up and doing, as they would be were they living now."

An Evaluation of the French Revolution

William Doyle

Although most would say that rapid and vast changes occurred during the French Revolution, it is difficult to evaluate the extent to which these changes were more apparent than real. Many historians have concluded that while the revolution stood for much, most of the promises made by the revolution were not carried out. Others argue that much that has been attributed to the revolution would probably have come about anyway. In the following selection William Doyle attempts to strike a balance between what was and was not accomplished by the revolution.

CONSIDER: *How Doyle determines what changes would in all probability have come about in any case; what Doyle attributes directly to the revolution; how Doyle's argument might be used by those opposing revolutions in general.*

The shadow of the Revolution, therefore, fell across the whole of the nineteenth century and beyond. Until 1917 few would have disputed that it was the greatest revolution in the history of the world; and even after that its claims to primacy remain strong. It was the first modern revolution, the archetypal one. After it, nothing in the European world remained the same, and we are all heirs to its influence. And yet, it can be argued, much that was attributed to it would in all probability have come about in any case. Before 1789 there were plenty of signs that the structure of French society was evolving towards domination by a single élite in which property counted for more than birth. The century-long expansion of the bourgeoisie which underlay this trend already looked irreversible; and greater participation by men of property in government, as constant experiments with provincial assemblies showed, seemed bound to come. Meanwhile many of the reforms the Revolution brought in were already being tried or thought about by the absolute monarchy—law codification, fiscal rationalization, diminution of venality, free trade, religious toleration. With all these changes under way or in contemplation,

SOURCE: From William Doyle, *The Oxford History of the French Revolution*, pp. 423–425. Copyright 1989. Reprinted by permission of Oxford University Press.

the power of government looked set for steady growth, too—which ironically was one of the complaints of the despotism-obsessed men of 1789. In the Church, the monastic ideal was already shrivelling and the status of parish priests commanding more and more public sympathy. Economically, the colonial trade had already peaked, and failure to compete industrially with Great Britain was increasingly manifest. In other structural areas, meanwhile, the great upheaval appears to have made no difference at all. Conservative investment habits still characterized the early nineteenth century, agricultural inertia and unentrepreneurial business likewise. And in international affairs, it is hard to believe that Great Britain would not have dominated the world's seas and trade throughout the nineteenth century, that Austro-Prussian rivalry would not have run much the course it did, or that Latin America would not have asserted its independence in some form or other, if the French Revolution had never happened. In all these fields, the effect was to accelerate or retard certain trends, but not to change their general drift.

Against all this, it is equally hard to believe that the specifically anti-aristocratic, anti-feudal revolutionary ideology of the Rights of Man would have emerged as it did without the jumble of accident, miscalculation, and misunderstanding which coalesced into a revolution in specifically French circumstances. It is equally hard to believe that anything as extraordinary as dechristianization would have occurred without the monumental misjudgement which produced the Revolution's quarrel with the Catholic Church. Without that quarrel, the dramatic revival in the authority of the papacy also seems inconceivable. Representative government may well have been on the horizon, but how long would the ideal of popular democracy have taken to establish itself without the example of the sansculotte movement? It certainly transformed and widened out of all recognition the cause of parliamentary reform in England—although the blood-stained figure of the sansculotte probably galvanized conservative resistance on the other side. Above all, the revolutionaries' decision to go to war, which all historians agree revolutionized the Revolution, destroyed an established pattern of warfare in a way no old regime government would otherwise have promoted. Arming the people was the last thing they would have dreamed of. The emergencies of that war in turn produced the scenes which have indelibly marked our memory of the Revolution: the Terror. Massacres were nothing new, and the worst ones of the 1790s occurred outside France. But there was something horribly new and unimaginable in the prospect of a government systematically executing its opponents by the cartload for months on end, and by a device which, however humane in concept, made the streets run with blood. And this occurred in what had passed for the most civilized country in Europe, whose writers had taught the eighteenth century to pride itself on its increasing mildness, good sense, and humanity. This great drama transformed the whole meaning of political change, and the contemporary world would be inconceivable if it had not happened.

In other words it transformed men's outlook.

✌ CHAPTER QUESTIONS

1. What seems to have motivated many of the revolutionaries, as revealed by the demands made prior to the French Revolution and the actions taken during the revolution?

2. What factors help explain why this revolution occurred in France, one of the most prosperous and powerful nations of Europe? What does this explanation add to the significance of the revolution?

3. With the advantage of hindsight, what might the monarchy have done to retain control and minimize revolutionary changes?

4. In what ways should the French Revolution be considered a middle-class revolution or a revolution of the notables?

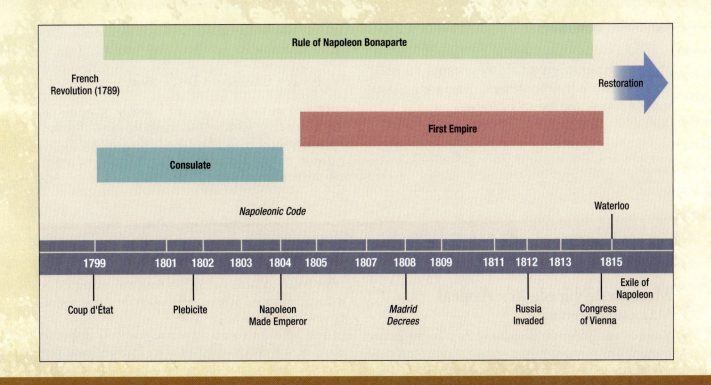

10 The Age of Napoleon

In 1799 members of the ruling Directory conspired with the well-known military leader Napoleon Bonaparte (1769–1821) to take over the French government by means of a *coup d'état.* It was successful, and Napoleon quickly asserted his own dominance over others. By 1802 he had full power, and by 1804 he was the self-proclaimed Emperor Napoleon I.

The period from 1799 to 1815 is generally known as the Age of Napoleon. Rising with opportunities presented by the French Revolution, Napoleon gained power not only in France, but directly and indirectly throughout much of continental Europe. Within France he crushed threats from both radicals and royalists who wanted to extend or reverse the French Revolution. Through administrative reforms, codification of laws, and settlement with the Church, he in-

stitutionalized some of the changes brought about by the revolution and took the heart out of others. Backed by the ideological force of the revolution and strong nationalism, his armies extended French rule, institutions, and influence throughout Europe. In 1814 Napoleon's forces, weakened by overextension and a disastrous Russian campaign, were defeated by a coalition of European powers. After Napoleon's defeat, the major powers, meeting at Vienna, attempted to establish a new stability that would minimize the revolutionary and Napoleonic experiences.

The sources in this chapter focus on the principal interpretive debate connected with Napoleon: How should Napoleon and his policies be understood? Is Napoleon best viewed as a moderate defender of the French Revolution or as an enlightened despot in the eighteenth-century tradition? To provide insight into these issues, the selections will examine Napoleon's rise to power and his ideas, external policies, and internal institutions.

For Classroom Discussion

What do you think of Napoleon? Should he be thought of as a progressive politician building on the French Revolution? Should he be thought of as a conservative and a conqueror? Use the selections by Blanning, Lyons, and Smith to debate these questions.

Primary Sources

Memoirs: Napoleon's Appeal
Madame de Remusat

Napoleon was neither the candidate of those longing to turn France to a more revolutionary course nor the favorite of those who wanted to return France to the legitimacy of the Ancien Régime. He came to power promising to uphold both revolutionary principles and order. Scholars have analyzed the question of why he was able to rise to power. Some see him as a military and political genius; others argue that he was an opportunist who took advantage of circumstances as they arose. One of the earliest analyses of Napoleon's rise to power was written by Madame de Remusat (1780–1821). As a lady in waiting to Empress Josephine and wife of a Napoleonic official, she observed Napoleon firsthand and described him in her Memoirs.

CONSIDER: *Why, according to Remusat, Napoleon was so appealing to the French; the means Napoleon used to secure his power.*

I can understand how it was that men worn out by the turmoil of the Revolution, and afraid of that liberty which had long been associated with death, looked for repose under the dominion of an able ruler on whom fortune was seemingly revolved to smile. I can conceive that they regarded his elevation as a degree of destiny and fondly believed that in the irrevocable they should find peace. I may confidently assert that those persons believed quite sincerely that Bonaparte, whether as consul or emperor, would exert his authority to oppose the intrigue of faction and would save us from the perils of anarchy.

None dared to utter the word "republic," so deeply had the Terror stained that name; and the government of the Directory had perished in the contempt with which its chiefs were regarded. The return of the Bourbons could only be brought about by the aid of a revolution; and the slightest disturbance terrified the French people, in whom enthusiasm of every kind seemed dead. Besides, the men in whom they had trusted had one after the other deceived them; and as, this time, they were yielding to force, they were at least certain that they were not deceiving themselves.

The belief, or rather the error, that only despotism could at that epoch maintain order in France was very widespread. It became the mainstay of Bonaparte; and it is due to him to say that he also believed it. The factions played into his hands by imprudent attempts which he turned to his own advantage. He had some grounds for his belief that he was necessary; France believed it, too; and he even succeeded in persuading foreign sovereigns that he constituted a barrier against republican influences, which, but for him, might spread widely. At the moment when Bonaparte placed the imperial crown upon his head there was not a king in Europe who did not believe that he wore his own crown more securely because of that event. Had the new emperor granted a liberal constitution, the peace of nations and of kings might really have been forever secured.

Memoirs: Napoleon's Secret Police
Joseph Fouché

Although historians have found various aspects of Napoleonic rule admirable, most condemn Napoleon's use of the secret police. Joseph Fouché, Duke of Otranto (1763–1820), headed this institution for most of the period between 1802 and 1810. Fouché combined the attributes of a powerful politician, a police officer, and an opportunist. In the following selection from his Memoirs, Fouché boasts of his accomplishments.

CONSIDER: *The credibility of this document; whether it was reasonable of Napoleon to have Fouché carry out these activities.*

With regard to the interior, an important spring was wanted, that of the general police, which might have rallied the past round the present, and guaranteed the security of the empire. Napoleon himself perceived the void, and, by an imperial decree of the 10th July, reestab-

SOURCE: From James Harvey Robinson, ed., *Readings in European History,* vol. II (Boston: Ginn, 1904), pp. 491–492.

SOURCE: Joseph Fouché, *Memoirs* (London: Gibbings and Co., 1894), pp. 188–191.

lished me at the head of the police; at the same time investing me with stronger functions than those which I had possessed, before the absurd fusion of the police with the department of justice. . . .

It will not be doubted that I had salaried spies in all ranks and orders; I had some of both sexes, hired at the rate of a thousand or two thousand francs per month, according to their importance and their services. I received their reports directly in writing, having a conventional mark. Every three months, I communicated my list to the emperor, in order that there might be no double employment; and also in order that the nature of the service, occasionally permanent, often temporary, might be rewarded either by places or remunerations.

As to the government's police abroad, it had two essential objects, namely, to watch friendly powers, and counteract hostile governments. In both cases, it was composed of individuals purchased or pensioned, and commissioned to reside near each government, or in each principal town, independent of numerous secret agents sent into all countries, either by the minister of foreign affairs, or by the emperor himself.

I also had my foreign spies. It was in my cabinet, also, that the foreign gazettes, prohibited to the perusal of the French people, were collected, abstracts of which were made for my own use. By that means, I held in my hands the most important strings of foreign politics; and I discharged, in conjunction with the chief of the government, a task capable of controlling or balancing that of the minister charged with foreign relations.

I was thus far from limiting my duties to *espionnage.* All the state prisons were under my control, as well as the *gendarmerie.* The delivery of the *visa* of passports belonged to me. To me was assigned the duty of watching amnestied individuals and foreigners. I established general commissariats in the principal towns of the kingdom, which extended the net-work of the police over the whole of France, and especially our frontiers.

My police acquired so high a renown, that the world went so far as to pretend that I had, among my secret agents, three nobles of the *ancien régime,* distinguished by princely titles, and who daily communicated to me the result of their observations.

I confess that such an establishment was expensive; it swallowed up several millions, the funds of which were secretly provided from taxes laid upon gambling and prostitution, and from the granting of passports. Notwithstanding all that has been said against gambling, reflecting and firm minds must allow, that in the actual state of society, the legal converting of vice into profit is a necessary evil. . . .

It became necessary to organize the gambling-houses upon a much larger scale, for the produce of them was not solely destined to reward my moving phalanxes of spies. I nominated as superintendent-general of the gambling-

houses in France, Perrein the elder, who already farmed them, and who, after the coronation, extended his privilege over all of the chief towns of the empire, upon condition of paying fourteen million yearly, independent of three thousand francs daily to the minister of the police, which, however, did not remain entirely in his hands.

Napoleon's Diary

Napoleon's accomplishments and place in history are explained in part by the type of individual he was. The principal sources of information on his personality are his diaries, memoirs, and letters, particularly the portions in which he reflects on himself. The following selection comes from diary entries made between 1798 and 1817.

CONSIDER: *Napoleon's opinions about what made him successful; Napoleon's analysis of his power and his personality; how Napoleon wants to be remembered.*

Paris, January 1, 1798

Paris has a short memory. If I remain longer doing nothing, I am lost. In this great Babylon one reputation quickly succeeds another. After I have been seen three times at the theatre, I shall not be looked at again; I shall therefore not go very frequently.

Paris, January 29, 1798

I will not remain here; there is nothing to be done. They will listen to nothing. I realize that if I stay my reputation will soon be gone. All things fade here, and my reputation is almost forgotten; this little Europe affords too slight a scope; I must go to the Orient; all great reputations have been won there. If the success of an expedition to England should prove doubtful, as I fear, the army of England will become the army of the East, and I shall go to Egypt.

The Orient awaits a man!

Milan, June 17, 1800

I have just reached Milan, somewhat fatigued.

Some Hungarian grenadiers and German prisoners passing by, who had already been prisoners in the campaigns of 1796 and 1797, recognized the First Consul. Many began to shout, with apparent enthusiasm: "Vive Bonaparte!"

What a thing is imagination! Here are men who don't know me, who have never seen me, but who only knew of me, and they are moved by my presence, they would do anything for me! And this same incident arises in all centuries and in all countries! Such is fanaticism! Yes, imagination rules the world. The defect of our modern institutions is that they do not speak to the imagination.

SOURCE: R. M. Johnston, ed., *The Corsican: A Diary of Napoleon's Life in His Own Words* (Boston: Houghton Mifflin Co., 1910), pp. 74, 140, 166, 492, 496.

By that alone can man be governed; without it he is but a brute.

December 30, 1802

My power proceeds from my reputation, and my reputation from the victories I have won. My power would fall if I were not to support it with more glory and more victories. Conquest has made me what I am; only conquest can maintain me.

Friendship is only a word; I love nobody; no, not even my brothers. Perhaps Joseph a little; even then it's a matter of habit, it's because he is my elder.—Duroc? Ah, yes, I love him; but why? His character attracts me: he is cool, dry, severe; and Duroc never sheds tears. As for me, you don't suppose I care; I know perfectly well I have no real friends. As long as I remain what I am, I shall have as many as I need so far as the appearance goes. Let the women whimper, that's their business, but for me, give me no sentiment. A man must be firm, have a stout heart, or else leave on one side war and government.

Saint Helena, March 3, 1817

In spite of all the libels, I have no fear whatever about my fame. Posterity will do me justice. The truth will be known; and the good I have done will be compared with the faults I have committed. I am not uneasy as to the result. Had I succeeded, I would have died with the reputation of the greatest man that ever existed. As it is, although I have failed, I shall be considered as an extraordinary man: my elevation was unparalleled, because unaccompanied by crime. I have fought fifty pitched battles, almost all of which I have won. I have framed and carried into effect a code of laws that will bear my name to the most distant posterity. I raised myself from nothing to be the most powerful monarch in the world. Europe was at my feet. I have always been of opinion that the sovereignty lay in the people. In fact, the imperial government was a kind of republic. Called to the head of it by the voice of the nation, my maxim was, *la carriére est ouverte aux talent* without distinction of birth or fortune, and this system of equality is the reason that your oligarchy hates me so much.

Saint Helena, August 28, 1817

Jesus was hanged, like so many fanatics who posed as a prophet, a messiah; there were several every year. What is certain is that at that epoch opinion was setting towards a single God, and those who first preached the doctrine were well received: circumstances made for it. It is just like in my case, sprung from the lower ranks of society I became an emperor, because circumstances, opinion, were with me.

Visual Sources

Napoleon Crossing the Alps

Jacques Louis David

Jacques Louis David was a leading painter of the late eighteenth and early nineteenth centuries and one of the first great painters to consciously devote his talents to the art of propaganda. A republican during the French Revolution, he painted a number of pictures supportive of the revolution and what it stood for. David argued that "the arts should . . . contribute forcefully to the education of the public" and that art "should have grandeur and a moral"; if a painting is properly presented, the "marks of heroism and civic virtue offered the eyes of the people will electrify its soul, and plant the seeds of glory and devotion to the fatherland."

When Napoleon rose to power, David became a Bonapartist. In 1800 he was asked by Napoleon to paint a picture of him leading his army across the Alps. The result, Napoleon Crossing the Alps *(figure 10.1), shows Napoleon in a heroic pose on a white charger following the glorious footsteps of Hannibal and Charlemagne (whose names are carved in the rocks below) across the Alps. Napoleon is pointing upward, probably both to heaven and to the top of the mountains, while a wind blows at his back—a traditional symbol of victory. Under the horse's belly are troops and cannon moving up the trail. In reality, Napoleon wisely rode a sure-footed mule. He also posed only briefly for David, informing him that "it is the character and what animates the physiognomy that needs to be painted. No one inquires if the portraits of great men are likenesses. It is enough that their genius lives in them."*

CONSIDER: *The way this painting and the circumstances surrounding its execution by David illustrate connections between politics and art of the period.*

Bonaparte Visiting the Plague Victims at Jaffa

Antoine-Jean Gros

Despite the British victory at Aboukir Bay in Egypt, which annihilated French sea power, Napoleon retained hopes of conquering the Near East by land. In February 1799, French forces moved northeast from Cairo to Gaza and Nazareth. Despite some victories, the campaign failed to establish French control over the area. Nevertheless, Napoleon tried to transform these disappointments by promoting paintings that created images of success in this campaign.

In 1804 Antoine-Jean Gros (1771–1835) presented a scene from the Near Eastern campaigns of 1799 that showed the heroic Napoleon displaying humanism, charity, and nobility. The painting (figure 10.2) records Napoleon, after the battle of Jaffa, entering the mosque courtyard (with its horseshoe arches and pointed arcades) of a pest house (plague hospital) at the Palestinian city of Jaffa in the Holy Land on March 11, 1799. Within lay victims of the bubonic plague, which had recently broken out among Arab defenders of the city and spread to the French. When the plague struck, Napoleon at first had his chief medical officer Desgenettes (just behind and to the right of Napoleon, who stands at the center of the painting) deny the presence of the sickness. Here Napoleon tries to stop the panic and inspire his troops by showing that he is not afraid of contamination and that the victims will be well cared for. At this moment the apparently immune and clearly fearless Napoleon reaches out and even touches the dreaded buboes (an inflamed swelling of the lymphatic glands that usually preceded death) of a French victim, perhaps conveying a sense that his touch might miraculously heal the stricken man. Just behind Napoleon, to the left, a more cautious officer holds a handkerchief to his face to ward off the stench of disease and death. In the foreground lay the dead and the agonized dying. At the left, an Arab physician in white robes attends the sick and an assistant carries bread for distribution to the needy. To the right, a blind man, leaning against a column, tries to approach Napoleon, and on the extreme bottom right a doctor, while caring for a soldier, succumbs himself. In the background are the white cubic houses and rising minarets of Jaffa. High in the center from the top of a Franciscan monastery flies triumphantly the French tricolor.

The surrounding facts differ from the historical image presented by this painting. During the battle of Jaffa, Napoleon

FIGURE 10.1 (© Réunion des Musées Nationaux/Art Resource, NY)

had agreed to protect the lives of enemy soldiers if they capitulated. But upon laying down their arms, Napoleon ordered the 3,000 prisoners massacred and plundered the town. By May 1799, French forces had retreated back to Egypt.

CONSIDER: *The message the artist intended to convey to viewers; how high quality art might be used for propaganda purposes.*

 ## Secondary Sources

Napoleon: The Authoritarian Statesman

Tim Blanning

As with most charismatic figures, it has been difficult to evaluate Napoleon objectively. Even before his death, a number of myths were developing about him. Since then much of the debate among scholars has dealt with whether Napoleon should be considered a defender or a destroyer of the revolution, and whether his rise to power reversed the revolutionary tide or consolidated it. In the following selection, Tim Blanning focuses on the consequences for France of Napoleon's rule and argues that he used statesman-like qualities to help create order.

CONSIDER: *What Blanning considers Napoleon's accomplishments within France; why Blanning calls Napoleon "statesman-like"; whether the primary and visual sources support this interpretation.*

SOURCE: Tim Blanning. *The Pursuit of Glory: Europe, 1648–1815* (New York: Viking, 2007), pp. 348–349.

FIGURE 10.2   (© Réunion des Musées Nationaux/Art Resource, NY)

It can safely be said that France had never been better governed, if quality is assessed in terms of effective obedience to orders issued by the centre. Almost everyone could be pleased by the dramatic improvement in public order which followed Bonaparte's seizure of power. The Vendée was pacified at long last by a judicious mixture of stick and carrot, the sectarian tit-for-tat killings in the Rhône valley were halted and everywhere banditry was suppressed. The prefects and their subordinates passed the acid test – the ability to enforce conscription – with flying colours, at least during the early years of the regime. Together with the repair of existing roads and the construction of new highways, physical communication enjoyed much-needed and long-overdue improvement. The other great failure of the successive revolutionary regimes, public finance, was also rectified. Building on preparatory work by the Directory and enjoying the benefit of a sustained recovery in the economy, Bonaparte established the Bank of France, stabilized the currency, improved revenue collection and brought the national debt under control. . . .

In restoring order to a revolution-torn country and continent, Bonaparte was at his most statesman-like in his search for reconciliation. Proscribing only irreconcilable royalists and Jacobins, he encouraged the rest of the émigrés to return home and rally to the regime. This policy was an undoubted success, as the appearance of aristocratic names among the list of prefects shows. His greatest eirenic triumph, however, was making peace with the Catholic Church by the Concordat of 1802. At a stroke, he took from the counter-revolutionaries their most potent appeal. It was some measure of the catastrophe which had befallen the papacy since 1789 that Pius VII was prepared to accept the terms offered, including recognition of the expropriation of ecclesiastical property and the subordination of Church to state. Although Bonaparte's vaulting ambition eventually led to a new schism, in the short and medium term the Concordat greatly facilitated his hold not only on France but on all Catholic Europe.

His other great positive achievement at home was the promulgation of six legal codes, the Civil Code of 1804 being both the first and the most important. It was renamed the Napoleonic Code in 1806, a not unreasonable personification as it was he who took the chair at most of the sessions of the drafting committee and who gave the final document his own unmistakable stamp. As it was imported into many other parts of Europe, it became the most important single legal document of modern European history. It has often been criticized on the grounds that Bonaparte's personal conservatism was reflected in the provisions dealing with property, women, the family and landed inheritance. No doubt these limitations would fall foul of some cosmic court of human rights, but compared with the chaos of the 400-odd legal codes of old regime France, the Napoleonic Code was a model of rationality and equity and was recognized as such by grateful recipients.

Napoleon Bonaparte and the Legacy of the French Revolution

Martyn Lyons

In recent years, some historians have taken a fresh look at Napoleon and the significance of his régime. In addition to examining his words and deeds, they stress the historical context of his rise to power and the break from the Old Régime of the Bourbon monarchy. In the following selection, Martyn Lyons argues that Napoleon was not an enlightened despot but rather the founder of the modern state, and that his régime was the fulfillment of the "bourgeois" Revolution of 1789–1799.

CONSIDER: *What Lyons means by founder of the modern state; how he disagrees with Bergeron and others who argue that Napoleon was an enlightened despot; in what ways Napoleon's régime was a fulfilment of the "bourgeois" Revolution of 1789–1799.*

Throughout this evolution, two main themes stand out. Napoleon was, as he is often described, the founder of the modern state. His régime was also the fulfilment of the bourgeois Revolution of 1789–99.

The new state, which emerged from the Revolution and was shaped by Napoleon, was a secular state, without a trace of the divine sanction which had been one of the ideological props of the old régime monarchy. It was a state based on a conscripted army and staffed by a professional bureaucracy. Administration was "rationalised," in the sense that corruption and favouritism were officially outlawed. The affairs of all citizens were dealt with in principle on a basis of equality and according to fixed regulations, instead of being at the mercy of a monarch's whim. Above all, the modern state was a well-informed state, which used its own machinery to collect data on the lives and activities of its subjects. As it knew them better, it policed them more closely and it taxed them more efficiently. . . .

In Napoleon's hands, however, the state had become the instrument of dictatorship. Although lip service was still paid to the princple of popular sovereignty, Napoleon negated its democratic essence by claiming that he alone embodied the indivisible rights of the people. He manipulated a series of plebiscites to consolidate his personal authority. Bonapartism was not, then, a military dictatorship, for its power was characteristically derived from repeated consultations with the popular will, in 1800, 1802, 1804 and 1815. It was, however, a régime which brought parliamentary life to an end and expressed utter contempt for the liberal intellectuals who defended the representative style of democracy. The imperial years of Bonapartism were anti-parliamentary and anti-liberal. In addition, the information media were strictly controlled by Napoleon's popular dictatorship. . . .

To compare Napoleon with the Bourbons is to sin by anachronism. Turning Napoleon into the last of the Enlightened Absolutists of the late eighteenth century means ignoring the momentous events that separate them. The French Revolution was a decisive historical rupture which places Louis XVI and Napoleon Bonaparte in totally different spheres. The historical role of the Enlightened Absolutists had been to rationalise the confused and creaking old régime state structure. Their aim was to squeeze more resources from it, without disturbing its fundamental framework which was based on inequality and privilege. They had no intention of undermining the society of orders itself. On the contrary, they stood at its pinnacle, and its existence justified their authority.

When Bonaparte came to power, the society of orders had been completely transformed by the French Revolution. Legal privilege and tax exemptions had been destroyed—a fact which Napoleon emphatically confirmed. Bonaparte's task was not to extract more resources from a traditional social structure; that traditional social structure, along with noble privilege, the guilds, the Parlements and provincial autonomies, had been swept away by the Revolution. The role of the Enlightened Absolutists was to rationalise the Old Régime, but Napoleon's was to rationalise the new one. His task was not to safeguard the social prestige of the aristocracy (to which the monarchies were dedicated, and to whom in 1789 Louis XVI had linked his own fate). Napoleon's role was rather to build the institutions which would realise new forms of equality of opportunity. . . .

Its social basis is what distinguishes the Napoleonic régime from the Bourbon monarchy, and makes it the heir of the Revolution. The social foundations of the Napoleonic régime, as this book has argued, lay in the bourgeois and peasant revolution of 1789.

The Consulate and Empire rested on the support of the *notables*, whom the régime itself helped to define

SOURCE: Martyn Lyons, *Napoleon Bonaparte and the Legacy of the French Revolution* (New York: St. Martin's Press, 1994), pp. 295–298.

and cultivate. The *notables* were gathered from the successful revolutionary bourgeoisie of landowners, professional men and administrators, together with elements of the commercial and manufacturing élites. They supported Napoleon because he preserved the social gains of the Revolution. He himself was an enduring symbol of careers open to talent. He perpetuated the abolition of seigneurialism and of aristocratic privilege. He confirmed the material gains of the bourgeoisie, especially the sale of the *biens nationaux*. He established a legal code which embodied equality before the law, and he introduced a system of secondary education which served the interests of the professional and administrative élite. The creation of the new imperial nobility seemed to many to be a retrograde step, but it could also be interpreted as an assertion of new social priorities. The new imperial nobility was intended to bury the old. The society of orders was obsolete and archaic. Instead of birth and connections, society now declared its new criteria for distinguished status: propertied wealth, personal talent and service to the state. . . . Napoleon was the consolidator of the bourgeois Revolution, but he was not the passive instrument of any class or social group.

Women and the Napoleonic Code

Bonnie G. Smith

However they evaluate Napoleon and his rule, most historians point to the set of rationally organized laws—the Napoleonic Code—as one of Napoleon's most important and lasting legacies. The Code embodied many principles of the Enlightenment and the French Revolution, and the Code was modified and adopted outside of France in Europe and the Western Hemisphere. While it has been generally considered a progressive legal system, historians now point out that it may have represented a step back for women. In the following selection from her comprehensive survey, Changing Lives: Women in European History Since 1700, *Bonnie G. Smith analyzes the significance of the Napoleonic Code for women.*

CONSIDER: *Ways the Code made women legally and economically dependent on men; what concept of woman's proper role the Code supported; what concept of man's proper role the Code supported.*

First, women acquired the nationality of their husbands upon marriage. This made a woman's relationship to the state an indirect one because it was dependent on her husband's. Second, a woman had to reside where her husband desired. Women could not participate in lawsuits or serve as witnesses in court or as witnesses to civil acts such as births, deaths, and marriages. Such a reduction in woman's civil status enhanced that of the individual male. Moreover, the Code reduced, if not eliminated, male accountability for sexual acts and thrust it squarely on women. For example, men were no longer susceptible to paternity suits or legally responsible for the support of illegitimate children. Women were weakened economically if they bore illegitimate children, whereas men were not so affected if they fathered them. Finally, female adultery was punished by imprisonment and fines unless the husband relented and took his wife back. Men, however, suffered no such sanctions unless they brought their sexual partner into the home. The sexual behavior of women was open to scrutiny and prescribed by law, whereas that of men, almost without exception, had no criminal aspect attached to it. Thus male sexuality was accepted with few limitations, but women's was only acceptable if it remained within strict domestic boundaries. The Napoleonic Code institutionalized the republican responsibility of women to generate virtue—a term that began to acquire sexual overtones to its civic definition.

The Napoleonic Code also defined the space women would occupy in the new regime as marital, maternal, and domestic—all public matters would be determined by men. This circumscription was made more effective by the way the property law undercut the possibilities for women's economic independence and existence in a world beyond the home. In general, a woman had no control over property. Even if she was married under a contract that ensured a separate accounting of her dowry, her husband still had administrative control of funds. This administrative power of the husband and father replaced arbitrary patriarchal rule and was more in tune with modern ideas of government. Instead of serving the king's whim, governmental officials served the best interests of the nation just as the father increased the well-being of the family. This kind of economic control of women held in all classes. Women's wages went to their husbands, and market women and others engaged in business could not do so without permission from their husbands. Once a woman gained permission she did acquire some kind of legal status, in that a business woman could be sued. On the other hand, she had no control of her profits—these always passed to her husband, and court records demonstrate the continuing enforcement of this kind of control. Moreover, the husband's right to a business woman's property meant that the property passed to his descendants rather than hers. All of these provisions meant that, in the strictest sense, women could not act freely or independently.

SOURCE: From Bonnie G. Smith, *Changing Lives: Women in European History Since 1700*, pp. 120–122. Copyright 1989 by D. C. Heath and Co. Reprinted by permission of the publisher.

The Napoleonic Code influenced many legal systems in Europe and the New World and set the terms for the treatment of women on a widespread basis. Establishing male power by transferring autonomy and economic goods from women to men, the Code organized gender roles for more than a century. "From the way the Code treats women, you can tell it was written by men," so older women reacted to the new decree. Women's publications protested the sudden repression after a decade of more equitable laws. Even in the 1820s, books explaining the Code to women always recognized their anger. The justification for the Code's provisions involved reminders about men's chivalrous character and women's weakness. Arguments were based on nature both to invoke the equality of all men and to reinforce the consequences of women's supposed physical inferiority. Looking at nature, one writer saw in terms of gender man's "greater strength, his propensity to be active and assertive in comparison to woman's weakness, lack of vigor and natural modesty." At the time the Code was written, the codifiers were looking at nature in two ways. In theorizing about men alone, nature was redolent of abstract rights. As far as women were concerned, however, nature became empirical in that women had less physical stature than men. Although short men were equal to tall men, women were simply smaller than men and thus were unequal.

According to jurists, therefore, women needed protection, and this protection was to be found within the domicile. The law, they maintained, still offered women protection from individual male brutality, in the rare cases when that might occur. Legislators thus used the law officially to carve out a private space for women in which they had no rights. At the same time, law codes were supposed to protect women from the abuses allowed in the first place. The small number of abuses that might result were not seen as significant drawbacks by the jurists. They saw the Code as "insuring the safety of patrimonies and restoring order in families." It mattered little to them that the old regime carried over for women in the form of an "estate"—a term that indicated an unchangeable lifetime situation into which people were born and would always remain. Estates had been abolished for men in favor of mobility, but it continued for women.

By the time the Napoleonic Code went into effect, little remained of liberal revolutionary programs for women except the provisions for equal inheritance by sisters and brothers. The Code cleared the way for the rule of property and for individual triumph. It ushered in an age of mobility, marked by the rise of the energetic and heroic. The Code gave women little room for that kind of acquisitiveness or for heroism. Instead, women's realm was to encompass virtue, reproduction, and family.

CHAPTER QUESTIONS

1. Considering the materials in this chapter, how would you explain Napoleon's rise to power and his effective exercise of it?

2. In what ways did Napoleon preserve and support the principles of the French Revolution? In what ways did he undermine these principles?

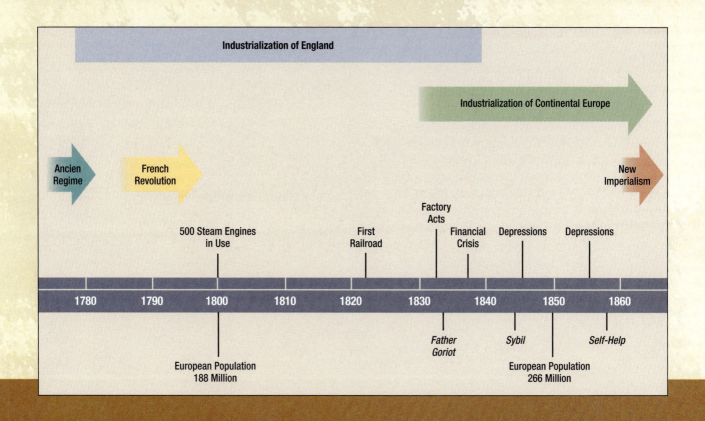

Industrialization of England

Industrialization of Continental Europe

Ancien Regime

French Revolution

New Imperialism

Factory Acts

500 Steam Engines in Use

First Railroad

Financial Crisis

Depressions

Depressions

| 1780 | 1790 | 1800 | 1810 | 1820 | 1830 | 1840 | 1850 | 1860 |

Father Goriot

Sybil

Self-Help

European Population 188 Million

European Population 266 Million

11 Industrialization and Social Change

The Industrial Revolution, which transformed economic life in the West, began in England in the eighteenth century. After the Napoleonic period it spread to Western Europe, and by the end of the nineteenth century it had touched most of Western civilization. The Industrial Revolution was characterized by unprecedented economic growth, the factory system of production, and the use of new, artificially powered machines for transportation and mechanical operations. The potential was tremendous; for the first time, human beings had the ability to produce far more than was needed to sustain a large percentage of the population. Whether that potential would be realized, and at what cost, remained to be seen.

In the wake of industrialization came great social changes. The middle and working classes were most affected by industrialization, and both grew in number and social influence as did the urban areas in which they worked and lived. But it was the middle class that benefited most, enjoying a rising standard of living, increased prestige, and growing political influence. Whether the working class benefited from industrialization during the early decades is a matter for debate among historians. Clearly it was this class that bore the burdens of urban social problems: overcrowded slums, poor sanitation, insufficient social services, and a host of related problems. The aristocracy, the peasantry, and the artisans—classes tied to the traditional agricultural economy and older means of production—slowly diminished in numbers and social importance as industrialization spread.

The selections in this chapter deal with the economic and social aspects of industrialization. Much-debated questions of economic history are addressed. Why did industrialization occur first in England? How did England differ from other areas that were relatively advanced economically? Most of the documents concern the human consequences of industrialization, questions of social history. The most popular area of interest, the effect of industrialization on the workers directly involved, is explored. What were the working conditions in the factories? How did industrialization affect the overall lifestyle of these people? Did their standard of living improve or diminish as a result of industrialization? The middle class is also examined, especially middle-class attitudes and values. How did the middle class view industrialization? What were its attitudes toward money? How did the attitudes of and toward women change?

This chapter centers on industrialization in the first half of the nineteenth century. It should be recognized that industrialization spread unevenly, and it was not until the second half of the nineteenth century and even the beginning of the twentieth century that industrialization spread to many areas in Southern and Eastern Europe.

❧ For Classroom Discussion

What were the benefits and burdens of industrialization? Use the selections by Disraeli, Engels, and Stearns to debate this issue.

 # Primary Sources

Testimony for the Factory Act of 1833: Working Conditions in England

Industrialization carried with it broad social and economic changes that were quickly felt by those involved. The most striking changes were in the working conditions in the new factories and mines. During the first decades of industrialization, there was little government control over working conditions and few effective labor organizations; laborers were thus at the mercy of factory owners who were pursuing profit in a competitive world. Investigations into conditions in factories and mines conducted by the British Parliament in the 1830s and 1840s led eventually to the enactment of legislation, such as the Factory Act of 1833. These parliamentary investigations provide us with extensive information about working conditions and attitudes toward them. The following selection contains three excerpts from a parliamentary commission's investigations into child labor in factories. The first is a summary by the commission of medical examiners from northeastern England. The second is the testimony of John Wright, a steward in a silk factory. The third is the testimony of William Harter, a silk manufacturer.

CONSIDER: *What these people perceived as the worst abuses of factory labor; the causes of the poor working conditions; how Harter might defend himself against the charges that he was abusing the working class; what biases the witnesses might hold.*

SOURCE: Commission for Inquiry into the Employment of Children in Factories, *Second Report, with Minutes of Evidence and Reports by the Medical Commissioners*, vol. V, Session 29 January–20 August, 1833 (London: His Majesty's Printing Office, 1833), pp. 5, 26–28.

TESTIMONY OF THE COMMISSION OF MEDICAL EXAMINERS

The account of the physical condition of the manufacturing population in the large towns in the North-eastern District of England is less favourable. It is of this district that the Commissioners state, "We have found undoubted instances of children five years old sent to work thirteen hours a day; and frequently of children nine, ten, and eleven consigned to labour for fourteen and fifteen hours." The effects ascertained by the Commissioners in many cases are, "deformity," and in still more "stunted growth, relaxed muscles, and slender conformation:" "twisting of the ends of the long bones, relaxation of the ligaments of the knees, ankles, and the like." "The representation that these effects are so common and universal as to enable some persons invariably to distinguish factory children from other children is, I have no hesitation in saying, an exaggerated and unfaithful picture of their general condition; at the same time it must be said, that the individual instances in which some one or other of those effects of severe labour are discernible are rather frequent than rare. . . .

"Upon the whole, there remains no doubt upon my mind, that under the system pursued in many of the factories, the children of the labouring classes stand in need of, and ought to have, legislative protection against the conspiracy insensibly formed between their masters and parents, to tax them to a degree of toil beyond their strength.

"In conclusion, I think it has been clearly proved that children have been worked a most unreasonable and cruel length of time daily, and that even adults have been expected to do a certain quantity of labour which scarcely any human being is able to endure. I am of opinion no child under fourteen years of age should work in a factory of any description for more than eight hours a day.

From fourteen upwards I would recommend that no individual should, under any circumstances, work more than twelve hours a day; although if practicable, as a physician, I would prefer the limitation of ten hours, for all persons who earn their bread by their industry."

TESTIMONY OF JOHN WRIGHT

How long have you been employed in a silk-mill?—More than thirty years.

Did you enter it as a child?—Yes, betwixt five and six.

How many hours a day did you work then?—The same thirty years ago as now.

What are those hours?—Eleven hours per day and two over-hours: over-hours are working after six in the evening till eight. The regular hours are from six in the morning to six in the evening, and two others are two over-hours: about fifty years ago they began working over-hours. . . .

Why, then, are those employed in them said to be in such a wretched condition?—In the first place, the great number of hands congregated together, in some rooms forty, in some fifty, in some sixty, and I have known some as many as 100, which must be injurious to both health and growing. In the second place, the privy is in the factory, which frequently emits an unwholesome smell; and it would be worth while to notice in the future erection of mills, that there be betwixt the privy door and the factory wall a kind of a lobby of cage-work. 3rdly, The tediousness and the everlasting sameness in the first process preys much on the spirits, and makes the hands spiritless. 4thly, The extravagant number of hours a child is compelled to labour and confinement, which for one week is seventy-six hours. . . . 5thly, About six months in the year we are obliged to use either gas, candles, or lamps, for the longest portion of that time, nearly six hours a day, being obliged to work amid the smoke and soot of the same; and also a large portion of oil and grease is used in the mills.

What are the effects of the present system of labour?—From my earliest recollections, I have found the effects to be awfully detrimental to the well-being of the operative; I have observed frequently children carried to factories, unable to walk, and that entirely owing to excessive labour and confinement. The degradation of the workpeople baffles all description: frequently have two of my sisters been obliged to be assisted to the factory and home again, until by-and-by they could go no longer, being totally crippled in their legs. And in the next place, I remember some ten or twelve years ago working in one of the largest firms in Macclesfield, (Messrs. Baker and Pearson,) with about twenty-five men, where they were scarce one half fit for His Majesty's service. Those that are straight in their limbs are stunted in their growth; much inferior to their fathers in point of strength. 3dly, Through excessive labour and confinement there is often a total loss of appetite; a kind of

langour steals over the whole frame—enters to the very core—saps the foundation of the best constitution—and lays our strength prostrate in the dust. In the 4th place, by protracted labour there is an alarming increase of cripples in various parts of this town, which has come under my own observation and knowledge. . . .

Are all these cripples made in the silk factories?—Yes, they are, I believe. . . .

TESTIMONY OF WILLIAM HARTER

What effect would it have on your manufacture to reduce the hours of labour to ten?—It would instantly much reduce the value of my mill and machinery, and consequently of far prejudice my manufacture.

How so?—They are calculated to produce a certain quantity of work in a given time. Every machine is valuable in proportion to the quantity of work which it will turn off in a given time. It is impossible that the machinery could produce as much work in ten hours as in twelve. If the tending of the machines were a laborious occupation, the difference in the quantity of work might not always be in exact proportion to the difference of working time; but in my mill, and silk-mills in general, the work requires the least imaginable labour; therefore it is perfectly impossible that the machines could produce as much work in ten hours as in twelve. The produce would vary in about the same ratio as the working time.

Sybil, or the Two Nations: Mining Towns
Benjamin Disraeli

Nineteenth-century novels contain some of the most effective descriptions of industrial life. In addition to providing such description, Sybil, or the Two Nations (1845), written by Benjamin Disraeli (1804–1881), a novelist and politician who also served as prime minister of England (1867–1868, 1874–1880), illustrates the thinking of a group of reforming Tory aristocrats, sometimes referred to as Young England. They hoped to gain working-class support against their political competitors, the liberal Whigs. In the following selection from this novel, Disraeli describes Marney, a rural mining town.

CONSIDER: *The physical consequences of industrialization for the land and the town; the worst aspects of industrial labor, according to Disraeli; how this description compares with Engels' views in the following excerpt; who, if anyone, Disraeli would blame for all this.*

SOURCE: Benjamin Disraeli, *Sybil, or the Two Nations* (New York: M. Walter Dunne, 1904), pp. 198–200.

The last rays of the sun contending with clouds of smoke that drifted across the country, partially illumined a peculiar landscape. Far as the eye could reach, and the region was level, except where a range of limestone hills formed its distant limit, a wilderness of cottages, or tenements that were hardly entitled to a higher name, were scattered for many miles over the land; some detached, some connected in little rows, some clustering in groups, yet rarely forming continuous streets, but interspersed with blazing furnaces, heaps of burning coal, and piles of smouldering ironstone; while forges and engine chimneys roared and puffed in all directions, and indicated the frequent presence of the mouth of the mine, and the bank of the coal-pit. Notwithstanding the whole country might be compared to a vast rabbit warren, it was nevertheless intersected with canals, crossing each other at various levels; and though the subterranean operations were prosecuted with so much avidity that it was not uncommon to observe whole rows of houses awry, from the shifting and hollow nature of the land, still, intermingled with heaps of mineral refuse, or of metallic dross, patches of the surface might here and there be recognised, covered, as if in mockery, with grass and corn, looking very much like those gentlemen's sons that we used to read of in our youth, stolen by the chimneysweeps, and giving some intimations of their breeding beneath their grimy livery. But a tree or a shrub, such an existence was unknown in this dingy rather than dreary region.

It was the twilight hour; the hour at which in southern climes the peasant kneels before the sunset image of the blessed Hebrew maiden; when caravans halt in their long course over vast deserts, and the turbaned traveller, bending in the sand, pays his homage to the sacred stone and the sacred city; the hour, not less holy, that announces the cessation of English toil, and sends forth the miner and the collier to breathe the air of earth, and gaze on the light of heaven.

They come forth: the mine delivers its gang and the pit its bondsmen; the forge is silent and the engine is still. The plain is covered with the swarming multitude: bands of stalwart men, broad-chested and muscular, wet with toil, and black as the children of the tropics; troops of youth, alas! of both sexes, though neither their raiment nor their language indicates the difference; all are clad in male attire; and oaths that men might shudder at issue from lips born to breathe words of sweetness. Yet these are to be, some are, the mothers of England! But can we wonder at the hideous coarseness of their language, when we remember the savage rudeness of their lives? Naked to the waist, an iron chain fastened to a belt of leather runs between their legs clad in canvas trousers, while on hands and feet an English girl, for twelve, sometimes for sixteen hours a day, hauls and hurries tubs of coals up subterranean roads, dark, precipitous, and plashy; circumstances that seem to have

escaped the notice of the Society for the Abolition of Negro Slavery. Those worthy gentlemen, too, appear to have been singularly unconscious of the sufferings of the little trappers, which was remarkable, as many of them were in their own employ.

See, too, these emerge from the bowels of the earth! Infants of four and five years of age, many of them girls, pretty and still soft and timid; entrusted with the fulfilment of responsible duties, the very nature of which entails on them the necessity of being the earliest to enter the mine and the latest to leave it. Their labour indeed is not severe, for that would be impossible, but it is passed in darkness and in solitude. They endure that punishment which philosophical philanthropy has invented for the direst criminals, and which those criminals deem more terrible than the death for which it is substituted. Hour after hour elapses, and all that reminds the infant trappers of the world they have quitted, and that which they have joined, is the passage of the coal-waggons for which they open the air-doors of the galleries, and on keeping which doors constantly closed, except at this moment of passage, the safety of the mine and the lives of the persons employed in it entirely depend.

The Condition of the Working Class in England

Friedrich Engels

To many contemporaries, child labor in factories and mines under harsh conditions was the most shocking change in working conditions brought on by industrialization. However, several investigators documented a whole range of problems facing England's industrial working class. One of the most famous of these investigators was Friedrich Engels (1820–1895), the son of a German textile manufacturer. Engels moved to England in the 1840s, where in addition to learning about business he traveled through cities visiting working-class areas and interviewing people. He would soon become a collaborator with his friend, Karl Marx, and one of the founders of modern socialism. The following excerpt is from the book that arose from his studies, The Condition of the Working Class in England, first published in 1845. Here Engels focuses on worker's living environment in England's industrial cities.

CONSIDER: *What Engels considers the worst health conditions facing the poor; Engels' analysis of how the environment affects the poor mentally as well as physically; how this description adds to the testimony before the commission on child labor (in a previous excerpt).*

SOURCE: Friedrich Engels, *The Condition of the Working Class in England,* trans. and ed. by W. O. Henderson and W. H. Chaloner. (Stanford, CA: Stanford University Press, 1968), pp. 110–111.

The way in which the vast mass of the poor are treated by modern society is truly scandalous. They are herded into great cities where they breathe a fouler air than in the countryside which they have left. They are housed in the worst ventilated districts of the towns; they are deprived of all means of keeping clean. They are deprived of water because this is only brought to their houses if someone is prepared to defray the cost of laying the pipes. River water is so dirty as to be useless for cleansing purposes. The poor are forced to throw into the streets all their sweepings, garbage, dirty water, and frequently even disgusting filth and excrement. The poor are deprived of all proper means of refuse disposal and so they are forced to pollute the very districts they inhabit. And this is by no means all. There is no end to the sufferings which are heaped on the heads of the poor. It is notorious that general overcrowding is a characteristic feature of the great towns, but in the working-class quarters people are packed together in an exceptionally small area. Not satisfied with permitting the pollution of the air in the streets, society crams as many as a dozen workers into a single room, so that at night the air becomes so foul that they are nearly suffocated. The workers have to live in damp dwellings. When they live in cellars the water seeps through the floor and when they live in attics the rain comes through the roof. The workers' houses are so badly built that the foul air cannot escape from them. The workers have to wear poor and ragged garments and they have to eat food which is bad, indigestible and adulterated. Their mental state is threatened by being subjected alternately to extremes of hope and fear. They are goaded like wild beasts and never have a chance of enjoying a quiet life. They are deprived of all pleasures except sexual indulgence and intoxicating liquors. Every day they have to work until they are physically and mentally exhausted. This forces them to excessive indulgence in the only two pleasures remaining to them. If the workers manage to survive this sort of treatment it is only to fall victims to starvation when a slump occurs and they are deprived of the little that they once had.

How is it possible that the poorer classes can remain healthy and have a reasonable expectation of life under such conditions? What can one expect but that they should suffer from continual outbreaks of epidemics and an excessively low expectation of life? The physical condition of the workers shows a progressive deterioration.

Self-Help: Middle-Class Attitudes

Samuel Smiles

Middle-class liberals were not totally unaware of the consequences of industrialization for society. Doctrines were developed that reflected and appealed to their attitudes. Such doctrines served to justify the position of the middle class, to support policies it usually favored, and to rationalize the poor state of the working class. Many of these doctrines appeared in Self-Help, *the popular book by Samuel Smiles, a physician, editor, secretary of two railroads, and author. First published in 1859,* Self-Help *became a best-seller in England and was translated into many languages. The following excerpt is a good example of the individualism and moral tone that appear throughout the book.*

CONSIDER: *How Smiles justifies his assertion that self-help is the only answer to problems; how Smiles would analyze the situation of the working class and how he would react to the testimony presented to the parliamentary commission on child labor.*

"Heaven helps those who help themselves" is a well tried maxim, embodying in a small compass the results of vast human experience. The spirit of self-help is the root of all genuine growth in the individual; and, exhibited in the lives of many, it constitutes the true source of national vigor and strength. Help from without is often enfeebling in its effects, but help from within invariably invigorates. Whatever is done *for* men or classes, to a certain extent takes away the stimulus and necessity of doing for themselves; and where men are subjected to over-guidance and over-government, the inevitable tendency is to render them comparatively helpless.

Even the best institutions can give a man no active help. Perhaps the most they can do is, to leave him free to develop himself and improve his individual condition. But in all times men have been prone to believe that their happiness and well-being were to be secured by means of institutions rather than by their own conduct. Hence the value of legislation as an agent in human advancement has usually been much overestimated. To constitute the millionth part of a Legislature, by voting for one or two men once in three or five years, however conscientiously this duty may be performed, can exercise but little active influence upon any man's life and character. Moreover, it is every day becoming more clearly understood, that the function of Government is negative and restrictive, rather than positive and active; being resolvable principally into protection—protection of life, liberty, and property. Laws, wisely administrated, will secure men in the enjoyment of the fruits of their labor, whether of mind or body, at a comparatively small personal sacrifice; but no laws, however stringent, can make the idle industrious, the shiftless provident, or the drunken sober. Such reforms can only be effected by means of individual action, economy, and self-denial; by better habits, rather than by greater rights. . . .

Indeed, all experience serves to prove that the worth and strength of a State depend far less upon the form of its institutions than upon the character of its men. For

SOURCE: Samuel Smiles, *Self-Help* (Chicago: Belford, Clarke, 1881), pp. 21–23, 48–49.

the nation is only an aggregate of individual conditions, and civilization itself is but a question of the personal improvement of the men, women, and children of whom society is composed.

National progress is the sum of individual industry, energy, and uprightness, as national decay is of individual idleness, selfishness, and vice. What we are accustomed to decry as great social evils, will for the most part be found to be but the outgrowth of man's own perverted life; and though we may endeavor to cut them down and extirpate them by means of Law, they will only spring up again with fresh luxuriance in some other form, unless the conditions of personal life and character are radically improved. If this view be correct, then it follows that the highest patriotism and philanthropy consist, not so much in altering laws and modifying institutions, as in helping and stimulating men to elevate and improve themselves by their own free and independent individual action.

One of the most strongly marked features of the English people is their spirit of industry, standing out prominent and distinct in their past history, and as strikingly characteristic of them now as at any former period. It is this spirit, displayed by the commons of England, which has laid the foundations and built up the industrial greatness of the empire. This vigorous growth of the nation has been mainly the result of the free energy of individuals, and it has been contingent upon the number of hands and minds from time to time actively employed within it, whether as cultivators of the soil, producers of articles of utility, contrivers of tools and machines, writers of books, or creators of works of art. And while this spirit of active industry has been the vital principle of the nation, it has also been its saving and remedial one, counteracting from time to time the effects of errors in our laws and imperfections in our constitution.

The career of industry which the nation has pursued, has also proved its best education. As steady application to work is the healthiest training for every individual, so is it the best discipline of a state. Honorable industry travels the same road with duty; and Providence has closely linked both with happiness. The gods, says the poet, have placed labor and toil on the way leading to the Elysian fields. Certain it is that no bread eaten by man is so sweet as that earned by his own labor, whether bodily or mental. By labor the earth has been subdued, and man redeemed from barbarism; nor has a single step in civilization been made without it. Labor is not only a necessity and a duty, but a blessing: only the idler feels it to be a curse. The duty of work is written on the thews and muscles of the limbs, the mechanism of the hand, the nerves and lobes of the brain—the sum of whose healthy action is satisfaction and enjoyment. In the school of labor is taught the best practical wisdom; nor is a life of manual employment, as we shall hereafter find, incompatible with high mental culture.

Father Goriot: Money and the Middle Class

Honoré de Balzac

With industrialization the middle class rose in status and wealth. Increasingly, money became a common denominator in society, and the middle class was in a position to benefit from this. But the emphasis on money had its painful side even for the relatively wealthy. Few have focused on this more profoundly and broadly than the French novelist Honoré de Balzac, who himself struggled with financial problems for much of his life. The following is an excerpt from his Father Goriot *(1834), in which Goriot, an old bourgeois, bemoans the way his daughters are treating him now that he is no longer so rich.*

CONSIDER: *How Goriot sees money as both the cause for and the solution to his problems; the connections Balzac makes between money, social structure, and family life; how a worker might react to Goriot's problems.*

"Ah! if I were rich still, if I had kept my money, if I had not given all to them, they would be with me now; they would fawn on me and cover my cheeks with their kisses! I should be living in a great mansion; I should have grand apartments and servants and a fire in my room; and *they* would be about me all in tears, and their husbands and their children. I should have had all that; now—I have nothing. Money brings everything to you; even your daughters. My money. Oh! where is my money? If I had plenty of money to leave behind me, they would nurse me and tend me; I should hear their voices; I should see their faces. Ah, God! who knows? They both of them have hearts of stone. I love them too much; it was not likely that they should love me. A father ought always to be rich; he ought to keep his children well in hand, like unruly horses. I have gone down on my knees to them. Wretches! this is the crowning act that brings the last ten years to a proper close. If you but knew how much they made of me just after they were married. (Oh! this is cruel torture!) I had just given them each eight hundred thousand francs; they were bound to be civil to me after that, and their husbands too were civil. I used to go to their houses: it was, 'My kind father' here, 'My dear father' there. There was always a place for me at their tables. I used to dine with their husbands now and then, and they were very respectful to me. I was still worth something, they thought. How should they know? I had not said anything about my affairs. It is worth while to be civil to a man who has given his daughters eight hundred thousand francs apiece; and they showed me every attention then—but it was all for my money.

SOURCE: Honoré de Balzac, *Father Goriot* (New York: Century Co., 1904), pp. 264–265.

Grand people are not great. I found that out by experience! I went to the theatre with them in their carriage; I might stay as long as I cared to stay at their evening parties. In fact, they acknowledged me their father; publicly they owned that they were my daughters. But I always was a shrewd one, you see, and nothing was lost upon me. Everything went straight to the mark and pierced my heart. I saw quite well that it was all sham and pretence, but there is no help for such things as these. I felt less at my ease at their dinner-table than I did downstairs here. I had nothing to say for myself. So these grand folks would ask in my son-in-law's ear, 'Who may that gentleman be?'—'The father-in-law with the dollars; he is very rich.'—'The devil, he is!' they would say, and look again at me with the respect due to my money."

Woman in Her Social and Domestic Character

Elizabeth Poole Sandford

Industrialization also had its effects on middle-class women. As the wealth and position of these women rose in a changing economic environment, previous models of behavior no longer applied. A variety of books and manuals appeared to counsel middle-class women on their proper role and behavior. The following is an excerpt from one of these, Woman in Her Social and Domestic Character *(1842), written by Mrs. John Sandford.*

CONSIDER: *Woman's ideal function in relation to her husband, according to this document; by implication, the role of the middle-class man in relation to his wife; possible explanations for this view of women.*

The changes wrought by Time are many. It influences the opinions of men as familiarity does their feelings; it has a tendency to do away with superstition, and to reduce every thing to its real worth.

It is thus that the sentiment for woman has undergone a change. The romantic passion which once almost deified her is on the decline; and it is by intrinsic qualities that she must now inspire respect. She is no longer the queen of song and the star of chivalry. But if there is less of enthusiasm entertained for her, the sentiment is more rational, and, perhaps, equally sincere; for it is in relation to happiness that she is chiefly appreciated.

And in this respect it is, we must confess, that she is most useful and most important. Domestic life is the chief source of her influence; and the greatest debt society

can owe to her is domestic comfort: for happiness is almost an element of virtue; and nothing conduces more to improve the character of men than domestic peace. A woman may make a man's home delightful, and may thus increase his motives for virtuous exertion. She may refine and tranquillize his mind,—may turn away his anger or allay his grief. Her smile may be the happy influence to gladden his heart, and to disperse the cloud that gathers on his brow. And in proportion to her endeavors to make those around her happy, she will be esteemed and loved. She will secure by her excellence that interest and regard which she might formerly claim as the privilege of her sex, and will really merit the deference which was then conceded to her as a matter of course. . . .

Perhaps one of the first secrets of her influence is adaptation to the tastes, and sympathy in the feelings, of those around her. This holds true in lesser as well as in graver points. It is in the former, indeed, that the absence of interest in a companion is frequently most disappointing. Where want of congeniality impairs domestic comfort, the fault is generally chargeable on the female side. It is for woman, not for man, to make the sacrifice, especially in indifferent matters. She must, in a certain degree, be plastic herself if she would mould others. . . .

To be useful, a woman must have feeling. It is this which suggests the thousand nameless amenities which fix her empire in the heart, and render her so agreeable, and almost so necessary, that she imperceptibly rises in the domestic circle, and becomes at once its cement and its charm.

⤙

Nothing is so likely to conciliate the affections of the other sex as a feeling that woman looks to them for support and guidance. In proportion as men are themselves superior, they are accessible to this appeal. On the contrary, they never feel interested in one who seems disposed rather to offer than to ask assistance. There is, indeed, something unfeminine in independence. It is contrary to nature, and therefore it offends. We do not like to see a woman affecting tremors, but still less do we like to see her acting the amazon. A really sensible woman feels her dependence. She does what she can; but she is conscious of inferiority, and therefore grateful for support. She knows that she is the weaker vessel, and that as such she should receive honor. In this view, her weakness is an attraction, not a blemish.

In every thing, therefore, that women attempt, they should show their consciousness of dependence. If they are learners, let them evince a teachable spirit; if they give an opinion, let them do it in an unassuming manner. There is something so unpleasant in female self-sufficiency that it not unfrequently deters instead of persuading, and prevents the adoption of advice which the judgment even approves.

SOURCE: Mrs. John Sandford (Elizabeth Poole Sandford), *Woman in Her Social and Domestic Character* (Boston: Otis, Broaders and Co., 1842), pp. 5–7, 15–16.

Women and the Working Class

Flora Tristan

As industrialization spread, working-class organizations developed. Opposed by governments and by the middle classes, these organizations faced great difficulties in creating a following and maintaining their existence. For the most part the new labor unions paid little attention to women and were dominated by men. However, there were women like Flora Tristan (1803–1844) who recognized the connections between the emancipation of women and forming working-class unions. In The Workers' Union (1844), Tristan made the following appeal to French workers.

CONSIDER: *The ways this might appeal to workers and particularly to working-class women; how this differs from the attitude of Elizabeth Poole Sandford or Samuel Smiles.*

(1) To constitute the working class by setting up a compact, solid, and indissoluble union.

(2) The workers' union to choose and pay a defender who shall represent the working class before the nation [workers were without the voting franchise because of the 200-franc tax requirement], so as to establish universal acceptance of this class' right to exist [as an organization].

(3) To proclaim the legitimacy of hands (*bras*) as property, 25 million French workers having no property other than their hands.

(4) To secure the recognition of every man and woman's right to work.

(5) To secure the recognition of every man and woman's right to moral, intellectual, and vocational training.

(6) To examine the possibilities of organizing the labor force in present social conditions.

(7) To construct workers' union buildings in every department of France which shall provide intellectual and vocational training for working-class children and admit working men and women who have been disabled on the job or are sick or old.

(8) To proclaim the urgent necessity of giving working-class women moral, intellectual, and vocational training so that they may improve the morals of the men.

(9) To proclaim the fact that juridical equality between men and women is the only means of achieving the unity of humanity.

SOURCE: Flora Tristan, *L'Union Ouvriére*, 2nd ed. (Paris, 1844), p. 108, in Julia O'Faolain and Lauro Martines, eds., *Not in God's Image*. Copyright © 1973 by Julia O'Faolain and Lauro Martines. Reprinted by permission of Harper & Row, Publishers, Inc.

 # Visual Sources

Gare Saint Lazare

Claude Monet

From a visual standpoint, industrial civilization was strikingly different from its predecessor. The 1877 painting (figure 11.1) of a railroad station in the heart of nineteenth-century Paris by the French Impressionist Claude Monet epitomizes the new industrial civilization. Steam, powerful engines, rapid transportation, and structures of iron and glass, all in an expanding urban environment, contrast sharply with the typical rural or urban images of previous eras.

CONSIDER: *The associations that a nineteenth-century viewer might have upon viewing this painting.*

FIGURE 11.1 (© Fogg Art Museum, Harvard University Art Museums, USA, Bequest from the Collection of Maurice Wertheim, Class of 1906/Bridgeman Art Library)

FIGURE 11.2 (© National Trust /Art Resource, NY)

Iron and Coal

William Bell Scott

In the caption to his 1860 painting of industrial activity in Tyneside, England (figure 11.2), British artist William Bell Scott (1811–1891) proudly proclaims: "In the Nineteenth Century the Northumbrians show the World what can be done with Iron and Coal." He may have painted the picture in response to a plea in a publication complaining that in most paintings "we miss . . . the poetry of the things about us; our railways, factories, mines, roaring cities, steam vessels, and the endless novelties and wonders produced everyday." Certainly this mid-nineteenth century painting celebrates these industrial "things." The foreground setting is an engineering workshop. In the center, three muscular workers hammer out molten iron. On the right is a drawing of a steam engine built by Robert Stephenson and Co., and indeed an example of that steam engine is crossing Stephenson's High Level Bridge in the background to the right. In the left foreground, a girl sits on an Armstrong gun with her father's lunch and an arithmetic book in her lap. In the shop are other industrial objects made of iron: an anchor, a marine air pump, and a heavy chain with a pulley. In back of the three workers a boy who works in the mines stands with a Davy safety lamp and looks down on the docks below. On the river a coal barge passes.

CONSIDER: *What image of industrial activity this painting presents to the viewer; what other images of industrial activity might an artist present.*

Illustration from *Life and Adventures of Michael Armstrong*

The following illustration (figure 11.3) is from a novel, Life and Adventures of Michael Armstrong (1840), by the well-known British author, Mrs. Frances Trollope. The illustration depicts several of the main elements of the Industrial Revolution in England. It shows the inside of a textile factory—a factory in the most advanced of the new industries. Thanks to mechanization and artificial power, a few workers can now do the work of many. The workers—men, women, and children—are obviously poor. In the background stands the stern middle-class owner talking with others of his class while in the foreground a child worker embraces his middle-class counterpart for some kindness he has displayed. The scene is reflective of the typical middle-class view of the poor and poverty—as problems of morals, to be treated with pity and philanthropic concern but not yet requiring substantial social or economic change.

CONSIDER: *The ways in which this illustration reflects aspects of industrialization touched on by other documents in this chapter; the similarities and differences between this illustration and Figure 18.2 in Chapter 18.*

Industrialization and Demographic Change

A comparison of maps 11.1 and 11.2, which show the population density of England in 1801 and 1851, respectively, reveals the relatively rapid increase in population and urbanization in certain areas of England during this period. The third map (map 11.3) shows where industry (mainly textiles, metallurgy, and mining) was concentrated in 1851. A comparison of all three maps reveals the connections among shifting population density, urbanization, and industrialization during this period of early, rapid modernization of England's economy.

CONSIDER: *What some of the geopolitical consequences of these connections between demographic and economic changes might be; what some of the social consequences of these same connections might be.*

FIGURE 11.3   (© Bettmann/Corbis)

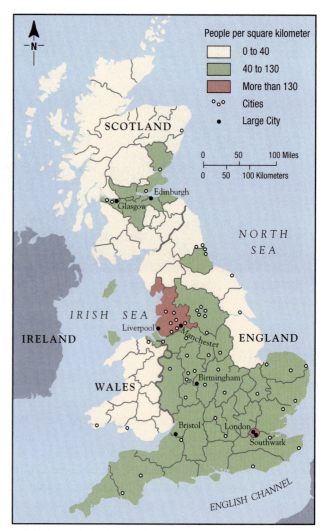

MAP 11.1   Population Density: England, 1801

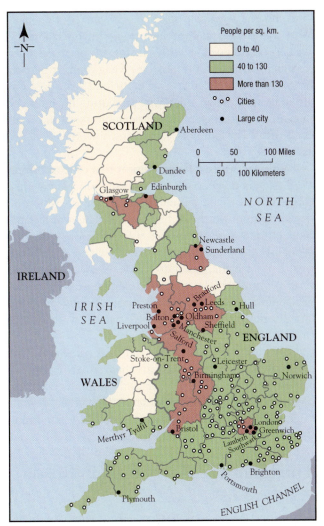

MAP 11.2   **Population Density: England, 1851**

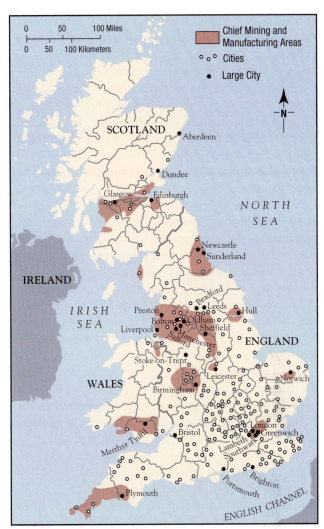

MAP 11.3   **Concentration of Industry in England, 1851**

Secondary Sources

The Making of Economic Society: England, the First to Industrialize

Robert L. Heilbroner

Although it is clear that industrialization occurred first in England, it is not apparent why this should be so. During the eighteenth century France was prosperous and economically advanced. Other countries such as Belgium and the Netherlands possessed certain economic advantages over England and might have industrialized earlier but did not. In the following selection Robert Heilbroner, an economist and economic historian, addresses the question of why England was first and points out the differences between England and most other European nations in the eighteenth century.

CONSIDER: *Why Heilbroner stresses the role of the "New Men" over the other factors he lists; any disadvantages England had to overcome; whether it was simply the circumstances that gave rise to the "New Men" or whether it was the "New Men" who took advantage of the circumstances when most men in most other nations would not have.*

Why did the Industrial Revolution originally take place in England and not on the continent? To answer the question we must look at the background factors which distinguished England from most other European nations in the eighteenth century.

SOURCE: Robert L. Heilbroner, *The Making of Economic Society.* Reprinted by permission of Prentice-Hall, Inc. (Englewood Cliffs, NJ, 1980), pp. 76–77, 80–81.

The first of these factors was simply that England was relatively wealthy. In fact, a century of successful exploration, slave-trading, piracy, war, and commerce had made her the richest nation in the world. Even more important, her riches had accrued not merely to a few nobles, but to a large upper-middle stratum of commercial bourgeoisie. England was thus one of the first nations to develop, albeit on a small scale, a prime requisite of an industrial economy: a "mass" consumer market. As a result, a rising pressure of demand inspired a search for new techniques.

Second, England was the scene of the most successful and thoroughgoing transformation of feudal society into commercial society. A succession of strong kings had effectively broken the power of the local nobility and had made England into a single unified state. As part of this process, we also find in England the strongest encouragement to the rising mercantile classes. Then too, as we have seen, the enclosure movement, which gained in tempo in the seventeenth and eighteenth centuries, expelled an army of laborers to man her new industrial establishments.

Third, England was the locus of a unique enthusiasm for science and engineering. The famous Royal Academy, of which Newton was an early president, was founded in 1660 and was the immediate source of much intellectual excitement. Indeed, a popular interest in gadgets, machines, and devices of all sorts soon became a mild national obsession: *Gentlemen's Magazine*, a kind of *New Yorker* of the period, announced in 1729 that it would henceforth keep its readers "abreast of every invention"—a task which the mounting flow of inventions soon rendered quite impossible. No less important was an enthusiasm of the British landed aristocracy for scientific farming: English landlords displayed an interest in matters of crop rotation and fertilizer which their French counterparts would have found quite beneath their dignity.

Then there were a host of other background causes, some as fortuitous as the immense resources of coal and iron ore on which the British sat; others as purposeful as the development of a national patent system which deliberately sought to stimulate and protect the act of invention itself. In many ways, England was "ready" for an Industrial Revolution. But perhaps what finally translated the potentiality into an actuality was the emergence of a group of new men who seized upon the latent opportunities of history as a vehicle for their own rise to fame and fortune. . . .

Pleasant or unpleasant, the personal characteristics fade beside one overriding quality. These were all men interested in expansion, in growth, in investment for investment's sake. All of them were identified with technological progress, and none of them disdained the productive process. An employee of Maudslay's once remarked, "It was a pleasure to see him handle a tool of any kind, but he was *quite splendid* with an 18-inch file." Watt was tireless in experimenting with his machines; Wedgwood stomped about his factory on his wooden leg scawling, "This won't do for Jos. Wedgwood," wherever he saw evidence of careless work. Richard Arkwright was a bundle of ceaseless energy in promoting his interests, jouncing about England over execrable roads in a post chaise driven by four horses, pursuing his correspondence as he traveled.

"With us," wrote a French visitor to a calico works in 1788, "a man rich enough to set up and run a factory like this would not care to remain in a position which he would deem unworthy of his wealth." This was an attitude entirely foreign to the rising English industrial capitalist. His work was its own dignity and reward; the wealth it brought was quite aside. Boswell, on being shown Watt and Boulton's great engine works at Soho, declared that he never forgot Boulton's expression as the latter declared, "I sell here, sir, what all the world desires to have—Power."

The new men were first and last *entrepreneurs*—enterprisers. They brought with them a new energy, as restless as it proved to be inexhaustible. In an economic, if not a political, sense, they deserve the epithet "revolutionaries," for the change they ushered in was nothing short of total, sweeping, and irreversible.

The Industrial Revolution in Russia
Peter N. Stearns

Before 1850 the industrial revolution was confined to Britain and a few limited areas in the West. Between 1850 and 1870, the coal mines, iron foundries, textile factories, steam engines, and railroads that had made Britain an industrial giant spread broadly into Western and Central Europe and North America. However, outside of these areas, no industrial revolution occurred until after the 1870s. Many historians have suggested reasons for this disparity between these areas of the West and elsewhere. In the following selection, Peter Stearns suggests reasons Russia was slow to industrialize.

CONSIDER: *What opportunities were available for industrial development in Russia; why, nevertheless, Russia did not industrialize sooner.*

Russia began to receive an industrial outreach from the West within a few decades of the advent of the industrial revolution. British textile machinery was imported beginning in 1843. Ernst Knoop, a German immigrant to Britain who had clerked in a Manchester cotton factory, set himself up as export agent to the Russians. He also

SOURCE: Peter N. Stearns, *The Industrial Revolution in World History* (Boulder, CO: Westview Press, 1993), pp. 72–73.

sponsored British workers who installed the machinery in Russia and told any Russian entrepreneur brash enough to ask not simply for British models but for alterations or adaptations: "That is not your affair; in England they know better than you." Despite the snobbism, a number of Russian entrepreneurs set up small factories to produce cotton, aware that even in Russia's small urban market they could make a substantial profit by underselling traditional manufactured cloth. Other factories were established directly by Britons.

Europeans and Americans were particularly active in responding to calls by the tsar's government for assistance in establishing railway and steamship lines. The first steamship appeared in Russia in 1815, and by 1820 a regular service ran on the Volga River. The first public railroad, joining St. Petersburg to the imperial residence in the suburbs, opened in 1837. In 1851 the first major line connected St. Petersburg and Moscow, along a remarkably straight route desired by Tsar Nicholas I himself. American engineers were brought in, again by the government, to set up a railroad industry so that Russians could build their own locomotives and cars. . . .

But Russia did not then industrialize. Modern industrial operations did not sufficiently dent established economic practices. The nation remained overwhelmingly agricultural. High percentage increases in manufacturing proceeded from such a low base that they had little general impact. Several structural barriers impeded a genuine industrial revolution. Russia's cities had never boasted a manufacturing tradition; there were few artisans skilled even in preindustrial methods. Only by the 1860s and 1870s had cities grown enough for an artisan core to take shape—in printing, for example—and even then large numbers of foreigners (particularly Germans) had to be imported. Even more serious was the system of serfdom that kept most Russians bound to agricultural estates. While some free laborers could be found, most rural Russians could not legally leave their land, and their obligation to devote extensive work service to their lords' estates reduced their incentive even for agricultural production. Peter the Great had managed to adapt serfdom to a preindustrial metallurgical industry by allowing landlords to sell villages and the labor therein for expansion of ironworks. But this mongrel system was not suitable for change on a grander scale, which is precisely what the industrial revolution entailed.

Furthermore, the West's industrial revolution, while it provided tangible examples for Russia to imitate, also produced pressures to develop more traditional sectors in lieu of structural change. The West's growing cities and rising prosperity claimed rising levels of Russian timber, hemp, tallow, and, increasingly, grain. These were export goods that could be produced without new technology and without altering the existing labor system. Indeed,

many landlords boosted the work-service obligations of the serfs in order to generate more grain production for sale to the West. The obvious temptation was to lock in an older economy—to respond to new opportunity by incremental changes within the traditional system and to maintain serfdom and the rural preponderance rather than to risk fundamental internal transformation.

Early Industrial Society: Progress or Decline?

Peter Stearns and Herrick Chapman

One of the most persistent debates over the early stages of the Industrial Revolution is whether a higher standard of living resulted for factory workers. A number of "optimistic" historians, relying primarily on statistical evidence such as wage rates, prices, and mortality rates, have argued that even during the early period factory workers experienced a rising standard of living. A group of more "pessimistic" historians, emphasizing qualitative data such as descriptions of the psychological, social, and cultural impact of the factory on workers' lives, argues that the standard of living declined for these workers during the first half of the nineteenth century. In the following selection Peter Stearns and Herrick Chapman focus on this debate, concluding that, at least for many workers, material conditions were modestly better.

CONSIDER: *The aspects of this selection that optimistic historians would emphasize and how pessimistic historians might respond; whether increased wage rates are a meaningful measure without a consideration of the psychological and social costs of that extra money.*

The question of whether conditions deteriorated or were improved by early factory employment has been hotly debated, particularly in the case of the British industrial revolution. There is evidence on both sides. Many have tried to prove that early industry was evil; others have asserted its beneficence. Even during the Industrial Revolution itself the question was argued with much partisan feeling. The issue is not merely an academic one. In order to understand the workers themselves, it is vital to know whether they experienced a deterioration in conditions as they entered industry. That the workers were in misery from a modern point of view cannot be denied; that they were severely limited in their conditions is obvious; but whether they felt themselves to be miserable, judging by the standards they knew, is far from clear. . . .

SOURCE: Reprinted with the permission of Macmillan College Publishing Company *Society in Upheaval*, 3rd ed., by Peter Stearns and Herrick Chapman. Copyright © 1992 by Macmillan College Publishing Company, Inc.

Furthermore, in England and elsewhere, rural conditions had usually been declining before the Industrial Revolution began. This was, after all, the main impulse for peasants to accept factory jobs. Peasant standards of living were low anyway; preindustrial society was simply poor. And the people entering industry were often drawn from the lowest categories of the peasantry. These were the people who suffered most from expanding population and declining domestic industry. There was deterioration of material conditions in the early industrial period, but it occurred primarily in the countryside among the landless and the domestic producers and among the unskilled in the slums of cities like London. When they found factory employment, workers seldom could note a significant worsening of their situation: many factory workers actually gained some ground in standard of living.

The worst problem for factory workers, as for the poorer classes even in premodern times, was the instability of conditions. Sick workers were rarely paid and sometimes lost their jobs. With age workers' skill and strength declined, and so did their earnings. Old workers, lacking property to fall back on, suffered from falling wages and frequent unemployment. Machine break-downs caused days and even weeks of unemployment. Most important, recurrent industrial slumps plunged many workers into profound misery. Wages fell, sometimes by as much as 50 percent; up to a quarter of the labor force lost their jobs. Some returned to the countryside to seek work or to roam in bands to find food. Some survived on charity; the charity rolls of manufacturing cities often embraced over half the working class, though only meager support was offered. Some sold or pawned their possessions. All reduced expenses by eating potatoes instead of bread and ignoring rent payments. Old age, finally, could bring disaster. Working-class life was thus punctuated by a number of personal and general crises, creating a sense of insecurity that haunted workers even in better times.

In prosperous years the worst feature of the average worker's material standard of living was housing. Rural cottages had often been flimsy and small, befouled by animals, but city housing was sometimes worse. . . .

With poor housing and urban crowding, along with the pressures of factory work itself, many workers were in poor health. Rates of infant mortality were high, and many workers had a life expectancy at birth only half as high as that of their employers. . . .

Unquestionably factory wages were better than those of the countryside. Highly skilled male workers, many of them former artisans, were paid three to six times as much as ordinary laborers. For early mechanization did not eliminate the need for skill, though it reduced the percentage of skilled workers and changed the skills required. Hence the men who built and installed machines or puddled iron or ran the more complex spinning machines required years to learn their trade fully. But even lesser-skilled workers could command a money wage that was higher than what was available in the countryside or to the transient workers of the cities. There was little left over for purchases beyond food, housing, and clothing. A bit of tobacco or a small contribution to a mutual aid group were all that the ordinary worker could afford. However, wages tended to go up with time. They definitely rose in England after 1840. The main factory centers in France saw an increase in real wages in the 1830s and 1840s, and there was improvement in Germany in the 1840s and 1850s, in Russia in the 1890s.

So it is safe to conclude that material conditions, though bad, provided modest gains and some solace for many workers during the early industrial period as a whole. On the average, conditions were better than the new workers' traditions had led them to expect.

The Family and Industrialization in Western Europe
Michael Anderson

The tremendous growth of interest in social history over the past twenty years has stimulated scholars from other disciplines to address historical questions. A number of sociologists have applied methods from their own discipline to social aspects of nineteenth-century industrialization. In the following selection Michael Anderson, a sociologist from the University of Edinburgh, discusses the effects of industrialization on the working-class family.

CONSIDER: *The specific ways in which the process of industrialization affected working-class families; how Anderson's interpretation might support the "optimists" or the "pessimists" in their debate over the effects of the Industrial Revolution on the working class; how the effects on middle-class families might differ.*

In industrial areas, then, the close interdependence of parents and children which was so important in peasant societies gave way, and this was reflected in changes in family relationships. The early stages of industrialization, however, probably changed relationships between husbands and wives much less, though freedom from such close supervision and a more private domestic situation may have allowed rather more affection to develop between them than had been the case in preindustrial peasant families. Husband and wife were no

SOURCE: Michael Anderson, "The Family and Industrialization in Western Europe," *The Forum Series.* Reprinted by permission of Forum Press (St. Louis, MO, 1978), p. 14. Copyright © 1978 by Forum Press.

longer cooperating in the same productive task, but this had never been universal anyway. There was, however, a continued need and possibility for both husbands and wives to work as producers to keep the family above the subsistence line. In a few areas wives actually left the house to work in the factories. More usually, as women had always done, the wives of factory workers worked at home producing small items of clothing, processing some kind of food or drink, taking in the middle class's washing, or running a small shop or lodging house. The manifold needs of an industrial community were thus met in a way which contributed to working class family solidarity while allowing mothers to supervise and care (perhaps rather better than before) for small children during the lengthening period before they were able to enter the labor force themselves.

Initially, then, it was only in a few areas, especially those specializing in mining, machine-making, metal manufacturing, shipbuilding and sawmilling, that a change occurred in the economic status of women and with it in their family situation. In these areas there were not enough openings for female wage employment and, in consequence, many women were forced into the almost totally new situation of full-time housewife. However, as more and more traditional tasks were taken over by the application of factory production methods to clothing and food preparation, the home increasingly became confined to consumption. Only then did the distinction between male productive work outside the home and female consumption-oriented work inside the home become common among the working class.

Though the evidence is patchy, it seems that, at least in some areas, this had an effect on relationships between husbands and wives. Since the husband became the only income producer, the rest of the family became more dependent on him than he was on them. Whatever the husband did, the wife had little power to resist. While the family as a whole relied materially on the father, he needed them only to the extent that he could obtain from them emotional or other rewards which he could not obtain elsewhere or to the extent to which public opinion in the neighborhood was effective in controlling his behavior (And with the weakened community control of large industrial cities, neighborhood control was often weak.). Thus, in the working class, the idea that a woman's place was in the home and that her role was essentially an inferior domestic one is not of great antiquity. Rather it seems only to have developed as a response to a major shift in the power balance between husbands and wives which reflected the new employment situation of late-nineteenth- and early-twentieth-century industrial society.

❧ CHAPTER QUESTIONS

1. Do you feel that industrialization should be considered a great boon, a mixed blessing, or a disaster for nineteenth-century Europeans? Why?

2. In retrospect, what policies might governments have adopted to minimize the pains of industrialization? What factors acted against the adoption of such policies?

3. In a debate over how industrialization should be evaluated, what would the arguments of middle-class liberals be? Of industrial workers? Of women?

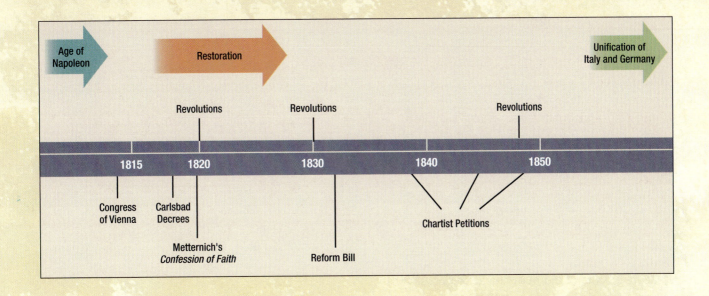

12 Reaction, Reform, Revolution, and Romanticism: 1815–1848

The European powers met at the Congress of Vienna (1814–1815) to decide how to proceed now that Napoleon had been defeated. Conservative sentiments, exemplified by the views of Prince Metternich of Austria, predominated at this congress. Although the final settlement was not punitive or humiliating to France, it did represent an effort by conservative leaders to reject changes instituted during the revolutionary and Napoleonic periods, to restore traditional groups and governments to power, and to resist liberalism and nationalism. As a result of this and other developments, the aristocracy regained some of its prominence, monarchs such as Louis XVIII (brother of Louis XVI) returned to power, and armies intervened (as in Spain and Italy) to crush threats to the status quo.

Nevertheless, movements for national liberation and liberal reform surfaced during the 1820s, 1830s, and 1840s.

In the 1820s and 1830s, Greece and Belgium gained independence and less successful nationalistic movements arose in Italy and Poland. Liberalism, encompassing demands for greater freedom, constitutional government, and political rights, was particularly strong in Western Europe. In England a series of legislative acts in the 1830s and 1840s clearly recognized liberal demands. In France a revolution in 1830 brought to power groups more open to liberal ideas.

A climax came in 1848, when revolutions erupted across Europe. Although each revolution was different, in general the middle and working classes demanded changes in the name of nationalism or liberalism. At first, established governments weakened or fell, but the revolutionaries found it difficult to remain unified once power was in their hands. Soon groups standing for authoritarian rule took advantage of this disunity and regained power.

The conservatism and liberalism that characterized so many of the political developments of this period were reflected in certain artistic and literary styles. Romanticism was the most important of these, reflecting, in different ways, both conservatism and liberalism. From its beginning in the late eighteenth century, it spread until it became the dominant cultural movement of the first half of the nineteenth century. Romanticism rejected the formalism of the previously dominant Classical style, refused to be limited by Enlightenment rationalism or the stark realism of everyday life, and emphasized emotion and freedom.

The sources in this chapter focus first on conservatism: What were some of the main characteristics of conservatism? What did it stand against? What policies fit with conservative attitudes? In what ways did the Congress of Vienna reflect the conservatism of the period? The next set of documents looks at liberalism and movements for reform: What did liberalism mean in the first half of the nineteenth century? What reforms did liberals demand? What was the nature of reform movements, as exemplified by Chartism in England? Third are the revolutions of 1848: In what ways did the revolutions of 1848 bring to a head some of the main trends of the period? Who might be considered the "winners" and "losers" in these revolutions? Finally sources on the nature of Romanticism, particularly as it is revealed in literature and art are reviewed: What were some of the ties between Romanticism and conservatism? How was Romanticism related to liberal and even revolutionary ideals? What emerges from these selections is a picture of Europeans trying to deal politically and culturally with the legacy of the French Revolution and the Enlightenment.

❧ For Classroom Discussion

What are the differences between nineteenth-century conservatism and liberalism? Use the source by Metternich, the excerpts from the Carlsbad Decrees and Bentham, and the analysis of Bramsted and Melhuish.

Primary Sources

Secret Memorandum to Tsar Alexander I, 1820: Conservative Principles

Prince Klemens von Metternich

The outstanding leader of the conservative tide that rose with the fall of Napoleon was Prince Klemens von Metternich (1773–1859). From his post as Austrian Minister of Foreign Affairs, Metternich hosted the Congress of Vienna and played a dominating role within Austria and among the conservative states of Europe between 1815 and 1848. Both in principle and in practice, he represented a conservatism that rejected the changes wrought by the French Revolution and stood against liberalism and nationalism. The following is an excerpt from a secret memorandum that Metternich sent to Tsar Alexander I of Russia in 1820, explaining his political principles. While not a sophisticated statement of political theory, it does reflect key elements of conservative attitudes and ideas.

CONSIDER: *What threats Metternich perceives; how Metternich connects "presumption" with the middle class; how this document reflects the experience of the revolutionary and Napoleonic periods; the kinds of policies that would logically flow from these attitudes.*

"L'Europe," a celebrated writer has recently said, "fait aujourd'hui pitié à l'homme d'esprit et horreur à l'homme vertueux."[1]

It would be difficult to comprise in a few words a more exact picture of the situation at the time we are writing these lines!

Kings have to calculate the chances of their very existence in the immediate future; passions are let loose, and league together to overthrow everything which society respects as the basis of its existence; religion, public morality, laws, customs, rights, and duties, all are attacked, confounded, overthrown, or called in question. The great mass of the people are tranquil spectators of these attacks and revolutions, and of the absolute want of all means of defense. A few are carried off by the torrent, but the wishes of the immense majority are to maintain a repose which exists no longer, and of which even the first elements seem to be lost. . . .

Having now thrown a rapid glance over the first causes of the present state of society, it is necessary to point out in a more particular manner the evil which threatens to deprive it, at one blow, of the real blessings, the fruits of genuine civilisation, and to disturb it in the midst of its enjoyments. This evil may be described in one word—presumption; the natural effect of the rapid

---

SOURCE: Prince Richard Metternich, ed., *Memoirs of Prince Metternich, 1815–1829*, vol. III, trans. Mrs. Alexander Napier (New York: Charles Scribner's Sons, 1881), pp. 454–455, 458–460, 468–469.

[1]Europe . . . is pitied by men of spirit and abhorred by men of virtue.

progression of the human mind towards the perfecting of so many things. This it is which at the present day leads so many individuals astray, for it has become an almost universal sentiment.

Religion, morality, legislation, economy, politics, administration, all have become common and accessible to everyone. Knowledge seems to come by inspiration; experience has no value for the presumptuous man; faith is nothing to him; he substitutes for it a pretended individual conviction, and to arrive at this conviction dispenses with all inquiry and with all study; for these means appear too trivial to a mind which believes itself strong enough to embrace at one glance all questions and all facts. Laws have no value for him, because he has not contributed to make them, and it would be beneath a man of his parts to recognise the limits traced by rude and ignorant generations. Power resides in himself; why should he submit himself to that which was only useful for the man deprived of light and knowledge? That which, according to him, was required in an age of weakness cannot be suitable in an age of reason and vigour amounting to universal perfection, which the German innovators designate by the idea, absurd in itself, of the Emancipation of the People! Morality itself he does not attack openly, for without it he could not be sure for a single instant of his own existence; but he interprets its essence after his own fashion, and allows every other person to do so likewise, provided that other person neither kills nor robs him.

In thus tracing the character of the presumptuous man, we believe we have traced that of the society of the day, composed of like elements, if the denomination of society is applicable to an order of things which only tends in principle towards individualising all the elements of which society is composed. Presumption makes every man the guide of his own belief, the arbiter of laws according to which he is pleased to govern himself, or to allow some one else to govern him and his neighbours; it makes him, in short, the sole judge of his own faith, his own actions, and the principles according to which he guides them. . . .

The Governments, having lost their balance, are frightened, intimidated, and thrown into confusion by the cries of the intermediary class of society, which, placed between the Kings and their subjects, breaks the sceptre of the monarch, and usurps the cry of the people—the class so often disowned by the people, and nevertheless too much listened to, caressed and feared by those who could with one word reduce it again to nothingness.

We see this intermediary class abandon itself with a blind fury and animosity which proves much more its own fears than any confidence in the success of its enterprises, to all the means which seem proper to assuage its thirst for power, applying itself to the task of per-

suading Kings that their rights are confined to sitting upon a throne, while those of the people are to govern, and to attack all that centuries have bequeathed as holy and worthy of man's respect—denying, in fact, the value of the past, and declaring themselves the masters of the future. We see this class take all sorts of disguises, uniting and subdividing as occasion offers, helping each other in the hour of danger, and the next day depriving each other of all their conquests. It takes possession of the press, and employs it to promote impiety, disobedience to the laws of religion and the State, and goes so far as to preach murder as a duty for those who desire what is good.

The Carlsbad Decrees, 1819: Conservative Repression

One way political leaders tried to assert conservatism against any perceived threats such as liberalism or nationalism was through international cooperation and action, a policy known as the Concert of Europe. Another way was through taking internal measures against the same threats, such as occurred in Germany in 1819 with the issuance of the Carlsbad Decrees. These decrees were pushed through the Diet of the German Confederation by Austria and Prussia, but particularly by Prince Metternich, in reaction to nationalist student movements against the principles of the Congress of Vienna. The following excerpts from those decrees concern the universities, the press, and all "revolutionary plots."

CONSIDER: *The purposes of these decrees and the means used to effect these purposes; whether these decrees are consistent with attitudes expressed by Metternich in the "confession of faith" he makes in his secret memorandum to Tsar Alexander I; the consequences of the effective enforcement of these decrees.*

PROVISIONAL DECREE RELATING TO THE UNIVERSITIES, UNANIMOUSLY ADOPTED SEPTEMBER 20, 1819

§2. The confederated governments mutually pledge themselves to remove from the universities or other public educational institutions all teachers who, by obvious deviation from their duty or by exceeding the limits of their functions, or by the abuse of their legitimate influence over the youthful minds, or by propagating harmful doctrines hostile to public order or subversive of existing

SOURCE: From James Harvey Robinson, ed., "The Reaction after 1815 and European Policy of Metternich," in *Translations and Reprints from the Original Sources of European History*, vol. I, no. 3, ed. Department of History of the University of Pennsylvania (Philadelphia: University of Pennsylvania Press, 1898), pp. 16–20.

governmental institutions, shall have unmistakably proved their unfitness for the important office intrusted to them. . . .

§3. Those laws which have for a long period been directed against secret and unauthorized societies in the universities, shall be strictly enforced. These laws apply especially to that association established some years since under the name Universal Students' Union (*Allgemeine Burschenschaft*), since the very conception of the society implies the utterly unallowable plan of permanent fellowship and constant communication between the various universities. The duty of especial watchfulness in this matter should be impressed upon the special agents of the government.

❦

PRESS LAWS FOR FIVE YEARS

§1. So long as this decree shall remain in force no publication which appears in the form of daily issues or as a serial not exceeding twenty sheets of printed matter shall go to press in any state of the Union without the previous knowledge and approval of the state officials.

❦

§6. . . . The Diet shall have the right, moreover, to suppress on its own authority, without being petitioned, such writings included in Section 1, in whatever German state they may appear, as in the opinion of a commission appointed by it, are inimical to the honor of the Union, the safety of individual states or the maintenance of peace and quiet in Germany. There shall be no appeal from such decisions and the governments involved are bound to see that they are put into execution.

❦

ESTABLISHMENT OF AN INVESTIGATING COMMITTEE AT MAINZ

ARTICLE I. Within a fortnight, reckoned from the passage of this decree, there shall convene, under the auspices of the Confederation, in the city and federal fortress of Mainz, an Extraordinary Commission of Investigation to consist of seven members including the chairman.

ARTICLE II. The object of the Commission shall be a joint investigation, as thorough and extensive as possible, of the facts relating to the origin and manifold ramifications of the revolutionary plots and demagogical associations directed against the existing Constitutional and internal peace both of the Union and of the individual states: of the existence of which plots more or less clear evidence is to be had already, or may be produced in the course of the investigation.

English Liberalism

Jeremy Bentham

The roots of liberalism are deep and varied, stretching back to the writings of John Locke in the seventeenth century and further. By the time liberalism started to flourish during the nineteenth century, it had a particularly strong English tradition. Perhaps the most influential of the early-nineteenth-century English liberals was Jeremy Bentham (1748–1832). He is best known as the author of the theory of utilitarianism and for advocating reform of many English institutions. The ideas and efforts of Bentham and his followers, who include James Mill and John Stuart Mill, formed one of the mainstreams of English liberalism and liberal reform in the nineteenth century. The first of the following two selections comes from Bentham's An Introduction to the Principles of Morals and Legislation *(1789) and focuses on the principle of utility. The second is from his* Manual of Political Economy *(1798) and indicates his views toward governmental economic policy.*

CONSIDER: *What exactly Bentham means by the principle of utility; what, according to the principle of utility, the proper role of government in general is; his explanation for the proper role of the government in economic affairs.*

I. Nature has placed mankind under the governance of two sovereign masters, *pain* and *pleasure*. It is for them alone to point out what we ought to do, as well as to determine what we shall do. On the one hand the standard of right and wrong, on the other chains of causes and effects, are fastened to their throne. They govern us in all we do, in all we say, in all we think: every effort we can make to throw off our subjection, will serve to demonstrate and confirm it. In words a man may pretend to abjure their empire: but in reality he will remain subject to it all the while. The *principle of utility* recognizes this subjection, and assumes it for the foundation of that system, the object of which is to rear the fabric of felicity by the hands of reason and of law. Systems which attempt to question it, deal in sounds instead of sense, in caprice instead of reason, in darkness instead of light.

But enough of metaphor and declamation: it is not by such means that moral science is to be improved.

II. The principle of utility is the foundation of the present work: it will be proper therefore at the outset to give an explicit and determinate account of what is meant by it. By the principle of utility is meant that principle which approves or disapproves of every action whatsoever, according to the tendency which it appears

SOURCES: Jeremy Bentham, *An Introduction to the Principles of Morals and Legislation* (Oxford: Clarendon Press, 1876), pp. 1–3; John Bowring, ed., *Bentham's Works,* vol. III (Edinburgh: William Tait, 1843), pp. 33–35.

to have to augment or diminish the happiness of the party whose interest is in question: or, what is the same thing in other words, to promote or to oppose that happiness. I say of every action whatsoever; and therefore not only of every action of a private individual, but of every measure of government.

III. By utility is meant that property in any object, whereby it tends to produce benefit, advantage, pleasure, good, or happiness (all this in the present case comes to the same thing) or (what comes again to the same thing) to prevent the happening of mischief, pain, evil, or unhappiness to the party whose interest is considered: if that party be the community in general, then the happiness of the community: if a particular individual, then the happiness of that individual.

IV. The interest of the community is one of the most general expressions that can occur in the phraseology of morals: no wonder that the meaning of it is often lost. When it has a meaning, it is this. The community is a fictitious *body*, composed of the individual persons who are considered as constituting as it were its *members*. The interest of the community then is, what?—the sum of the interests of the several members who compose it.

V. It is in vain to talk of the interest of the community, without understanding what is the interest of the individual. A thing is said to promote the interest, or to be *for* the interest, of an individual, when it tends to add to the sum total of his pleasures: or, what comes to the same thing, to diminish the sum total of his pains.

VI. An action then may be said to be conformable to the principle of utility, or, for shortness sake, to utility (meaning with respect to the community at large) when the tendency it has to augment the happiness of the community is greater than any it has to diminish it.

VII. A measure of government (which is but a particular kind of action, performed by a particular person or persons) may be said to be conformable to or dictated by the principle of utility, when in like manner the tendency which it has to augment the happiness of the community is greater than any which it has to diminish it. . . .

✒

The practical questions, therefore, are how far the end in view is best promoted by individuals acting for themselves? and in what cases these ends may be promoted by the hands of government?

With the view of causing an increase to take place in the mass of national wealth, or with a view to increase of the means either of subsistence or enjoyment, without some special reason, the general rule is, that nothing ought to be done or attempted by government. The motto, or watchword of government, on these occasions, ought to be—*Be quiet.*

For this quietism there are two main reasons:

1. Generally speaking, any interference for this purpose on the part of government is needless. The wealth of the whole community is composed of the wealth of the several individuals belonging to it taken together. But to increase his particular portion is, generally speaking, among the constant objects of each individual's exertions and care. Generally speaking, there is no one who knows what is for your interest so well as yourself—no one who is disposed with so much ardour and constancy to pursue it.

2. Generally speaking, it is moreover likely to be pernicious, viz. by being unconducive, or even obstructive, with reference to the attainment of the end in view. Each individual bestowing more time and attention upon the means of preserving and increasing his portion of wealth, than is or can be bestowed by government, is likely to take a more effectual course than what, in his instance and on his behalf, would be taken by government.

It is, moreover, universally and constantly pernicious in another way, by the restraint or constraint imposed on the free agency of the individual. . . .

. . . With few exceptions, and those not very considerable ones, the attainment of the maximum of enjoyment will be most effectually secured by leaving each individual to pursue his own maximum of enjoyment, in proportion as he is in possession of the means. Inclination in this respect will not be wanting on the part of any one. Power, the species of power applicable to this case—viz. wealth, pecuniary power—could not be given by the hand of government to one, without being taken from another; so that by such interference there would not be any gain of power upon the whole.

The gain to be produced in this article by the interposition of government, respects principally the head of knowledge. There are cases in which, for the benefit of the public at large, it may be in the power of government to cause this or that portion of knowledge to be produced and diffused, which, without the demand for it produced by government, would either not have been produced, or would not have been diffused.

We have seen above the grounds on which the general rule in this behalf—*Be quiet*—rests. Whatever measures, therefore, cannot be justified as exceptions to that rule, may be considered as *non agenda* on the part of government. The art, therefore, is reduced within a small compass: *security* and *freedom* are all that industry requires. The request which agriculture, manufactures and commerce present to governments, is modest and reasonable as that which Diogenes made to Alexander: "*Stand out of my sunshine.*" We have no need of favour—we require only a secure and open path.

Liberalism: Progress and Optimism
The Economist, 1851

Liberals usually believed in progress and were optimistic about their own times and the future. By mid-century, liberalism was most widespread in England, Europe's dominant economic power. English liberals living in the mid-nineteenth century were therefore particularly confident and proud, as indicated by the following excerpts from two 1851 articles published in The Economist. *This journal appealed to England's prosperous middle class.*

CONSIDER: *What liberals considered the great improvements of the first half of the nineteenth century; who benefited most from these changes; how conservatives or socialists might respond.*

Economists are supposed to be, by nature and occupation, cold, arithmetical, and unenthusiastic. We shall not, we hope, do discredit to this chapter when we say that we consider it a happiness and a privilege to have had our lot cast in the first fifty years of this century. . . .

It has witnessed a leap forward in all the elements of material well-being such as neither scientific vision nor poetic fancy ever pictured. It is not too much to say that, in wealth, in the arts of life, in the discoveries of science and their application to the comfort, the health, the safety, and the capabilities of man, in public and private morality, in the diffusion if not in the advancement of knowledge, in the sense of social charity and justice, in religious freedom, and in political wisdom,—the period of the last fifty years has carried us forward faster and further than any other half-century in modern times . . . in many of the particulars we have enumerated, it has witnessed a more rapid and astonishing progress than *all* the centuries which have preceded it. In several vital points the difference between the 18th and the 19th century, is greater than between the first and the 18th, as far as civilised Europe is concerned.

❧

When we refer to a few only of the extraordinary improvements of the half century just elapsed—such as the 35 years' peace, so far as morals are concerned; such as the philanthropic and just conviction that the welfare of the multitude, not of one or two classes, is the proper object of social solicitude; the humane direction which the mind has received towards the abolition of slavery; the amelioration of all penal systems, and the doubts that have been generated of their utility; the advances in religious toleration, and in forbearing one with another:

and such as the application of steam to locomotives on water and land, and the consequent vast extension of communication all over the world, so far as physics are concerned;—such as the invention and general introduction of gas; the use of railroads and electric telegraphs; the extended application of machinery to all the arts of life, almost putting an end to very severe injurious bodily toil, except in agriculture, in which, though the labourers are speedily doubled up with rheumatism, and become, from poverty and excessive labour in all kinds of weather, prematurely old, great improvements have nevertheless been made:—when we refer to a few events of this kind, we become convinced that the half century just elapsed is more full of wonders than any other on record.

The First Chartist Petition: Demands for Change in England

Movements for reform occurred throughout Europe between 1815 and 1848 despite the efforts of conservatives to quash them. Eventually almost all countries in Europe experienced the revolutions conservatives feared so much. One exception was England, but even there political movements threatened to turn into violent revolts against the failure of the government to change. The most important of these was the Chartist movement, made up primarily of members of the working class who wanted reforms for themselves. The following is an excerpt from the first charter presented to the House of Commons in 1838. Subsequent charters were presented in 1842 and 1848. In each case the potential existed for a mass movement to turn into a violent revolt, and in each case Parliament rejected the Chartist demands. Only later in the century were most of these demands met.

CONSIDER: *The nature of the Chartists' demands; by what means the Chartists hoped to achieve their ends; how Metternich might analyze these demands.*

Required, as we are universally, to support and obey the laws, nature and reason entitle us to demand that in the making of the laws the universal voice shall be implicitly listened to. We perform the duties of freemen; we must have the privileges of freemen. Therefore, we demand universal suffrage. The suffrage, to be exempt from the corruption of the wealthy and the violence of the powerful, must be secret. The assertion of our right necessarily involves the power of our uncontrolled exercise. We ask for the reality of a good, not for its

SOURCE: *The Economist* (London), vol. IX, January 4, 1851, p. 5; January 18, 1851, p. 57.

SOURCE: From R. G. Gammage, *History of the Chartist Movement,* 2nd ed. (Newcastle-on-Tyne, England: Browne and Browne, 1894), pp. 88–90.

semblance, therefore we demand the ballot. The connection between the representatives and the people, to be beneficial, must be intimate. The legislative and constituent powers, for correction and for instruction, ought to be brought into frequent contact. Errors which are comparatively light, when susceptible of a speedy popular remedy, may produce the most disastrous effects when permitted to grow inveterate through years of compulsory endurance. To public safety, as well as public confidence, frequent elections are essential. Therefore, we demand annual parliaments. With power to choose, and freedom in choosing, the range of our choice must be unrestricted. We are compelled, by the existing laws, to take for our representatives men who are incapable of appreciating our difficulties, or have little sympathy with them; merchants who have retired from trade and no longer feel its harrassings; proprietors of land who are alike ignorant of its evils and its cure; lawyers by whom the notoriety of the senate is courted only as a means of obtaining notice in the courts. The labours of a representative who is sedulous in the discharge of his duty are numerous and burdensome. It is neither just, nor reasonable, nor safe, that they should continue to be gratuitously rendered. We demand that in the future election of members of your honourable house, the approbation of the constituency shall be the sole qualification, and that to every representative so chosen, shall be assigned out of the public taxes, a fair and adequate remunerative for the time which he is called upon to devote to the public service. The management of his mighty kingdom has hitherto been a subject for contending factions to try their selfish experiments upon. We have felt the consequences in our sorrowful experience. Short glimmerings of uncertain enjoyment, swallowed up by long and dark seasons of suffering. If the self-government of the people should not remove their distresses, it will, at least, remove their repinings. Universal suffrage will, and it alone can, bring true and lasting peace to the nation; we firmly believe that it will also bring prosperity. May it therefore please your honourable house, to take this our petition into your most serious consideration, and to use your utmost endeavours, by all constitutional means, to have a law passed, granting to every male of lawful age, sane mind, and unconvicted of crime, the right of voting for members of parliament, and directing all future elections of members of parliament to be in the way of secret ballot, and ordaining that the duration of parliament, so chosen, shall in no case exceed one year, and abolishing all property qualifications in the members, and providing for their due remuneration while in attendance on their parliamentary duties.

"And your petitioners shall ever pray."

An Eyewitness Account of the Revolutions of 1848 in Germany
Annual Register, 1848

In 1848 revolutions broke out throughout Europe. The February Revolution in France seemed to act as a spark for revolutions elsewhere, particularly in the German states. Indeed, within a few days of the outbreak in France, the established governments of the German states were faced with demands for change, demonstrations, and revolutions. The following is an account by an eyewitness of some of the events in Germany during March 1848, as reported in the London Annual Register.

CONSIDER: *Whether this indicates any pattern to the revolutionary activities; the nature of the demands for change; how the established governments reacted.*

In order to give a clear and distinct narrative of the complicated events which have taken place during the present year in Germany, we have had to consider carefully the question of arrangement; for, independently of the revolutionary movements in the separate kingdoms, there has been a long-sustained attempt to construct a new German nationality on the basis of a Confederation of all the states, with one great Parliament or Diet, and a Central Executive at Frankfort. . . .

It was in the southwestern states of Germany that the effects of the French Revolution began first to manifest themselves. On the 29th of February the Grand Duke of Baden received a deputation from his subjects who demanded liberty of the press, the establishment of a national guard, and trial by jury. They succeeded in their object, and M. Welcker, who had distinguished himself as a Liberal leader, was appointed one of the ministers.

On the 3d of March, the Rhenish provinces, headed by Cologne, followed the same example. On the 4th similar demonstrations took place at Wiesbaden and Frankfort, and on the 5th at Düsseldorf. At Cologne, on the 3d of March, the populace asembled in crowds before the Stadthaus, or town hall, where the town council were sitting, and demanded the concession of certain rights, which were inscribed on slips of paper and handed about amongst the mob. They were as follows: (1) Universal suffrage; all legislation and government to proceed from the people. (2) Liberty of the press and freedom of speech. (3) Abolition of the standing army and the armament of the people, who are to elect their own officers. (4) Full rights of public

SOURCE: Louis L. Snyder, ed., *Documents of German History* (New Brunswick, NJ: Rutgers University Press, 1958), pp. 174–175.

meeting. (5) Protection to labor, and a guarantee for the supply of all necessaries. (6) State education for all children.

The military were, however, called out, and the streets were cleared without much difficulty.

At Wiesbaden, in Nassau, a large concourse of people met opposite the palace on the 4th, and demanded a general arming of the people under their own elective leaders; entire liberty of the press; a German Parliament; right of public meeting; public and oral trial by jury; the control of the duchy domain; convocation of the second chamber to frame a new electoral law on the basis of population, and to remove all restrictions on religious liberty. The Duke was absent at Berlin, but the Duchess, from the balcony of the palace, assured the people that their demands would be fully conceded by the Duke, her stepson. Subsequently appeared a proclamation in which the Duchess *guaranteed* the concession of these demands; and on the same day, in the afternoon, the Duke returned, and, immediately addressing the people, he ratified all the concessions made by the Duchess and his ministers.

The Tables Turned: The Glories of Nature

William Wordsworth

Romantic themes were reflected in poetry as much as in other cultural forms. The British poet William Wordsworth (1770–1850) focused early on romantic themes in his work. He emphasized the connection between the individual and the glories of nature. Wordsworth gained much recognition in his own lifetime and was eventually appointed Poet Laureate of England. The following poem, "The Tables Turned," was first published in 1798.

SOURCE: Edward Dowden, ed., *The Poetical Works of William Wordsworth*, vol. IV (London: George Bell and Sons, 1893), pp. 198–199.

CONSIDER: *How this poem might be viewed as a rejection of the Enlightenment; the ways in which this poem relates to themes stressed by Châteaubriand in an excerpt later in this chapter.*

Up! up! my Friend, and quit your books;
Or surely you'll grow double:

Up! up! my Friend, and clear your looks;
Why all this toil and trouble?

The sun, above the mountain's head,
A freshening lustre mellow
Through all the long green fields has spread,
His first sweet evening yellow.

Books! 'tis a dull and endless strife:
Come, hear the woodland linnet,
How sweet his music! on my life,
There's more of wisdom in it.

And hark! how blithe the throstle sings!
He, too, is no mean preacher:
Come forth into the light of things,
Let Nature be your Teacher.

She has a world of ready wealth,
Our minds and hearts to bless—
Spontaneous wisdom breathed by health,
Truth breathed by cheerfulness.

One impulse from a vernal wood
May teach you more of man,
Of moral evil and of good,
Than all the sages can.

Sweet is the lore which Nature brings;
Our meddling intellect
Mis-shapes the beauteous forms of things:—
We murder to dissect.

Enough of Science and of Art;
Close up those barren leaves;
Come forth, and bring with you a heart
That watches and receives.

Visual Sources

Abbey Graveyard in the Snow

Caspar David Friedrich

Abbey Graveyard in the Snow (*figure 12.1*) *was painted by the well-known North German artist Caspar David Friedrich in 1819. In the center are the ruins of a Gothic choir of a monastic church surrounded by a snow-covered graveyard* and *leafless winter forest. To the left a procession of monks follows a coffin into the ruins.*

This painting exemplifies many elements typical of Romanticism, particularly German Romanticism. The scene, while visually accurate, goes beyond realism: The light is too perfectly placed, the church remains are too majestic, the surrounding forest is too symmetrical a frame, and the funeral procession is out of place (funerals did not take place in ruins). By implication, this painting rejects the limits of Enlightenment rationalism and the reality of nineteenth-century urban life. Instead, a Romantic version of the Middle Ages, the spirituality of nature, and the glories of Christianity are evoked. The Romantic longing to be overwhelmed by eternal nature is suggested, particularly by the rendering of small human figures in a large landscape. Romanticism typically exalted the emotional over the rational, even if it was a melancholy sensitivity that was being displayed.

CONSIDER: *The ways in which the Romanticism of this painting is consistent with that of Wordsworth's poetry, and with Châteaubriand's description of a Gothic cathedral, which follows.*

FIGURE 12.1   (© Bildarchiv Preussischer Kulturbesitz/Art Resource, NY)

The Genius of Christianity

René de Châteaubriand

The Romantic movement of the late eighteenth century and first half of the nineteenth century was in part a rebellion against new trends such as rationalism, urbanization, and secularism. Many historians have noted specific connections between Romanticism and conservatism, particularly in the longing for a less complex life, the respect for traditional religion, and the sense of unity between rural life and human institutions. This is illustrated in the following selection from The Genius of Christianity *by René de Châteaubriand (1768–1848), a conservative French politician and writer. Published in 1802, it gained considerable popularity and helped Châteaubriand achieve a leading position among French conservatives. Here Châteaubriand describes the Gothic churches of the Middle Ages.*

CONSIDER: *Why this description might appeal to members of the aristocracy and the Catholic Church; by implication, the aspects of Châteaubriand's own times that he was attacking; how this complements Friedrich's painting.*

You could not enter a Gothic church without feeling a kind of awe and a vague sentiment of the Divinity. You were all at once carried back to those times when a

fraternity of cenobites, after having meditated in the woods of their monasteries, met to prostrate themselves before the altar and to chant the praises of the Lord, amid the tranquillity and the silence of night. Ancient France seemed to revive altogether; you beheld all those singular costumes, all that nation so different from what it is at present; you were reminded of its revolutions, its productions, and its arts. The more remote were these times the more magical they appeared, the more they inspired ideas which always end with a reflection on the nothingness of man and the rapidity of life. . . .

The forests of Gaul were, in their turn, introduced into the temples of our ancestors, and those celebrated woods of oaks thus maintained their sacred character. Those ceilings sculptured into foliage of different kinds, those buttresses which prop the walls and terminate abruptly like the broken trunks of trees, the coolness of the vaults, the darkness of the sanctuary, the dim twilight of the aisles, the secret passages, the low doorways,—in a word, every thing in a Gothic church reminds you of the labyrinths of a wood; every thing excites a feeling of religious awe, of mystery, and of the Divinity.

The two lofty towers erected at the entrance of the edifice overtop the elms and yew-trees of the church-yard, and produce the most picturesque effect on the azure of heaven. Sometimes their twin heads are illumined by the first rays of dawn; at others they appear crowned with a capital of clouds or magnified in a foggy atmosphere. The birds themselves seem to make a mistake in regard to them, and to take them for the trees of the forest; they hover over their summits, and perch upon their pinnacles. But, lo! confused noises suddenly

SOURCE: Viscount de Châteaubriand, *The Genius of Christianity,* trans. Charles I. White (Baltimore, MD: John Murphy, 1856), pp. 385–387.

issue from the top of these towers and scare away the af-frighted birds. The Christian architect, not content with building forests, has been desirous to retain their mur-murs; and, by means of the organ and of bells, he has at-tached to the Gothic temple the very winds and thunders that roar in the recesses of the woods. Past ages, conjured up by these religious sounds, raise their venerable voices from the bosom of the stones, and are heard in every cor-ner of the ancient Sibyl; loud-tongued bells swing over your head, while the vaults of death under your feet are profoundly silent.

Liberty Leading the People: Romanticism and Liberalism

Eugène Delacroix

A number of historical themes of the first half of the nine-teenth century are combined in Liberty Leading the People *(1830) by the French painter Eugène Delacroix (figure 12.2).*

The painting shows an important event of the revolution of 1830 in Paris—revolutionaries fighting off government troops at a bridge in the center of the city. The revolutionaries are led by a feminine figure symbolizing liberty and carrying a Re-publican flag in one hand, a gun in the other. She is followed by people of all classes and ages.

In both style and content this painting reveals some of the connections between liberalism and Romanticism. The scene represents the high moral purposes of the revolution: the people struggling for the ideals of liberalism and nationalism. Despite the turmoil of the event, the people's faces convey a calm, firm assurance of the rightness and the outcome of their liberal cause. At the same time, the style of the painting is in the Romantic tradition, above all in its emphasis on heroism and the attainment of ideal goals—here liberal goals—beyond the normal expectations of life.

CONSIDER: *The ways in which this painting represents what Metternich and the Congress of Vienna struggled against.*

FIGURE 12.2 (© Erich Lessing/Art Resource, NY)

Working Class Disappointments: Rue Transnonain, April 15, 1834

Honoré Daumier

The 1830 revolutions may have brought victories to the middle class in some countries, but the working class was soon disappointed. In the years after 1830, the new regime in France not only did little to ease conditions for workers but actually passed legislation restricting their rights to organize. In 1834, outraged by the institution of the repressive Law on Associations (which would ban all unauthorized associations with more than 20 members in the name of order) and suffering from brutal labor conditions (silk weavers usually worked 16 to 20 hours a day), a workers' insurrection erupted in Lyon. After four days of bloodshed that left hundreds dead, government troops put down the uprising. A smaller insurrection also broke out in Paris, where armed insurgents began building barricades on the streets. This too was put down by government troops.

In this 1834 lithograph (figure 12.3), Honoré Daumier (1808–1879), a republican critic of the government and illustrator for two political periodicals, depicted the aftermath of this action, focusing on an event at 12 rue Transnonain in a working-class neighborhood of Paris. There, government troops believed they were being fired upon from an apartment house window. On the night of April 14–15, they stormed up the stairs to the apartment complex and shot, stabbed, and clubbed to death eight innocent men, a woman, and a child. Daumier shows the dead victims strewn in a bedroom. In the center, next to an overturned chair and propped up on the bed, lies a father whose body is riddled with wounds. Beneath him is his infant, his bashed-in bleeding skull showing from under the nightshirt. On the right is the dead grandfather and in the darkened left is the body of the mother. On the floor are the bloody footprints of the murderers. French officials quickly confiscated all the copies of this print they could find.

CONSIDER: What this reveals about the policies of even the more "liberal" governments that came to power during the 1830 revolutions; why governmental officials tried to confiscate all copies of this print.

RUE TRANSNONAIN, LE 15 AVRIL 1834

FIGURE 12.3   (© Erich Lessing/Art Resource, NY)

Secondary Sources

The Congress of Vienna

Hajo Holborn

Hindsight allows historians to evaluate diplomatic events with a sharply critical eye. Often great settlements between nations have been criticized for not taking into account the historical forces that would soon undo the stability that the peace treaties were supposed to establish. Although this critical view applies to the Congress of Vienna, there are historians who see it as relatively successful, particularly in comparison with the settlement after World War I. One of these historians is Hajo Holborn of Yale University. In the following selection Holborn evaluates the Congress of Vienna from the point of view of what was realistic for the parties at that time.

CONSIDER: *Why Holborn feels that the Congress of Vienna produced a constructive peace treaty; how other historians might criticize this view.*

The Vienna settlement created a European political system whose foundations lasted for a full century. For a hundred years there occurred no wars of world-wide scope like those of the twenty-odd years after 1792. Europe experienced frightful wars, particularly between 1854 and 1878, but none of them was a war in which all the European states or even all the great European powers participated. The European wars of the nineteenth century produced shifts of power, but they were shifts within the European political system and did not upset that system as such.

The peace settlement of Vienna has more often been condemned than praised. The accusation most frequently levelled against the Congress of Vienna has been that it lacked foresight in appraising the forces of modern nationalism and liberalism. Foresight is, indeed, one of the main qualities that distinguishes the statesman from the mere political professional. But even a statesman can only build with the bricks at hand and cannot hope to construct the second floor before he has modelled the first by which to shelter his own generation. His foresight of future developments can often express itself only by cautious attempts at keeping the way open for an evolution of the new forces.

It is questionable how successful the Congress of Vienna was in this respect. None of the Congress representatives was a statesman or political thinker of the first historic rank. All of them were strong partisans of conservatism or

outright reaction, and they found the rectitude of their convictions confirmed by the victory of the old powers over the revolutionary usurper. Still, they did not make a reactionary peace. They recognized that France could not live without a constitutional charter, and they knew, too, that the Holy Roman Empire was beyond resurrection. The new German Confederation represented a great improvement of the political conditions of Germany if one remembers that in Germany as well as in Italy the national movements were not strong enough to serve as pillars of a new order. In eastern Europe, furthermore, the modern ideas of nationality had hardly found more than a small academic and literary audience. A peace treaty cannot create new historical forces; it can only place the existing ones in a relationship most conducive to the maintenance of mutual confidence and least likely to lead to future conflict. The rest must be left to the ever continuing and never finished daily work of the statesmen.

In this light the Vienna settlement was a constructive peace treaty.

Western Liberalism

E. K. Bramsted and K. J. Melhuish

Although liberalism varied throughout Europe in accordance with the circumstances facing each country, there were broad similarities among the various liberal ideas and demands during the first half of the nineteenth century. In the following selection E. K. Bramsted and K. J. Melhuish summarize the common elements of liberal doctrine and attitudes in Europe.

CONSIDER: *How these doctrines and attitudes differ from conservatism; why liberalism would be more appealing to the middle class than to the aristocracy or the working class.*

In spite of the variations in the three main strands of liberalism, the features which classic liberals from Locke to John Stuart Mill had in common should not be overlooked. Rooted largely in the outlook of Enlightenment there was a constant emphasis on man's fundamental rationality and reasonableness. Privileges of the ruling strata based on mere tradition and custom were questioned and often rejected. Everywhere we encounter a strong urge to expand the rights of the individual and to reduce the powers of the State and of the government. However widely their arguments differed, liberal thinkers of the period . . . argued mainly in favour of the rights and the social usefulness of the individual citizen and stressed the need for parliamentary control of the powers of the government and of the accountability of its civil servants. Throughout, liberalism presumed a pluralism of existing political and religious opinions; everywhere it tended to make a plea for the rights of minorities, rights which should be protected. Civil disabilities on account of religious or political dissent were to be abolished, provided the dissenters kept their activities within the rule of the law. The right to own property and the obligation of the government to safeguard it were essential features of the liberal ideology. It was not accidental that most liberals insisted on property qualifications to be attached to the right to vote. . . .

While by no means all liberals shared Guizot's famous slogan *"Enrichissez vous!,"*[2] people without property were not much respected by most of them, but were regarded as the concern of charity, if not of socialists and anarchists. Instead liberals busied themselves with the belief in a rational political order, based on a constitution and promoted by a government with limited powers. Ministers were to be responsible to Parliament.

The belief in progress, in an advancing civilization, was another characteristic of most liberal thought. . . . The continuous improvement of mankind, helped by the advance of science and the new self-confidence of the diligent middle classes, was never seriously doubted.

The European Revolutions, 1848–1851

Jonathan Sperber

The revolutions of 1848 have been at the center of historical debate for a long time. To some, 1848 represents the end of the system set up by the Congress of Vienna; to others, it represents the great battle between the forces of liberalism and conservatism; and to still others, it represents the point at which liberalism, nationalism, socialism, and Romanticism met. Perhaps the most persistent historiographical tradition views 1848 as a point at which history made a "wrong" turn. Aspects of this historical debate are summarized in the following selection by Jonathan Sperber.

CONSIDER: *The differences between the three major interpretative traditions concerning the revolutions of 1848; which of these interpretations makes the most sense to you.*

---

[2]Make yourself wealthy.

SOURCE: Jonathan Sperber, *The European Revolutions, 1848–1851.* Cambridge: Cambridge University Press, 1994, pp. 1–2.

The European revolutions of 1848 have not always received the kindest of treatment at the hands of historians. Gentle mockery, open sarcasm and hostile contempt have frequently set the tone for narrative and evaluation. More favorable treatments of the period have not been much of an improvement, since their poetic interpretations have subtly downgraded the revolutions as serious political movements, not to be compared to the real business of 1789 and 1917. We might point to three major interpretative traditions.

One is characterized by its description of 1848 as the "romantic revolution." Historians writing along these lines apostrophize the barricade fighting born from a combination of youthful enthusiasm and romantic poetry; they evoke a revolution reaching its climax in the brief euphoria of liberation in March 1848, the "springtime of the peoples" as the contemporary German phrase described it. In this version, attention is often focused on the romantically heroic deeds of individual great figures: Lajos Kossuth travelling from village to village in the Hungarian plain, to rally the peasants against the invading Habsburg armies; Giuseppe Garibaldi leading the improvised armies of the Roman Republic against the French expeditionary force; Daniele Manin single handedly rallying the Venetians to fight the Austrians against terrible odds. It was all great and glorious, but primarily in gesture and pathos—whether it really accomplished anything is quite another matter.

Rather darker is another version of the 1848 revolutions, that views them primarily as farce, a revolution made by revolutionaries who were at best incompetent dilettantes, at worst cowards and blowhards who stole away from the scene when the going got rough. This version features the story of the Parisian revolutionary observing from his window a demonstrating crowd go by, springing up from his chair, and rushing out, proclaiming, "I am their leader; I must follow them." Another typical victim of retrospective contempt is the Frankfurt National Assembly, the all-German parliament. Historians have had their fun with the "professors' parliament," mocking its lengthy debates about whether Germany should be a *Bundesstaat* or a *Staatenbund*, noting how, after a year of deliberation, the deputies voted to name the King of Prussia emperor, only to discover that he had no interest in the post.

The third and probably most substantial of the historians' versions of 1848 directs attention to the failure of the revolutions of that year to establish new regimes, pointing out that after a shorter or longer—and usually shorter—interval, the authorities overthrown at the onset of the revolution returned to power. Historians working in this tradition contrast the failed revolutions of the mid-nineteenth century with the more successful ones in 1789 and 1917, and offer a variety of explanations for the differences.

The Revolutions of 1848

John Weiss

The scholarly debate over the revolutions of 1848 continues, but in recent years several historians have suggested a new interpretation. The following selection by John Weiss is an example of this new trend. Here he deemphasizes the role of liberalism, stressing instead the role played by artisans and peasants in the revolutions.

CONSIDER: *According to Weiss, the social and economic causes of the revolutions; how Weiss supports his conclusion that it is misleading to label these revolutions liberal.*

The revolutions of 1848 were the last in Europe, excluding those caused by defeat in war. Their suppression also marked the last triumph of the semi-feudal varieties of conservatism discussed previously. It is misleading to label these revolutions liberal, as is usually done. The revolutions were started and maintained by artisans and peasants who were either fighting to maintain some elements of the traditional order, or whose status had been dislocated by the intrusion of liberal commercial capitalism. It is true that liberals assumed leadership once the outbreaks had started, but they wanted reform, not revolution. Moreover, the liberals did not represent the middle class as a whole, but only the politically aware professional groups—lawyers, civil servants, educators and students. There was no mass following for liberal reforms in Europe, and the middle classes in general had no clearly perceived class enemy blocking their social mobility as in 1789. Consequently they were much more wary of the potential for social upheaval from below.

SOURCE: From John Weiss, *Conservatism in Europe*, p. 56. Reprinted by permission of Thames & Hudson, Ltd.

The liberal leaders of the revolutions were isolated from their own class and, as it turned out, had little to offer the artisans and peasants in revolt that could not as easily have been granted by conservatives. Only in Hungary and Italy, where nationalism incited mass risings against the Austrians, were the revolutions truly violent and sweeping. Elsewhere, we find only urban revolts accompanied by sporadic peasant uprisings. Excluding France, frightened conservative élites were never overthrown; they merely made paper concessions and withdrew temporarily until the weakness of the revolutionaries was evident, whereupon they returned in force. East of France traditionalists could still dominate the forms of social upheaval characteristic of pre-industrial society. In 1848 the industrial proletariat played almost no role whatsoever, and the outbreaks had familiar traditional causes: 1846 and 1847 were the years of the most terrible crop failures of nineteenth-century Europe, from which stemmed famine, inflation, shrinking markets and unemployment.

⚜ CHAPTER QUESTIONS

1. In a debate between liberals and conservatives of the early nineteenth century over how the French Revolution should be evaluated, what points would each side make?

2. In what ways might conservatives find Romanticism to their liking? What aspects of Romanticism might appeal to liberals?

3. Analyze nineteenth-century conservatism, liberalism, and Romanticism as alternative ways in which Europeans attempted to deal with the changes in Western civilization that had been occurring since the second half of the eighteenth century.

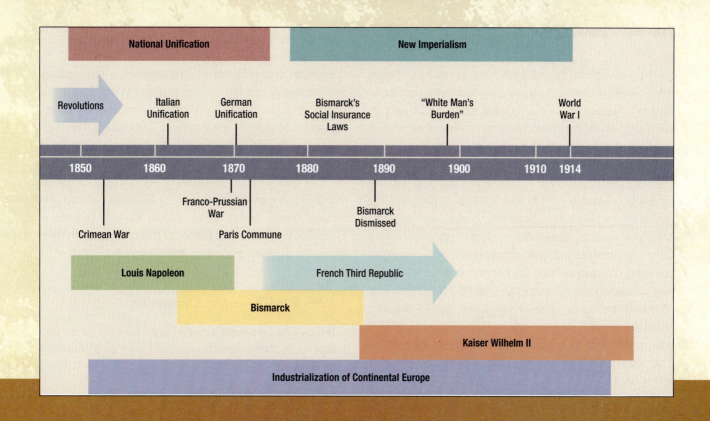

13 The National State, Nationalism, and Imperialism: 1850–1914

Between 1850 and 1914 Europe was characterized politically by the development of the national state, the spread of nationalism, and the rise of the "new imperialism." The development of the national state took place after 1848. Governments, responding to economic and social pressures, increased their involvement in the economic and social life of their countries. This was apparent both in liberal England and in more conservative France under Louis Napoleon. There were similar trends during the national unification movements in Italy and particularly in Germany, where the state took on a wide range of new functions.

Nationalism had deep roots, notably in the experience of and reactions to the French Revolution and the Napoleonic invasions. Nationalism also played a central role in the revolutions of 1848. During the second half of the nineteenth century, nationalism continued to grow and to be capitalized upon by national governments. The most striking manifestations of nationalism came in the successful unification movements in Italy and Germany.

The rise of the new imperialism occurred in the latter decades of the nineteenth century. The European powers engaged in a sudden quest for control over new territories in Asia and Africa. Explorers, missionaries, traders, troops, and government officials quickly followed one another into these lands and established direct political control. In this process the West greatly increased its dominance over much of the rest of the world, bringing Western culture and institutions to the indigenous societies whether they wanted it or not.

The sources in this chapter explore each of these three developments. Some of the documents concentrate on the growth of the national state, particularly in Germany, where the authoritarian government expanded in an effort to adapt to the social and economic pressures of the times. Some of the questions addressed are: How did the government in Germany react to demands for social legislation? What was the role of conservative forces in the German unification process, and how did other powers deal with Prussia's drive to unify Germany? Other documents concern nationalism, particularly its meaning, its appeal, and its connections to liberalism and conservatism. What role did nationalism play in the unification movements in Germany and Italy? How was nationalism tied to the new imperialism of the period? Finally, most of the selections deal with imperialism, for not only was imperialism of far-reaching significance for much of the world, it has been a topic of considerable debate among historians. What were the nationalistic and economic motives for imperialism? What were some of the attitudes toward imperialism, particularly as reflected in materials glorifying it as a Christian and humanitarian movement? What roles did women play in colonial societies?

Throughout these selections there is evidence for an increasing competitiveness among European states and political strains within those states. As will be seen in Chapter 26, these contributed to the outbreak of World War I and the revolutions that accompanied it.

✑ For Classroom Discussion

What caused nineteenth-century imperialism? Use the selections by Fabri, Hobsbawm, and Hayes to debate this question.

Primary Sources

Speeches on Pragmatism and State Socialism

Otto von Bismarck

The revolutions of 1848 were ultimately a blow to idealistic reform. Thereafter, governments pursued more limited goals. They tended to resort to more authoritarian measures, to avoid doctrinaire policies, and even to adopt certain programs of opposing groups in the hopes of weakening determined opposition to the government. Otto von Bismarck (1815–1898) did this in Germany. Born into a noble Prussian family, Bismarck rose to the position of chief minister under the king in 1862. The first selection below is from an 1862 speech to the Reichstag, in which he argues that the idealism of 1848 must be replaced by a conservative realism.

Bismarck remained in power until 1890. During this time he and his conservative supporters faced opposition from some liberals and from a growing number of socialists representing the working class. In the 1880s Bismarck supported some of the workers' demands for social insurance

SOURCE: Louis L. Snyder, ed., *Documents of German History* (New Brunswick, NJ: Rutgers University Press, 1958), p. 202; William H. Dawson, *Bismarck and State Socialism* (London: Swan Sonnenschein and Co., 1890), pp. 29, 34–35, 63–64, 118–119.

and pushed through such legislation as the German Workers' Insurance Laws. The remaining excerpts below Bismarck's speeches indicate the rationale behind these policies.

CONSIDER: *What Bismarck means when he says the great questions of the day will be decided by iron and blood; how Bismarck justifies his support of "socialist" policies; why Bismarck would support such policies; what conservatives have to gain and who stands to lose by enactment of these policies.*

IRON AND BLOOD

. . . It is true that we can hardly escape complications in Germany, although we do not seek them. Germany does not look to Prussia's liberalism, but to her power. The south German States—Bavaria, Württemberg, and Baden—would like to indulge in liberalism, and because of that no one will assign Prussia's role to them! Prussia must collect her forces and hold them in reserve for an opportune moment, which has already come and gone several times. Since the Treaty of Vienna, our frontiers have not been favorably designed for a healthy body politic. Not by speeches and majorities will the great questions of the day be decided—that was the mistake of 1848 and 1849—but by iron and blood.

STATE SOCIALISM

Herr Richter has called attention to the responsibility of the State for what it does. But it is my opinion that the State can also be responsible for what it does not do. I do not think that doctrines like those of "*Laissez-faire, laissez-aller*," "Pure Manchesterdom in politics," "He who is not strong enough to stand must be knocked down and trodden to the ground," "To him that hath shall be given, and from him that hath not shall be taken away even that which he hath,"—that doctrines like these should be applied in the State, and especially in a monarchically, paternally governed State. On the other hand, I believe that those who profess horror at the intervention of the State for the protection of the weak lay themselves open to the suspicion that they are desirous of using their strength—be it that of capital, that of rhetoric, or whatever it be—for the benefit of a section, for the oppression of the rest, for the introduction of party domination, and that they will be chagrined as soon as this design is disturbed by any action of the Government.

❦

Give the working-man the right to work as long as he is healthy; assure him care when he is sick; assure him maintenance when he is old. If you do that, and do not fear the sacrifice, or cry out at State Socialism directly the words "provision for old age" are uttered,—if the State will show a little more Christian solicitude for the working-man, then I believe that the gentlemen of the Wyden (Social-Democratic) programme will sound their bird-call in vain, and that the thronging to them will cease as soon as working-men see that the Government and legislative bodies are earnestly concerned for their welfare.

Yes, I acknowledge unconditionally a right to work, and I will stand up for it as long as I am in this place. But here I do not stand upon the ground of Socialism, which is said to have only begun with the Bismarck Ministry, but on that of the Prussian common law.

❦

Many measures which we have adopted to the great blessing of the country are Socialistic, and the State will have to accustom itself to a little more Socialism yet. We must meet our needs in the domain of Socialism by reformatory measures if we would display the wisdom shown in Prussia by the Stein-Hardenberg legislation respecting the emancipation of the peasantry. That was Socialism, to take land from one person and give it to another—a much stronger form of Socialism than a monopoly. But I am glad that this Socialism was adopted, for we have as a consequence secured a free and very well-to-do peasantry, and I hope that we shall in time do something of the sort for the labouring classes. Whether I, however, shall live to see it—with the general opposition which is, as a matter of principle, offered to me on all sides, and which is wearying me—I cannot say. But you will be compelled to put a few drops of social oil into the recipe which you give to the State—how much I do not know. . . . The establishment of the freedom of the peasantry was Socialistic; Socialistic, too, is every expropriation in favour of railways; Socialistic to the utmost extent is the aggregation of estates—the law exists in many provinces—taking from one and giving to another, simply because this other can cultivate the land more conveniently; Socialistic is expropriation under the Water Legislation, on account of irrigation, etc., where a man's land is taken away from him because another can farm it better; Socialistic is our entire poor relief, compulsory school attendance, compulsory construction of roads, so that I am bound to maintain a road upon my lands for travellers. That is all Socialistic, and I could extend the register further; but if you believe that you can frighten any one or call up specters with the word "Socialism," you take a standpoint which I abandoned long ago, and the abandonment of which is absolutely necessary for our entire imperial legislation.

❦

The whole matter centres in the question, Is it the duty of the State, or is it not, to provide for its helpless citizens? I maintain that it is its duty, that it is the duty not only of the "*Christian* State," as I ventured once to call it when speaking of "practical Christianity," but of every State. It would be foolish for a corporation to undertake matters which the individual can attend to alone; and similarly the purposes which the parish can fulfill with justice and with advantage are left to the parish. But there are purposes which only the State as a whole can fulfill. To these belong national defence, the general system of communications, and, indeed, everything spoken of in article 4 of the constitution. To these, too, belong the help of the necessitous and the removal of those just complaints which provide Social Democracy with really effective material for agitation. This is a duty of the State, a duty which the State cannot permanently disregard. . . . As soon as the State takes this matter [of insurance] in hand—and I believe it is its duty to take it in hand—it must seek the cheapest form of insurance, and, not aiming at profit for itself, must keep primarily in view the benefit of the poor and needy. Otherwise we might leave the fulfillment of certain State duties—such as poor relief, in the widest sense of the words, is amongst others—like education and national defence with more right to share companies, only asking ourselves, Who will do it most cheaply? who will do it most effectively? If provision for the necessitous in a greater degree than is possible with the present poor relief legislation is a State duty, the State must take the matter in hand; it cannot rest content with the thought that a share company will undertake it.

If an establishment employing twenty thousand or more workpeople were to be ruined . . . we could not allow these men to hunger. We should have to resort to real State Socialism and find work for them, and this is what we do in every case of distress. If the objection were right that we should shun State Socialism as we would an infectious disease, how do we come to organise works in one province and another in case of distress—works which we should not undertake if the labourers had employment and wages? In such cases we build railways whose profitableness is questionable; we carry out improvements which otherwise would be left to private initiative. If that is Communism, I have no objection at all to it; though with such catchwords we really get no further.

The Duties of Man

Giuseppe Mazzini

Nationalism, a growing force since the French Revolution, tended to be associated with liberal and humanitarian ideals during the first half of the nineteenth century. After 1848 it became more pragmatic and conservative, as illustrated by the unification of Germany and Italy. Yet it was still based on some of the earlier ideals. These ideals are illustrated in both the life and writings of the Italian patriot Giuseppe Mazzini (1805–1872). Mazzini was a revolutionary for most of his life and strove continuously for an independent and united Italian Republic. His revolutionary efforts in the 1830s and 1840s failed; unification was ultimately accomplished under the more pragmatic leadership of Cavour in the 1860s. But his ideas represented a strong strain of mid-nineteenth-century nationalism both in Italy and in other countries. The following is an excerpt from Mazzini's most famous essay, The Duties of Man, *addressed to Italian workingmen.*

CONSIDER: *The bases for Mazzini's nationalism; why these ideas might be appealing to the Italian working class; why Bismarck might approve of these ideas and whether there is anything he might reject.*

Your first duties—first as regards importance—are, as I have already told you, towards Humanity. You are *men* before you are either citizens or fathers. If you do not embrace the whole human family in your affection, if you do not bear witness to your belief in the Unity of that family, consequent upon the Unity of God, and in that fraternity among the peoples which is destined to reduce that unity to action; if, wheresoever a fellow-creature suffers, or the dignity of human nature is violated by falsehood or tyranny—you are not ready, if able, to aid the unhappy, and do not feel called upon to combat, if able, for the redemption of the betrayed or oppressed—you violate your law of life, you comprehend not that Religion which will be the guide and blessing of the future.

But what can each of you, singly, *do* for the moral improvement and progress of Humanity? You can from time to time give sterile utterance to your belief; you may, on some rare occasions, perform some act of *charity* towards a brother man not belonging to your own land;—no more. But charity is not the watchword of the Faith of the Future. The watchword of the faith of the future is *Association,* and fraternal co-operation of all towards a common aim; and this is as far superior to all charity, as the edifice which all of you should unite to raise would be superior to the humble hut each one of you might build alone, or with the mere assistance of lending and borrowing stone, mortar, and tools.

But, you tell me, you cannot attempt united action, distinct and divided as you are in language, customs, tendencies, and capacity. The individual is too insignificant, and Humanity too vast. The mariner of Brittany prays to God as he puts to sea: *Help me, my God! my boat is so small and thy ocean so wide!* And this prayer is the true expression of the condition of each one of you, until you find the means of infinitely multiplying your forces and powers of action.

This means was provided for you by God when he gave you a country; when, even as a wise overseer of labour distributes the various branches of employment according to the different capacities of the workmen, he divided Humanity into distinct groups or nuclei upon the face of the earth, thus creating the germ of Nationalities. Evil governments have disfigured the divine design. Nevertheless you may still trace it, distinctly marked out—at least as far as Europe is concerned—by the course of the great rivers, the direction of the higher mountains, and other geographical conditions. They have disfigured it by their conquests, their greed, and their jealousy even of the righteous power of others; disfigured it so far that if we except England and France—there is not perhaps a single country whose present boundaries correspond to that design.

SOURCE: Emilie Ashurst Venturi, *Joseph Mazzini: A Memoir* (London: Alexander & Shepheard, 1875), pp. 312–315.

These governments did not, and do not, recognise any country save their own families or dynasty, the egotism of caste. But the Divine design will infallibly be realized. Natural divisions, and the spontaneous, innate tendencies of the peoples, will take the place of the arbitrary divisions sanctioned by evil governments. The map of Europe will be redrawn. The countries of the Peoples, defined by the vote of free men, will arise upon the ruins of the countries of kings and privileged castes, and between these countries harmony and fraternity will exist. And the common work of Humanity, of general amelioration and the gradual discovery and application of its Law of life, being distributed according to local and general capacities, will be wrought out in peaceful and progressive development and advance. Then may each one of you, fortified by the power and the affection of many millions, all speaking the same language, gifted with the same tendencies, and educated by the same historical tradition, hope, even by your own single effort, to be able to benefit all Humanity.

O my brothers, love your Country! Our country is our Home, the house that God has given us, placing therein a numerous family that loves us, and whom we love; a family with whom we sympathise more readily, and whom we understand more quickly than we do others; and which, from its being centred round a given spot, and from the homogeneous nature of its elements, is adapted to a special branch of activity. Our country is our common workshop, whence the products of our activity are sent forth for the benefit of the whole world; wherein the tools and implements of labour we can most usefully employ are gathered together: nor may we reject them without disobeying the plan of the Almighty, and diminishing our own strength.

Militant Nationalism

Heinrich von Treitschke

The idea of nationalism and nationalistic movements gained great power throughout the nineteenth century. While favored by a variety of liberal and conservative thinkers and groups during the first half of the century, nationalism became more militant, extreme, and racist in the second half of the century, particularly in central Europe. One of the most influential proponents of this militant nationalism in Germany was Heinrich von Treitschke (1834–1896), a historian at the University of Berlin. In

the following selections from his works, Treitschke puts forth his views on national character, the state, war, and Jews.

CONSIDER: *What might be appealing about these views; possible reasons for Treitschke's views of the English and Jews; what policies might logically flow from these ideas.*

ON THE GERMAN CHARACTER

Depth of thought, idealism, cosmopolitan views; a transcendent philosophy which boldly oversteps (or freely looks over) the separating barriers of finite existence; familiarity with every human thought and feeling, the desire to traverse the worldwide realm of ideas in common with the foremost intellects of all nations and all times. All that has at all times been held to be characteristic of the Germans and has always been praised as the essence of German character and breeding. . . .

ON THE STATE

The state is a moral community, which is called upon to educate the human race by positive achievement. Its ultimate object is that a nation should develop in it, a nation distinguished by a real national character. To achieve this state is the highest moral duty for nation and individual alike. All private quarrels must be forgotten when the state is in danger.

At the moment when the state cries out that its very life is at stake, social selfishness must cease and party hatred be hushed. The individual must forget his egoism, and feel that he is a member of the whole body.

The most important possession of a state, its be-all and end-all, is power. He who is not man enough to look this truth in the face should not meddle in politics. The state is not physical power as an end in itself, it is power to protect and promote the higher interests. Power must justify itself by being applied for the greatest good of mankind. It is the highest moral duty of the state to increase its power.

The true greatness of the state is that it links the past with the present and future; consequently, the individual has no right to regard the state as a means for attaining his own ambitions in life. Every extension of the activities of the state is beneficial and wise if it arouses, promotes, and purifies the independence of free and reasoning men; it is evil when it kills and stunts the independence of free men. It is men who make history. . . .

Only the truly great and powerful states ought to exist. Small states are unable to protect their subjects against external enemies; moreover, they are incapable

SOURCE: Louis L. Snyder, ed., *Documents of German History* (New Brunswick, NJ: Rutgers University Press, 1958), pp. 259–62.

of *Kultar* in great dimensions. Weimar produced a Goethe and a Schiller; still these poets would have been greater had they been citizens of a German national state. . . .

ON WAR

The idea of perpetual peace is an illusion supported only by those of weak character. It has always been the weary, spiritless, and exhausted ages which have played with the dream of perpetual peace. A thousand touching portraits testify to the sacred power of the love which a righteous war awakes in noble nations. It is altogether impossible that peace be maintained in a world bristling with arms, and even God will see to it that war always recurs as a drastic medicine for the human race. Among great states the greatest political sin and the most contemptible is feebleness. It is the political sin against the Holy Ghost.

War is elevating because the individual disappears before the great conception of the state. The devotion of the members of a community to each other is nowhere so splendidly conspicuous as in war.

Modern wars are not waged for the sake of goods and chattels. What is at stake is the sublime moral good of national honor, which has something in the nature of unconditional sanctity, and compels the individual to sacrifice himself for it.

ON THE ENGLISH

The hypocritical Englishman, with the Bible in one hand and a pipe of opium in the other, possesses no redeeming qualities. The nation was an ancient robber-knight, in full armor, lance in hand, on every one of the world's trade routes.

The English possess a commercial spirit, a love of money which has killed every sentiment of honor and every distinction of right and wrong. English cowardice and sensuality are hidden behind unctuous, theological fine talk which is to us free-thinking German heretics among all the sins of English nature the most repugnant. In England all notions of honor and class prejudices vanish before the power of money, whereas the German nobility has remained poor but chivalrous. That last indispensable bulwark against the brutalization of society—the duel—has gone out of fashion in England and soon disappeared, to be supplanted by the riding whip. This was a triumph of vulgarity. The newspapers, in their accounts of aristocratic weddings, record in exact detail how much each wedding guest has contributed in the form of presents or in cash; even the youth of the nation have turned

their sports into a business, and contend for valuable prizes, whereas the German students wrought havoc on their countenances for the sake of a real or imaginary honor.

ON JEWS

The Jews at one time played a necessary role in German history, because of their ability in the management of money. But now that the Aryans have become accustomed to the idiosyncrasies of finance, the Jews are no longer necessary. The international Jew, hidden in the mask of different nationalities, is a disintegrating influence; he can be of no further use to the world. It is necessary to speak openly about the Jews, undisturbed by the fact that the Jewish press befouls what is purely historical truth.

Does Germany Need Colonies?
Friedrich Fabri

Imperialism swept through Europe with extraordinary force in the late nineteenth century. Probably the most apparent motive for the new imperialism was economic. With each conquest, people expected to develop new commerce and particularly new markets for manufactured goods. But there was another, perhaps even more important motive: nationalism. The step between the increasingly assertive nationalism of the time and the new imperialism was a short one. Both of these views are reflected by Friedrich Fabri in his 1879 pamphlet, "Does Germany Need Colonies?" A former inspector of a German missionary association in South West Africa, Fabri emphasizes Germany's "cultural mission" in becoming an imperial power.

CONSIDER: *What arguments Fabri mounts to justify Germany's acquisition of colonies; what Fabri means by Germany's "cultural mission" and how that relates to imperialism.*

Should not the German nation, so seaworthy, so industrially and commercially minded, more than other peoples geared to agricultural colonization, and possessing a rich and available supply of labor, all these to a greater extent than other modern culture-peoples, should not this nation successfully hew a new path on the road of imperialism? We are convinced beyond doubt that the colonial question has become a matter of life-or-death for the

SOURCE: Louis L. Snyder, *The Imperialism Reader* (New York: D. Van Nostrand, 1962), pp. 18–20 as excerpted.

development of Germany. Colonies will have a salutary effect on our economic situation as well as on our entire national progress.

Here is a solution for many of the problems that face us. In this new Reich of ours there is so much bitterness, so much unfruitful, sour, and poisoned political wrangling, that the opening of a new, promising road of national effort will act as a kind of liberating influence. Our national spirit will be renewed, a gratifying thing, a great asset. A people that has been led to a high level of power can maintain its historical position only as long as it understands and proves itself to be *the bearer of a culture-mission*. At the same time, this is the only way to stability and to the growth of national welfare, the necessary foundation for a lasting expansion of power.

At one time Germany contributed only intellectual and literary activity to the tasks of our century. That era is now over. As a people we have become politically minded and powerful. But if political power becomes the primal goal of a nation, it will lead to harshness, even to barbarism. We must be ready to serve for the ideal, moral, and economic culture-tasks of our time. The French national-economist, Leroy Beaulieu, closed his work on colonization with these words: "That nation is the greatest in the world which colonizes most; if she does not achieve that rank today, she will make it tomorrow."

No one can deny that in this direction England has by far surpassed all other countries. Much has been said, even in Germany, during the last few decades about the "disintegrating power of England." Indeed, there seems to be something to it when we consider the Palmerston era and Gladstonian politics. It has been customary in our age of military power to evaluate the strength of a state in terms of its combat-ready troops. But anyone who looks at the globe and notes the steadily increasing colonial possessions of Great Britain, how she extracts strength from them, the skill with which she governs them, how the Anglo-Saxon strain occupies a dominant position in the overseas territories, he will begin to see the military argument as the reasoning of a philistine.

The fact is that England tenaciously holds on to its world-wide possessions with scarcely one-fourth the manpower of our continental military state. That is not only a great economic advantage but also a striking proof of the solid power and cultural fiber of England. . . .

It would be wise for us Germans to learn about colonial skills from our Anglo-Saxon cousins and to begin a friendly competition with them. When the German Reich centuries ago stood at the pinnacle of the states of Europe, it was the Number One trade and sea power. If the New Germany wants to protect its newly won position of power for a long time, it must heed its *Kultur-mission* and, above all, delay no longer in the task of renewing the call for colonies.

The White Man's Burden

Rudyard Kipling

Imperialism was often glorified both by those actively involved in it and by the public at home. Part of this glorification involved perceiving imperialism as a Christian and nationalistic venture. More broadly it involved portraying imperialism as a heroic deed carried out by idealistic leaders of Western civilization in an effort to spread the "benefits" of "true civilization" to "less advanced" peoples of the world. One of the most popular expressions of this is found in the writings of Rudyard Kipling (1865–1936), particularly in his poem "The White Man's Burden," written in 1899 to celebrate the American annexation of the Philippines.

CONSIDER: *What Kipling means by "the White Man's burden"; how Kipling justifies imperialism; why such a justification might be so appealing.*

Take up the White Man's burden—
   Send forth the best ye breed—
Go, bind your sons to exile
   To serve your captives' need;
To wait, in heavy harness,
   On fluttered folk and wild—
Your new-caught sullen peoples,
   Half devil and half child.

Take up the White Man's burden—
   In patience to abide,
To veil the threat of terror
   And check the show of pride;
By open speech and simple,
   An hundred times made plain,
To seek another's profit
   And work another's gain.

Take up the White Man's burden—
   The savage wars of peace—
Fill full the mouth of Famine,
   And bid the sickness cease;

SOURCE: Rudyard Kipling, "The White Man's Burden," *McClure's Magazine,* vol. XII, no. 4 (February 1899), pp. 290–291.

And when your goal is nearest
    (The end for others sought)
Watch sloth and heathen folly
    Bring all your hope to nought.

Take up the White Man's burden—
    No iron rule of kings,
But toil of serf and sweeper—
    The tale of common things.
The ports ye shall not enter,
    The roads ye shall not tread,
Go, make them with your living
    And mark them with your dead.

Take up the White Man's burden,
    And reap his old reward—
The blame of those ye better
    The hate of those ye guard—
The cry of hosts ye humour
    (Ah, slowly!) toward the light:—
"Why brought ye us from bondage,
    Our loved Egyptian night?"

Take up the White Man's burden—
    Ye dare not stoop to less—
Nor call too loud on Freedom
    To cloke your weariness.
By all ye will or whisper,
    By all ye leave or do,
The silent sullen peoples
    Shall weigh your God and you.

Take up the White Man's burden!
    Have done with childish days—
The lightly-proffered laurel,
    The easy ungrudged praise:
Comes now, to search your manhood
    Through all the thankless years,
Cold, edged with dear-bought wisdom,
    The judgment of your peers.

Controlling Africa: The Standard Treaty

Royal Niger Company

Europeans used many means to gain control over African lands, the most obvious being force. However, more subtle means included "treaties," or what the Europeans could

SOURCE: Edwart Hertslet, ed., *The Map of Africa by Treaty,* 2nd ed. (London: Her Majesty's Stationary Office, 1896), vol. I, pp. 467–468.

consider "legal contracts." During the scramble for Africa, African chieftains signed hundreds of these documents. The following document is an example of one of these "standard treaties" issued in the 1880s by the British firm, the Royal Niger Company. The company had already been granted a trade monopoly over the area around the Niger River in West Africa by the British government and was competing with the French for control over that area. The treaties would eventually form the basis for creating the British colony of Nigeria.

CONSIDER: *What the treaties offered to each side; what the Africans were giving up; why the British found this way of gaining control so appealing.*

We, the undersigned Chiefs of _____, with the view to the bettering of the condition of our country and people, do this day cede to the Royal Niger Company, for ever, the whole of our territory extending from _____.

We also give to the said Royal Niger Company full power to settle all native disputes arising from any cause whatever, and we pledge ourselves not to enter into any war with other tribes without the sanction of the said Royal Niger Company.

We understand that the said Royal Niger Company have full power to mine, farm, and build in any portion of our country.

We bind ourselves not to have any intercourse with any strangers or foreigners except through the said Royal Niger Company.

In consideration of the foregoing, the said Royal Niger Company (Chartered and Limited) bind themselves not to interfere with any of the native laws or customs of the country, consistently with the maintenance of order and good government.

The said Royal Niger Company agree to pay native owners of land a reasonable amount for any portion they may require.

The said Royal Niger Company bind themselves to protect the said Chiefs from the attacks of any neighboring aggressive tribes.

The said Royal Niger Company also agree to pay the said Chiefs _____ measures native value.

We, the undersigned witnesses, do hereby solemnly declare that the _____ Chiefs whose names are placed opposite their respective crosses have in our presence affixed their crosses of their own free will and consent, and that the said _____ has in our presence affixed his signature.

Done in triplicate at _____, this _____ day of _____, 188 _____.

Declaration by interpreter I, _____, of _____, do hereby solemnly declare that I am well acquainted with the language of the country, and that on the _____ day of _____, 188 _____, I truly and faithfully explained the above Agreement to all the Chiefs present, and that they understood its meaning.

Visual Sources

Melancholia

Jacek Malczewski

Some of the pessimistic and introspectic undercurrents from the 1880s emerge in Polish artist Jacek Malczewski's (1854–1929) 1894 canvas (figure 13.1). In the background on the far left, the introspective Malczewski sits in his studio, painting. From his canvas pours a swirling, struggling stream of children already bearing arms. They quickly mature into adults. Afire with nationalistic passion, some rally around a flag, which symbolizes their efforts to liberate Poland from foreign rule. Below them lie the corpses of those who have died in nineteenth-century rebellions for independence. In the foreground, figures holding unbroken chains suggest the uprisings' failures. On the right drift two more portraits of the artist. Behind him, aged Polish survivors float toward the window, where a grieving figure of death awaits them and their life-long dreams of Polish nationhood.

CONSIDER: *What this reveals about the force of nationalism during this period; what disturbing trends of the late nineteenth century this painting suggests.*

_____

SOURCE: Musdeum Narodowe, Posen/Artothek.

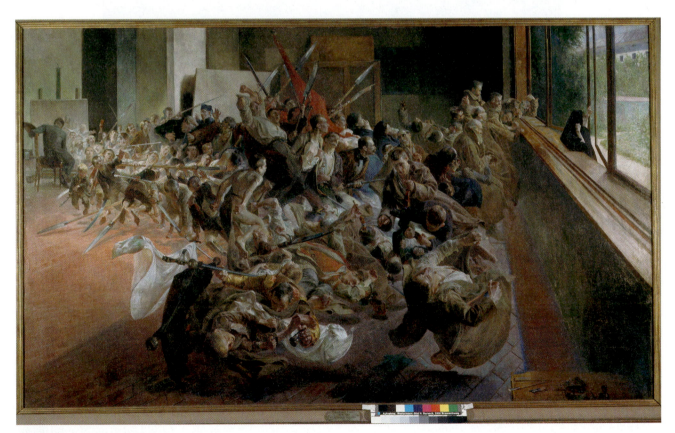

FIGURE 13.1   (© Westermann/Artothek)

FIGURE 13.2 (© Bettmann/Corbis)

Imperialism Glorified

George Harcourt

The following 1900 painting by George Harcourt (figure 13.2) conveys some of the meaning of imperialism to Europeans. First displayed at the Royal Academy in 1900, it shows British soldiers leaving by train for the Boer War in South Africa. The soldiers are clearly cast in the role of masculine heroes, both in their own eyes and in the eyes of civilians, young and old. This is further evidenced by the couple in the center, representing the epitome of sentimentalized British masculinity and femininity. For many, imperialism enabled Europeans to have a sense of adventure and to prove their superiority to themselves and the rest of the world. Avoided in this picture is the reality of the bloodshed and exploitation to be experienced by these same soldiers and the populations of the colonized lands.

CONSIDER: *How this painting fits with Kipling's description of "the White Man's burden."*

American Imperialism in Asia: Independence Day 1899

The Spanish-American War of 1898 led to the Spanish defeat and withdrawal from Cuba, Puerto Rico, and the Philippines. It also occasioned an impassioned debate in the United States about whether America should follow in Europe's footsteps

FIGURE 13.3 (© New York Public Library/Art Resource, NY)

and acquire colonies. The "liberation" of the Philippines led to a ten-year war against Philippine insurgents who fought for independence from both Spain and the United States. American imperialists were interested in the Philippines in large part because it gave them access to trade and investments in other Asian countries, especially the fabled China market that would be able to buy untold quantities of American goods. In this cartoon (figure 13.3) we see Uncle Sam about to bayonet a Filipino youth who is trying to defend himself with a sword, suggesting the massive difference in power between the U.S. Army and the Philippine insurgents. In back of Uncle Sam, then President McKinley waves the flag, suggesting the patriotism and jingoism that was seen to be behind American imperialism.

CONSIDER: How Americans were able to rationalize their support for colonialism with their long opposition to European imperialism.

Imperialism in Africa

Map 13.1 shows the approximate divisions among indigenous peoples in the centuries prior to European colonization. Map 13.2 (on p. 183) highlights political and cultural divisions in nineteenth-century Africa prior to 1880. Map 13.3 (on p. 184) shows the colonial partition of Africa between 1880 and 1914.

Together these maps indicate a number of things about imperialism in Africa. First, the manner and speed with which Africa was divided demonstrate the intense competition involved in this late-nineteenth-century imperial expansion. Second, the European partition of Africa did not take account of the already established social, political, cultural, and ethnic divisions among Africans. From this geopolitical perspective alone, one can imagine some of the disruption to native societies and cultures caused by imperialism. Third, these maps help explain problems experienced by Africans after decolonization occurred. The new African nations were generally formed on the basis of the arbitrary political lines established by European colonizers. Thus many African countries had to deal with persisting divisions and rivalries among their populations, stemming from the nineteenth-century partition of Africa.

CONSIDER: How these maps help explain the effects of imperialism on Africans.

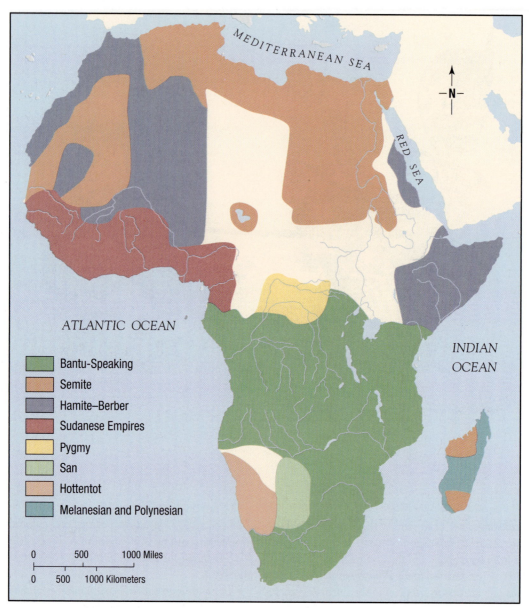

MAP 13.1　Divisions Among Indigenous Peoples

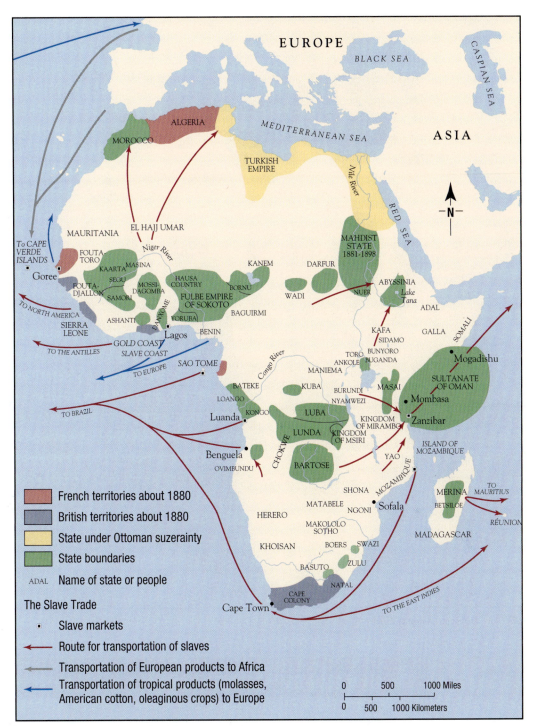

EUROPE

BLACK SEA

CASPIAN SEA

MEDITERRANEAN SEA

ASIA

ALGERIA

MOROCCO

TURKISH
EMPIRE

Nile River

RED SEA

N

To CAPE
VERDE
ISLANDS

MAURITANIA

EL HAJJ UMAR

Niger River

MAHDIST
STATE
1881-1898

Goree

FOUTA-
TORO

KAARTA MASINA

KANEM

DARFUR

ABYSSINIA

SEGU

MOSSI-
DAGOMBA

HAUSA
COUNTRY

BORNU

WADI

NUER

Lake
Tana

ADAL

FOUTA-
DJALLON

SAMORI

FULBE EMPIRE
OF SOKOTO

BAGUIRMI

KAFA
SIDAMO

GALLA

SOMALI

TO NORTH AMERICA

ASHANTI

YORUBA

TORO
ANKOLE

BUNYORO
BUGANDA

SIERRA
LEONE

DAHOMEY

BENIN

Mogadishu

GOLD COAST

Lagos

TO THE ANTILLES

SLAVE COAST

Congo River

MANIEMA

MASAI

SULTANATE
OF OMAN

SAO TOME

TO EUROPE

BATEKE

KUBA

BURUNDI

NYAMWEZI

Mombasa

LOANGO

LUBA

Zanzibar

TO BRAZIL

Luanda

KONGO

KINGDOM
OF MIRAMBO

CHOKWE

LUNDA

KINGDOM
OF MSIRI

ISLAND OF
MOZAMBIQUE

Benguela

BARTOSE

YAO

TO
MAURITIUS

OVIMBUNDU

MOZAMBIQUE

MERINA

SHONA

BETSILOE

RÉUNION

MATABELE

NGONI

Sofala

HERERO

MAKOLOLO
SOTHO

MADAGASCAR

KHOISAN

BOERS

SWAZI

BASUTO

ZULU

NATAL

CAPE
COLONY

Cape Town

TO THE EAST INDIES

French territories about 1880

British territories about 1880

State under Ottoman suzerainty

State boundaries

ADAL Name of state or people

The Slave Trade

▪ Slave markets

→ Route for transportation of slaves

→ Transportation of European products to Africa

→ Transportation of tropical products (molasses,
   American cotton, oleaginous crops) to Europe

0   500   1000 Miles

0   500   1000 Kilometers

MAP 13.2   Political and Cultural Divisions

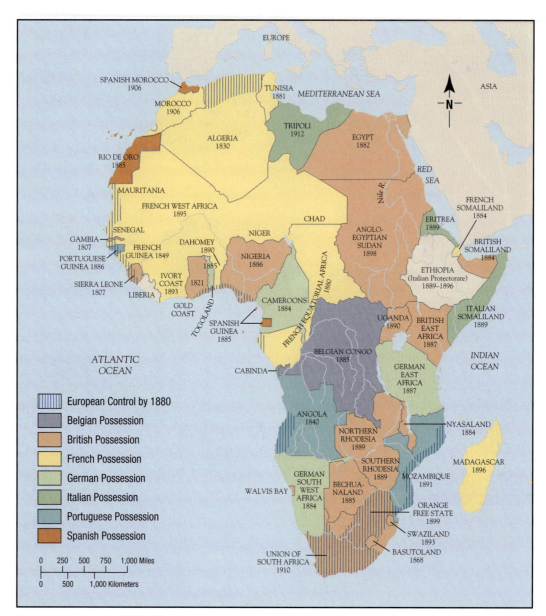

MAP 13.3 European Control of Africa

Legend:
- European Control by 1880
- Belgian Possession
- British Possession
- French Possession
- German Possession
- Italian Possession
- Portuguese Possession
- Spanish Possession

Secondary Sources

A Sterner Plan for Italian Unity: Nationalism, Liberalism, and Conservatism

Raymond Grew

During the first half of the nineteenth century, nationalism was most often connected to liberalism. After the revolu-tions of 1848 there were increasing ties between national-ism and conservatism, particularly in the movements for national unification. In the following selection Raymond Grew, an advocate of comparative history from the University of Michigan, analyzes the relationships among nationalism, liberalism, and conservatism in a comparative context.

SOURCE: Raymond Grew, *A Sterner Plan for Italian Unity*. Reprinted by permission of Princeton University Press (Princeton, NJ, 1963), pp. 465–466. Copyright © 1963 by Princeton University Press.

CONSIDER: *How nationalism could appeal to both liberals and conservatives; why, during the second half of the nine-teenth century, liberal ideals were often sacrificed in the name of nationalism.*

Insofar as politics was the public battle of ideas and interests, then nationalism was a denial of politics. For in stressing the values of unity, loyalty, and duty, nationalism saw political dispute as a source of weakness. It denied that there was conflict in the true interests of classes, groups or regions. The effect of nationalism was therefore inherently conservative in that it provided reason for supporting anyone thought to wield the power of the state effectively in behalf of national unity and strength, Disraeli or Gladstone, Napoleon III or Bismarck. Since order and unity, the cry of the political conservative, are essential to a strong state, and since, to the nationalist, most worthy ends required that strength, the nationalist was always tempted under pressure to move toward the political right, to sacrifice liberty to unity, discussion to authority, ends to means.

Yet the origins of nationalism were usually liberal and reformist; for everywhere it was a demand for change, the doctrine of the modernizers who, while they had too much to lose to want a social revolution, were self-consciously aware that theirs was an "underdeveloped" country. Nationalism could make its denial of politics effective because its ends were so clear, so easily defined in the model of the modern state. For the French that model had been England; for the Italians it was England and France. Italian nationalists were usually liberals, but their liberalism was primarily an admiration for the achievements of the liberal state. Because their model already existed, they looked directly to it, anxious to achieve an efficient bureaucracy, a responsible government, a progressive economic structure, all based on accepted and universally applied laws. Nationalism was a program to obtain these things quickly, not to evolve toward them but, if necessary, to superimpose them. The hurry to achieve these goals where nationalism itself was seriously opposed made a doctrinaire concern for means appear pedantic and unrealistic. Italian nationalists needed nothing so brutal as cynicism to justify "postponement" of controversy or the choice of practical means, though often this meant whittling away at the practices necessary to viable liberalism.

German Unification

David Blackbourn

As in the case of Italy, nationalism in Germany during the first half of the nineteenth century was closely connected to liberalism. This was particularly so in the early stages of the revolutions of 1848. But with the failure of liberal

SOURCE: David Blackbourn, *The Long Nineteenth Century: A History of Germany, 1780–1918* (New York: Oxford University Press, 1998), pp. 247–248.

nationalists to gain the concrete changes they strove for, steps toward unification over the next two decades followed a path blazed by Bismarck and the conservatives, who used three wars to help achieve unity in 1871. In the following selection, David Blackbourne analyzes the international environment that allowed the drive for German unification to succeed.

CONSIDER: *Why the great powers allowed Prussia to unify Germany without intervening; why Russia and Great Britain were "distracted"; what the other powers might have done to counter Prussia.*

Germany was unified as a result of three wars that created a new power in the centre of Europe. Why did the other great powers allow this to come about? An important part of the answer is obviously the success of Prussian arms when put to the test. It cannot be emphasized too much that unification was, in the last resort, achieved on the battlefield. But other elements smoothed the Prussian path to success. Russia had suffered military humiliation in the Crimean war, and was absorbed during the 1860s in a bout of internal reforms. Early Russian industrialization also depended on Russo-German trade, and placed a premium on good relations with the emerging German power. . . . Britain had pressing colonial problems; it was primarily suspicious of French ambitions on the Continent, and viewed the emerging Germany as a power that neither threatened fundamental British interests nor possessed a significant navy. Add to this the general British approval of national self-determination (as in Italy), the high regard for German culture, and Gladstone's concern with domestic issues, and it is clear why British sympathizers comfortably outnumbered those suspicious of Prussian "militarism." If we turn to the two powers directly defeated by Prussia on the road to unification, it is their weakness rather than their benevolent neutrality that requires emphasis. Austria was desperately isolated in this period. Vienna had failed to repair the alliance with Russia, broken by the Crimean war; and the great irony of the Austrian position, as well as the central weakness, was the fact that its principal ally, Prussia, was also its archrival in German affairs. Compounding these problems were the perpetual difficulties created by the subject nation-alities of the far-flung Habsburg monarchy, Hungarians, Italians and Slavs. This was an important part of the background to 1866; then, during the Franco-Prussian war, the restlessness of the Czechs and Poles pushed Vienna into a more pro-"German" stance. Last, but not least, France under Napoleon III was the loose cannon in European affairs, an adventurist power that excited universal suspicion and found none to mourn its fate in 1870.

The Age of Empire
Eric J. Hobsbawn

Imperialism has been interpreted from a number of perspectives since the early twentieth century. The way that scholars view imperialism often reveals much about their own political and ideological views. Some of the earliest interpretations, such as those by J. H. Hobson and V. I. Lenin, were economic. They criticized imperialism as an outgrowth of capitalism, Hobson from the perspective of a liberal socialist, Lenin as a Marxist theorist and political leader. Economic interpretations of imperialism, often in newer versions, remain popular. This is illustrated in the following selection by the British historian E. J. Hobsbawn, who has written extensively on nineteenth-century Western civilization.

CONSIDER: *Why Hobsbawn considers economic results irrelevant to economic motives for imperialism; why Hobsbawn calls imperialism a natural by-product of the international economy; why political actions are secondary to the economic motives for imperialism.*

A more convincing general motive for colonial expansion was the search for markets. The fact that this was often disappointed is irrelevant. The belief that the "overproduction" of the Great Depression could be solved by a vast export drive was widespread. Businessmen, always inclined to fill the blank spaces on the map of world trade with vast numbers of potential customers, would naturally look for such unexploited areas: China was one which haunted the imagination of salesmen—what if every one of those 300 millions bought only one box of tin-tacks?—and Africa, the unknown continent, was another. The Chambers of Commerce of British cities in the depressed early 1880s were outraged by the thought that diplomatic negotiations might exclude their traders from access to the Congo basin, which was believed to offer untold sales prospects, all the more so as it was being developed as a paying proposition by that crowned businessman, King Leopold II of the Belgians. . . .

But the crux of the global economic situation was that a number of developed economies simultaneously felt the same need for new markets. If they were sufficiently strong their ideal was "the open door" on the markets of the underdeveloped world; but if not strong enough, they hoped to carve out for themselves territories which, by virtue of ownership, would give national business a monopoly position or at least a substantial advantage. Partition of the unoccupied parts of the

Third World was the logical consequence. In a sense, this was an extension of the protectionism which gained ground almost everywhere after 1879. . . . To this extent the "new imperialism" was the natural by-product of an international economy based on the rivalry of several competing industrial economies, intensified by the economic pressures of the 1880s. It does not follow that any particular colony was expected to turn into Eldorado by itself, though this is what actually happened in South Africa, which became the world's greatest gold-producer. Colonies might simply provide suitable bases or jumping-off points for regional business penetration. . . .

At this point the economic motive for acquiring some colonial territory becomes difficult to disentangle from the political action required for the purpose, for protectionism of whatever kind is economy operating with the aid of politics. . . . Once rival powers began to carve up the map of Africa or Oceania, each naturally tried to safeguard against an excessive portion (or a particularly attractive morsel) going to the others. Once the status of a great power thus became associated with raising its flag over some palm-fringed beach (or, more likely, over stretches of dry scrub), the acquisition of colonies itself became a status symbol, irrespective of their value.

Imperialism as a Nationalistic Phenomenon
Carlton J. H. Hayes

Although the economic interpretation of imperialism has not lost its strength, other views have been offered recently as supplements and sometimes as direct alternatives to an economic interpretation. A direct alternative appears in the following selection by Carlton J. H. Hayes. One of the earliest historians to develop a sophisticated understanding of nationalism, Hayes argues that economic motives were at best secondary; on the whole, imperialism was a nationalistic phenomenon.

CONSIDER: *The evidence Hayes uses to reject economic interpretations of nationalism; how Hobsbawn might reply to this interpretation; the ways in which this view fits with the documents on nationalism in this chapter.*

The founding of new colonial empires and the fortifying of old ones antedated the establishment of neomercantilism, and that the economic arguments adduced

SOURCE: From *The Age of Empire* by Eric Hobsbawn. Copyright © 1987 by E. J. Hobsbawn. Reprinted by permission of Pantheon Books, a division of Random House, Inc.

SOURCE: Excerpted from *A Generation of Materialism, 1871–1900*, pp. 223–224, by Carlton J. H. Hayes. Copyright 1941 by Harper & Row Publishers, Inc. Copyright renewed 1969 by Mary Evelyn Hayes. Reprinted by permission of HarperCollins Publishers, Inc.

in support of imperialism seem to have been a rationalization *ex post facto*. In the main, it was not Liberal parties, with their super abundance of industrials and bankers, who sponsored the outward imperialistic thrusts of the '70's and early '80's. Instead, it was Conservative parties, with a preponderantly agricultural clientele notoriously suspicious of moneylenders and big business, and, above all, it was patriotic professors and publicists regardless of political affiliation and unmindful of personal economic interest. These put forth the economic arguments which eventually drew bankers and traders and industrialists into the imperialist camp.

Basically the new imperialism was a nationalistic phenomenon. It followed hard upon the national wars which created an all-powerful Germany and a united Italy, which carried Russia within sight of Constantinople, and which left England fearful and France eclipsed. It expressed a resulting psychological reaction, an ardent desire to maintain or recover national prestige. France sought compensation for European loss in oversea gain. England would offset her European isolation by enlarging and glorifying the British Empire. Russia, halted in the Balkans, would turn anew to Asia, and before long Germany and Italy would show the world that the prestige they had won by might inside Europe they were entitled to enhance by imperial exploits outside. The lesser powers, with no great prestige at stake, managed to get on without any new imperialism, though Portugal and Holland displayed a revived pride in the empires they already possessed and the latter's was administered with renewed vigor. . . .

Most simply, the sequence of imperialism after 1870 appears to have been, first, pleas for colonies on the ground of national prestige; second, getting them; third, disarming critics by economic argument; and fourth, carrying this into effect and relating the results to the neomercantilism of tariff protection and social legislation at home.

The Tools of Empire

Daniel R. Headrick

Recently some historians have focused on exactly how the spread of imperial rule took place during the second half of the 19th century. They argue that the tools of colonial conquest constituted an important explanation for that burst of colonial expansion occurring when it did. In the following selection from his influential book, The Tools of Empire: Technology

SOURCE: Daniel R. Headrick, *The Tools of Empire: Technology and European Imperialism in the Nineteenth Century* (New York: Oxford University Press, 1981), pp. 205–206.

and European Imperialism in the Nineteenth Century, Daniel R. Headrick focuses on the ways key inventions and innovations enabled Europeans to conquer new lands with such relative ease.

CONSIDER: *How, according to Headrick, technology helps explain the events of imperial expansion; whether Headrick's argument undermines an economic or nationalistic interpretation of imperialism or adds to those interpretations.*

Imperialism in the mid-century was predominantly a matter of British tentacles reaching out from India toward Burma, China, Malaya, Afghanistan, Mesopotamia, and the Red Sea. Territorially, at least, a much more impressive demonstration of the new imperialism was the scramble for Africa in the last decades of the century. Historians generally agree that from a profit-making point of view, the scramble was a dubious undertaking. Here also, technology helps explain events.

Inventions are most easily described one by one, each in its own technological and socioeconomic setting. Yet the inner logic of innovations must not blind us to the patterns of chronological coincidence. Though advances occurred in every period, many of the innovations that proved useful to the imperialists of the scramble first had an impact in the two decades from 1860 to 1880. These were the years in which quinine prophylaxis made Africa safer for Europeans; quick-firing breechloaders replaced muzzleloaders among the forces stationed on the imperial frontiers; and the compound engine, the Suez Canal, and the submarine cable made steamships competitive with sailing ships, not only on government-subsidized mail routes, but for ordinary freight on distant seas as well. Europeans who set out to conquer new lands in 1880 had far more power over nature and over the people they encountered than their predecessors twenty years earlier had; they could accomplish their tasks with far greater safety and comfort. . . .

What the breechloader, the machine gun, the steamboat and steamship, and quinine and other innovations did was to lower the cost, in both financial and human terms, of penetrating, conquering, and exploiting new territories. So cost-effective did they make imperialism that not only national governments but lesser groups as well could now play a part in it. The Bombay Presidency opened the Red Sea Route; the Royal Niger Company conquered the Caliphate of Sokoto; even individuals like Macgregor Laird, William Mackinnon, Henry Stanley, and Cecil Rhodes could precipitate events and stake out claims to vast territories which later became parts of empires. It is because the flow of new technologies in the nineteenth century made imperialism so cheap that it reached the threshold of acceptance among the peoples and governments of Europe, and led nations to become empires. Is this not as important a factor in the scramble for Africa as the political, diplomatic, and business motives that historians have stressed?

Gender and Empire

Margaret Strobel

While most of the Europeans who served as soldiers, officials, and administrators in overseas colonies were men, women also traveled to the colonies, lived there, and participated in these overseas societies. Their position as unequals to men in their own societies but superior to colonized men and women added complexity to their roles and to controversies over imperial practices. In the following selection, Margaret Strobel analyzes the situation facing these women and how they related to colonized peoples in Africa and Asia.

CONSIDER: *The ways European women benefited from imperialism; how these women may have viewed imperialism differently than men.*

European women had a complex, varied, and often contradictory relationship to the African and Asian territories controlled by the European powers in the nineteenth and twentieth centuries. As members of the "inferior sex" within the "superior race" (to use contemporary formulations), women were afforded options by imperialism that male dominance in the colonies then limited. By the twentieth century, some European women were attacking aspects of the racial, political, and economic inequalities of the colonial relationship. But the vast majority of them supported and contributed to the imperial venture. These women benefited from the economic and political subjugation of indigenous peoples and shared many of the accompanying attitudes of racism, paternalism, ethnocentrism, and national chauvinism. For most of them,

life in the colonies provided opportunities not found in Europe, where their options were limited by their social class, a "shortage" of marriageable men, difficulty in finding adequate employment, or the lack of "heathen souls" to be converted. At the same time, women continuously experienced, sometimes challenged, and sometimes reproduced the economic, political, and ideological subordination of women. As wives of colonial officials, they subordinated their lives to a male-centered administrative environment. As educators of indigenous women, they reproduced the European notions of bourgeois or Victorian domesticity and female dependence. Even missionary women, whose commitment to career and calling was in some ways a challenge to those very notions, accepted the patriarchal ideology and bureaucracy of the Church and promoted conventional European gender roles to African and Asian women. . . .

In one sense, European women's marginal status within a male-dominated colonial society and structure provided an opportunity. People outside the dominant culture have a different perspective that derives from their different experience and position within the social structure. Perhaps European women's marginal position within the dominant colonial society enabled them to see aspects of imperialism differently. European women frequently saw the needs of indigenous women where male administrators were blind to them. Some chose to use their skills, enhanced power, and status as members of the colonizing society on behalf of indigenous people. In so doing, they contributed, if not always intentionally, to the dismantling of the empire.

❧ CHAPTER QUESTIONS

1. What historical links are there between nationalism, the national state, and imperialism during the nineteenth century? How might all three be connected to industrialization?

2. How would you explain the rise of imperialism in the late nineteenth century?

3. In what ways have some of our perceptions of imperialism changed since the late nineteenth century?

SOURCE: Margaret Strobel, "Gender, Race, and Empire in Nineteenth- and Twentieth-Century Africa and Asia," in Renate Bridenthal et al., eds., *Becoming Visible: Women in European History,* 3rd ed. (New York: Houghton Mifflin Co., 1998), pp. 390, 410.

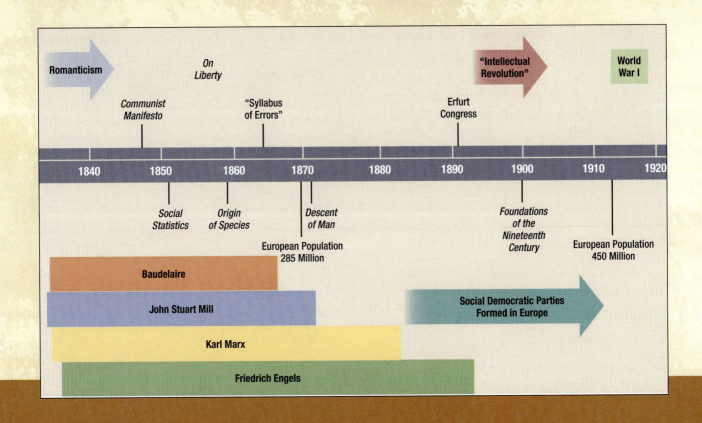

14 Culture, Thought, and Society: 1850–1914

From the mid–nineteenth century to 1914 the urban middle class dominated Europe socially and culturally. It was this class that was benefiting most from the continuing industrialization of the period. As the urban middle class grew in numbers and wealth, it asserted its own values and assumptions. Increasingly this class set the standards of lifestyle, thought, and culture. At the same time, these standards were attacked from all sides, particularly by those sensitive to the problems of the working class. The contrast between the standards being established by the middle class and the challenges to those standards marks this period as one of great social, cultural, and intellectual ferment.

The selections in this chapter exemplify some of the main social, cultural, and intellectual developments of this period. Three broad questions are addressed. First, what

were some of the main elements of the middle-class style of life? Some of the materials show how this lifestyle was reflected in the physical setting of the middle class; others concentrate on the role women and the family played in this style of life. Second, what were some of the dominant intellectual currents favored by the middle class? Here liberalism as it was evolving toward the end of the century and ideas generally referred to as Social Darwinism are examined. Third, what were some of the main challenges to middle-class ideas and institutions? The most pervasive of these were Marxism and related social doctrines, but there were also conservative challenges, such as those from the Catholic Church and the challenges of racism.

What emerges from these sources is a picture of a dynamic society with a vast array of cultural and intellectual developments. In the decades following the outbreak of

World War I, many would look back to this period as one of unusual progress. Some of the twentieth-century developments that in retrospect make the second half of the nineteenth century seem such a positive time will be examined in the next chapter.

 For Classroom Discussion

How might some sources be used to reveal the nature of the middle-class style of life? Use the painting by Eastman Johnson, the document "Women as Chemists," the illustration from The Ages of Woman, and the analysis by Riemer and Fout.

 Primary Sources

The Origin of Species *and* The Descent of Man

Charles Darwin

The nineteenth century was a period of great scientific ideas and discoveries. Perhaps the most important and certainly the most controversial was Darwin's theory of evolution. Charles Darwin (1809–1882), a British naturalist, gathered data while on voyages in the southern Pacific. He used those data to develop his theory of evolution by natural selection. This theory of evolution, particularly as applied to human beings, challenged Biblical accounts of creation. He argued that all life, including human life, evolved from lower forms. Evolution was slow and extended over a much longer period than had been assumed. Natural selection, or survival of the fittest, determined how species evolved. Darwin first formulated his findings and theory in an 1844 essay. However, it was only after 1859, when he published The Origin of Species by Means of Natural Selection, *that his ideas became well known and widely controversial. The first of two selections below is from that book. The second is from* The Descent of Man, *which he published in 1871.*

CONSIDER: *Why his ideas might be so welcome by some, so disturbing to others; the possible psychological impact of his ideas; how those favoring Biblical accounts might respond.*

. . . [C]an we doubt (remembering that many more individuals are born than can possibly survive) that individuals having any advantage, however slight, over others, would have the best chance of surviving and of procreating their kind? On the other hand, we may feel sure that any variation in the least degree injurious would be rigidly destroyed. This preservation of favourable individual differences and variations, and the destruction of those which are injurious, I have called Natural Selection, or the Survival of the Fittest. . . .

Natural selection acts solely through the preservation of variations in some way advantageous, which consequently endure. Owing to the high geometrical rate of increase of all organic beings, each area is already fully stocked with inhabitants; and it follows from this, that as the favoured forms increase in number, so, generally, will the less favoured decrease and become rare. Rarity, as geology tells us, is the precursor to extinction.

The main conclusion here arrived at, and now held by many naturalists who are well competent to form a sound judgment, is that man is descended from some less highly organized form. The grounds upon which this conclusion rests will never be shaken, for the close similarity between man and the lower animals in embryonic development, as well as in innumerable points of structure and constitution, both of high and of the most trifling importance,—the rudiments which he retains, and the abnormal reversions to which he is occasionally liable,—are facts which cannot be disputed. They have long been known, but until recently they told us nothing with respect to the origin of man. Now when viewed by the light of our knowledge of the whole organic world, their meaning is unmistakable. The great principle of evolution stands up clear and firm, when these groups of facts are considered in connection with others, such as the mutual affinities of the members of the same group, their geographical distribution in past and present times, and their geological succession. It is incredible that all these facts should speak falsely. He who is not content to look, like a savage, at the phenomena of nature as disconnected, cannot any longer believe that man is the work of a separate act of creation. . . .

We have seen that man incessantly presents individual differences in all parts of his body and in his mental faculties. These differences or variations seem to be induced by the same general causes, and to obey the same laws as with the lower animals. In both cases similar laws of inheritance prevail. Man tends to increase at a greater rate than his means of subsistence; consequently he is occasionally subjected to a severe struggle for existence, and natural selection will have effected whatever lies

SOURCES: Charles Darwin, *The Origin of Species by Means of Natural Selection*, 6th ed. (London: John Murray, 1872), pp. 63, 85; Charles Darwin, *The Descent of Man* (New York: D. Appleton and Co., 1883), pp. 606–607, 619.

within its scope. A succession of strongly-marked variations of a similar nature is by no means requisite; slight fluctuating differences in the individual suffice for the work of natural selection. . . .

[M]an with all his noble qualities, with sympathy which feels for the most debased, with benevolence which extends not only to other men but to the humblest living creature, with his god-like intellect which has penetrated into the movements and constitution of the solar system—with all these exalted powers—Man still bears in his bodily frame the indelible stamp of his lowly origin.

Social Statics: Liberalism and Social Darwinism

Herbert Spencer

The works of Herbert Spencer (1820–1903) epitomize the assertive liberal philosophy favored by successful mid-nineteenth-century industrialists. This was a period in which capitalism was relatively unrestrained and social legislation was only in its infancy. It was also the beginning of thinking from a biological and evolutionary perspective, as best evidenced by the publication of Charles Darwin's Origin of Species in 1859. Spencer reflected all this in his massive writings. He rose from being a railroad engineer to become editor of the London Economist—which espoused the views of industrial capitalism—and an independent author. Always a supporter of laissez-faire, he was best known for his advocacy of social evolution and acceptance of Darwinian ideas applied to society (Social Darwinism). Modern scholars consider him a founder of sociology. The following is an excerpt from Social Statics first published in 1851.

CONSIDER: *Why Spencer's views would be so appealing to the industrial middle class; on what grounds certain groups might oppose these views; the social policies that would flow from these ideas; ways these views reflect Darwin's ideas.*

Pervading all Nature we may see at work a stern discipline which is a little cruel that it may be very kind. . . . It seems hard that an unskillfulness which with all his efforts he cannot overcome, should entail hunger upon the artizan. It seems hard that a labourer incapacitated by sickness from competing with his stronger fellows, should have to bear the resulting privations. It seems hard that widows and orphans should be left to struggle for life or death. Nevertheless, when regarded not separately but in connexion with the interests of universal humanity, these harsh fatalities are seen to be full of beneficence—the same beneficence which brings to early graves the children of diseased parents, and singles out the intemperate and the debilitated as the victims of an epidemic.

There are many very amiable people who have not the nerve to look this matter fairly in the face. Disabled as they are by their sympathies with present suffering, from duly regarding ultimate consequences, they pursue a course which is injudicious, and in the end even cruel. We do not consider it true kindness in a mother to gratify her child with sweetmeats that are likely to make it ill. We should think it a very foolish sort of benevolence which led a surgeon to let his patient's disease progress to a fatal issue, rather than inflict pain by an operation. Similarly, we must call those spurious philanthropists who, to prevent present misery, would entail greater misery on future generations. That rigorous necessity which, when allowed to operate, becomes so sharp a spur to the lazy and so strong a bridle to the random, these paupers' friends would repeal, because of the wailings it here and there produces. Blind to the fact that under the natural order of things society is constantly excreting its unhealthy, imbecile, slow, vacillating, faithless members, these unthinking, though well-meaning, men advocate an interference which not only stops the purifying process, but even increases the vitiation—absolutely encourages the multiplication of the reckless and incompetent by offering them an unfailing provision, and *discourages* the multiplication of the competent and provident by heightening the difficulty of maintaining a family. And thus, in their eagerness to prevent the salutary sufferings that surround us, these sigh-wise and groan-foolish people bequeath to posterity a continually increasing curse.

On Liberty

John Stuart Mill

During the second half of the nineteenth century, liberalism in theory and practice started to change. In general, it became less wedded to laissez-faire policies and less optimistic than it was during the first half of the nineteenth century. This change is reflected in the thought of John Stuart Mill (1806–1873). He was the most influential British thinker of the mid-nineteenth century and probably the leading liberal theorist of the period. When he was young he favored the early liberalism of his father, James Mill, a well-known philosopher, and Jeremy Bentham, the author of utilitarianism. Over time he perceived difficulties with this early liberalism and new dangers. He modified his liberal ideas, a change that would later be reflected in liberal political policies of the late

SOURCE: Herbert Spencer, *Social Statics* (New York: D. Appleton and Co., 1896), pp. 149–151.

SOURCE: John Stuart Mill, *Utilitarianism, Liberty, and Representative Government* (London: J. M. Dent and Sons Ltd., Everyman Library, 1910), pp. 66–68.

*nineteenth and early twentieth centuries. In the following se-
lection from* On Liberty *(1859), his most famous work, Mill
analyzes this evolution of liberalism starting with the aims of
liberals during the first half of the nineteenth century.*

CONSIDER: *What Mill feels was the essence of early liberalism; what crucial changes occurred to transform liberalism;
what Mill means by tyranny of the majority.*

The aim, therefore, of patriots was to set limits to the
power which the ruler should be suffered to exercise over
the community; and this limitation was what they meant
by liberty. It was attempted in two ways. First, by obtaining
a recognition of certain immunities, called political liberties or rights, which it was to be regarded as a breach of
duty in the ruler to infringe, and which if he did infringe,
specific resistance, or general rebellion, was held to be justifiable. A second, and generally a later expedient, was the
establishment of constitutional checks, by which the consent of the community, or of a body of some sort, supposed
to represent its interests, was made a necessary condition
to some of the more important acts of the governing power.
To the first of these modes of limitation, the ruling power,
in most European countries, was compelled, more or less,
to submit. It was not so with the second; and, to attain
this, or when already in some degree possessed, to attain it
more completely, became everywhere the principal object
of the lovers of liberty. And so long as mankind were content to combat one enemy by another, and to be ruled by a
master, on condition of being guaranteed more or less effi-
caciously against his tyranny, they did not carry their aspirations beyond this point.

A time, however, came, in the progress of human affairs, when men ceased to think it a necessity of nature
that their governors should be an independent power,
opposed in interest to themselves. It appeared to them
much better that the various magistrates of the State
should be their tenants or delegates, revocable at their
pleasure. In that way alone, it seemed, could they have
complete security that the powers of government would
never be abused to their disadvantage. By degrees this
new demand for elective and temporary rulers became
the prominent object of the exertions of the popular
party, wherever any such party existed; and superseded,
to a considerable extent, the previous efforts to limit
the power of rulers. As the struggle proceeded for making
the ruling power emanate from the periodical choice of the
ruled, some persons began to think that too much importance had been attached to the limitation of the
power itself, *That* (it might seem) was a resource against
rulers whose interests were habitually opposed to those of
the people. What was now wanted was, that the rulers
should be identified with the people; that their interest
and will should be the interest and will of the nation. The

nation did not need to be protected against its own will.
There was no fear of its tyrannising over itself. Let the
rulers be effectually responsible to it, promptly removable
by it, and it could afford to trust them with power of which
it could itself dictate the use to be made. Their power was
but the nation's own power, concentrated, and in a form
convenient for exercise. This mode of thought, or rather
perhaps of feeling, was common among the last generation of European liberalism, in the Continental section of
which it still apparently predominates. . . .

In time, however, a democratic republic came to occupy a large portion of the earth's surface, and made itself
felt as one of the most powerful members of the community of nations; and elective and responsible government
became subject to the observations and criticisms which
wait upon a great existing fact. It was now perceived that
such phrases as "self-government," and "the power of the
people over themselves," do not express the true state of
the case. The "people" who exercise the power are not always the same people with those over whom it is exercised; and the "self-government" spoken of is not the
government of each by himself, but of each by all the rest.
The will of the people, moreover, practically means the
will of the most numerous or the most active *part* of the
people; the majority, or those who succeed in making
themselves accepted as the majority; the people, consequently, *may* desire to oppress a part of their number; and
precautions are as much needed against this as against
any other abuse of power. The limitation, therefore, of
the power of government over individuals loses none of
its importance when the holders of power are regularly
accountable to the community, that is, to the strongest
party therein. This view of things, recommending itself
equally to the intelligence of thinkers and to the inclination of those important classes in European society to
whose real or supposed interests democracy is adverse,
has had no difficulty in establishing itself; and in political
speculations "the tyranny of the majority" is now generally included among the evils against which society requires to be on its guard.

Like other tyrannies, the tyranny of the majority was
at first, and is still vulgarly, held in dread, chiefly as operating through the acts of the public authorities. But reflecting persons perceived that when society is itself the
tyrant—society collectively over the separate individuals
who compose it—its means of tyrannising are not re-
stricted to the acts which it may do by the hands of its political functionaries. Society can and does execute its
own mandates: and if it issues wrong mandates instead of
right, or any mandates at all in things with which it ought
not to meddle, it practises a social tyranny more formidable than many kinds of political oppression, since, though
not usually upheld by such extreme penalties, it leaves
fewer means of escape, penetrating much more deeply

into the details of life, and enslaving the soul itself. Protection, therefore, against the tyranny of the magistrate is not enough: there needs protection also against the tyranny of the prevailing opinion and feeling; against the tendency of society to impose, by other means than civil penalties, its own ideas and practices as rules of conduct on those who dissent from them; to fetter the development, and, if possible, prevent the formation, of any individuality not in harmony with its ways, and compel all characters to fashion themselves upon the model of its own. There is a limit to the legitimate interference of collective opinion with individual independence: and to find that limit, and maintain it against encroachment, is as indispensable to a good condition of human affairs, as protection against political despotism.

Women as Chemists [Pharmacists]
Our Sisters

Most occupations were defined as inappropriate for middle-class women. What few occupations were appropriate were often explained to middle-class women in "how to" guides that appeared in books and women's magazines, often written by women. The following is an excerpt from "What to Do with Our Daughters, or Remunerative Employment of Women—Women as Chemists [Pharmacists]," an 1897 article published in Our Sisters, *a popular magazine addressed to middle-class women.*

CONSIDER: *What makes pharmacy appropriate for women; what kinds of activities are inappropriate for women as pharmacists and women in general.*

The Pharmaceutical Society, in opening up its ranks to women, has provided them with an eminently suitable calling. There is no lack of persons of both sexes who still loudly proclaim that a woman doctor is a thing unsexed. These persons could scarcely bring their arguments to bear against Pharmacy, and maintain that there is anything essentially unfeminine in the making up of drugs and pills. The calling of a chemist does not necessitate the possession on the part of a woman of all those faculties and qualities generally summed up as "strong-mindedness." In the peaceful seclusion of a drug shop, a woman chemist, unlike a doctor or a nurse, is not brought face to face with those stern realities: disease, pain, deformity, death. True, she works in with the doctor and the nurse, and her share in the healing of the sick is

SOURCE: "What to Do with Our Daughters, or Remunerative Employment of Women—Women as Chemists," *Our Sisters*, February 1897, pp. 85–86, in Eleanor S. Riemer and John C. Fout, eds., *European Women: A Documentary History, 1789–1945* (New York: Schocken Books, 1980), p. 45.

responsible enough; but for all that, her life work involves no such wear and tear, no such physical and mental strain, no such constant demands upon her endurance, patience, and staying power. Should her services be required for an operation to which some chemists devote attention, namely, tooth drawing, and should she not feel equal to the occasion, she need only refer the sufferer from toothache either to a dentist or a male colleague around the corner!

The Communist Manifesto
Karl Marx and Friedrich Engels

Although initially only one of many radical doctrines, Marxism proved to be the most dynamic and influential challenge to industrial capitalism and middle-class civilization in general. Its most succinct and popular statement is contained in the Communist Manifesto, *written by Karl Marx (1818–1883) and Friedrich Engels (1820–1895) and first published in 1848. Karl Marx was born in Germany, studied history and philosophy, and entered a career as a journalist, writer, and revolutionary. For most of his life he lived in exile in London. His collaborator, Friedrich Engels, was also born in Germany and lived in England, but there he helped manage his family's cotton business in Manchester. Their doctrines directly attacked the middle class and industrial capitalism, presenting communism as a philosophically, historically, and scientifically justified alternative that would inevitably replace capitalism. They saw themselves as revolutionary leaders of the growing proletariat (the working class). The following is a selection from the* Communist Manifesto.

CONSIDER: *The appeal of the ideas presented here; the concrete policies advocated by Marx and Engels; the historical and intellectual trends reflected in the Manifesto.*

A specter is haunting Europe—the specter of Communism. All the powers of old Europe have entered into a holy alliance to exorcise this specter; Pope and Czar, Metternich and Guizot, French radicals and German police spies.

Where is the party in opposition that has not been decried as Communistic by its opponents in power? Where the opposition that has not hurled back the branding reproach of Communism, against the more advanced opposition parties, as well as against its reactionary adversaries?

Two things result from this fact.

I. Communism is already acknowledged by all European powers to be in itself a power.

SOURCE: Karl Marx and Friedrich Engels, *Manifesto of the Communist Party*, 2nd ed. (New York: National Executive Committee of the Socialist Labor Party, 1898), pp. 30–32, 41–43, 60.

II. It is high time that Communists should openly, in the face of the whole world, publish their views, their aims, their tendencies, and meet this nursery tale of the Specter of Communism with a Manifesto of the party itself.

To this end the Communists of various nationalities have assembled in London, and sketched the following manifesto to be published in the English, French, German, Italian, Flemish and Danish languages.

❧

In what relation do the Communists stand to the proletarians as a whole?

The Communists do not form a separate party opposed to other working class parties.

They have no interests separate and apart from those of the proletariat as a whole.

They do not set up any sectarian principles of their own by which to shape and mould the proletarian movement.

The Communists are distinguished from the other working class parties by this only: 1. In the national struggles of the proletarians of the different countries, they point out and bring to the front the common interests of the entire proletariat, independently of all nationality. 2. In the various stages of development which the struggle of the working class against the bourgeoisie has to pass through, they always and everywhere represent the interests of the movement as a whole.

The Communists, therefore, are on the one hand, practically, the most advanced and resolute section of the working class parties of every country, that section which pushes forward all others; on the other hand, theoretically, they have over the great mass of the proletariat the advantage of clearly understanding the line of march, the conditions, and the ultimate general results of the proletarian movement.

The immediate aim of the Communists is the same as that of all the other proletarian parties: formation of the proletariat into a class, overthrow of the bourgeois supremacy, conquest of political power by the proletariat.

The theoretical conclusions of the Communists are in no way based on ideas or principles that have been invented, or discovered, by this or that would-be universal reformer.

They merely express, in general terms, actual relations springing from an existing class struggle, from a historical movement going on under our very eyes. The abolition of existing property relations is not at all a distinctive feature of Communism.

All property relations in the past have continually been subject to historical change, consequent upon the change in historical conditions.

The French revolution, for example, abolished feudal property in favor of bourgeois property.

The distinguishing feature of Communism is not the abolition of property generally, but the abolition of bourgeois property. But modern bourgeois private property is the final and most complete expression of the system of producing and appropriating products, that is based on class antagonisms, on the exploitation of the many by the few.

In this sense the theory of the Communists may be summed up in the single sentence: Abolition of private property.

We have seen above that the first step in the revolution by the working class is to raise the proletariat to the position of the ruling class; to win the battle of democracy.

The proletariat will use its political supremacy to wrest, by degrees, all capital from the bourgeoisie; to centralize all instruments of production in the hands of the State, *i.e.*, of the proletariat organized as the ruling class; and to increase the total of productive forces as rapidly as possible.

Of course, in the beginning this cannot be effected except by means of despotic inroads on the rights of property and on the conditions of bourgeois production; by means of measures, therefore, which appear economically insufficient and untenable, but which, in the course of the movement, outstrip themselves, necessitate further inroads upon the old social order and are unavoidable as a means of entirely revolutionizing the mode of production.

These measures will, of course, be different in different countries.

Nevertheless in the most advanced countries the following will be pretty generally applicable:

1. Abolition of property in land and application of all rents of land to public purposes.

2. A heavy progressive or graduated income tax.

3. Abolition of all right of inheritance.

4. Confiscation of the property of all emigrants and rebels.

5. Centralization of credit in the hands of the State, by means of a national bank with State capital and an exclusive monopoly.

6. Centralization of the means of communication and transport in the hands of the State.

7. Extension of factories and instruments of production owned by the State; the bringing into cultivation of waste lands, and the improvement of the soil generally in accordance with a common plan.

8. Equal liability of all to labor. Establishment of industrial armies, especially for agriculture.

9. Combination of agriculture with manufacturing industries: gradual abolition of the distinction between town and country, by a more equable distribution of the population over the country.

10. Free education for all children in public schools. Abolition of children's factory labor in its present form. Combination of education with industrial production, etc., etc.

When, in the course of development, class distinctions have disappeared and all production has been concentrated in the hands of a vast association of the whole nation, the public power will lose its political character. Political power, properly so called, is merely the organized power of one class for oppressing another. If the proletariat during its contest with the bourgeoisie is compelled, by the force of circumstances, to organize itself as a class, if, by means of a revolution, it makes itself the ruling class, and, as such, sweeps away by force the old conditions of production, then it will, along with these conditions, have swept away the conditions for the existence of class antagonisms, and of classes generally, and will thereby have abolished its own supremacy as a class.

In place of the old bourgeois society with its classes and class antagonisms we shall have an association in which the free development of each is the condition for the free development of all.

Socialist Women: Becoming a Socialist

Anna Maier

Between 1850 and 1914 numerous working-class women joined unions and various working-class political organizations. As socialism became more popular in the last decades of the nineteenth century, more and more working-class women were attracted to socialist organizations. At first, most socialist leaders took little account of the specific needs of women workers, but over time more attention was paid to women's issues and women gained leadership roles within socialist organizations. In the following selection Anna Maier describes how she became a socialist by joining the Social Democrats in Austria during the 1890s.

CONSIDER: *What experiences led Anna Maier to become a socialist; the consequences of her becoming a socialist.*

SOURCE: Adelheid Popp, ed., *A Commemorative Book: Twenty Years of the Austrian Women Workers' Movement* (Vienna, 1912), pp. 107–109, in Eleanor S. Riemer and John C. Fout, eds., *European Women: A Documentary History, 1789–1945* (New York: Schocken Books, 1980), pp. 94–95.

When I turned thirteen my mother took me by the hand and we went to see the manager of a tobacco factory to get me a job. The manager refused to hire me but my mother begged him to change his mind, since she explained, my father had died. I was hired. When I was getting ready to go to work the next day, my mother told me that I was to keep quiet and do what I was told. That was easier said than done. The treatment you received in this factory was really brutal. Young girls were often abused or even beaten by the older women. I rebelled strongly against that. I tried anything that might help improve things for me. As a child I was very pious and used to listen enthusiastically to the priests telling stories from the Bible. So, when things were going badly for me [at work], I would go to church on Sundays where I prayed so intently that I saw or heard nothing going on around me. When I went back to work on Monday, things were not any better and sometimes they were worse. I asked myself: Can there be a higher power that rewards good and punishes evil? I said to myself, no, that cannot be.

Several years went by. The *Women Workers' Newspaper* [*Arbeiterinnen-Zeitung*] began to appear and a few issues were smuggled into the factory by one of the older women. The more I was warned to stay away from this woman, the more I went to her to ask her if she would lend me a copy of the newspaper since I didn't have enough money to buy my own. At that time work hours were very long and the pay was very low. When my friend lent me a copy of the newspaper, I had to keep it hidden and I couldn't even let my mother see it if I took it home. I came to understand many things, my circle of acquaintances grew and when a political organization was founded in Sternberg, the workers were urged to join—only the men, the women were left out. A party representative came to us since I was already married by then. When he came by for the third time I asked him if I wasn't mature enough to become a member of the organization. He was embarrassed but replied: "When do you want to?" So I joined and I am a member of the party to this day.

I attended all the meetings, took part in all the demonstrations and it was not long before I was punished by the manager of the factory. I was taken off a good job and put in a poorer one just because I had become a Social Democrat. Nothing stopped me though; I said to myself, if this official is against it, out of fear to be sure, then it can't be all bad. When the tobacco workers' union was founded in November 1899, I joined and we had some big battles before we were able to make progress. Through these two organizations I have matured into a class-conscious fighter and I am now trying to win over mothers to the cause so that future children of the proletariat will have a happier youth than I had.

Why We Are Militant

Emmeline Pankhurst

The movement for female suffrage had deep roots in the nineteenth century, but gained force toward the end of the century. Various women's organizations in the West circulated petitions, led marches, and held demonstrations to support their demands for the right to vote. In the years before World War I, women's groups became more militant in the face of refusals by governmental officials to act. In Britain, Emmeline Pankhurst (1858–1928) helped organize the Women's Social and Political Union, which conducted assaults on private property and hunger strikes to promote the cause of women's suffrage. In the following excerpt from a 1913 speech, Pankhurst explains why her group is so militant.

CONSIDER: *The problems facing women who wanted to gain the right to vote; how Pankhurst explains why it became necessary for women to revolt; what arguments government officials might use to oppose Pankhurst.*

I know that in your minds there are questions like these; you are saying, "Woman Suffrage is sure to come; the emancipation of humanity is an evolutionary process, and how is it that some women, instead of trusting to that evolution, instead of educating the masses of people of their country, instead of educating their own sex to prepare them for citizenship, how is it that these militant women are using violence and upsetting the business arrangements of the country in their undue impatience to attain their end?" . . .

Meanwhile, during the '80's, women, like men, were asking for the franchise. Appeals, larger and more numerous than for any other reform, were presented in support of Woman's Suffrage. Meetings of the great corporations, great town councils, and city councils, passed resolutions asking that women should have the vote. More meetings were held, and larger, for Woman Suffrage than were held for votes for men, and yet the women did not get it. Men got the vote because they were and would be violent. The women did not get it because they were constitutional and law-abiding. Why, is it not evident to everyone that people who are patient where mis-government is concerned may go on being patient! Why should anyone trouble to help them? I take to myself some shame that through all those years, at any rate from the early '80's, when I first came into the Suffrage movement, I did not learn my political lessons.

I believed, as many women still in England believe, that women could get their way in some mysterious manner, by purely peaceful methods. We have been so accustomed, we women, to accept one standard for men and another standard for women, that we have even applied that variation of standard to the injury of our political welfare.

Having had better opportunities of education, and having had some training in politics, having in political life come so near to the "superior" being as to see that he was not altogether such a fount of wisdom as they had supposed, that he had his human weaknesses as we had, the twentieth century women began to say to themselves. "Is it not time, since our methods have failed and the men's have succeeded, that we should take a leaf out of their political book?" . . .

Well, I say the time is long past when it became necessary for women to revolt in order to maintain their self respect in Great Britain. The women who are waging this war are women who would fight, if it were only for the idea of liberty—if it were only that they might be free citizens of a free country—I myself would fight for that idea alone. But we have, in addition to this love of freedom, intolerable grievances to redress. . . .

Well, in Great Britain, we have tried persuasion, we have tried the plan of showing (by going upon public bodies, where they allowed us to do work they hadn't much time to do themselves) that we are capable people. We did it in the hope that we should convince them and persuade them to do the right and proper thing. But we had all our labour for our pains, and now we are fighting for our rights, and we are growing stronger and better women in the process. We are getting more fit to use our rights because we have such difficulty in getting them.

Syllabus of Errors

Pope Pius IX

Critics of middle-class liberalism were not limited to those demanding more rapid, radical changes such as the Marxists. From the time of the French Revolution, the conservative Catholic Church was usually hostile to most of the changes favored by the middle class and by doctrines of liberalism. Indeed, in the decades just after mid-century, when it had become apparent that traditional society was on the wane, the Church became more intransigent than ever. In 1864 Pius IX, who served as pope from 1846 to 1878, issued the famous "Syllabus of Errors," in which most of the major forces of the

SOURCE: Jane Marcus, ed., *Suffrage and the Pankhursts* (New York: Routledge and Kegan Paul, 1987), pp. 153–156.

SOURCE: From William E. Gladstone, *The Vatican Decrees in Their Bearing on Civil Allegiance: A Political Expostulation* (New York: Harper and Brothers, 1875), pp. 109–129.

nineteenth century were formally rejected. The following excerpts from that document should be read with care; they present views the Church specifically rejected as errors, not views accepted by the Church.

CONSIDER: Why Pius IX took this stand; the dilemma faced by Catholics who were also middle class and liberal; the groups that might favor the Church's view as expressed here.

15. Every man is free to embrace and profess the religion he shall believe true, guided by the light of reason.

16. Men may in any religion find the way of eternal salvation, and obtain eternal salvation.

❧

39. The commonwealth is the origin and source of all rights, and possesses rights which are not circumscribed by any limits.

❧

45. The entire direction of public schools, in which the youth of Christian states are educated, except (to a certain extent) in the case of episcopal seminaries, may and must appertain to the civil power, and belong to it so far that no other authority whatsoever shall be recognized as having any right to interfere in the discipline of the schools, the arrangement of the studies, the taking of degrees, or the choice and approval of the teachers.

❧

47. The best theory of civil society requires that popular schools open to the children of all classes, and, generally, all public institutes intended for instruction in letters and philosophy, and for conducting the education of the young, should be freed from all ecclesiastical authority, government, and interference, and should be fully subject to the civil and political power, in conformity with the will of rulers and the prevalent opinions of the age.

❧

56. Moral laws do not stand in need of the divine sanction, and there is no necessity that human laws should be conformable to the laws of nature, and receive their sanction from God.

57. Knowledge of philosophical things and morals, and also civil laws, may and must depart from divine and ecclesiastical authority.

❧

78. In the present day, it is no longer expedient that the Catholic religion shall be held as the only religion of the State, to the exclusion of all other modes of worship.

❧

80. The Roman Pontiff can and ought to reconcile himself to, and agree with, progress, liberalism, and civilization as lately introduced.

Foundations of the Nineteenth Century: Racism

Houston Stewart Chamberlain

During the second half of the nineteenth century, elements of nationalism, Darwinism, and Romanticism were combined by various writers to produce racist theories and provide justification for the growth of racist views. One of the most famous of these writers was Houston Stewart Chamberlain (1855–1927), an Englishman who moved to Germany and became a naturalized German. There he wrote Foundations of the Nineteenth Century *(1900), which soon became a popular success. In it he stressed the importance of racism for the development of civilization. The following selection from that book deals with the "German race."*

CONSIDER: *The characteristics of the "German race"; the ways in which this selection reflects racist thought; how this might relate to German nationalism.*

Let us attempt a glance into the depths of the soul. What are the specific intellectual and moral characteristics of this Germanic race? Certain anthropologists would fain teach us that all races are equally gifted; we point to history and answer: that is a lie! The races of mankind are markedly different in the nature and also in the extent of their gift, and the Germanic races belong to the most highly gifted group, the group usually termed Aryan. Is this human family united and uniform by bonds of blood? Do these stems really all spring from the same root? I do not know and I do not much care; no affinity binds more closely than elective affinity, and in this sense the Indo-European Aryans certainly form a family. . . .

Physically and mentally the Aryans are pre-eminent among all peoples; for that reason they are by right, as the Stagirite expresses it, the lords of the world. Aristotle puts the matter still more concisely when he says, "Some men are by nature free, others slaves"; this perfectly expresses the moral aspect. For freedom is by no means an

SOURCE: Houston Stewart Chamberlain, *Foundations of the Nineteenth Century*, vol. I (New York: Howard Fertig, 1968), pp. 542–543.

abstract thing, to which every human being has fundamentally a claim; a right to freedom must evidently depend upon capacity for it, and this again presupposes physical and intellectual power. One may make the assertion, that even the mere conception of freedom is quite unknown to most men. Do we not see the *homo syriacus* develop just as well and as happily in the position of slave as of master? Do the Chinese not show us another example of the same nature? Do not all historians tell us that the Semites and half-Semites, in spite of their great intelligence, never succeeded in founding a State that lasted, and that because every one always endeavoured to grasp all power for himself, thus showing that their capabilities were limited to despotism and anarchy, the two opposites of freedom?

Judaism in Music: Anti-Semitism

Richard Wagner

One of the darkest aspects of racist thought during the second half of the nineteenth century was its growing stress on anti-Semitism. Anti-Semitism has a long history, but it welled up with new strength after mid-century, particularly in Germany, where it became an important social and political force. An example of this bitter anti-Semitism comes from the pen of the great German composer, Richard Wagner (1813–1883). The following is an excerpt from "Judaism in Music," an article he published in a German journal in 1850.

CONSIDER: *The elements of Wagner's anti-Semitism; the support he uses for his arguments against the Jew; how this relates to the ideas of Houston Stewart Chamberlain.*

SOURCE: Louis L. Snyder, ed., *Documents of German History* (New Brunswick, NJ: Rutgers University Press, 1958), pp. 192–193.

It is necessary for us to explain the *involuntary repugnance* we possess for the nature and personality of the Jews. . . . According to the present constitution of the world, the Jew in truth is already more than emancipate: He rules, and will rule, as long as Money remains the power before which all our doings and our dealings lose their force. . . . The public art taste has been brought between the busy fingers of the Jews, who reside over an art bazaar. . . . The Jew's outward appearance always has something disagreeably foreign about it. . . .

The Jew speaks the language of the nation in whose midst he dwells from generation to generation, but he always speaks it as an alien. Our whole European art and civilization have remained to the Jew a foreign tongue. In this speech, this art, the Jew can only after-speak and after-patch—cannot truly make a poem of his words, an artwork of his doings. In the peculiarities of Semitic pronunciation the first thing that strikes our ear as quite outlandish and unpleasant, in the Jew's production of the voice sounds, is a creaking, squeaking, buzzing snuffle. . . . The Jew who is innately incapable of enouncing himself to us artistically through either his outward appearance or his speech, and least of all through his singing, has, nevertheless, been able in the widest-spread of modern art varieties, to wit, in Music, to reach the rulership of public taste. . . . Control of money through usury has led the Jews to power, for modern culture is accessible to none but the well-to-do. . . .

The Jews have never produced a true poet. [Heinrich Heine] reached the point where he duped himself into a poet, and was rewarded by his versified lies being set to music by our own composers. He was the conscience of Judaism, just as Judaism is the evil conscience of our modern civilization.

 Visual Sources

The Hatch Family: The Upper Middle Class

Eastman Johnson

The following 1871 portrait of the Hatch family by the American artist Eastman Johnson (figure 14.1) shows a number of elements of the condition, style of life, and values of the upper middle class. Both the quality and quantity of the furnishings and the clothes indicate how materially well to do this family is. The clothes and demeanor convey the strong sense of propriety; yet the activities of the children

and the position of their toys denote how child-centered this family is. The appropriate gender roles are suggested: the father at center right in an authoritative pose, with pen in hand sitting at his desk, the grandfather on the left, keeping up on the news by reading a paper, the mother on the right, generally surveying her children, and the grandmother on the left, knitting. The large painting on the left as well as the sculptures on the right show this family to be properly supportive and appreciative of the arts. The large bookcase on the right indicates a respect for literature and learning. Heavy curtains largely block out the outside world; values

FIGURE 14.1   (Image copyright © The Metropolitan Museum of Art/Art Resource, NY)

of domesticity and privacy are evident.

CONSIDER: What lessons the nineteenth-century viewer might learn from this portrait.

The Ages of Woman

This mid-nineteenth-century French engraving (figure 14.2) shows an idealized image of the ages of woman. In the center, three religious scenes represent the purity of woman's origins, place on earth, and final destination. Around this foundation is the woman at nine ages, from the happy playful child of ten years old to the solitary honorable grandmother of ninety years role as a middle-class wife, mother, and grandmother.

CONSIDER: What image of women's proper nature and role this conveys to nineteenth-century viewers; how this fits with the Eastman Johnson portrait and the analysis of European women by Riemer and Fout that follows; how an image of the ages of man might differ.

FIGURE 14.2   (© Musee Nat. des Arts et Traditions Populaires, Paris, France, Lauros/Giraudon/Bridgeman Art Library)

Lunch Hour: The Working Class

Käthe Kollwitz

Accompanying the rise to prominence of the upper middle class was the growth of the urban working class, the two economically dependent on each other but in strikingly different conditions. This 1909 drawing by the German artist Käthe Kollwitz *(figure 14.3), entitled* Lunch Hour, *gives an impression of the condition and spirit of the German working class. The workers seem to be part of an almost undifferentiated mass, dully and similarly clothed, eating low-quality meals in uncomfortable circumstances, and above all displaying a physical and psychological fatigue and a pervasive sense of discouragement.*

CONSIDER: *How this drawing relates to the views of Marx and Engels.*

The Stages of a Worker's Life

Léon Frédéric

Léon Frédéric (1856–1940), for a time Belgium's most famous painter, tried to encompass all stages of a worker's life in this large 1895 triptych (figure 14.4). In the foreground of the central panel, children on the right play cards while on the left they carry and nibble bread. Their parents and young couples stand just behind them; in the background are the aged members of the working class whose ultimate fate is marked by the distant but approaching funeral coach. The left side panel depicts the man's work world, where men of all ages, from adolescence to old age, engage in manual labor or observe it. In the foreground they are

FIGURE 14.3 (Käthe Kollwitz: *Lunch Hour.* Black charcoal and ink on paper. Nagel/Timm 469. Private Collection. Photo courtesy Galerie St. Etienne, New York)

digging while in the middle ground they struggle with heavy beams. Behind them are the factories where they work. The right side panel shows women's world, all mothering and

FIGURE 14.4 (© Réunion des Musées Nationaux/Art Resource, NY. © 2010 Artists Rights Society (ARS), New York/SABAM, Brussels)

nurturing with babies in their arms and at their breasts. Behind them are market stalls where they shop. Here is a vision of workers' lives in a nutshell: hard manual labor for men, childrearing and food preparation for women, and at the end old age and death for all.

CONSIDER: Whether this seems like a realistic depiction of workers' lives; how, in content and tone, a corresponding depiction of middle-class lives might look.

The City
Jacob Steinhardt

During the decades surrounding the turn of the century, great cities like Brussels, Paris, Milan, London, and Berlin became thriving embodiments of modern life. But many artists revealed disturbing undersides to these modern urban centers.

The 1913 canvas, The City (figure 14.5), by German expressionist artist Jacob Steinhardt (1887–1968) is one apt example. In this painting, throngs of people and modern streetcars push through the city boulevards at night. Electric lights from street lamps and store windows blaze; around corners, people half-disappear into shadows. In the left foreground, a man sleeps, perhaps dreaming. Above him a distracted nude woman (probably a prostitute) sits framed at a window, while above her haunting figures revel and lean out to ogle the action. Buildings loom over the people below. The scene evokes the frenzy, decadence, and danger of the modern city—the dark side of the years leading up to the "Great War."

CONSIDER: How this painting suggests the stresses of city life during the years before World War I.

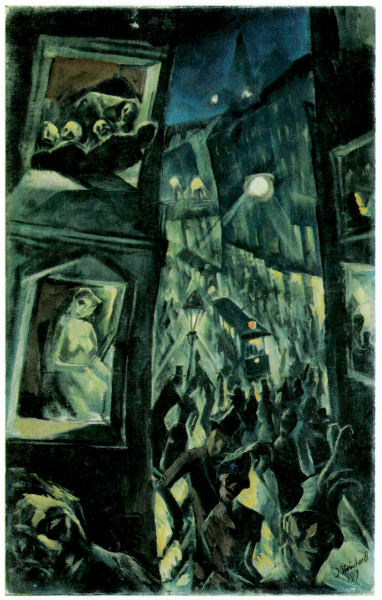

FIGURE 14.5   (© Bildarchiv Preussischer Kulturbesitz/Art Resource, NY)

 ## Secondary Sources

The Decline of Political Liberalism
F. H. Hinsley

Despite the apparent failures of 1848, political liberalism was at its zenith during the middle of the nineteenth century. By the last two decades of the century it was clearly on the decline or was at least evolving in striking new ways. This

SOURCE: F. H. Hinsley, "Introduction," in *The New Cambridge Modern History,* vol. XI, F. H. Hinsley, ed. (Cambridge, England: Cambridge University Press, 1962), pp. 32–34. Reprinted by permission of the publisher.

evolution is analyzed in the following selection from The New Cambridge Modern History by F. H. Hinsley of Cambridge.

CONSIDER: The causes of the decline of political liberalism; the intellectual or ideological developments that occurred in the second half of the nineteenth century, as reflected by the decline of political liberalism.

The politics of the age was distinguished, even in the least authoritarian of states, as much by the growth of authority as by the extension of democracy; and less by the extension of democracy and the democratisation of government than by an advance towards the democratisation of government policies and of the political context in which governments operated. It is these facts which account for the collapse of liberalism—for its exhaustion in more democratic countries as well as for its frustration in less democratic circumstances and its distortion in situations that were in between.

In the advanced countries of western Europe during the 1870's, when liberalism was at its zenith in its European home, liberal governments, abandoning the liberal opposition to the power of the state and seeing the state as the most effective means of securing the liberal conception of freedom in changed circumstances, accepted the early steps towards the inevitable extension of the functions of government and the use of unprecedented state compulsion on individuals for social ends—embracing the notion of state education, legalising trade unions, justifying public health measures, adopting even insurance and factory legislation. No governments in such countries, whatever their political complexion, could, indeed, have opposed such developments. From the end of the 1870's, however, they were overrun and overturned in those countries by the further progress of those twin forces, the masses and the modern state. Every advance in the role of the state, every new aspect of the social problem, every recognition of the emergence of the masses, every new turn of policy—whether towards protectionism and imperialism or towards social regulation and the extension of the franchise—conflicted with the liberal belief in freedom of contract and of enterprise, in free trade, in individual liberty, in public economy, in the minimum of government interference. Liberalism's great contribution, the constitutional state, and its guiding principles, the freedom of the individual, legal equality and conflict with the Church, were—to the varying extents that they had been already established in these states—taken over by more empirical and conservative politicians. Liberalism became more doctrinaire and more narrowly associated with urban and big business interests—even while industrial organisation itself, with the movement from personal to corporate control, was deserting it. The liberal parties split into moderate (national, social or imperialist) and radical wings on these current issues and lost office. Liberal rule or its equivalent ended in Great Britain in 1885, in Germany in 1878, in Austria and the Netherlands in 1879, in Sweden in 1880, in Belgium in 1884, in France in 1885. In Italy under Depretis and Crispi and in some states beyond western Europe liberal parties remained in power. But, liberal only in name, they embraced protectionism and imperialism, undertook social regulation and retained of the old liberal creed only opposition

to the extension of the franchise and to the pretensions of the Church. In these states, as in even more authoritarian countries, authentic liberalism remained a relevant if a weakened basis for opposition to established authority. But even in that role, and even when it was not proscribed by the increased possibilities of repression, it was doomed to frustration by the growth of the need for social regulation and strong government and by the demand for those things by the mass of the population.

The Unfinished Revolution: Marxism Interpreted

Adam B. Ulam

Critical analyses of Marx and Marxism abound and from almost all points of view. From the historian's perspective, one of the most useful ways to approach Marx and Marxism is to place both in their historical context. This is done in the following excerpt from The Unfinished Revolution *by Adam Ulam, a professor of government at Harvard who has written extensively on the history of Marxism and the Soviet Union. Here he attempts to explain aspects of both the content and the appeal of Marxism by pointing to intellectual traditions affecting Marx and social realities conditioning those who accepted it.*

CONSIDER: *Why Marxism is most appealing during the early period of industrialization; how Ulam would explain the apparent failure of Marxism to take hold in twentieth-century nations such as the United States; what Ulam means when he calls Marx a child of rationalistic optimism; how a more pro-Marxist scholar might respond to this interpretation.*

Here, then, is a theory attuned even more closely than other parts of Marxism to the facts and feelings of an early period of industrialization. The class struggle is the salt of Marxism, its most operative revolutionary part. As a historical and psychological concept, it expresses a gross oversimplification, but it is the oversimplification of a genius. The formula of the class struggle seizes the essence of the mood of a great historical moment—a revolution in basic economy—and generalizes it into a historical law. It extracts the grievances of groups of politically conscious workers in Western Europe, then a very small part of the whole proletariat, and sees in it the portent and meaning of the awakening of the whole working class everywhere. The *first* reaction of the worker to industrialization, his feelings of

SOURCE: Adam B. Ulam, *The Unfinished Revolution* (New York: Random House, Inc., 1960), pp. 42–44. Reprinted by permission of the author.

grievance and impotence before the machine, his employer, and the state which stands behind the employer, are assumed by Marx to be typical of the general reactions of the worker to industrialization. What does change in the process of the development of industry is that the worker's feeling of impotence gives way to class consciousness, which in turn leads him to class struggle and socialism. Marx's worker is the historical worker, but he is the historical worker of a specific period of industrial and political development.

Even in interpreting the psychology of the worker of the transitional period, Marx exhibited a rationalistic bias. The worker's opposition to the capitalist order is a total opposition to its laws, its factories, and its government. But this revolutionary consciousness of the worker is to take him next to Marxist socialism, where he will accept the factory system and the state, the *only* difference being the abolition of capitalism. Why shouldn't the revolutionary protest of the worker flow into other channels: into rejection of industrialism as well as capitalism, into rejection of the socialist as well as the capitalist state? It is here that Marx is most definitely the child of his age, the child of rationalistic optimism: the workers will undoubtedly translate their anarchistic protests and grievances into a sophisticated philosophy of history. They will undoubtedly realize that the forces of industrialism and modern life, which strip them of property, status, and economic security, are in themselves benevolent in their ultimate effects and that it is only capitalism and the capitalists which make them into instruments of oppression. The chains felt by the proletariat are the chains of the industrial system. The chains Marx urges them to throw off are those of capitalism. Will the workers understand the difference? And if they do, will they still feel that in destroying capitalism they have a "world to win"?

Understanding Nineteenth-Century Industrialization and Urban Life

C. A. Bayly

Efforts to understand industrialization and the expansion of urban life during the nineteenth century have long preoccupied historians. As C. A. Bayly argues in the following selection, contemporary intellectuals, politicians, social thinkers, and artists were also concerned with these topics.

CONSIDER: *The ways historians' ideas about industrialization might be changing; how industrialization and city life affected politics.*

The nineteenth-century intelligentsia regarded industrialization and the expansion of urban life as the most important features of their age. They were both right and wrong. Historians have demonstrated that industrialization came relatively late in the century, was often rural, and that its effects, though powerful, were quite patchy even as late as 1914. The idea that industrialization gave rise to a large, homogeneous, self-conscious working class is also now difficult to sustain. Yet the contemporary intellectuals were right in the sense that, as political, social, and even artistic symbols, the idea of the working class and the modern city had been invested with great power by the end of the century. Politicians of the right and left alike acted with an eye to encouraging or placating what they believed to be a growing and powerful working class. Most social thinkers and artists were equally preoccupied with the life of the modern city, whether they feared the moral and aesthetic corruption which it spawned or celebrated the liberation and equality which it offered.

Even if industrial capitalists and a stock-owning middle class had not been able to grasp unchallenged political power before 1900, industrialization and the politics of cities had registered powerful effects from at least the mid-century. In the 1850s, European rulers took a more active role in sponsoring railways, telegraphs, the development of war industries, and the planning of cities. Even that modestly inclined state, the US federal government, flexed its muscles here. Japanese and Chinese authorities soon followed suit. These interventions gave the nationalism and empire building of the late nineteenth century a broader scope and a harder, more aggressive edge.

European Women

Eleanor S. Riemer and John C. Fout

In recent years many historians have pointed out the limitations facing middle-class women between 1850 and 1914. As investigations into women's history have multiplied and deepened, new interpretations have been made. In the following selection the historians Eleanor S. Riemer and John C. Fout argue that middle-class women during this period increasingly questioned their roles and often expanded their activities into new, important areas.

CONSIDER: *How middle-class women's maternal and housewifely roles were justified; ways in which middle-class*

SOURCE: C. A. Bayly, *The Birth of the Modern World, 1780–1914* (Oxford: Blackwell Publishing, 2004), p. 198.

SOURCE: From *European Women: A Documentary History, 1789–1945,* edited by Eleanor S. Riemer and John C. Fout. Copyright © 1980 by Schocken Books, Inc. Reprinted by permission of Schocken Books, published by Pantheon Books, a division of Random House, Inc.

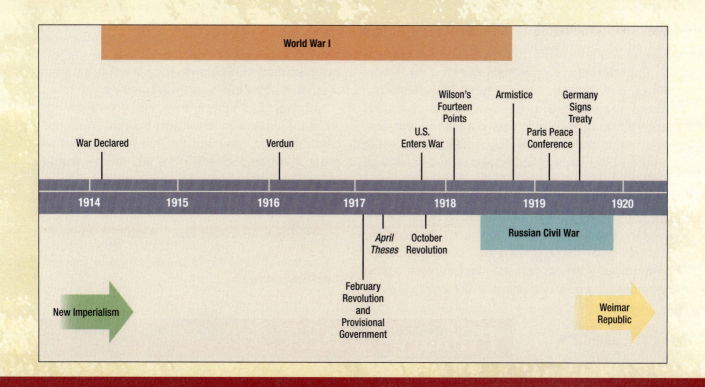

15 War and Revolution: 1914–1920

Historians usually mark the end of the nineteenth century not at the turn of the century but with the outbreak of World War I in 1914. Although a number of wars took place after 1815, none covered all of Europe, none was long, and none was very costly. Indeed, many Europeans optimistically believed that the Western nations had become too economically interdependent and culturally mature to become involved in massive wars ever again. At the outbreak of World War I no one expected it to be so widespread or long-lasting. In fact, the fighting continued for four years before the war was finally concluded. The destruction was so unprecedented and the fighting so brutal that many people questioned whether Western civilization had progressed at all. The war was such a strain that the most modernized nations, England, France, and Germany, for example, mobilized the total resources of their societies, while less modernized nations like Russia were unable to support the effort.

Revolutions occurred in a number of areas, most notably in Germany, the Austro-Hungarian Empire, and Russia. The revolutions in Russia were the most significant. In March 1917 the tsarist government was swept from power by relatively moderate, liberal groups. In November of that year the new Provisional Government was toppled by the Bolsheviks, who initiated a Communist regime that proved surprisingly resilient. Under this government, the Soviet Union was to become a significant force in world politics.

In some ways the Paris Peace Conference in 1919 brought the period to a close, but the problems facing diplomats and heads of state meeting in Versailles were overwhelming. The Soviet Union was not invited to the conference, and the Germans were virtually ignored. Few left the conference satisfied, and many harbored resentments that would color domestic and international politics during the 1920s and 1930s.

This chapter focuses on World War I and the Russian Revolution. With World War I, the two major issues for historians are the cause and the settlement. What caused this apparently unwanted war to break out and who, if anyone, was most to blame? Was the Peace of Paris a success or a failure? Some of the selections also explore tactics used to fight the war, people's experiences during the war, and the results of the war. Other documents deal with the ways the war affected women. With the Russian Revolution, the question is not only why it occurred but also how and why the Bolsheviks—through most of 1917 only a small party—were ultimately able to gain and maintain power against extremely long odds. A number of documents illustrate Lenin's strategy and Bolshevik policy as well as the variety of scholarly efforts to answer these questions.

Many feel that the events during this period of war constituted a fundamental break with the past. The significance of World War I and the Russian Revolution are shown in the developments in the two decades that followed. These will be covered in Chapters 27 and 28.

❧ For Classroom Discussion

What caused World War I? Use the sources by Strachan and Strandmann.

Primary Sources

Reports from the Front: The Battle for Verdun, 1916

The widely anticipated short war typified by heroic offensive thrusts failed to materialize. Instead, it turned into a long, extraordinarily brutal struggle. On the Western front, opposing armies slaughtered each other from their trenches. There are numerous reports of life at the front, such as the following account by a French Army officer of the battle for Verdun in 1916.

CONSIDER: *Why the defense was at such an advantage; why there was a willingness to sacrifice so much for such small advances.*

The Germans attacked in massed formation, by big columns of five or six hundred men, preceded by two waves of sharpshooters. We had only our rifles and our machine guns, because the 75's could not get to work.

Fortunately the flank batteries succeeded in catching the Boches on the right. It is absolutely impossible to convey what losses the Germans must suffer in these attacks. Nothing can give the idea of it. Whole ranks are mowed down, and those that follow them suffered the same fate. Under the storm of machine gun, rifle and 75 fire, the German columns were plowed into furrows of death. Imagine if you can what it would be like to rake water. Those gaps filled up again at once. That is enough to show with what disdain of human life the German attacks are planned and carried out.

In these circumstances German advances are sure. They startle the public, but at the front nobody attaches any importance to them. As a matter of fact, our trenches are so near those of the Germans that once the barbed wire is destroyed the distance between them can be covered in a few minutes. Thus, if one is willing to suffer a loss of life corresponding to the number of men necessary to cover the space between the lines, the other trench can always be reached. By sacrificing thousands of men, after a formidable bombardment, an enemy trench can always be taken.

There are slopes on Hill 304 where the level of the ground is raised several meters by mounds of German corpses. Sometimes it happens that the third German wave uses the dead of the second wave as ramparts and shelters. It was behind ramparts of the dead left by the first five attacks, on May 24th, that we saw the Boches take shelter while they organized their next rush.

We make prisoners among these dead during our counterattacks. They are men who have received no hurt, but have been knocked down by the falling of the human wall of their killed and wounded neighbors. They say very little. They are for the most part dazed with fear and alcohol, and it is several days before they recover.

Dulce et Decorum Est: Disillusionment

Wilfred Owen

The experience of World War I was profoundly disillusioning to those who believed in nineteenth-century ideals. After World War I, Europe was no longer characterized by the sense of optimism, progress, and glory that had typified Europe for most of the period between the eighteenth century and 1914. This is

SOURCE: From *Source Records of the Great War,* vol. IV, ed. Charles F. Horne (New York: National Alumni, 1923), pp. 222–223.

SOURCE: C. Day Lewis, *Collected Poems of Wilfred Owen.* Reprinted by permission of New Directions and Chatto & Windus, p. 55. Copyright © Chatto & Windus, Ltd., 1946, 1963, and The Owen Estate.

evidenced in war poems that no longer glorified the struggle but instead conveyed a sense of the horror and futility about it. One of the best of these antiwar poets was Wilfred Owen, born in England in 1893 and killed in action in 1918, one week before the armistice. The following poem has the ironic ending, "It is sweet and proper to die for one's country."

CONSIDER: *The psychological consequences of war for the soldiers; other ways this same disillusionment might be shown in novels, plays, paintings, or even historical analyses of the time.*

DULCE ET DECORUM EST

Bent double, like old beggars under sacks,
Knock-kneed, coughing like hags, we cursed through
 sludge,
Till on the haunting flares we turned our backs
And towards our distant rest began to trudge.
Men marched asleep. Many had lost their boots
But limped on, blood-shod. All went lame; all blind;
Drunk with fatigue; deaf even to the hoots
Of tired, outstripped Five-Nines that dropped behind.

Gas! Gas! Quick, boys!—An Ecstasy of fumbling,
Fitting the clumsy helmets just in time;
But someone still was yelling out and stumbling
And flound'ring like a man in fire or lime . . .
Dim, through the misty panes and thick green light,
As under a green sea, I saw him drowning.
In all my dreams, before my helpless sight,
He plunges at me, guttering, choking, drowning.

If in some smothering dreams you too could pace
Behind the wagon that we flung him in,
And watch the white eyes writhing in his face,
His hanging face, like a devil's sick of sin;
If you could hear, at every jolt, the blood
Come gargling from the froth-corrupted lungs,
Obscene as cancer, bitter as the cud
Of vile, incurable sores on innocent tongues,—
My friend, you would not tell with such high zest
To children ardent for some desperate glory,
The old Lie: Dulce et decorum est
Pro patria mori.

The Home Front

Evelyn Blücher

As each year of the war dragged on, support from the home front became more crucial. For most people living away from the battle lines, conditions usually grew worse as the military drew resources and supplies for the armed forces. In the following selection, Evelyn Blücher, an English wife of a German officer, describes the difficulties of life in Berlin during the winter of 1917.

CONSIDER: *What seemed to bother people on the home front most; differences in the hardships faced by people in the countryside; what powers governments needed to manage the home fronts.*

In a small town near here, a sad little ceremony took place the other day. The ancient church bell, which had rung the people from the cradle to the grave for 300 years and more, was requisitioned by the military authorities. The grief felt by the inhabitants was so great that they determined to do their ancient friend all the honor that they could; and after having performed the regular funeral service for the dead over it, a procession was formed, headed by the priest in his vestments, with his acolytes swinging their incense, and the inhabitants following the bell, which was covered with wreaths and flowers and handed over to the military authorities under tears and protestations.

As coffee and tea have entirely run out, all sorts of berries and leaves are being used as a surrogate. Chestnuts are used for feeding the deer, and it is interesting to see the children, who are not old enough to work otherwise, busy plucking and collecting the different things.

Nothing seems to be left unused—salad-oil being extracted from every kind of fruit-stone, and an excellent oil for greasing machinery is being pressed from the seeds of sunflowers. It is marvelous how much has been produced in this way, and it is only a pity we cannot use the latter for cooking and eating purposes too.

The difficulty of getting butter is increasing daily, and one has to use all one's power of persuasion to be able to entice a miserable quarter of a pound of it, after having begged in vain at quite a number of small peasants' houses. . . .

Lighting will prove a great problem this winter, as there is almost no petroleum or methylated spirits to be had; gas-light is next to impossible, on account of the small quantity allowed, and electric-light is also limited. . . .

This darkness is especially unpleasant for the people in the town who have to wait for the vegetables and fruit coming in from the country. Our gardener, who goes in daily, tells me that they stand for hours and hours patiently waiting to get but a pound of cabbage, onions, etc., which are all very scarce indeed. Luckily for the purchasers, maximum prices have been settled on all eatables, or it would be impossible for the poorer classes to get anything at all. . . .

The food question is always the most important topic of the day. The less there is of it, the more do we talk of it. The Austrians have already eaten up their stores, and are grumbling and turning to Germany for fresh supplies.

SOURCE: Evelyn Blücher, *An English Wife in Berlin* (New York: E. P. Dutton, 1920), pp. 183–184, 231.

It is rather like turning from a sandy desert to a rocky mountain for nourishment. . . .

We ourselves have little to eat but smoked meat and dried peas and beans, but in the towns they are considerably worse off. The potatoes have come to a premature end, and in Berlin the population have now a portion of 1 lb. per head a week, and these even are bad. The cold winds of this wintry June have retarded the growth of vegetables, and there is almost nothing to be had. We are all waiting hungrily for the harvest and the prospect of at least more bread and flour.

Program of the Provisional Government in Russia

In the spring of 1917 a revolution finally toppled the disintegrating tsarist government in Russia. A relatively moderate, liberal Provisional Government was formed under the leadership of men like Prince Lvov and Paul Miliukov. While the Provisional Government had to share and even compete for power with the more radical workers' political organizations—the soviets—it initially acted with speed to make important changes. The following is the early program of the Provisional Government, issued on March 16, 1917.

CONSIDER: *The attitudes revealed by this document; the nature of the reforms initiated; what this implies about the problems under the tsarist government and the discontents that supported the revolution.*

Citizens, the Provisional Executive Committee of the members of the Duma, with the aid and support of the garrison of the capital and its inhabitants, has triumphed over the dark forces of the Old Régime to such an extent as to enable it to organize a more stable executive power. . . .

The Cabinet will be guided in its actions by the following principles:

1. An immediate general amnesty for all political and religious offenses, including terrorist acts, military revolts, agrarian offenses, etc.

2. Freedom of speech and press; freedom to form labor unions and to strike. These political liberties should be extended to the army in so far as war conditions permit.

3. The abolition of all social, religious and national restrictions.

4. Immediate preparation for the calling of a Constituent Assembly, elected by universal and secret vote, which shall determine the form of government and draw up the Constitution for the country.

5. In place of the police, to organize a national militia with elective officers, and subject to the local self-government body.

6. Elections to be carried out on the basis of universal, direct, equal, and secret suffrage.

7. The troops that have taken part in the revolutionary movement shall not be disarmed or removed from Petrograd.

8. On duty and in war service, strict military discipline should be maintained, but when off duty, soldiers should have the same public rights as are enjoyed by other citizens.

The Provisional Government wishes to add that it has no intention of taking advantage of the existence of war conditions to delay the realization of the above-mentioned measures of reform.

April Theses: The Bolshevik Opposition

V. I. Lenin

Faced with a continuing war and deep discontent, the Provisional Government soon came under attack by people like Vladimir Ilyich Lenin (1870–1924), who called for more radical changes. Lenin, who spent much of his life as a revolutionary—often in exile—had risen to the leadership of the Bolshevik faction of the Russian Marxists. He combined the skills of a superb Marxist theoretician and a revolutionary organizer. In April 1917 the Germans aided his return to Russia in an effort to weaken the new government there. On his arrival, Lenin presented his April Theses, at first criticized by Russian Marxists but eventually accepted by the Bolshevik Central Committee.

CONSIDER: *Why Lenin rejects support for the Provisional Government; to whom this program might be appealing and why; the ways in which this program is particularly Marxist.*

1. In our attitude towards the war, which under the new government of Lvov and Co. unquestionably remains on Russia's part a predatory imperialist war owing to the capitalist nature of that government, not the slightest concession to a "revolutionary defencism" is permissible. . . .

2. The specific feature of the present situation in Russia is that the country is *passing* from the first stage of the revolution—which, owing to the insufficient class-consciousness and organisation of the proletariat,

SOURCE: Frank A. Golder, ed., *Documents of Russian History, 1914–1917,* trans. Emanuel Aronsberg (New York: Prentice-Hall, Inc., 1927).

SOURCE: From V. I. Lenin, *Collected Works,* vol. XXIV (Moscow: Progress Publishers, 1964), pp. 21–24. Reprinted by permission of the Copyright Agency of the U.S.S.R

placed power in the hands of the bourgeoisie—to its *second* stage, which must place power in the hands of the proletariat and the poorest sections of the peasants. . . .

3. No support for the Provisional Government; . . .

5. Not a parliamentary republic—to return to a parliamentary republic from the Soviets of Workers' Deputies would be a retrograde step—but a republic of Soviets of Workers', Agricultural Labourers' and Peasants' Deputies throughout the country, from top to bottom. Abolition of the police, the army and the bureaucracy.

   The salaries of all officials, all of whom are elective and displaceable at any time, not to exceed the average wage of a competent worker.

6. The weight of emphasis in the agrarian programme to be shifted to the Soviets of Agricultural Labourers' Deputies.

   Confiscation of all landed estates.

   Nationalisation of *all* lands in the country, the land to be disposed of by the local Soviets of Agricultural Labourers' and Peasants' Deputies. The organisation of separate Soviets of Deputies of Poor Peasants.

   The setting up of a model farm on each of the large estates (ranging in size from 100 to 300 dessiatines, according to local and other conditions, and to the decisions of the local bodies) under the control of the Soviets of Agricultural Labourers' Deputies and for the public account.

7. The immediate amalgamation of all banks in the country into a single national bank, and the institution of control over it by the Soviet of Workers' Deputies.

8. It is not our *immediate* task to "introduce" socialism, but only to bring social production and the distribution of products at once under the *control* of the Soviets of Workers' Deputies.

Speech to the Petrograd Soviet— November 8, 1917: The Bolsheviks in Power

V. I. Lenin

The Provisional Government fell in a revolution in November 1917. Under the leadership of Lenin and Leon Trotsky (1877–1940), the tightly organized Bolsheviks quickly took control. On November 8, 1917, Lenin made the following speech to a meeting of the Petrograd Soviet.

CONSIDER: *The policies Lenin supported and how they compare with the program in his* April Theses; *the ways in which Lenin was relying on forces outside of Russia to sustain the initial success of this revolution.*

Comrades, the workmen's and peasants' revolution, the need of which the Bolsheviks have emphasized many times, has come to pass.

What is the significance of this revolution? Its significance is, in the first place, that we shall have a soviet government, without the participation of bourgeoisie of any kind. The oppressed masses will of themselves form a government. The old state machinery will be smashed into bits and in its place will be created a new machinery of government by the soviet organizations. From now on there is a new page in the history of Russia, and the present, third Russian revolution shall in its final result lead to the victory of Socialism.

One of our immediate tasks is to put an end to the war at once. But in order to end the war, which is closely bound up with the present capitalistic system, it is necessary to overthrow capitalism itself. In this work we shall have the aid of the world labor movement, which has already begun to develop in Italy, England, and Germany.

A just and immediate offer of peace by us to the international democracy will find everywhere a warm response among the international proletariat masses. In order to secure the confidence of the proletariat, it is necessary to publish at once all secret treaties.

In the interior of Russia a very large part of the peasantry has said: Enough playing with the capitalists; we will go with the workers. We shall secure the confidence of the peasants by one decree, which will wipe out the private property of the landowners. The peasants will understand that their only salvation is in union with the workers.

We will establish a real labor control on production.

We have now learned to work together in a friendly manner, as is evident from this revolution. We have the force of mass organization which has conquered all and which will lead the proletariat to world revolution.

We should now occupy ourselves in Russia in building up a proletarian socialist state.

Long live the world-wide socialistic revolution.

The Fourteen Points

Woodrow Wilson

Each nation entered World War I for its own mixture of pragmatic and idealistic reasons. In considering their war aims and a possible peace settlement, governments did not

SOURCE: Frank A. Golder, ed., *Documents of Russian History, 1914–1917,* Emanuel Aronsberg, trans. Reprinted by permission of Prentice-Hall, Inc., pp. 618–619. Copyright © 1927 by Prentice-Hall, Inc.

SOURCE: Woodrow Wilson, "Fourteen Points," *Congressional Record,* vol. LVI, part I (1918), Washington, D.C.: U.S. Government Printing Office, pp. 680–681.

anticipate the changes that would occur in this unexpectedly long and costly war. By 1918 various governments had fallen and the United States had entered the conflict. On January 8, 1918, in an address to a joint session of the U.S. Congress, President Woodrow Wilson (1856–1924) presented his Fourteen Points, a delineation of American war aims and proposals for a peace settlement. The Fourteen Points served as a basis for debate at the Paris Peace Conference in 1919 and represented the most idealistic statement of what might be gained in a final peace settlement.

CONSIDER: *The ideals that hold these points together; the grievances recognized and unrecognized in these points; the assumptions about what measures would preserve peace in the postwar world.*

We entered this war because violations of right had occurred which touched us to the quick and made the life of our own people impossible unless they were corrected and the world secured once for all against their recurrence. What we demand in this war, therefore, is nothing peculiar to ourselves. It is that the world be made fit and safe to live in; and particularly that it be made safe for every peace-loving nation which, like our own, wishes to live its own life, determine its own institutions, be assured of justice and fair dealing by the other peoples of the world as against force and selfish aggression. All the peoples of the world are in effect partners in this interest, and for our own part we see very clearly that unless justice be done to others it will not be done to us. The program of the world's peace, therefore, is our program; and that program, the only possible program, as we see it, is this:

I. Open covenants of peace, openly arrived at, after which there shall be no private international understandings of any kind but diplomacy shall proceed always frankly and in the public view.

II. Absolute freedom of navigation upon the seas, outside territorial waters, alike in peace and in war, except as the seas may be closed in whole or in part by international action. . . .

III. The removal, so far as possible, of all economic barriers and the establishment of an equality of trade conditions among all the nations consenting to the peace and associating themselves for its maintenance.

IV. Adequate guarantees given and taken that national armaments will be reduced to the lowest point consistent with domestic safety.

V. A free, open-minded, and absolutely impartial adjustment of all colonial claims, based upon a strict observance of the principle that in determining all such questions of sovereignty the interests of the populations concerned must have equal weight with the equitable claims of the government whose title is to be determined.

VI. The evacuation of all Russian territory and such a settlement of all questions affecting Russia as will secure the best and freest cooperation of the other nations of the world in obtaining for her an unhampered and unembarrassed opportunity for the independent determination of her own political development and national policy and assure her of a sincere welcome into the society of free nations under institutions of her own choosing; and, more than a welcome, assistance also of every kind that she may need and may herself desire. . . .

VII. Belgium, the whole world will agree, must be evacuated and restored, without any attempt to limit the sovereignty which she enjoys in common with all other free nations. . . .

VIII. All French territory should be freed and the invaded portions restored, and the wrong done to France by Prussia in 1871 in the matter of Alsace-Lorraine, which has unsettled the peace of the world for nearly fifty years, should be righted, in order that peace may once more be made secure in the interest of all.

IX. A readjustment of the frontiers of Italy should be effected along clearly recognizable lines of nationality.

X. The peoples of Austria-Hungary, whose place among the nations we wish to see safeguarded and assured, should be accorded the freest opportunity of autonomous development.

XI. Rumania, Serbia, and Montenegro should be evacuated; occupied territories restored; Serbia accorded free and secure access to the sea; and the relations of the several Balkan states to one another determined by friendly counsel along historically established lines of allegiance and nationality; and international guarantees of the political and economic independence and territorial integrity of the several Balkan states should be entered into.

XII. The Turkish portions of the present Ottoman Empire should be assured a secure sovereignty, but the other nationalities which are now under Turkish rule should be assured an undoubted security of life and an absolutely unmolested opportunity of autonomous development. . . .

XIII. An independent Polish state should be erected which should include the territories inhabited by indisputably Polish populations. . . .

XIV. A general association of nations must be formed under specific covenants for the purpose of affording mutual guarantees of political independence and territorial integrity to great and small states alike.

In regard to these essential rectifications of wrong and assertions of right we feel ourselves to be intimate partners of all the governments and peoples associated together against the Imperialists. We cannot be separated in interest or divided in purpose. We stand together until the end. . . .

We have no jealousy of German greatness, and there is nothing in this program that impairs it. We grudge her no achievement or distinction of learning or of pacific enterprise such as have made her record very bright and very enviable. We do not wish to injure her or to block in any way her legitimate influence or power. . . .

Neither do we presume to suggest to her any alteration or modification of her institutions. But it is necessary. . . . that we should know whom her spokesmen speak for when they speak to us, whether for the Reichstag majority or for the military party and the men whose creed is imperial domination. . . .

An evident principle runs through the whole program I have outlined. It is the principle of justice to all peoples and nationalities, and their right to live on equal terms of liberty and safety with one another, whether they be strong or weak. . . . The people of the United States could act upon no other principle; and to the vindication of this principle they are ready to devote their lives, their honor, and everything that they possess. The moral climax of this the culminating and final war for human liberty has come, and they are ready to put their own strength, their own highest purpose, their own integrity and devotion to the test.

Visual Sources

World War I: The Front Lines

The following figure (figure 15.1) displays the physical and psychological realities of life on the Western front during World War I. The war is being fought from trenches with soldiers at machine guns guarding land made barren by artillery barrages, throwing hand grenades at the often unseen enemy, and using poison gas (note the gas mask). It is difficult to find in such a scene a sense of a progressive civilization, of the dignity of the individual, or of reasoned interaction among nations— the ideals held by nineteenth-century Western civilization. Considering the use of such weapons, we can easily imagine the carnage and the sense of futility that resulted from the "heroic" offensive charges of the foot soldiers that were so common for most of the war.

CONSIDER: *How this supports the description of life on the front lines during the Verdun battle.*

The Paths of Glory
C. R. W. Nevinson

The brutality of World War I ended dreams of heroic battles and courageous military deeds. The 1917

painting (figure 15.2) by English artist C. R. W. Nevinson (1889–1946), with its ironic title, The Paths of Glory, *spoke eloquently to this disturbing reality.*

In this image, the bodies of two British soldiers—easily identified by their brown uniforms and flat helmets—lie in a desolate battlefield in northern France. This battle has ended, and it is unclear how their anonymous deaths contributed to the war or to any supposed glory. The only

FIGURE 15.1

FIGURE 15.2   (© Snark/Art Resource, NY)

objects left standing are the wooden stakes holding up the rows of barbed wire that have entangled these two individuals. Already the bodies are dissolving into earth. "Words such as glory, honor, courage, or hallow [became] obscene" in the face of the carnage that resulted, wrote the American author and veteran Ernest Hemingway. Nevinson's painting, echoing these sentiments, was hung in a British gallery in March 1918. Military authorities immediately condemned it.

CONSIDER: *Why British military authorities condemned this painting; how this image might represent the realities of battle during World War I.*

World War I: The Home Front and Women

The following picture of a British war plant (figure 15.3) gives an idea of how industrialization and technology have helped turn any extended war into a massive strain. Large factories had to be built or converted to the production of war munitions, here heavy artillery shells. A new labor force had to be trained, often involving a change of values: Here women and older men

predominate to make up for the drain on manpower caused by the armed services. Finally, this picture suggests the enormous logistical organization and government cooperation with capitalist enterprises necessary to keep a modern war effort going.

The need for labor on the home front resulted in large numbers of women entering the labor force or changing jobs. The following two charts indicate the changing employment of women in Great Britain between 1914 and 1918: chart 15.1 for all employment, chart 15.2 for industrial employment.

FIGURE 15.3   (The Art Archive/The Imperial War Museum)

Chart 15.1 Women in the Labor Force, Great Britain, 1914–1918

Numbers of women working	In July 1914	In July 1918	In July 1918, over (+) or under (−) numbers in July 1914
On their own account or as employers	430,000	470,000	+40,000
In industry	2,178,600	2,970,000	+792,000
In domestic service	1,658,000	1,258,000	−400,000
In commerce, etc.	505,500	934,500	+429,000
In national and local government, including education	262,200	460,200	+198,000
In agriculture	190,000	228,000	+38,000
In employment of hotels, public houses, theatres, etc.	181,000	220,000	+39,000
In transport	18,200	117,200	+99,000
In other, including professional employment and as home workers	542,500	652,500	+110,000
Altogether in occupations	5,966,000	7,311,000	+1,345,000
Not in occupations but over 10	12,946,000	12,496,000	−450,000
Under 10	4,809,000	4,731,000	−78,000
Total females	23,721,000	24,538,000	+817,000

Chart 15.2 Women in Industry, Great Britain, 1914–1918

Trades	Estimated number of females employed in July 1914	Estimated number of females employed in July 1918	Difference between numbers of females employed in July 1914, and July 1918	Percentage of females to total number of workpeople employed July 1914	Percentage of females to total number of workpeople employed July 1918	Estimated number of females directly replacing males in Jan. 1918
Metal	170,000	594,000	+424,000	9	25	195,000
Chemical	40,000	104,000	+64,000	20	39	35,000
Textile	863,000	827,000	−36,000	58	67	64,000
Clothing	612,000	568,000	−44,000	68	76	43,000
Food, drink, and tobacco	196,000	235,000	+39,000	35	49	60,000
Paper and printing	147,500	141,500	−6,000	36	48	21,000
Wood	44,000	79,000	+35,000	15	32	23,000
China and earthenware	32,000					
Leather	23,100	197,100	+93,000	4	10	62,000
Other	49,000					
Government establishments	2,000	225,000	+223,000	3	47	197,000
Total	2,178,600	2,970,600	+792,000	26	37	704,000

SOURCE: *Women in Industry: Report of the War Cabinet Committee on Women in Industry* (London: His Majesty's Stationery Office, 1919).

CONSIDER: *The ways in which a modern war effort affects a nation's people and economy, even though the war is being fought on foreign soil; the potential significance for women of these changes in employment.*

Revolutionary Propaganda

This 1922 poster (figure 15.4) celebrating the fifth anniversary of the Russian revolution reflects some of the message and appeal of the Communists during the revolution of 1917 and the years that followed. Here Lenin, in a worker's suit, tie, and cap, stands on a globe as if leading a worldwide Communist revolution. He proclaims, "Let the ruling class tremble before the Communist revolution." Behind him the rising sun marks the glorious dawn of the communist era. To his left and right, together in alliance, are agricultural and industrial workers—the revolutionary mainstays and beneficiaries of the new order—carrying a banner proclaiming, "Proletariat of All Countries, Unite." Below are the tools of their trades and symbols of Russia's Communist revolution— the hammer and sickle.

CONSIDER: *What might be particularly appealing about this poster; what image of the Russian revolution it incorporates.*

FIGURE 15.4   (© Sovfoto/Eastfoto)

 ## Secondary Sources

Germany and the Coming of War
Hartmut Pogge von Strandmann

In an attempt to understand the origins of World War I and why it lasted so long, many scholars focus on the role of Germany, but differ greatly on what the underpinnings of German involvement were. In the following selection Hartmut Pogge von Strandmann analyzes what made war acceptable to the German population and what sustained the war efforts for four years.

CONSIDER: *Ways in which forces for war within Germany were part of Europeanwide developments; why, according to the author, there was support for the war effort in Germany;*

how this analysis of Germany compares to Stromberg's analysis for the origins of the war.

However strongly the political and military leadership was influenced by the public and its political debates, the war was not started for domestic reasons nor to defend a social status quo. The concept of expansion based on a military victory found enough support to command a consensus among the military, political, and business leaders of Wilhelmine Germany. The drive to the east and to the west was underpinned by an imperialist culture which spread the virtues of Social Darwinism, the conquest of markets, the penetration of spheres of influence, competition between capitalist partners, the winning of living-space, and the rising power of the state. Buoyed up by an assumed military superiority, general economic strength and particular industrial vigour, widespread optimism and a mood of belligerence, the military and political leaders found, when they made the decision to push for war, that this

SOURCE: From Hartmut Pogge von Strandmann, "Germany and the Coming of War," in *The Coming of the First World War,* p. 123, eds. R. J. W. Evans and Hartmut Pogge von Strandmann. © 1988 Oxford University Press. Reprinted by permission of Oxford University Press.

was an acceptable option to many Germans, possibly even to the majority. The notion of "cultural despair" is of limited value. There were no signs of panic and no indications that Wilhelmine Germany could not continue to muddle through politically for years to come. Confidence, determination, and the belief in victory were the ingredients of a willingness to fight an expansionist war, disguised as a defensive or preventive action, which was widely shared by political and military leaders, political groupings, as well as large sectors of the population. This consensus enabled Germany to sustain the war effort until the military defeats of August and September 1918.

The Outbreak of the First World War

Hew Strachan

How did people in countries throughout Europe react to the outbreak of World War I? While some perceptive observers dreaded the consequences of such a war, a wide range of people seemed to welcome it with great enthusiasm. In the following selection, Hew Strachan analyzes this enthusiastic acceptance of the war and its significance.

CONSIDER: *Why intellectuals might have welcomed the war; what Strachan means when he argues that "enthusiasm was the conspicuous froth, the surface element only"; the importance of this enthusiasm for our understanding of World War I.*

The enthusiasm with which Europe went to war was therefore composed of a wide range of differing responses. Its universality lay in their convergence and not in their component parts. Intellectuals welcomed war as an instrument with which to change pre-war society; many of those who joined up did so to defend it. For the latter, the foundations were as much psychological as ideological; community and conformity gave shape to lives disordered by the upheavals which the war caused.[72] The common denominator may more accurately be described as passive acceptance, a willingness to do one's duty; enthusiasm was the conspicuous froth, the surface element only.

The mood relied in large part on an ignorance of the conditions of modern war. The bulk of popular literature continued to portray war as a matter of individual courage and resource, to use imagery more appropriate to knights-errant and the days of chivalry. 'Where then are horse and rider? Where is my sword?', Wilhelm Lamszus

had asked ironically in *Das Menschenschlachthaus* (the slaughterhouse of mankind), published in 1912. Like H. G. Wells in Britain, Lamszus had recognized that the next war would represent the triumph of the machine over human flesh.[73] But the inherent optimism of the human condition, the belief that the best will occur rather than the worst, the intimations of immortality to which youth is subject, persuaded many that technical progress would make war less lethal, not more so. The *Breisgauer Zeitung* assured its readers on 1 August that their chances of coming back in one piece from this war were greater than in previous wars. The modern battlefield was much less bloody because of the extended distances at which fighting occurred. Moreover, high-velocity bullets were of smaller calibre and therefore passed through the body with less damage. Such wounds as were inflicted could be rapidly treated thanks to the advances of modern medicine.[74] British regular soldiers who had served in South Africa did not share the general exuberance; recent knowledge of war—in their case that with Japan in 1904—may also have contributed to the reluctance of Russian reservists.[75] But in France, Germany, and Austria-Hungary no such experience of combat could clutter their idealized views.

Popular enthusiasm played no part in causing the First World War. And yet without a popular willingness to go to war the world war could not have taken place. The statesmen had projected internal collapse as a consequence of prolonged fighting. Instead, the societies of all the belligerents remained integrated until at least 1917, and in large part into 1918. The underlying conviction of the war's necessity, of the duty of patriotic defence, established in 1914, remained the bedrock of that continuing commitment.

The Revolution in War and Diplomacy

Gordon A. Craig

The technology and tactics used in World War I were strikingly different from those used in previous wars. This, combined with the war's length and the waning distinction between civilian and military targets, made it difficult for people to perceive the enemy in terms other than extreme hatred. This was reflected in the demands for retribution made both

SOURCE: Hew Strachan, *The Outbreak of the First World War* (Oxford: Oxford University Press, 2004), pp. 205–206.

SOURCE: Gordon A. Craig, "The Revolution in War and Diplomacy," Jack J. Roth, ed., *World War I: A Turning Point in Modern History.* Reprinted by permission of Alfred A. Knopf, Inc., pp. 12–14. Copyright © 1967 by Alfred A. Knopf, Inc.

during and at the end of the war, inevitably affecting the peace settlements that followed. In the following selection Gordon Craig of Princeton and Stanford, a noted military and diplomatic historian who has done extensive work on German history, analyzes these attitudes and their causes while comparing World War I with previous wars.

CONSIDER: *How the primary documents on the experience of World War I relate to this interpretation; why it was difficult for governments of belligerent nations to compromise; whether this description of what happened in World War I is likely to be true for almost any extended twentieth-century war.*

The war of 1914 was the first total war in history, in the sense that very few people living in the belligerent countries were permitted to remain unaffected by it during its course. This had not been true in the past. Even during the great wars against Napoleon many people could go on living as if the world were at peace. . . .

This kind of detachment, which was true also of the wars in Central Europe in the 1860s, was wholly impossible during World War I. This was, for one thing, the first war in which the distinction between soldier and civilian broke down, a development that was partly due to the expansion of warfare made possible by . . . technological innovations. . . . When dirigibles began to drop bombs over London and submarines began to sink merchant ships, war had invaded the civilian sphere and the battle line was everywhere. . . .

Moreover . . . precisely because war became so total and was so prolonged, it also became ideological, taking on a religious cast that had not characterized warfare in the West since the Thirty Years' War. . . .

The civilian . . . could not look the enemy in the face and recognize him as another man; he knew only that it was "the enemy," an impersonal, generalized concept, that was depriving him of the pleasures of peace. As his own discomfort grew, his irritation hardened into a hatred that was often encouraged by government propagandists who believed that this was the best way of maintaining civilian morale. Before long, therefore, the enemy was considered to be capable of any enormity and, since this was true, any idea of compromise with him became intolerable. The foe must be beaten to his knees, no matter what this might cost in effort and blood; he must be made to surrender unconditionally; he must be punished with peace terms that would keep him in permanent subjection.

The result of this was . . . that rational calculation of risk versus gain, of compromise through negotiation . . . became virtually impossible for the belligerent governments.

Women, Work, and World War I
Bonnie S. Anderson and Judith P. Zinsser

As men were drawn into the armed forces during World War I and there were new demands for arms and other goods to support the war effort, the demand for women workers grew. Women entered the work force in great numbers, often taking jobs previously offered only to men. Historians have pointed to this as a crucial change for women, but recently other historians question how much women, in the long run, benefited from their experiences as workers during World War I. In the following excerpt from A History of Their Own, *Bonnie S. Anderson and Judith P. Zinsser argue that the changes for women were fewer and less long-lasting than generally assumed.*

CONSIDER: *Why, according to Anderson and Zinsser, changes for women were more apparent than real, more short-term than long-lasting; how employers, governments, and the mass media undermined changes for women; how this document relates to the visual sources on the home front and women.*

The improved standard of living, smaller family size, maternity benefits, protective legislation, unions, and new jobs comprised the most important changes in the lives of urban working-class women between the 1870s and the 1920s. Compared to these changes, the impact of World War I (1914–1918) on these women's lives was relatively minor. While middle- and upper-class women often reported that the war freed them from nineteenth-century attitudes limiting both work and personal life, working-class women's lives changed relatively little. Unlike more privileged women, working-class women were used to earning income outside the home, and their entry into war work was more likely to be exploitative than liberating. Unlike more privileged women, working-class women and girls had rarely been shielded by a "double standard" of sexual behavior for women and men; rather, working-class women made the maintenance of the double standard possible for men of property. For working-class women in the cities, the growth of the new white-collar job was the one new trend fostered by the war which was not reversed afterward. Otherwise, World War I brought only a temporary suspension of the normal conditions of work outside the home, and traditional patterns returned in the postwar era.

SOURCE: Excerpts from *A History of Their Own,* vol. II, by Bonnie Anderson and Judith Zinsser. Copyright © 1988 by Harper & Row, Publishers, Inc., pp. 112–114. Reprinted by permission of Harper & Row, Publishers, Inc.

As soon as the war broke out, European governments moved to suspend protective legislation for women for the duration. Just as nations expected working-class men to serve in the military, so they exhorted working-class women to serve in the factories, taking the places of the men who had joined the armed forces. Drawn by high wages as well as patriotism, women thronged into these new, previously male jobs. . . .

Governments initially insisted that women receive equal pay for doing a job formerly done by a man, but this policy was largely ineffective: factories tended to divide up jobs into smaller operations and pay women at a lesser rate. Women's industrial wages rose during the war, both relative to men's and absolutely, but they still remained measurable as a percentage of male earnings. In Paris, women in metallurgy earned only 45 percent of what men earned before the war; by 1918, the women earned 84 percent of what men earned. In Germany, women's industrial earnings relative to men's rose by about 5 percent. Both women and men seemed to view the changes brought by the war as temporary. After the war, the men would return to their jobs, the women would leave men's work, and all would return to normal. . . .

As soon as the war was over, all belligerent governments acted quickly to remove women from "men's" jobs. In England, these women were made "redundant" and let go; in France, they were offered a bonus payment if they left factory work; and in Germany, the government issued regulations calling for women to be dismissed before men if necessary. These policies were effective: by 1921, fewer French and English women worked in industry than had before the war. Women's earnings decreased to return to lower percentages of men's, and the promise of "equal remunerations for work of equal value" made in the Versailles Treaty of 1919 remained a dead letter. Mass media concentrated on the relatively superficial changes in women's clothing, hair styles, and use of cosmetics and ignored the deeper continuities which structured most women's lives.

Peace and Diplomacy

Arthur Walworth

Historians have traditionally condemned the settlement of World War I worked out at Versailles. They usually argue that it compared poorly with the previous Vienna settlement ending the Napoleonic Wars. Yet some historians have challenged this view, arguing that the circumstances of peacemaking were extraordinarily difficult at the end of World War I. In the following selection Arthur Walworth analyzes the pressures and obstacles facing the peacemakers.

CONSIDER: *The choices and compromises the diplomats would have to make; in these circumstances, what the diplomats might have done; how Walworth's interpretation compares to that of Craig.*

A belligerent spirit of nationalism, fortified by the patriotic sacrifices that war had called forth, ran strong and limited the freedom of the peacemakers to pursue the distant goals of idealists. The prevailing hatred toward the defeated enemy made it difficult for diplomats to make a rational peace without being denounced as "pro-German." The wisest of the statesmen realized, after the cessation of the fighting, that unless they were able to reverse the baneful psychology of wartime quickly, no enduring peace could be signed, much less dictated.

Furthermore, the European democracies during the war had set up obstacles that would embarrass the diplomats in the making of peace. Under the necessity of survival the governments of the Allied powers had made secret commitments to the satisfaction of national aspirations. The 1915 Treaty of London, concluded in order to bring Italy into the conflict on the side of the Allies, had promised that nation a frontier that would place hundreds of thousands of Austrians and Slavs under Italian rule. To persuade the Japanese to step up their naval activity, Japan had been offered concessions in China and a share of Germany's islands in the Pacific. Although agreements to which Russia was a party became invalid when the Soviet government made peace with Germany, nevertheless the interests of France, Great Britain, and Italy in the lands of the Ottoman Empire remained as they had been defined in understandings reached in 1916 and 1917. These secret understandings gained force from popular indignation against the violations of treaty obligations at the time of the outbreak of war in 1914.

The settlement at the war's end could not disregard the commitments and the national aspirations that existed in 1919 and that no one could expect to alter quickly. Compromises were inevitable. For one thing, there had to be an accommodation among various prescriptions for dealing with the German enemy. At the end of the war the European diplomats were of two minds about a policy to preserve the peace. One, the more appealing to the English-speaking authorities, would avoid peace terms that might incite violent reactions among the vanquished and also would provide for a continuing process of adjustment. The other, advocated by the French, would create alliances with a preponderance of

SOURCE: From Arthur Walworth, *Wilson and His Peacemakers*, pp. xii–xiii. Copyright 1986 W. W. Norton. Reprinted by permission of W. W. Norton & Company, Inc.

military power that could put down any opposition. During the long war of attrition France's deficiency in manpower had worsened; it was clear that the French nation, fighting alone, could not hope to withstand another onset of German might.

The Russian Revolution

Robert Service

Historians often respond to the challenge of explaining the occurrence of a major revolution by constructing a complex set or theory of causes. For Marxist historians, the Russian Revolution was of extraordinary importance. These historians and others point to long-term economic and social factors as crucial in causing this revolution. Many historians, however, argue that the causes were more immediate and less complex. Robert Service, a respected author of several works on Russian history, takes a middle ground, focusing on a few circumstances as the key causes for the revolution. In the following selection, Service analyzes the revolution that toppled the tsar's government in February 1917, as well as the rise to power of Lenin and the Bolsheviks in October 1917.

CONSIDER: *The problems facing the Russian Empire; how Tsar Nicholas II placed himself in "double jeopardy"; why the Bolsheviks resorted to terror.*

Under the tsars, the Russian Empire faced many problems and approval of the state's demands and purposes was largely absent from society. The technological gap was widening between Russia and the other capitalist powers. Military security posed acute problems; administrative and educational co-ordination remained frail. Political parties had little impact on popular opinion, and the State Duma was to a large extent ignored. Furthermore, the traditional propertied classes made little effort to engender a sense of civic community among the poorer members of society. While most Russians lacked a strong sense of nationhood, several non-Russian nations had a sharp sense of national resentment. The Russian Empire was a restless, unintegrated society.

Nicholas II, the last tsar, had put himself in double jeopardy. He had seriously obstructed and annoyed the emergent elements of a civil society: the political parties, professional associations and trade unions. But he also

stopped trying to suppress them entirely. The result was a constant challenge to the tsarist regime. The social and economic transformation before the First World War merely added to the problems. Those groups in society which had undergone impoverishment were understandably hostile to the authorities. Other groups had enjoyed improvement in their material conditions; but several of these, too, posed a danger since they felt frustrated by the nature of the political order. It was in this situation that the Great War broke out and pulled down the remaining stays of the regime. The result was the February Revolution of 1917 in circumstances of economic collapse, administrative dislocation and military defeat. Vent was given to a surge of local efforts at popular self-rule; and workers, peasants and military conscripts across the empire asserted their demands without impediment.

These same circumstances made liberalism, conservatism and fascism impractical for a number of years ahead: some kind of socialist government was by far the likeliest outcome in those years. Yet it was not inevitable that the most extreme variant of socialism—Bolshevism—should take power. What was scarcely avoidable was that once the Bolsheviks made their revolution, they would not be able to survive without making their policies even more violent and regimentative than they already were. Lenin's party had much too little durable support to remain in government without resort to terror. This in turn placed limits on their ability to solve those many problems identified by nearly all the tsarist regime's enemies as needing to be solved. The Bolsheviks aspired to economic competitiveness, political integration, inter-ethnic co-operation, social tranquillity, administrative efficiency, cultural dynamism and universal education. But the means they employed inevitably vitiated their declared ends.

SOURCE: Robert Service, *A History of Twentieth-Century Russia* (Cambridge, MA: Harvard University Press, 1998), pp. 545–547.

❧ CHAPTER QUESTIONS

1. In what ways was World War I an outgrowth of the major trends of the late nineteenth century? Why is World War I nevertheless often considered a dividing line between the nineteenth and twentieth centuries?

2. What role did World War I play in explaining the Russian Revolution and the Bolsheviks' rise to power?

3. What was there about the causes and process of World War I that made the peace settlement at the end of the war so difficult?

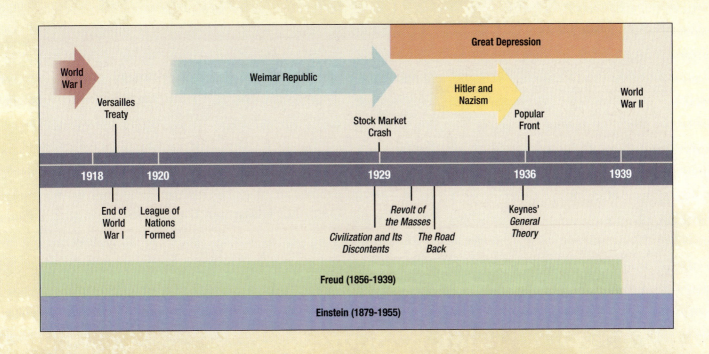

					Great Depression		

World War I

Versailles Treaty

Weimar Republic

Stock Market Crash

Hitler and Nazism

Popular Front

World War II

| 1918 | 1920 | | 1929 | | 1936 | | 1939 |

End of World War I

League of Nations Formed

Civilization and Its Discontents

Revolt of the Masses

The Road Back

Keynes' General Theory

Freud (1856-1939)

Einstein (1879-1955)

16 Democracy, Depression, and Instability: The 1920s and 1930s

The two decades following World War I were marked by instability and uncertainty. Except in Russia, where the Bolsheviks had taken power, it appeared that liberal democracy had been established throughout Europe as a result of World War I. But soon a trend toward authoritarianism appeared, with many nations suffering from political fluctuations. The economic problems left from World War I and the immediate postwar period did not disappear despite a brief period of fragile prosperity in the mid-1920s. In 1929 the stock market crash in New York initiated the Great Depression in the United States, which quickly spread to Europe. Huge numbers of people suffered economically, and governments were pressured to effect radical solutions to the problems. Not surprisingly, there were great social strains through all of this. The difficulty of

recovering from World War I was exacerbated by this political and economic instability. Swept by uncertainty about the present and the future, society seemed to polarize into opposing classes and around competing ideologies.

A similar uncertainty characterized intellectual trends. The optimism and faith in rationality typical of the eighteenth and nineteenth centuries gave way to movements such as relativism in the physical and social sciences, Freudianism in psychology, and seeming anarchy in the arts. The West was no longer so confident, and events of the 1920s and 1930s added to that lack of confidence.

The selections in this chapter exemplify these trends. Historians usually focus on Germany during the 1920s in describing the general unrest and the efforts made to respond to it. What was the nature of the political and economic disorder in Germany during the 1920s? In what ways was there a sense that things were out of hand and that the population was composed of many opposing factions? The Great Depression dealt the worst blow to the industrial economy. How did the Depression make the future of capitalism uncertain? What policies were pursued by governments to deal with the Depression? How was the Depression related to political disorder during the 1930s? What was the long-term significance of the Depression? Finally, a general sense of disillusionment and uncertainty characterized intellectual life. In what ways was disillusionment particularly strong for the generation that came of age in 1914? In what ways was there a feeling that nineteenth-century ideals were gone and that twentieth-century people might be worse off than their predecessors?

A gloomy picture of life during the 1920s and 1930s emerges from these materials. The growth of totalitarianism during this period, to be examined in the next chapter, will add to this negative image.

✍ For Classroom Discussion

In what ways is the interwar period best seen as one of decline, disruption, and pessimism? Use the sources by Crossman, Whol, Freud, and Ortega y Gasset.

 # Primary Sources

The Road Back
Erich Maria Remarque
and
Restless Days
Lilo Linke

With the establishment of the Weimar Republic at the end of World War I, Germany had a government system much like those of the other Western democracies. But the German government was burdened with tremendous economic problems, continued social turmoil, and inexperienced politicians laboring with the legacy of World War I. This society and its mood are particularly well reflected in the cultural productions of the period, for example, in the following selections from Erich Maria Remarque and Lilo Linke. Remarque, whose All Quiet on the Western Front *(1929) and* The Road Back *(1931) were two of the most popular books of the period, was a German soldier during World War I. The first selection is from* The Road Back, *which focuses on the life in Germany faced by the returning soldier. The second selection is from Linke's autobiography,* Restless Days.

CONSIDER: *Any connections between World War I and subsequent economic problems; the political problems facing the Weimar Republic; how such an environment might prove fertile for the rise of a political figure like Hitler.*

SOURCE: Excerpt from *The Road Back* by Erich Maria Remarque. "Der Weg Zurück." Copyright © 1931 by Ullstein, A.G.: Copyright renewed 1958 by Erich Maria Remarque; Lilo Linke, *Restless Days.* Reprinted by permission of Alfred A. Knopf, Inc., pp. 388–389. Copyright © 1935 by Alfred A. Knopf, Inc., and renewed © 1963 by Lilo Linke.

Demonstrations in the streets have been called for this afternoon. Prices have been soaring everywhere for months past, and the poverty is greater even than it was during the war. Wages are insufficient to buy the bare necessities of life, and even though one may have the money it is often impossible to buy anything with it. But ever more and more gin palaces and dance halls go up, and ever more and more blatant is the profiteering and swindling.

Scattered groups of workers on strike march through the streets. Now and again there is a disturbance. A rumour is going about that troops have been concentrated at the barracks. But there is no sign of it as yet.

Here and there one hears cries and counter-cries. Somebody is haranguing at a street corner. Then suddenly everywhere is silence.

A procession of men in the faded uniforms of the front-line trenches is moving slowly toward us.

It is formed up by sections, marching in fours. Big white placards are carried before: *Where is the Fatherland's gratitude?—The War Cripples are starving.*

The men with one arm are carrying the placards, and they look around continually to see if the procession is still coming along properly behind them, for they are the fastest.

These are followed by men with sheep dogs on short, leather leads. The animals have the red cross of the blind at their collars. . . .

Behind the blind come the men with one eye, the tattered faces of men with head wounds: wry, bulbous mouths, faces without noses and without lower jaws, entire faces one great red scar with a couple of holes where formerly were a mouth and a nose. But above this desolation, quiet, questioning, sad human eyes.

On these follow the long lines of men with legs amputated. Some already have artificial limbs that spring forward obliquely as they walk and strike clanking on the pavement, as if the whole man were artificial, made up of iron and hinges. Others have their trouser legs looped up and made fast with safety pins. These go on crutches or sticks with black rubber pads.

Then come the shakers, the shell-shocked. Their hands, their heads, their clothes, their bodies quake as though they still shudder with horror. They no longer have control of themselves; the will has been extinguished, the muscles and nerves have revolted against the brain, the eyes become void and impotent.

❧

It was no good to go on assuming that a common basis for all the different groups and classes in Germany could be found. The break between them became daily wider and more irreparable. The plebiscite of the Right "against the Young Plan and the war-guilt lie" proved just as unsuccessful as those arranged in former years by the Left, but the poison of the defamatory agitation remained in the body of the community, and we watched its effects with anxiety.

In my own family the political antagonism was growing past endurance. In October Fritz had finished his apprenticeship in an old-established export house, at the precise moment when the firm went bankrupt—a minor incident compared with such events as the breakdown of the Frankfurt General Insurance Company and the Civil Servants' Bank or the enforced reorganization and amalgamation of the Deutsche Bank and the DiscontoGesellschaft, which all happened in the course of the year and dangerously damaged the whole economic life of Germany. Yet for my brother the bankruptcy of his firm overshadowed all other happenings, since it meant that he lost his job. His three years' training was in vain—there was not a single export firm which was not forced to dismiss as many of its employees as possible. . . .

"Yes, that's just it—millions! If it isn't my fault, whose fault is it? I tell you—your friends, the French, the English, the Americans, all those damnable nations who inflict on us one dishonorable penalty after the other—they are to blame for all this. Before the war the whole world bought German goods. My firm exported to Africa, to the German colonies. Hundreds of thousands we turned over every year. But they have robbed us of our colonies, of all our foreign markets. They have stolen the coal-mines in the Saar and in Upper Silesia, they squeeze millions of marks out of our bleeding country. We'll never rise again unless we free ourselves by another war."

"Don't be foolish, Fritz. Things are bad in the whole world."

"I don't care about the world, I care only about Germany, which you and your pacifists have delivered into the hands of our enemies. I despise you, you are not worthy to call yourself a German."

With Germany's Unemployed

Heinrich Hauser

No nation was hit harder by the Great Depression than Germany. By 1932 it had more than six million unemployed workers and countless people wandering homeless along its streets and roads. Many sought help in city shelters. The plight of these people—like that of millions in other nations—is reflected in the following account by Heinrich Hauser.

CONSIDER: *Who Hauser observed along Germany's highways; the psychological effects of the hardships on these people; how such conditions might lead many to turn to Adolf Hitler and the Nazis.*

An almost unbroken chain of homeless men extends the whole length of the great Hamburg-Berlin highway.

There are so many of them moving in both directions, impelled by the wind or making their way against it, that they could shout a message from Hamburg to Berlin by word of mouth. . . . All the highways in Germany over which I traveled this year presented the same aspect. . . .

But most of the hikers paid no attention to me. They walked separately or in small groups, with their eyes on the ground. And they had the queer, stumbling gait of barefooted people, for their shoes were slung over their shoulders. Some of them were guild members,—carpenters with embroidered wallets, knee breeches, and broad felt hats; milkmen with striped red shirts, and bricklayers with tall black hats,—but they were in a minority. Far more numerous were those whom one could assign to no special profession or craft—unskilled young people, for the most part, who had been unable to find a place for themselves in any city or town in Germany, and who had never had a job and never expected to have one. There was something else that had never been seen before—whole families that had piled all their goods into baby carriages and wheelbarrows that they were pushing along as they plodded forward in dumb despair. It was a whole nation on the march.

I saw them—and this was the strongest impression that the year 1932 left with me—I saw them, gathered into groups of fifty or a hundred men, attacking fields of potatoes. I saw them digging up the potatoes and throwing them into sacks while the farmer who owned the field watched them in despair and the local policeman looked on gloomily from the distance. I saw them staggering toward the lights of the city as night fell, with their sacks on their backs. What did it remind me of? Of the War, of

SOURCE: Heinrich Hauser, "With Germany's Unemployed," *Living Age,* vol. 344, no. 4398 (March 1933), pp. 27–29, 37–38.

the worst periods of starvation in 1917 and 1918, but even then people paid for the potatoes. . . .

I entered the huge Berlin municipal lodging house in a northern quarter of the city. . . .

My next recollection is sitting at table in another room on a crowded bench that is like a seat in a fourth-class railway carriage. Hundreds of hungry mouths make an enormous noise eating their food. The men sit bent over their food like animals who feel that someone is going to take it away from them. They hold their bowl with their left arm part way around it, so that nobody can take it away, and they also protect it with their other elbow and with their head and mouth, while they move the spoon as fast as they can between their mouth and the bowl. The portions, for men on a normal diet, would be extraordinarily large. There must be about a quart of stew in each bowl, and it's not bad, either. There is fat and strength in it. But I am only halfway through mine when all my neighbors have finished and are looking at me enviously. I give the rest to the Saxon, who looks at me in amazement. "Stomach ache," I say. In the twinkling of an eye the rest has disappeared.

Wash basins are brought in on the other side of the room. Everyone washes his own bowl here, for he will need it again for his morning meal.

Program of the Popular Front— January 11, 1936

The Great Depression of the 1930s was a major blow to Western stability. In many areas it led to the fall of established governments and the rise of right-wing groups. In France in 1934, Socialists and Communists, in part fearing the rise of fascism, drew together into the Popular Front. In 1936, under the leadership of Léon Blum (1872–1950), the Popular Front came to power, but only for about two years. The following is an excerpt from the program of the Popular Front, January 11, 1936.

CONSIDER: *The ways in which this document reflects the turmoil of public life during the 1930s; how the Popular Front proposes to deal with the Depression; to what groups such a program would most appeal and why.*

I. *Defence of Freedom.*
  1. A general amnesty.
  2. Measures against the Fascist Leagues:
    (*a*) The effective disarmament and dissolution of all semi-military formations, in accordance with the law.
    (*b*) The enforcement of legal measures in cases of incitement to murder or any attempt against the safety of the State. . . .
  4. The Press:
    (*a*) The repeal of the laws and decrees restricting freedom of opinion. . . .
      (iii) Measures ending the private monopoly of commercial advertising and the scandals of financial advertising, and preventing the formation of newspaper trusts.
    (*c*) Organization by the State of wireless broadcasts with a view to assuring the accuracy of wireless news and the equality of political and social organizations in relation to radio.
  5. Trade Union Liberties:
    (*a*) Application and observance of trade union freedom for all.
    (*b*) Recognition of women's labour rights. . . .
II. *Defence of Peace.*
  1. Appeal to the people, and especially the working classes, for collaboration in the maintenance and organization of peace.
  2. International collaboration within the framework of the League of Nations for collective security, by defining the aggressor and by joint application of sanctions in cases of aggression.
  3. Ceaseless endeavour to pass from armed peace to disarmed peace, first by a convention of limitation, and then by the general, simultaneous and effectively controlled reduction of armaments.
  4. Nationalization of war industries and suppression of private trade in armaments.
  5. Repudiation of secret diplomacy; international action and public negotiation to bring back to Geneva the states which have left it, without weakening the essential principles of the League of Nations, which are the principles of collective security and indivisible peace. . . .
III. *Economic Demands.*
  1. Restoration of purchasing power destroyed or reduced by the crisis.
    (*a*) Against unemployment and the crisis in industry.
      (i) Establishment of a national unemployment fund.
      (ii) Reduction of the working week without reduction of the weekly wage.
      (iii) Bringing your workers into employment by establishing a system of adequate pensions for aged workers.

SOURCE: From David Thomson, *Democracy in France.* Reprinted by permission of Oxford University Press (Oxford, England, 5th ed., 1969), pp. 310–314.

(iv) Rapid execution of a public works programme, both urban and rural, linking local investments with schemes financed by the State and local authorities. . . .

2. Against the robbery of investors and for the better organization of credit:

(a) Regulation of banking business. . . .

(c) In order to remove credit and investment from the control of the economic oligarchy, the Bank of France must cease to be a private concern, and "The Bank of France" must become "France's Bank.". . .

IV. *Financial Purification*. . . .

3. Democratic reform of the system of taxation as to relax the fiscal burden blocking economic recovery, and raising revenue by measures against large fortunes. Rapid steepening of income tax on incomes above 75,000 francs a year; reorganization of death duties; special taxes on monopoly profits, but in such a way as to have no effects on retail prices. Measures against tax evasions, in connexion with transferable ("bearer") securities.

The Revolt of the Masses

José Ortega y Gasset

The disillusionment of the 1920s and 1930s, often associated with the effects of World War I, is reflected in many of the more profound attempts to understand Western civilization and the human condition. But this intellectual trend should not be seen only as a reaction to World War I. In The Revolt of the Masses *(1930), one of the most influential works of the period, José Ortega y Gasset (1883–1955) laments the population increase, the rise of the "masses," and the decline of the elite, cultured, liberal civilization of the nineteenth century. Ortega, a strong liberal and antimonarchist, became professor of metaphysics at the University of Madrid in 1910 and Spain's leading intellectual. Anticipating the defeat of the Republicans, he fled Spain in 1936. In the following excerpt from* The Revolt of the Masses, *he introduces the themes he will deal with in the rest of the book.*

CONSIDER: *Why the rise to power of the masses is so serious; how Ortega distinguishes the "masses" from the "qualified minorities"; whether he presents a valid criticism of modern democracy.*

SOURCE: Fosé Ortega y Gasset, *The Revolt of the Masses.* Reprinted by permission of W. W. Norton & Co., Inc. (New York, 1932), pp. 11, 16, 18.

There is one fact which, whether for good or ill, is of utmost importance in the public life of Europe at the present moment. This fact is the accession of the masses to complete social power. As the masses, by definition, neither should nor can direct their own personal existence, and still less rule society in general, this fact means that actually Europe is suffering from the greatest crisis that can afflict peoples, nations, and civilisation. Such a crisis has occurred more than once in history. Its characteristics and its consequences are well known. So also is its name. It is called the rebellion of the masses. . . .

There exist, then, in society, operations, activities, and functions of the most diverse order, which are of their very nature special, and which consequently cannot be properly carried out without special gifts. For example: certain pleasures of an artistic and refined character, or again the functions of government and of political judgment in public affairs. Previously these special activities were exercised by qualified minorities, or at least by those who claimed such qualification. The mass asserted no right to intervene in them; they realised that if they wished to intervene they would necessarily have to acquire those special qualities and cease being mere mass. They recognised their place in a healthy dynamic social system. . . .

The characteristic of the hour is that the commonplace mind, knowing itself to be commonplace, has the assurance to proclaim the rights of the commonplace and to impose them wherever it will. As they say in the United States: "to be different is to be indecent." The mass crushes beneath it everything that is different, everything that is excellent, individual, qualified and select. Anybody who is not like everybody, who does not think like everybody, runs the risk of being eliminated. And it is clear, of course, that this "everybody" is not "everybody." "Everybody" was normally the complex unity of the mass and the divergent, specialised minorities. Nowadays, "everybody" is the mass alone. Here we have the formidable fact of our times, described without any concealment of the brutality of its features.

Civilization and Its Discontents

Sigmund Freud

Psychoanalysis became one of the most powerful intellectual influences in the twentieth century. In part, it was based on the older eighteenth- and nineteenth-century optimism about

SOURCE: Sigmund Freud, *Civilization and its Discontents*, in *The Standard Edition of the Complete Psychological Works of Sigmund Freud*, James Strachey, trans. and ed. Reprinted by permission of W. W. Norton & Co., Inc. (New York, 1961), pp. 58–59, 92, The Hogarth Press, Ltd., Sigmund Freud Copyrights Ltd., and The Institute of Psycho-Analysis.

the power of human rationality and scientific investigation: It assumed that human behavior could be even more deeply understood than before through scientific observation and that rational understanding could alleviate pain and problems. In other ways, however, it reflected the late-nineteenth- and early-twentieth-century attack on rationality: It argued that much of human behavior is irrational, unconscious, and instinctual. Finally, it echoed some of the pessimism fostered by the experience of World War I: Civilization was increasingly threatened by deep, antisocial drives such as those for sex or aggression. Sigmund Freud (1856–1939), the person most responsible for developing psychoanalysis, was a Viennese neurologist who became increasingly interested in psychoanalysis as a theory of human behavior, as a method of investigation, and as a treatment for certain illnesses. The following is a selection from Civilization and Its Discontents *(1929), written in the aftermath of World War I and toward the end of Freud's life. In it Freud speaks of the fragility of civilization.*

CONSIDER: *How this selection reflects the experience of World War I; the ways in which this document reflects and contributes to the sense of uncertainty common in this period; similarities between Ortega and Freud.*

The element of truth behind all this, which people are so ready to disavow, is that men are not gentle creatures who want to be loved, and who at the most can defend themselves if they are attacked; they are, on the contrary, creatures among whose instinctual endowments is to be reckoned a powerful share of aggressiveness. As a result, their neighbour is for them not only a potential helper or sexual object, but also someone who tempts them to satisfy their aggressiveness on him, to exploit his capacity for work without compensation, to use him sexually without his consent, to seize his possessions, to humiliate him, to cause him pain, to torture and to kill him. *Homo homini lupus.*[1] Who, in the face of all his experience of life and of history, will have the courage to dispute this assertion? As a rule this cruel aggressiveness waits for some provocation or puts itself at the service of some other purpose, whose goal might also have been reached by milder measures. In circumstances that are favourable to it, when the mental counter-forces which ordinarily inhibit it are out of action, it also manifests itself spontaneously and reveals man as a savage beast to whom consideration towards his own kind is something alien. Anyone who calls to mind the atrocities committed during racial migrations or the invasions of the Huns, or by the people known as

Mongols under Jenghiz Khan and Tamerlane, or at the capture of Jerusalem by the pious Crusaders, or even, indeed, the horrors of the recent World War—anyone who calls these things to mind will have to bow humbly before the truth of this view.

The existence of this inclination to aggression, which we can detect in ourselves and justly assume to be present in others, is the factor which disturbs our relations with our neighbour and which forces civilization into such a high expenditure [of energy]. In consequence of this primary mutual hostility of human beings, civilized society is perpetually threatened with disintegration. The interest of work in common would not hold it together; instinctual passions are stronger than reasonable interests. Civilization has to use its utmost efforts in order to set limits to man's aggressive instincts and to hold the manifestations of them in check by psychical reaction-formations. Hence, therefore, the use of methods intended to incite people into identifications, and aim-inhibited relationships of love, hence the restriction upon sexual life, and hence too the ideal's commandment to love one's neighbour as oneself—a commandment which is really justified by the fact that nothing else runs so strongly counter to the original nature of man. In spite of every effort, these endeavours of civilization have not so far achieved very much. It hopes to prevent the crudest excesses of brutal violence by itself assuming the right to use violence against criminals, but the law is not able to lay hold of the more cautious and refined manifestations of human aggressiveness.

❧

The fateful question for the human species seems to me to be whether and to what extent their cultural development will succeed in mastering the disturbance of their communal life by the human instinct of aggression and self-destruction. It may be that in this respect precisely the present time deserves a special interest. Men have gained control over the forces of nature to such an extent that with their help they would have no difficulty in exterminating one another to the last man. They know this, and hence comes a large part of their current unrest, their unhappiness and their mood of anxiety. And now it is to be expected that the other of the two "Heavenly Powers," eternal Eros, will make an effort to assert himself in the struggle with his equally immortal adversary. But who can foresee with what success and with what result?[2]

---

[1] "Man is a wolf to man." Derived from Plautus, *Asinaria* II, iv, 88.

[2] The final sentence was added in 1931—when the menace of Hitler was already becoming apparent.

Visual Sources

Decadence in the Weimar Republic

George Grosz

The following 1921 drawing by the German artist George Grosz (figure 16.1) shows some of the problems facing Western societies, particularly Germany, shortly after World War I. The wealthy few indulge in leisure activities while guards protect their factories. The rest of the people are crippled veterans, bankrupt businessmen, old women, young children, and the poor. They appear to feel isolated, distrustful, and out of place. The subject matter of this drawing is typical of art and literature that attacked capitalism and militarism between the wars.

CONSIDER: *How this drawing relates to the selection by Linke or the one by Remarque.*

Unemployment and Politics in the Weimar Republic

Economic and political developments often go hand in hand. Many historians argue that this was particularly the case in Germany during the 1920s and

FIGURE 16.1 (© The Granger Collection, New York)

Chart 16.1 Elections to the German Reichstag, 1924–1932

	May 4, 1924	December 7, 1924	May 20, 1928	September 14, 1930	July 31, 1932	November 6, 1932
Number of Eligible Voters (in millions)	38.4	39.0	41.2	43.0	44.2	44.2
Votes Cast (in millions)	29.7	30.7	31.2	35.2	37.2	35.7
National Socialist German Workers Party	1,918,000 6.6%	908,000 3%	810,000 2.6%	6,407,000 18.3%	13,779,000 37.3%	11,737,000 33.1%
German Nationalist People's Party (Conservative)	5,696,000 19.5%	6,209,000 20.5%	4,382,000 14.2%	2,458,000 7%	2,187,000 5.9%	3,131,000 8.8%
Center Party (Catholic)	3,914,000 13.4%	4,121,000 13.6%	3,712,000 12.1%	4,127,000 11.8%	4,589,000 12.4%	4,230,000 11.9%
Democratic Party (The German State Party)	1,655,000 5.7%	1,921,000 6.3%	1,506,000 4.9%	1,322,000 3.8%	373,000 1%	339,000 1%
Social Democratic Party	6,009,000 20.5%	7,886,000 26%	9,153,000 29.8%	8,576,000 24.5%	7,960,000 21.6%	7,251,000 20.4%
Communist Party	3,693,000 12.6%	2,712,000 9%	3,265,000 10.6%	4,590,000 13.1%	5,370,000 14.3%	5,980,000 16.9%

early 1930s. Chart 16.1 and Chart 16.2 deal with the Weimar Republic in Germany between 1924 and 1932. The first shows election results by political parties to the Reichstag; the second shows unemployment figures.

CONSIDER: The relationship between unemployment and voting patterns.

Unemployment During the Great Depression, 1930–1938

While the Great Depression of the 1930s had worldwide consequences, it didn't affect all countries equally. One way of comparing the course of the Depression in different countries is to examine national unemployment, perhaps the most telling

Chart 16.2 Unemployment in Germany, 1924–1932

1924	1928	1930	July 31, 1932	October 31, 1932
978,000	1,368,000	3,076,000	5,392,000	5,109,000

SOURCE: Joachim Remak, ed., *The Nazi Years: A Documentary History* (Englewood Cliffs, NJ: Simon & Schuster, Inc., 1969), p. 44.

Chart 16.3 National Unemployment, 1930–1938

Year	Germany Number	Germany Percentage	Japan Number	Japan Percentage
1930	3,075,580	—	369,408	5.3%
1931	4,519,704	23.7%	422,755	6.1
1932	5,575,492	30.1	485,681	6.8
1933	4,804,428	25.8	408,710	5.6
1934	2,718,309	14.5	372,941	5.0
1935	2,151,039	11.6	356,044	4.6
1936	1,592,655	8.1	338,365	4.3
1937	912,312	4.5	295,443	3.7
1938 (June)	429,475	2.0	230,262	2.9

Year	Great Britain Number	Great Britain Percentage	United States Number	United States Percentage
1930	1,464,347	11.8%	4,340,000	8.7%
1931	2,129,359	16.7	8,020,000	15.9
1932	2,254,857	17.6	12,060,000	23.6
1933	2,110,090	16.4	12,830,000	24.9
1934	1,801,913	13.91	1,340,000	21.7
1935	1,714,844	13.1	10,610,000	20.1
1936	1,497,587	11.2	9,030,000	16.9
1937	1,277,928	9.4	7,700,000	14.3
1938 (Nov.)	1,529,133	10.8	10,390,000	19.0

FIGURE 16.2 (Library of Congress [LC-USZC4-3236])

index of the depth of the Great Depression and its social consequences. Chart 16.3 traces unemployment numbers and unemployment as a percentage of the civilian labor force in four countries between 1930 and 1938.

CONSIDER: *Which countries suffered more than others; where unemployment persisted the longest; possible reasons why Japan was not hit so hard as other countries.*

Unemployment and the Appeal to Women

The Nazi party used unemployment as part of its political appeal to women, as revealed in the following 1931 poster (figure 16.2). It states: "Women! Millions of Men Are Without Work. Millions of Children Are Without a Future. Save the German Family! Vote for Adolf Hitler!"

CONSIDER: *Why certain political parties gained and others lost as unemployment grew during the Depression years; how these charts relate to the drawing by Grosz, the selections by Linke and Remarque, and the Nazi poster; ways this poster was designed to appeal, in particular to German women.*

Secondary Sources

The Generation of 1914: Disillusionment

Robert Wohl

The end of World War I raised hopes and expectations among large numbers of people. In a few years those hopes and expectations turned into disappointment and disillusion, coloring the two decades between World Wars I and II. In the following selection Robert Wohl analyzes the origins and meaning of this disillusionment, focusing on the shared experiences of the generation of Europeans who were born during the 1890s and who had to shoulder much of the burden of the war.

SOURCE: Reprinted by permission of the publishers from *The Generation of 1914* by Robert Wohl. Cambridge, MA: Harvard University Press. Copyright © 1979 by the President and Fellows of Harvard College.

CONSIDER: *Why the first few years of peace were so crucial for the creation of cynicism and disillusion among survivors of the war; the forms disillusion took; possible consequences of the developments of 1917–1920 according to Wohl.*

When we think of the army of returning veterans during the 1920s, we see them through the eyes of Remarque and Hemingway as a generation of men crippled, both physically and morally, by their service in the war. Many no doubt were. Yet it is a fact that the famed cynicism and disillusionment of the survivors were, to a great extent, a product of the first few years of peace. To understand this mood of disillusionment we must recall the attitudes and expectations that soldiers brought home with them, attitudes and expectations that were also widespread among the younger population as a whole.

Many soldiers had, like Omodeo, come to think that the war must have a secret meaning that only the future would reveal; they found it necessary to believe that their sacrifice and suffering would not be in vain; and they clung to the hope that the war would turn out to have been a rite of purification with positive results. Sensing this feeling and realizing its importance, political leaders in all countries encouraged the fighting and civilian sectors of the population to expect from peace not merely an end to bloodshed but a real alteration and improvement in the tenor and quality of life. It was said, and widely believed, that class barriers would fall; that selfishness would give way to cooperation; that harmony would reign; that conflict among nations would cease; and that everyone's sacrifice and suffering would somehow be compensated.

These expectations were often encapsulated in the word "revolution," but people of different social backgrounds assigned very different meanings to the term. Governments encouraged these hopes with their propaganda, and in 1918 Wilson came to incarnate the dream of renovation. The Wilsonian vision of a world safe for democracy merged with the equally vague idea of a revolution carried out by returning soldiers in the name of the values of manhood and self-sacrifice they had discovered on the battlefield. . . .

Disillusionment comes in many forms. The special form it took in Europe in the 1920s had to do with the development of the political situation and the frustration of apocalyptic hopes. Between 1917 and 1920 a revolutionary wave broke over every European country. Armies grew restive and mutinied; urban populations staged riots and insurrections over dwindling food supplies and rising prices; unions swelled in membership far beyond their prewar size; and workers began to challenge factory owners for the control of production. . . .

This disillusionment was felt by men and women of all age-groups in all parts of Europe; but the feeling of betrayal and defeat was especially strong among returning veterans born in the 1890s. They suffered from a tremendous sense of anticlimax, and the younger they were the more disoriented they felt. . . .

The developments of 1917–1920 engendered disappointment and frustration; they gave rise to bitterness and cynicism; but among young war veterans, the dream of cultural and political renewal did not die. Brought up in a crepuscular atmosphere of cultural crisis, subjected while still young to the ordeal of the war, witnesses during the immediate postwar years to a wave of revolution that swept away century-old empires and shook to its foundations every European institution, intellectuals born in the last two decades of the nineteenth century could not divest themselves of the feeling that the apocalypse had only been postponed and that any restoration of the postwar era would be temporary. The survival of the revolutionary regime in Russia, the creation of Communist parties throughout Europe, the victory of the Fascist movement in Italy, the collapse of parliamentary government in Spain, the difficulties that Great Britain and France experienced in regaining their prewar dynamism, and the onset of the worldwide economic crisis in 1929 confirmed these intellectuals in their belief that the world of their childhood was dead and that a new postwar world was being born.

Government and the Governed: The Interwar Years

R. H. S. Crossman

Many scholars saw the 1920s as a period of failure and missed opportunities. This was particularly true of liberal or left-wing scholars from Western democracies, for they looked for the origins of the disastrous rise of dictatorships and the Great Depression in those years. The following selection by R. H. S. Crossman exemplifies this perspective. Educated at Oxford, Crossman became a leading figure in the Labour Party's left wing and wrote numerous works on philosophy and politics. Here, in a work published in 1940, Crossman analyzes the period between 1918 and 1933.

CONSIDER: *Opportunities that were missed in 1918 and 1919; policies that the Western democracies might have initiated during this period that could have changed the course of events.*

Seen in retrospect, the period from 1918–1933 is marked by a growing lethargy in the victor nations. Neither at home nor abroad did democracy undertake a single great constructive enterprise. Victory seemed to have deprived France and Britain of their dynamic: their Conservatives ceased to be ardent imperialists, and their Socialists lost their revolutionary fervour. A spirit of collective pacifism possessed them, and made the people content with the lazy approval of high ideals, the verbal condemnation of injustice, chicanery and oppression. Holding all the power, the Western democracies disdained to use it, so long as the status quo was in any way tolerable. The attitude of America was not dissimilar, except that here the League idea was rejected and the Monroe doctrine was still regarded as America's contribution to world peace.

A myth is only justifiable if it stimulates to action. But "Collective Pacifism" was a sedative, not a stimulant. It intoxicated the democracies with a feeling of moral

SOURCE: R. H. S. Crossman, *Government and the Governed*. Reprinted by permission of G. P. Putnam's Sons (New York, 1940), pp. 255–257. Copyright © 1940 by G. P. Putnam's Sons.

superiority and well-being, while it sapped their sense of responsibility. Gradually statesmen and peoples alike began to believe that the League of Nations was a force able to do the work which previously fell to the various nations. Instead of relying on themselves and on cooperation with their allies, they began to rely on the League to preserve peace. Since the League had no coercive power at its disposal, this trust was wholly unjustified.

No one Party or section of the population can be blamed for this collapse of democratic morale. The great opportunity had been missed in 1918–19: and it was difficult for the Western democracies to recover from that failure. They had encouraged nationalism as the basis of government; they had retained economic imperialism and permitted international finance to function independently of government policy. In brief, they had as far as possible returned to pre-war conditions. Having done so, they sought to humanize them. That they failed is an indication that good intentions and kindness, unbacked by resolution and knowledge, may disguise injustices but never eradicate them. Kindness and good-will no doubt console the patient suffering from cancer, but they will not cure the cancer; and the patient whose practitioner only displays these qualities, may, in his intolerable agonies, turn to a quack and curse the Christian humanity which his practitioner displays.

The Great Depression in Europe

James M. Laux

Most scholars agree that the Great Depression was very important, but they disagree over its precise significance. For Marxists, it was the greatest in a series of periodic economic crises inevitably flowing from the capitalist system and an indication that this system would soon collapse. For liberal economic historians, it was an indictment of conservative, nationalistic economic policies that would be forced to give way to modern Keynesian policies characterized by greater government activity and planning. For others, it was a crucial cause of the rise of Nazism and World War II itself. In the following selection James Laux analyzes the impact of the Great Depression, emphasizing various changes in attitude that stemmed from it.

CONSIDER: *Whether, as some scholars argue, the Great Depression forced governments to modify* laissez-faire *just enough to save capitalism as a whole; why economic planning appeared more attractive after the experience of the Depression.*

The Depression, perhaps, had the most serious impact in Europe on people's thinking about economic matters. Looking back on the experience, most Europeans agreed that the orthodoxy of laissez-faire no longer held. They would not again accept the view that a government must interfere as little as possible in the operation of the economic system. Governments must accept wider responsibilities than balancing their own budgets. The value of the currency in terms of gold must give way to economic expansion if the two appear to conflict. Laissez-faire already was wheezing and laboring in the 1920s; after the decade of the 1930s it was nearly prostrate. As so often happens, a philosophy came along to justify this changed attitude, a new approach to theoretical economics worked out by the Englishman John Maynard Keynes. The most influential economist of the twentieth century, Keynes published his classic work in 1936, *The General Theory of Employment, Interest and Money.* He argued that governments can and should manipulate capitalist economies, by running surpluses or deficits, by investing heavily in public works, by changing the size of the money and credit supply, and by altering rates of interest. In his analysis he emphasized the total economy, the relations among savings, investment, production, and consumption, what is called macroeconomics, rather than an investigation of a single firm or sector. A critic of socialism, Keynes scorned the significance of government ownership of production facilities, but promoted government intervention in an economy to make capitalism work better.

Bolstering this view were the remarkable production achievements of many European industrial states during the two world wars. In these crises national economies expanded military production enormously under government direction. Many asked why such techniques could not be applied in peacetime also, but to make consumer products rather than tools of destruction.

The upshot was that by 1945 if not 1939 most Europeans abandoned the idea that they lived at the mercy of an impersonal economic system whose rules could not be changed and accepted the proposition that the economy could operate the way people wanted it to. From this it was a short step to the concept of planning the future development of the economy—both the whole and particular segments of it. Economic planning became an acceptable posture for capitalist societies and enjoyed a considerable reputation. Some of those who supported it perhaps underestimated the possible merits of free markets as guiding production decisions and did seem to assume that planners somehow possess more wisdom than ordinary human beings.

Economic nationalism was a more immediate result of the Depression—the policy that short-run national economic interests have highest priority and that international

SOURCE: James M. Laux, from "The Great Depression in Europe" (*The Forum Series*). Reprinted by permission of Forum Press (St. Louis, MO, 1974), pp. 13–14. Copyright © 1974 by Forum Press.

economic cooperation and trade must give way before narrowly conceived national interests. Economic nationalism showed its sharpest teeth in those European states where political nationalism reached a peak—Germany, Italy, and the Soviet Union. Its strength declined in western Europe after the Second World War as people saw once again that economic prosperity among one's neighbors could bring great benefits to oneself. In an expanding continental or world economy everyone can get richer. But one wonders if economic nationalism may not revive in western Europe, especially if it seems a popular policy in a crisis.

The Great Depression had important political repercussions too. In Germany, the Depression's tragic gloom made the dynamism of the Nazi movement seem more attractive. It is difficult to imagine the Nazis achieving power without the Depression and its pervasive unemployment in the background. In France, the Depression convinced many that the regime of the Third Republic had lost its élan and relevance to twentieth-century problems, but the lack of a widely popular alternative meant that the Republic could limp along until a disastrous military defeat brought it down. In Britain, the Depression was less serious and no fundamental challenge to the political regime developed. The Conservatives held power for most of the interwar period and their failure to work actively to absorb the large unemployment that continued there until late in the 1930s brought widespread rancor and bitterness against them. Doubts as to the Conservatives' ability to manage a peacetime economy led to the first majority Labour government in the 1945 election. More profoundly, the years of heavy unemployment bred a very strong anticapitalist sentiment in much of British labor, a sentiment that led them after the war to demand moves toward socialism, such as nationalization of major industries.

The Depression helped convince Europeans that their governments must try to manage their economies. Most agreed that full employment and expanding output should be the goals. They did not agree on the means to achieve these ends.

✤ CHAPTER QUESTIONS

1. Which developments focused on in this chapter are most closely related to the experience and results of World War I?

2. In what ways do the trends of the 1920s and 1930s support the argument that Western civilization reached its apogee between 1789 and 1914 and that starting with World War I it was clearly on the decline? What factors might be pointed out to mitigate or counter this interpretation?

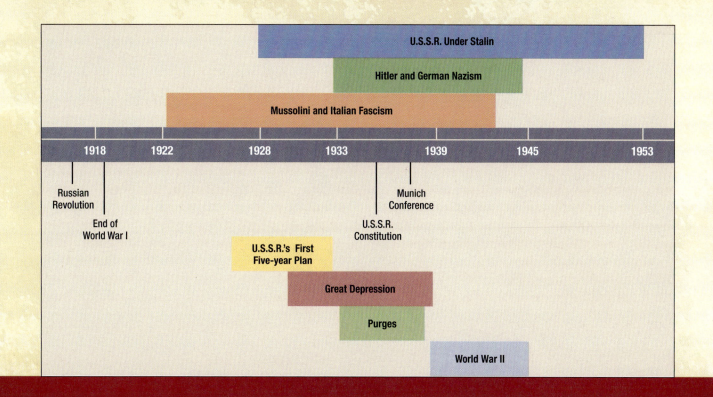

17 Communism, Fascism, and Authoritarianism

The end of World War I and the arrangements made at the Paris Peace Conference in 1919 seemed to represent success for parliamentary democracy. But during the 1920s and 1930s, that success proved to be more apparent than real. The 1917 revolution had already brought a Communist regime to power in Russia. During the following two decades, Communist parties spread throughout Europe and were perceived as a great threat, but they did not come to power outside of the Soviet Union. Authoritarian movements of the right became the most immediate danger to parliamentary democracy. The first of these movements was Mussolini's fascism, which became dominant in Italy in 1922. By the end of the decade regimes in Eastern and Southern Europe were becoming more authoritarian. This trend became stronger during the Depression of the 1930s. There was a retreat toward nationalistic economic policies and greater central control by governments attempting to deal with the despair, destruc-

tion, and dislocation accompanying the Depression. In Central, Eastern, and Southern Europe, the Depression fueled already strong tendencies toward dictatorships and fascism. The most extreme of rightist ideology was Hitler's Nazism, which became dominant in Germany in 1933. By the end of that decade, Europe was embroiled in a new World War even greater than World War I.

Historians and social scientists looking at this period sometimes focus on the rise of "totalitarianism." This is a controversial term that is hard to evaluate objectively. Generally, it refers to a form of government that shares certain traits. It rejects individualism, a single party is in power, and the state controls almost all aspects of life (economic activities, social organizations, cultural institutions, the military, and politics). It has one official, revolutionary ideology, and terror, propaganda, and mass communications are used as tools of power. Yet there have been important differences among states that have been called totalitarian.

Communism in Russia under Stalin and its professed opposite, Nazism in Germany, sprang from different sources and ideologies. Even though German Nazism and Italian fascism resembled each other, some scholars question whether Italian fascism was thorough and effective enough to be considered totalitarian. Other nationalistic authoritarian regimes of the right, from Eastern Europe to Spain and Portugal, shared only certain elements of fascism. Nevertheless, many scholars still argue that the concept of totalitarianism does provide us with a tool to use in interpreting important developments between the two world wars.

This chapter addresses a number of broad questions. What were the main features of these regimes? How were they similar to and different from one another? How can their appeal and the power they commanded over people be explained? In what ways were they related to nineteenth- and early-twentieth-century trends?

The selections in this chapter survey Communism, fascism, and authoritarianism from a variety of perspectives. What characteristics do these regimes share and how do these regimes differ from parliamentary systems? The selections on Mussolini and Italian fascism focus on the ideology of fascism and its historical place. An effort is made to distinguish German Nazism from Italian fascism, to analyze Nazism's appeal, to understand the extremes—including the policy of genocide—possible under such a system, and to evaluate the role of Hitler in shaping Nazism. Three of the most controversial aspects of Stalin and Russian communism are examined: Stalin's justification for the policy against the *kulaks* in 1929, his analysis of democracy as part of his defense of the 1936 Soviet Constitution, and his massive purges of the 1930s.

In addition to offering broad insights into Communism, fascism, and authoritarianism during the 1920s and 1930s, the selections in this chapter provide some of the background of World War II, which will be covered in the next chapter.

✍ For Classroom Discussion

How do you explain the appeal of Nazism? Use evidence from the primary sources by Joseph Goebbels and Eugene Kogon and the interpretation by Klaus Fischer.

Primary Sources

The Doctrine of Fascism

Benito Mussolini

Italy was the first European power to turn to fascism. The country was one of the victors in World War I, but the war was costly and Italy did not gain much. After the war the country was marked by instability, weak governments, and an apparent threat from the left. Benito Mussolini (1883–1945), a former leader of the Socialist party and a veteran of the war, organized the Italian Fascist party in 1919. Strongly nationalistic, the party stood against the Versailles Treaty, left-wing radicalism, and the established government. After leading his Blackshirts in a march on Rome in 1922, Mussolini was invited by King Victor Emmanuel III to form a government. Over the next few years Mussolini effectively eliminated any opposition and installed his fascist state system, which would last some twenty years. The following document contains excerpts from "The Political and Social Doctrine of Fascism," an article signed by Mussolini and written with the philosopher Giovanni Gentile that originally appeared in

the Enciclopedia Italiana in 1932. It describes the ideological foundations of Italian fascism. These excerpts emphasize the rejection of traditional democracy, liberalism, and socialism as well as faith in the authoritarian, fascist state.

CONSIDER: *The greatest sources of appeal in the doctrine according to Mussolini; the ways in which this doctrine can be considered a rejection of major historical trends that had been developing over the previous century; the government policies that would logically flow from such a doctrine.*

Fascism, the more it considers and observes the future and the development of humanity quite apart from political considerations of the moment, believes neither in the possibility nor the utility of perpetual peace. It thus repudiates the doctrine of Pacifism—born of a renunciation of the struggle and an act of cowardice in the face of sacrifice. War alone brings up to its highest tension all human energy and puts the stamp of nobility upon the peoples who have the courage to meet it. . . .

The Fascist accepts life and loves it, knowing nothing of and despising suicide; he rather conceives of life as duty and struggle and conquest, life which should be high and full, lived for oneself, but above all for others—those who are at hand and those who are far distant, contemporaries, and those who will come after. . . .

SOURCE: Benito Mussolini, "The Political and Social Doctrine of Fascism," *International Conciliation*, No. 306 (January 1935), pp. 7–17. Originally published by the Carnegie Endowment for International Peace, as part of the *International Conciliation Series*.

Such a conception of life makes Fascism the complete opposite of that doctrine, the base of so-called scientific and Marxian Socialism, the materialist conception of history. . . . Fascism, now and always, believes in holiness and in heroism; that is to say, in actions influenced by no economic motive, direct or indirect. . . .

Fascism repudiates the conception of "economic" happiness, to be realized by Socialism and, as it were, at a given moment in economic evolution to assure to everyone the maximum of well-being. Fascism denies the materialist conception of happiness as a possibility, and abandons it to its inventors, the economists of the first half of the nineteenth century. . . .

After Socialism, Fascism combats the whole complex system of democratic ideology, and repudiates it, whether in its theoretical premises or in its practical application. Fascism denies that the majority, by the simple fact that it is a majority, can direct human society; it denies that numbers alone can govern by means of a periodical consultation, and it affirms the immutable, beneficial, and fruitful inequality of mankind, which can never be permanently leveled through the mere operation of a mechanical process such as universal suffrage. . . .

Fascism denies, in democracy, the absurd conventional untruth of political equality dressed out in the garb of collective irresponsibility, and the myth of "happiness" and indefinite progress. But if democracy may be conceived in diverse forms—that is to say, taking democracy to mean a state of society in which the populace are not reduced to impotence in the State—Fascism may write itself down as "an organized, centralized, and authoritative democracy."

Fascism has taken up an attitude of complete opposition to the doctrines of Liberalism, both in the political field and the field of economics. . . . Fascism uses in its construction whatever elements in the Liberal, Social, or Democratic doctrines still have a living value; it maintains what may be called the certainties which we owe to history, but it rejects all the rest—that is to say, the conception that there can be any doctrine of unquestioned efficacy for all times and all peoples. Given that the nineteenth century was the century of Socialism, of Liberalism, and of Democracy, it does not necessarily follow that the twentieth century must also be a century of Socialism, Liberalism, and Democracy: political doctrines pass, but humanity remains; and it may rather be expected that this will be a century of authority, a century of the Left, a century of Fascism. For if the nineteenth century was a century of individualism (Liberalism always signifying individualism) it may be expected that this will be the century of collectivism, and hence the century of the State. It is a perfectly logical deduction that a new doctrine can utilize all the still vital elements of previous doctrines. . . .

The foundation of Fascism is the conception of the State, its character, its duty, and its aim. Fascism conceives of the State as an absolute, in comparison with which all individuals or groups are relative, only to be conceived of in their relation to the State. The conception of the Liberal State is not that of a directing force, guiding the play and development, both material and spiritual, of a collective body, but merely a force limited to the function of recording results: on the other hand, the Fascist State is itself conscious, and has itself a will and a personality—thus it may be called the "ethic" State. . . .

If every age has its own characteristic doctrine, there are a thousand signs which point to Fascism as the characteristic doctrine of our time. For if a doctrine must be a living thing, this is proved by the fact that Fascism has created a living faith; and that this faith is very powerful in the minds of men, is demonstrated by those who have suffered and died for it.

Fascism has henceforth in the world the universality of all those doctrines which, in realizing themselves, have represented a stage in the history of the human spirit.

Mein Kampf
Adolf Hitler

The most extreme and racist form of fascism arose in Germany under the Nazis, led by Adolf Hitler (1889–1945). After serving in World War I, Hitler joined and soon took control of the small National Socialist German Workers party. In the early 1930s, after years of relative obscurity, the Nazi party gained popularity with a nationalistic program attacking the Versailles Treaty, the Weimar Republic, the Communists, and above all the Jews. In 1933 Hitler was appointed chancellor and Germany was soon transformed into a Nazi state. Hitler's ideology, his mental processes, and some of the ideas behind Nazism are illustrated in his rather formless book Mein Kampf *("My Struggle"). It was written in 1924 while he was in jail for his efforts to overthrow the government of Bavaria in southern Germany. With the growing popularity of the Nazi party in the early 1930s, the book became a best-seller. In these selections from* Mein Kampf, *Hitler displays his anti-Semitism, argues that a racial analysis is central to an understanding of history, and indicates his vision of German expansion eastward at the expense of Russia.*

SOURCE: Adolf Hitler, *Mein Kampf*, R. Manheim, trans. Reprinted by permission of Houghton Mifflin Company (New York, 1943), pp. 290–296, 300–302, 305–308, 312–320, 323–327, 580–583, 649–655, and the Hutchinson Publishing Group Ltd. (London, 1943). Copyright © 1943 and © renewed 1971 by Houghton Mifflin Co. (U.S. Rights), and by the Hutchinson Publishing Group Ltd. (Canadian Rights).

CONSIDER: *How Hitler connects the Jews, the Marxists, and German expansion eastward; on what points Mussolini might agree with Hitler here; the ways in which these ideas might be appealing, popular, or acceptable in the historical circumstances of Germany in the early 1930s.*

If we were to divide mankind into three groups, the founders of culture, the bearers of culture, the destroyers of culture, only the Aryan could be considered as the representative of the first group. From him originate the foundations and walls of all human creation, and only the outward form and color are determined by the changing traits of character of the various peoples. He provides the mightiest building stones and plans for all human progress and only the execution corresponds to the nature of the varying men and races. . . .

Blood mixture and the resultant drop in the racial level is the sole cause of the dying out of old cultures; for men do not perish as a result of lost wars, but by the loss of that force of resistance which is contained only in pure blood.

All who are not of good race in this world are chaff. . . .

With satanic joy in his face, the black-haired Jewish youth lurks in wait for the unsuspecting girl whom he defiles with his blood, thus stealing her from her people. With every means he tries to destroy the racial foundations of the people he has set out to subjugate. Just as he himself systematically ruins women and girls, he does not shrink back from pulling down the blood barriers for others, even on a large scale. It was and it is Jews who bring the Negroes into the Rhineland, always with the same secret thought and clear aim of ruining the hated white race by the necessarily resulting bastardization, throwing it down from its cultural and political height, and himself rising to be its master.

For a racially pure people which is conscious of its blood can never be enslaved by the Jew. In this world he will forever be master over bastards and bastards alone.

And so he tries systematically to lower the racial level by a continuous poisoning of individuals.

And in politics he begins to replace the idea of democracy by the dictatorship of the proletariat.

In the organized mass of Marxism he has found the weapon which lets him dispense with democracy and in its stead allows him to subjugate and govern the peoples with a dictatorial and brutal fist.

He works systematically for revolutionization in a twofold sense: economic and political.

Around peoples who offer too violent a resistance to attack from within he weaves a net of enemies, thanks to his international influence, incites them to war, and finally, if necessary, plants the flag of revolution on the very battlefields.

In economics he undermines the states until the social enterprises which have become unprofitable are taken from the state and subjected to his financial control.

In the political field he refuses the state the means for its self-preservation, destroys the foundations of all national self-maintenance and defense, destroys faith in the leadership, scoffs at its history and past, and drags everything that is truly great into the gutter.

Culturally he contaminates art, literature, the theater, makes a mockery of natural feeling, overthrows all concepts of beauty and sublimity, of the noble and the good, and instead drags men down into the sphere of his own base nature.

Religion is ridiculed, ethics and morality represented as outmoded, until the last props of a nation in its struggle for existence in this world have fallen.

Now begins the great last revolution. In gaining political power the Jew casts off the few cloaks that he still wears. The democratic people's Jew becomes the blood-Jew and tyrant over peoples. In a few years he tries to exterminate the national intelligentsia and by robbing the peoples of their natural intellectual leadership makes them ripe for the slave's lot of permanent subjugation.

The most frightful example of this kind is offered by Russia, where he killed or starved about thirty million people with positively fanatical savagery, in part amid inhuman tortures, in order to give a gang of Jewish journalists and stock exchange bandits domination over a great people.

The end is not only the end of the freedom of the peoples oppressed by the Jew, but also the end of this parasite upon the nations. After the death of his victim, the vampire sooner or later dies too. . . .

❧

And so we National Socialists consciously draw a line beneath the foreign policy tendency of our pre-War period. We take up where we broke off six hundred years ago. We stop the endless German movement to the south and west, and turn our gaze toward the land in the east. At long last we break off the colonial and commercial policy of the pre-War period and shift to the soil policy of the future.

If we speak of soil in Europe today, we can primarily have in mind only Russia *and her vassal border states.*

Here Fate itself seems desirous of giving us a sign. By handing Russia to Bolshevism, it robbed the Russian nation of that intelligentsia which previously brought about and guaranteed its existence as a state. For the organization of a Russian state formation was not the result of the political abilities of the Slavs in Russia, but only a wonderful example of the state-forming efficacity of the German element in an inferior race. Numerous mighty empires on earth have been created in this way. Lower nations led by Germanic organizers and overlords have more than once grown to be mighty state formations and have endured as long as the racial nucleus of the creative state race maintained itself. For centuries Russia drew nourishment from this Germanic nucleus of its upper leading strata. Today it can be regarded as almost totally exterminated and extinguished. It has been replaced by the Jew. Impossible as it is for the Russian by himself to shake off the yoke of the Jew by his own resources, it is equally impossible for the Jew to maintain the mighty empire forever. He himself is no element of organization, but a ferment of decomposition. The Persian empire in the east is ripe for collapse. And the end of Jewish rule in Russia will also be the end of Russia as a state. We have been chosen by Fate as witnesses of a catastrophe which will be the mightiest confirmation of the soundness of the folkish theory.

Nazi Propaganda Pamphlet

Joseph Goebbels

Propaganda was strongly emphasized by the Nazis as a method of acquiring and maintaining power. Joseph Goebbels (1897–1945), an early leader in the Nazi party, was made chief of propaganda in 1929, minister for propaganda and national enlightenment in 1933, and a member of Hitler's cabinet council in 1938. The following is an excerpt from a 1930 pamphlet, written by Goebbels, describing why the Nazis are nationalists, "socialists," and against Jews and Marxists.

CONSIDER: *How this document reflects the character of life in Germany during the 1920s; to whom this document was designed to appeal and in what ways it might be a convincing piece of propaganda; in tone, quality, and ideas, how this compares with Mussolini's "Doctrine of Fascism"; how Nazi "socialism" differs from more traditional or Marxist conceptions of socialism.*

WHY ARE WE NATIONALISTS?

We are NATIONALISTS because we see in the NATION the only possibility for the protection and the furtherance of our existence.

The NATION is the organic bond of a people for the protection and defense of their lives. He is nationally minded who understands this IN WORD AND IN DEED.

Today, in GERMANY, NATIONALISM has degenerated into BOURGEOIS PATRIOTISM, and its power exhausts itself in tilting at windmills. It says GERMANY and means MONARCHY. It proclaims FREEDOM and means BLACK-WHITE-RED.

WE ARE NATIONALISTS BECAUSE WE, AS GERMANS, LOVE GERMANY. And because we love Germany, we demand the protection of its national spirit and we battle against its destroyers.

SOURCE: From Louis L. Snyder, *The Weimar Republic.* Reprinted by permission of D. Van Nostrand Co. (New York, 1966), pp. 201–203. Copyright © 1966 by Litton Educational Publishing, Inc.

WHY ARE WE SOCIALISTS?

We are SOCIALISTS because we see in SOCIALISM the only possibility for maintaining our racial existence and through it the reconquest of our political freedom and the rebirth of the German state. SOCIALISM has its peculiar form first of all through its comradeship in arms with the forward-driving energy of a newly awakened nationalism. Without nationalism it is nothing, a phantom, a theory, a vision of air, a book. With it, it is everything, THE FUTURE, FREEDOM, FATHERLAND!

It was a sin of the liberal bourgeoisie to overlook THE STATE-BUILDING POWER OF SOCIALISM. It was the sin of MARXISM to degrade SOCIALISM to a system of MONEY AND STOMACH.

SOCIALISM IS POSSIBLE ONLY IN A STATE WHICH IS FREE INSIDE AND OUTSIDE.

DOWN WITH POLITICAL BOURGEOIS SENTIMENT: FOR REAL NATIONALISM!

DOWN WITH MARXISM: FOR TRUE SOCIALISM!

UP WITH THE STAMP OF THE FIRST GERMAN NATIONAL SOCIALIST STATE!

AT THE FRONT THE NATIONAL SOCIALIST GERMAN WORKERS PARTY!

WHY DO WE OPPOSE THE JEWS?

We are ENEMIES OF THE JEWS, because we are fighters for the freedom of the German people. THE JEW IS THE CAUSE AND THE BENEFICIARY OF OUR MISERY. He has used the social difficulties of the broad masses of our people to deepen the unholy split between Right and Left among our people. He has made two halves of Germany. He is the real cause for our loss of the Great War.

The Jew has no interest in the solution of Germany's fateful problems. He CANNOT have any. FOR HE LIVES ON THE FACT THAT THERE HAS BEEN NO SOLUTION. If we would make the German people a unified community and give them freedom before the world, then the Jew can have no place among us. He has the best trumps in his hands when a people lives in inner and outer slavery. THE JEW IS RESPONSIBLE FOR OUR MISERY AND HE LIVES ON IT.

That is the reason why we, AS NATIONALISTS and AS SOCIALISTS, oppose the Jew. HE HAS CORRUPTED OUR RACE, FOULED OUR MORALS, UNDERMINED OUR CUSTOMS, AND BROKEN OUR POWER.

THE JEW IS THE PLASTIC DEMON OF THE DECLINE OF MANKIND.

WE ARE ENEMIES OF THE JEWS BECAUSE WE BELONG TO THE GERMAN PEOPLE. THE JEW IS OUR GREATEST MISFORTUNE.

It is not true that we eat a Jew every morning at breakfast.

It is true, however, that he SLOWLY BUT SURELY ROBS US OF EVERYTHING WE OWN.

THAT WILL STOP, AS SURELY AS WE ARE GERMANS.

The German Woman and National Socialism [Nazism]

Guida Diehl

From the beginning, the Nazi party stood against any expansion of women's political or economic roles. Indeed, the Nazi policy was to keep women in their own separate sphere as mothers and wives and remove them from jobs and politics—the man's sphere. Nevertheless, many women supported the Nazi party and joined Nazi women's organizations. The following selection is from a book published in 1933 by Guida Diehl, a leader of pro-Nazi women's organizations.

CONSIDER: *The ways this might appeal to German women; how this fits with other ideals of Nazism.*

This tumultuous age with all its difficulties and challenges must create a new type of woman capable of partaking in the achievements of the Third Reich and of fulfilling the womanly task that awaits her.

Let us not forget that this new woman holds her honor high above all else. A man's honor rests on fulfilling the tasks of public life entrusted to him. He safeguards his honor by doing his work honorably and with firmness of character and pride. A woman's honor rests on the province specifically entrusted to her, for which she is responsible, the province where new life is to grow: love, marriage, family, motherhood. A woman who does not accept this responsibility, who misuses this province for mere enjoyment, who will not let herself be proudly wooed before she surrenders—which is nature's way— who does not in marriage provide a new generation with the basis of a family—such a woman desecrates her honor. For we live in a time when womanly worth and dignity, womanly honor and pride, are of the utmost importance for the future of the nation, for the next generation. Therefore, the proud safeguarding of her honor must be an essential characteristic of this new type of woman. The German man wants to look up again to the German maid, the German woman. He wants to admire in her this dignity, this pride, this safeguarding of her honor and her heroic fighting spirit along with her native, cheerful simplicity. He wants to know again that German women and

German fidelity go hand in hand, and that it is worthwhile to live and die for such German womanhood.

The Theory and Practice of Hell: The Nazi Elite

Eugene Kogon

The SS was Hitler's special corps, serving as his bodyguard and elite police force. Members of the SS usually became extremely dedicated to the ideas and practices of Nazism and carried out its precepts with extraordinary ruthlessness. The following is a statement from an SS officer recorded in a 1937 interview conducted by Eugene Kogon, less than one year before Kogon was arrested and taken to the concentration camp at Buchenwald. The officer was being trained as one of the elite of the Nazi state. Here he reveals his assumptions as a committed follower of Hitler and Nazism.

CONSIDER: *The role this officer assumes the SS will play in the Nazi state and the ways this role was particularly appropriate to a fascist system; how this document helps account for the appeal of the SS to those deciding to join it; how the ideas revealed here might serve as psychological justification for some of the atrocities committed by the SS.*

"What we trainers of the younger generation of Führers aspire to is a modern governmental structure on the model of the ancient Greek city states. It is to these aristocratically run democracies with their broad economic basis of serfdom that we owe the great cultural achievements of antiquity. From five to ten percent of the people, their finest flower, shall rule; the rest must work and obey. In this way alone can we attain that peak performance we must demand of ourselves and of the German people.

"The new Führer class is selected by the SS—in a positive sense by means of the National Political Education Institutes (*Napola*) as a preparatory stage, of the *Ordensburgen* as the academies proper of the coming Nazi aristocracy, and of a subsequent active internship in public affairs; in a negative sense by the extermination of all racially and biologically inferior elements and by the radical removal of all incorrigible political opposition that refuses on principle to acknowledge the philosophical basis of the Nazi State and its essential institutions.

"Within ten years at the latest it will be possible for us in this way to dictate the law of Adolf Hitler to Europe, put a halt to the otherwise inevitable decay of the continent, and build up a true community of nations, with Germany as the leading power keeping order."

SOURCE: Guida Diehl, *The German Woman and National Socialism* (Eisenach, 1933), pp. 111–113, in Eleanor S. Riemer and John C. Fout, eds., *European Women: A Documentary History, 1789–1945* (New York: Schocken Books, 1980), pp. 108–109.

SOURCE: Excerpt from *The Theory and Practice of Hell* by Eugene Kogon. Copyright © 1950 by Farrar, Straus & Giroux, Inc. Reprinted by permission of Farrar, Straus & Giroux, Inc.

The Informed Heart: Nazi Concentration Camps

Bruno Bettelheim

Organized, official racial persecution, particularly of the Jews, was a direct consequence of Nazi theories, attitudes, and practices. During the 1920s and early 1930s, however, the extent of the persecution was unanticipated. The most extreme form of this occurred in the late 1930s, with the introduction of forced labor and concentration camps, later to be followed by camps in which a policy of literal extermination was pursued resulting in the killing of millions of Jews and others. In the following selection Bruno Bettelheim, a psychoanalyst in Austria at the time and later a leading psychoanalyst in the United States, describes his experiences in the concentration camps at Dachau and Buchenwald. He focuses on the dehumanizing processes involved and some of the ways prisoners adapted in an effort to survive.

CONSIDER: *The methods used to gain control over the prisoners; the psychological means developed by Bettelheim and other prisoners to cope with and survive this experience; how the existence, nature, and functioning of these camps reflect the theory and practice of Nazi totalitarianism.*

Usually the standard initiation of prisoners took place during transit from the local prison to the camp. If the distance was short, the transport was often slowed down to allow enough time to break the prisoners. During their initial transport to the camp, prisoners were exposed to nearly constant torture. The nature of the abuse depended on the fantasy of the particular SS man in charge of a group of prisoners. Still, they all had a definite pattern. Physical punishment consisted of whipping, frequent kicking (abdomen or groin), slaps in the face, shooting, or wounding with the bayonet. These alternated with attempts to produce extreme exhaustion. For instance, prisoners were forced to stare for hours into glaring lights, to kneel for hours, and so on.

From time to time a prisoner got killed, but no prisoner was allowed to care for his or another's wounds. The guards also forced prisoners to hit one another and to defile what the SS considered the prisoners' most cherished values. They were forced to curse their God, to accuse themselves and one another of vile actions, and their wives of adultery and prostitution. . . .

The purpose of this massive initial abuse was to traumatize the prisoners and break their resistance; to change at least their behavior if not yet their personalities. This could be seen from the fact that tortures became less and less violent to the degree that prisoners stopped resisting and complied immediately with any SS order, even the most outrageous. . . .

It is hard to say just how much the process of personality change was speeded up by what prisoners experienced during the initiation. Most of them were soon totally exhausted; physically from abuse, loss of blood, thirst, etc.; psychologically from the need to control their anger and desperation before it could lead to a suicidal resistance. . . .

If I should try to sum up in one sentence what my main problem was during the whole time I spent in the camps, it would be: to protect my inner self in such a way that if, by any good fortune, I should regain liberty, I would be approximately the same person I was when deprived of liberty. So it seems that a split was soon forced upon me, the split between the inner self that might be able to retain its integrity, and the rest of the personality that would have to submit and adjust for survival. . . .

I have no doubt that I was able to endure the horrors of the transport and all that followed, because right from the beginning I became convinced that these dreadful and degrading experiences were somehow not happening to "me" as a subject, but only "me" as an object. . . .

All thoughts and feelings I had during the transport were extremely detached. It was as if I watched things happening in which I took part only vaguely. . . .

This was taught me by a German political prisoner, a communist worker who by then had been at Dachau for four years. I arrived there in a sorry condition because of experiences on the transport. I think that this man, by then an "old" prisoner, decided that, given my condition, the chances of my surviving without help were slim. So when he noticed that I could not swallow food because of physical pain and psychological revulsion, he spoke to me out of his rich experience: "Listen you, make up your mind: do you want to live or do you want to die? If you don't care, don't eat the stuff. But if you want to live, there's only one way: make up your mind to eat whenever and whatever you can, never mind how disgusting. Whenever you have a chance, defecate, so you'll be sure your body works. And whenever you have a minute, don't blabber, read by yourself, or flop down and sleep."

Witness to the Holocaust

Fred Baron

In the 1940s, the Nazis instituted the "final solution" to exterminate Jews and others that Hitler considered enemies of the state. The Nazis built several huge death camps, employing terror and factory-like methods to kill their victims. Only a

SOURCE: Bruno Bettelheim, *The Informed Heart: Autonomy in a Mass Age.* Reprinted by permission of Macmillan Publishing Co., Inc. Copyright © 1960 by The Free Press, a corporation.

SOURCE: Rhoda G. Lewin, ed., *Witnesses to the Holocaust: An Oral History.* Boston: Twayne Publishers, 1990, pp. 10–12.

few survived, but some who did managed to tell the story. One of these was Fred Baron, an Austrian Jew who was sent to the death camp at Auschwitz in occupied Poland. Here he tells of his deportation and experiences at the camp.

CONSIDER: *The methods used by Nazis to gain obedience and effect extermination; the nature of life for those in the camps.*

Deportation: I was marched with the local Jewish population—men, women, and children—eight or ten hours, to a small railroad station. Nobody told us where we were going. We were forced into railroad cars, 100 to 120 in one car, like sardines, without food, without water, without any sanitary facility. The cars were sealed and we stood there for maybe half a day before even moving. Finally, began the slow trip to nowhere.

There were children in our car, and old people. People got sick, died, and some went insane. It was an absolute, indescribable hell. I really don't know how many days and nights we were in that living hell on wheels.

When we finally stopped, they tore open the railroad cars and we were blinded by light, because our eyes were just not used to light any more. We saw funny-looking characters wearing striped pajama-like uniforms with matching caps, with great big sticks in their hands. They were screaming and yelling in all languages to jump out of the cars.

I didn't know where I was. All around us were barracks and barbed wire and machine gun towers, and in the distance I saw what looked like a huge factory with black smoke coming out of chimneys. I noticed a peculiar smell in the air and also a fine dust, subduing the light. The sunshine was not bright but there were birds singing. It was a beautiful day.

We were marched through a meadow filled with yellow flowers and one of the fellows next to me just turned and walked straight into the meadow. The guards cried out to him to stop, but he didn't hear or he didn't want to. He just kept slowly marching into the meadow, and then they opened up with machine guns and the man fell down dead. And that was my reception to Auschwitz.

Auschwitz: We were separated, men and women, and formed rows of fives. I found myself in front of a very elegantly dressed German officer. He was wearing boots and white gloves and he carried a riding whip, and with the whip he was pointing left or right, left or right. Whichever direction he pointed, guards pushed the person in front of him either left or right. I was twenty-one years old and in pretty good shape, but older people were sent to the other side and marched away.

We had to undress and throw away all belongings except our shoes. We were chased through a cold shower, and we stood shivering in the night air until we were told to march to a barracks. We were handed prisoner uniforms—a jacket, pants, and a sort of beanie—and a

metal dish. We didn't really know what happened yet. We were absolutely numb.

A non-Jewish kapo, an Austrian with a hard, weather-beaten face, told us, "You have arrived at hell on earth." He had been in prison since 1938, and he gave us basic concepts on how to stay alive.

"Don't trust anybody," he said, "don't trust your best friend. Look out for yourself. Be selfish to the point of obscenity. Try and stay alive from one minute to the other one. Don't let down for one second. Always try and find out where the nearest guards are and what they are doing. Don't volunteer for anything. And don't get sick, or you will be a goner in no time."

Auschwitz was gigantic—row and rows of barracks as far as the eye could see, subdivided by double strings of electric barbed wire. There were Hungarians and Polish Jews and a great number of Greeks, many Dutch Jews, some French, Germans.

Food was our main interest in life. In the morning we received what they called coffee—black water. We worked until noon, then we got a bowl of soup. In the evening we received another bowl of either vegetable or soup, a little piece of bread, and sometimes a tiny little piece of margarine or sugar or some kind of sausage. And that was the food for the day.

Suicides happened all the time, usually by hanging, at night. One fellow threw himself in front of a truck. It just broke his arm, but the S.S. guards beat him to a pulp, and in the morning he was dead.

A tremendous number of transports were coming in. The gas chambers could not keep up, so they were burning people in huge pits. Some of the smaller children were thrown in alive. We could hear the screams day and night, but sometimes the human mind can take just so much and then it just closes up and refuses to accept what is happening just 100, 200 feet away.

Problems of Agrarian Policy in the U.S.S.R.: Soviet Collectivization

Joseph Stalin

Joseph Stalin (1879–1953) rose from his working-class origins to become a leading member of the Bolsheviks before the 1917 revolution, the general secretary of the Russian Communist party in 1922, and the unchallenged dictator of the U.S.S.R. by 1929. In 1927 Stalin and the leadership of the Russian Communist party decided on a policy for the planned industrialization of the U.S.S.R.—the First Five-Year Plan. At the same time they decided on a policy favoring the collectivization

SOURCE: J. V. Stalin, "Problems of Agrarian Policy in the U.S.S.R.," in *Problems of Leninism,* ed. J. V. Stalin (Moscow: Foreign Languages, 1940), pp. 303–305, 318–321. Reprinted by permission of the Copyright Agency of the U.S.S.R.

of agriculture. By 1929 Stalin made that policy more drastic, using massive coercion against the kulaks (relatively rich independent peasants). Kulaks resisted this enforced collectivization and widespread death and destruction resulted. Nevertheless, by 1932 much of Russian agriculture was collectivized. The following is an excerpt from a 1929 speech delivered by Stalin at the Conference of Marxist Students of the Agrarian Question. In it he explains and justifies the policy of collectivization and the need to eliminate the kulaks as a class.

CONSIDER: *The relations of this policy toward the kulaks to the policy for the planned industrialization of the U.S.S.R.; how Stalin justifies this policy as "socialist" as opposed to "capitalist"; the differences between Stalin's attitudes and ideas toward the kulaks and Hitler's toward the Jews.*

Can we advance our socialized industry at an accelerated rate while having to rely on an agricultural base, such as is provided by small peasant farming, which is incapable of expanded reproduction, and which, in addition, is the predominant force in our national economy? No, we cannot. Can the Soviet government and the work of Socialist construction be, for any length of time, based on two *different* foundations; on the foundation of the most large-scale and concentrated Socialist industry and on the foundation of the most scattered and backward, small-commodity peasant farming? No, they cannot. Sooner or later this would be bound to end in the complete collapse of the whole national economy. What, then, is the solution? The solution lies in enlarging the agricultural units, in making agriculture capable of accumulation, of expanded reproduction, and in thus changing the agricultural base of our national economy. But how are the agricultural units to be enlarged? There are two ways of doing this. There is the *capitalist* way, which is to enlarge the agricultural units by introducing capitalism in agriculture—a way which leads to the impoverishment of the peasantry and to the development of capitalist enterprises in agriculture. We reject this way as incompatible with the Soviet economic system. There is a second way: the *Socialist* way, which is to set up collective farms and state farms, the way which leads to the amalgamation of the small peasant farms into large collective farms, technically and scientifically equipped, and to the squeezing out of the capitalist elements from agriculture. We are in favour of this second way.

And so, the question stands as follows: either one way or the other, either *back*—to capitalism or *forward*—to Socialism. There is no third way, nor can there be. The "equilibrium" theory makes an attempt to indicate a third way. And precisely because it is based on a third (non-existent) way, it is Utopian and anti-Marxian. . . .

Now, as you see, we have the material base which enables us to *substitute* for kulak output the output of the collective farms and state farms. That is why our offensive against the kulaks is now meeting with undeniable

success. That is how the offensive against the kulaks must be carried on, if we mean a real offensive and not futile declamations against the kulaks.

That is why we have recently passed from the policy of *restricting* the exploiting proclivities of the kulaks to the policy of *eliminating the kulaks as a class.*

Well, what about the policy of expropriating the kulaks? Can we permit the expropriation of kulaks in the regions of solid collectivization? This question is asked in various quarters. A ridiculous question! We could not permit the expropriation of the kulaks as long as we were pursuing the policy of restricting the exploiting proclivities of the kulaks, as long as we were unable to launch a determined offensive against the kulaks, as long as we were unable to substitute for kulak output the output of the collective farms and state farms. At that time the policy of not permitting the expropriation of the kulaks was necessary and correct. But now? Now the situation is different. Now we are able to carry on a determined offensive against the kulaks, to break their resistance, to eliminate them as a class and substitute for their output the output of the collective farms and state farms. Now, the kulaks are being expropriated by the masses of poor and middle peasants themselves, by the masses who are putting solid collectivization into practice. Now, the expropriation of the kulaks in the regions of solid collectivization is no longer just an administrative measure. Now, the expropriation of the kulaks is an integral part of the formation and development of the collective farms. That is why it is ridiculous and fatuous to expatiate today on the expropriation of the kulaks. You do not lament the loss of the hair of one who has been beheaded.

There is another question which seems no less ridiculous: whether the kulak should be permitted to join the collective farms. Of course not, for he is a sworn enemy of the collective-farm movement. Clear, one would think.

Report to the Congress of Soviets, 1936: Soviet Democracy

Joseph Stalin

In 1936 a new constitution for the U.S.S.R. was established. Although in form it was democratic and apparently rather liberal, in fact it did nothing to challenge Stalin's power or the Communist party as the only legitimate political organization. Part of the problem has to do with differing conceptions of the word "democracy." In the following selection from his report to the Extraordinary Eighth Congress of Soviets of the U.S.S.R. in 1936, Stalin defends the constitution, comparing the meanings of "democracy" and "political freedom" in the U.S.S.R. with their significance in other societies.

SOURCE: James H. Meisel and Edward S. Kozera, eds., *Materials for the Study of the Soviet System* (Ann Arbor, MI: The George Wahr Publishing Co., 1950), pp. 236–237. Reprinted by permission of the publisher.

CONSIDER: *The concerns revealed by this document; why Stalin goes to such pains to justify the new constitution; the legitimacy of the distinction made between democracy in capitalist countries and democracy in the U.S.S.R.*

I must admit that the draft of the new Constitution does preserve the regime of the dictatorship of the working class, just as it also preserves unchanged the present leading position of the Communist Party of the U.S.S.R. [Loud applause.] If the esteemed critics regard this as a flaw in the Draft Constitution, that is only to be regretted. We Bolsheviks regard it as a merit of the Draft Constitution. [Loud applause.]

As to freedom for various political parties, we adhere to somewhat different views. A party is a part of a class, its most advanced part. Several parties, and, consequently, freedom for parties, can exist only in a society in which there are antagonistic classes whose interests are mutually hostile and irreconcilable—in which there are, say, capitalists and workers, landlords and peasants, kulaks and poor peasants, etc. But in the U.S.S.R. there are no longer such classes as the capitalists, the landlords, the kulaks, etc. In the U.S.S.R. there are only two classes, workers and peasants, whose interests—far from being mutually hostile—are, on the contrary, friendly. Hence there is no ground in the U.S.S.R. for the existence of several parties, and, consequently, for freedom for these parties. In the U.S.S.R. there is ground only for one party, the Communist Party. In the U.S.S.R. only one party can exist, the Communist Party, which courageously defends the interests of the workers and peasants to the very end. . . .

They talk of democracy. But what is democracy? Democracy in capitalist countries, where there are antagonistic classes, is, in the last analysis, democracy for the strong, democracy for the propertied minority. In the U.S.S.R., on the contrary, democracy is democracy for the working people, i.e., democracy for all. But from this it follows that the principles of democratism are violated, not by the draft of the new Constitution of the U.S.S.R., but by the bourgeois constitutions. That is why I think that the Constitution of the U.S.S.R. is the only thoroughly democratic Constitution in the world.

Visual Sources

Nazi Mythology

Richard Spitz

The following (figure 17.1) is an example of Nazi propaganda art, with its characteristic blend of realistic style and romantic vision. It shows Nazi soldiers and civilian folk marching in brotherly comradeship toward Valhalla, the final resting place of Aryan heroes. Above them, Nazi flags and wounded soldiers are being lifted together toward the same heavens. Stereotypes, rather than distinct individuals, are shown: The soldiers all look almost the same, and on the right there are representatives of civilian youth, middle-aged and elderly people, farmers, and workers. Those being glorified are all males and almost all soldiers. Viewers of this picture are supposed to feel proud, to feel that sacrifices for the state will be rewarded and that the greatest glory comes from military service. In subject and style, this picture represents a rejection of the major twentieth-century artistic trends.

CONSIDER: *How this picture fits the image and ideals of Nazism as reflected in the documents by Hitler and Goebbels and the statements of the SS officer.*

Socialist Realism

K. I. Finogenov

The following example of socialist realism (figure 17.2) has great similarities to Nazi art: its realistic style, its romantic vision, its propagandistic purpose. In this case, however, the emphasis on economic themes is greater than that on military themes. Painted in 1935 by K. I. Finogenov, it shows Communist party and government leaders, led by Stalin, on a modern Soviet farm. On the right an expert checks the soil. In the background a new tractor is displayed. All the figures are relatively well dressed; no one looks like a peasant farmer.

CONSIDER: *How this picture relates to the role of the government in the Soviet Union and to Stalin's place in it; what insight into the agricultural policy during the 1930s the picture is supposed to convey; how the image presented here fits with Stalin's explanation of collectivization; how this picture compares with that of Joseph II in Chapter 8 (figure 8.3).*

Authoritarianism and Totalitarianism, 1919–1937

The following map (map 17.1) shows the spread of authoritarian and totalitarian governments in Europe between 1919 and 1937. Although no firm rules apply here, those countries retaining parliamentary democratic forms of government generally had a longer tradition of democratic institutions, were more satisfied winners in World War I,

FIGURE 17.1 (Photograph by Garner. Courtesy of Army Art Collection, U.S. Army Center of Military History)

FIGURE 17.2 (© Tass/Sovfoto/Eastfoto)

MAP 17.1   The Spread of Authoritarian Governments

and were located in more advanced industrialized areas in northwestern Europe.

CONSIDER: *Taking account of the relevant geography, historical background, and experience of World War I, the*

commonalities of two or more countries that became dictatorships or changed to right-wing authoritarian regimes.

Secondary Sources

Fascism in Western Europe

H. R. Kedward

Both fascism and communism, as they were practiced during the first half of the twentieth century, are traditionally categorized as totalitarian systems. Yet fascism is typically placed on the extreme

right of the political spectrum, communism on the extreme left. Indeed, the two usually consider each other archenemies. In the following selection H. R. Kedward, a British historian at the University of Sussex, takes account of these facts in developing and diagraming a working political definition of fascism.

CONSIDER: *Why the extreme left should be placed next to the extreme right on the political spectrum, even though they consider each other enemies; the historical developments that justify using the second diagram for the twentieth century and*

SOURCE: H. R. Kedward, *Fascism in Western Europe: 1900–1945.* Reproduced by kind permission of Blackie and Son Ltd. (Bishopbriggs, Glasgow, 1971), pp. 240–241.

the first for the nineteenth century; the characteristics of fascism according to Kedward.

It could be argued that the best way to define fascism is not in a positive but in a negative way, by references to its opposites, but this too presents difficulties. At one time its opposite was naturally assumed to be communism, since fascism was said to be on the extreme Right of politics and communism on the extreme Left. This appeared self-evident when the traditional semicircle of political parties was drawn, i.e.:

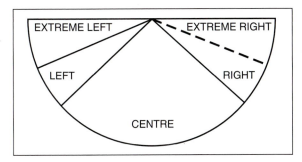

Such a diagram served the political scene of the 19th century when socialism was on the extreme Left and autocratic conservatism on the extreme Right, but in the 20th century a new diagram is needed in the form of a circle, i.e.:

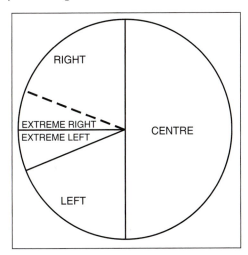

This circular image does greater justice to the realities of 20th-century politics by recognizing that extreme Left and extreme Right, communism and fascism, converge at many points and are in some cases indistinguishable. Doriot, for example, moved with ease from French communism to his Fascist P.P.F. without changing his attitudes or methods, and most of the conclusions on Nazi culture . . . could be applied to Stalinism. The circle, however, does not minimize the differences which kept the two systems apart. Travelling the longest route round the circle, it is a very long way indeed from extreme Left to extreme Right. Thus communism and fascism are as distinct in some respects as they are similar in others.

This was most clearly apparent in the Spanish Civil War. If one looked at methods, the Communists were as violent, as authoritarian and as tightly organized as the Fascists; they were both supported by dictators, Stalin on the one hand and Hitler and Mussolini on the other, and they were both as intolerant of any deviation from the party line. They were next to each other on the circle. But if one looked at this history and their ideology the two had little in common: the Communists stood in the Marxist tradition and aimed at proletarian revolution, while the Fascists had their national values and a vision of an organic society. They were quite distinct.

Fascism therefore will only be partly defined by its opposition to communism. It is perhaps more profitable to look for its political opposites across the circle in the centre, where one finds progressive conservatism, liberalism and radical individualism. It is at least historically true that in the countries where these political attitudes were most entrenched—Britain, France and Belgium—neither fascism nor communism came to power.

The Rise of Fascism

F. L. Carsten

Historians have employed a variety of perspectives in an effort to understand the rise of fascism during the two decades following World War I. Focusing on the appeal of fascism, several historians have analyzed what social classes and groups of people supported fascist movements. In the following selection F. L. Carsten argues that while fascism appealed to all social groups, certain groups responded more strongly to it than others.

CONSIDER: *Why fascism might have been particularly appealing to the lower middle classes; what other groups it appealed to and why.*

Unlike many middle-class or working-class parties, the Fascists appealed to all social groups, from the top to the bottom of the social scale. Excluded were only those who were their favourite objects of attack: the profiteers, the parasites, the financial gangsters, the ruling cliques, the rapacious capitalists, the reactionary landowners. But even there exceptions were made if it suited the Leader's book. There is no doubt, however, that certain social groups responded much more strongly to the Fascist appeal than others. This is particularly true of those who were uprooted and threatened by social and economic change, whose position in society was being undermined, who had lost their

SOURCE: From F. L. Carsten, *The Rise of Fascism*, pp. 232–234. Copyright 1980. Reprinted by permission of the Regents of the University of California Press and the University of California.

traditional place, and were frightened of the future. These were, above all, the lower middle classes—or rather certain groups within them: the artisans and independent tradesmen, the small farmers, the lower grade government employees and white-collar workers. Perhaps even more important in the early stages were the former officers and non-commissioned officers of the first world war for whom no jobs were waiting, who had got accustomed to the use of violence, and felt themselves deprived of their "legitimate" rewards. In Italy, in Germany, and elsewhere the "front" generation played a leading part in the rise of Fascism. For its members fighting was a way of life which they transferred to the domestic scene. They loved battles for their own sake. It is no accident that the most important Fascist movements had their origin in the year 1919, the year of the Hungarian and Munich Soviet republics, of civil war which aroused fear and hatred in many hearts. Those who had been badly frightened did not easily forget. The occupation of the factories in northern Italy in the following year had the same effect. . . .

Apart from the groups already mentioned, there were the youngsters at school and university who became ardent believers in Fascism at an early stage. They were fed up with the existing society, bored with their daily duties, and strongly attracted by a movement which promised a radical change, which they could invest with a romantic halo. These youths came from middle-class or lower middle-class families. They could not easily find the way into the Communist camp. But they found the weak and changing governments of the post-war period utterly unattractive. In the Weimar Republic, in the post-war Italian kingdom, in the corrupt governments of Rumania, in the powerless governments of Spain, there was nothing to fire the enthusiasm of youth: they were dreary and pedestrian, the offices filled with mediocrities and time-servers. It was this, rather than any economic threat, that led so many idealist students into the Fascist camp. Similarly, many young officers and soldiers of the post-war generation were attracted by visions of national greatness and the promise of a revision of the peace treaties. A perusal of the autobiographical notes compiled by men who joined the National Socialist Party in its early years shows that pride of place belongs to a strong nationalism, the desire to see Germany strong and united again, freed from the "chains of Versailles", and also from the faction fights and the 'horse-trading' of the political parties. This often went together with hatred of the Communists and Socialists, and with anti-Semitism. Those who joined the Party were usually very young; they loved the frequent fights and battles in which they got involved together with their comrades, as well as the uniforms and the propaganda marches.

Hitler and Nazism
Klaus P. Fischer

It is difficult to analyze Nazism without focusing on its leader, Adolf Hitler. The close connection between Nazism and Hitler raises two questions of particular importance for historians. First, what was the role of the individual in shaping history—here, of Hitler in shaping German Nazism? Second, to what extent were Hitler and Nazism uniquely German developments related to particular characteristics of Germany's past? Klaus Fischer, a German historian and author of the widely respected Nazi Germany: A New History, *addresses these issues. In this excerpt, he focuses in particular on who supported Hitler.*

CONSIDER: *Whether Hitler and Nazism should be considered as uniquely German or as an extreme of a broader historical trend affecting the West as a whole during the 1920s and 1930s; who made up the "hard core" of his followers; the role played by Hitler in creating the appeal of Nazism.*

With the appointment of Adolf Hitler as chancellor, Germany would be plunged into an abyss, a dark age of unprecedented evil. Although Hitler's much-heralded Thousand-Year Reich would last for only twelve years, the world has never witnessed the perpetration of so much evil in such a short period. The historiographic effect has been to produce a series of optical illusions in the eyes of many historians who have described the rise and fall of the Third Reich. The evil that Hitler unleashed had the effect of magnifying the Twelve-Year Reich within the stream of history, prompting many historians to postulate fallacious or misleading theories of political causation and psychological motivation. Since the amount of destruction the Nazis unleashed on the world was so great, historians have assumed that such evil must be rooted deeply in German history and in the German character, an assumption that, ironically, inspired some slanderous explanations of the sort that Nazi racialists had developed as their own stock-in-trade during the Third Reich. For some Germanophobic historians the Nazi experience still serves as *the* pivot around which explanations about German history as a whole are formulated. At its most extreme, this has resulted in the practice of twisting many personalities or events in German history into a prefiguration of Adolf Hitler and Auschwitz. And what has been perpetrated on the past has also been extended into the future, for Hitler's shadow is still stretching beyond the present into the future.

SOURCE: Klaus P. Fischer, *Nazi Germany: A New History* (New York: The Continuum Publishing Co., 1995), pp. 259–262.

The opposite of the Germanophobic approach is the exculpatory, which holds that the Nazi experience was an aberration unrelated to previous events or institutions in German history. Some even claim that it was a unique event, an eruption of evil whose roots reside outside historical time and place. These arguments are as inauthentic as their opposite, though they may satisfy some Germans who would like to believe that they were unwitting and innocent victims of Hitler's lust for aggression. Dodging behind various covers—ignorance (we knew nothing), obeying orders, comparative trivialization (you were as bad as we were), or simple denial—some revisionist historians have tried to whitewash the record by claiming that the Nazis, though perhaps misguided, wanted the best for Germany and did not commit most of the heinous crimes attributed to them by their opponents. . . .

It is important to remind ourselves that Hitler was not Germany and Germany was not Hitler, as one ridiculous Nazi slogan insisted. If this is the case, who supported Hitler and what was the nature of the movement he inspired? . . . The followers by conviction represented the hard core of the Nazi movement. They were overwhelmingly male, and there is some justification to the famous Nazi boast that National Socialism was "a male event." The hard core consisted largely of recalcitrant and demobilized soldiers who could not reconcile their inherited militarism with the democratic beliefs of the Weimar Republic. . . .

If economic stability had been restored and maintained during the Weimar Republic, the Nazi movement would have never amounted to anything more than a small, xenophobic group of unregenerate misfits, but with the economic collapse, first of 1923 and then of 1929, it began to amalgamate misguided sympathizers who joined out of economic self-interest because they had been frightened into believing that the only alternative was the destruction of the middle class and the triumph of Communism. In order of precedent, the following groups were amalgamated step-by-step into the Nazi movement—the lower middle classes, who were afraid of being deprived of their social status; substantial elements of the more prosperous *Mittlestand* who fell victim to scare tactics that their businesses or possessions were subject to immanent expropriation by Communism; and disenchanted workers whose loyalty to nation exceeded their loyalty to class.

In the end, however, it was Hitler's organizational and charismatic genius that made it possible for the Nazi Party to attract a broad segment of the German population. Party membership lists and electoral data reveal that the Nazi Party was able to appeal beyond its hard-core followers and attract apparently incompatible social groups. Hitler seems to have known intuitively that voting patterns are shaped not only by class affiliation but by group prejudices. Hitler reasoned that if he could successfully nationalize the masses, indoctrinating them with ethnic prejudices, he could effectively diffuse economic divisions and reintegrate heterogeneous elements into one national community. . . .

The Weimar Republic failed because there were not enough strongly committed republicans to save it. In normal times, the republic might have been able to muddle through, as illustrated by its modest resurgence in the middle years (1924–29); but in times of turbulent and chaotic changes, its weaknesses became fatal liabilities. Amid a climate of mutual fear and paranoia, many Germans regressed to a "quick-fix," authoritarian solution; and given the predominance of right-wing, nationalistic attitudes, such a solution was bound to originate from the political right.

Dictatorship in Russia: Stalin's Purges

Stephen J. Lee

In 1934 a colleague of Stalin was assassinated by a member of the Communist party. Shortly afterward, Stalin initiated mass purges of the Communist party. By 1939, when the purges had ended, vast numbers of people had been executed or imprisoned. Analysts have tried to explain these purges in a variety of ways. In the following selection Stephen Lee describes this historical controversy.

CONSIDER: *How the interpretations differ; which interpretation makes the most sense to you; whether purges, or their like, are an inherent or predictable characteristic of any totalitarian regime.*

The most spectacular and notorious of all Stalin's policies was his deliberate creation of a state of total terror. His direct responsibility for this has never been questioned and plenty of evidence was provided by Khrushchev in 1956. . . .

Although the enormity of Stalin's purges defy a completely logical explanation, a number of motives have been suggested. One is that Stalin had a disastrously flawed personality. Khrushchev, for example, later emphasized his brutality, vindictiveness, pathological distrust and "sickly" suspicion. More recently, Tucker has maintained that, in addition to serving a political function, the trials also rationalized "Stalin's own paranoid tendency." A second reason for the purges is that Stalin

SOURCE: From Stephen J. Lee, *The European Dictatorships, 1918–1945*, pp. 53–55. Copyright 1987. Reprinted by permission of the authors and Methuen & Co. as publishers.

was never one to resort to half measures. He aimed to wipe out the entire generation of Bolsheviks who had assisted Lenin between 1917 and 1924. This alone would guarantee Stalin as the sole heir to Lenin and would secure his position for a lifetime. Most of the threats to his power were latent and would possibly not reveal themselves for several years. They should, nevertheless, be dealt with as soon as possible. Since these latent threats were impossible to identify, a large number of people who would ultimately prove innocent of any form of opposition to Stalin, would also have to go. It was only by having such a clean sweep that Stalin could make sure of eradicating those who would be a threat. . . .

A third explanation of the purges is that they were ideologically necessary. Stalin argued that he was merely continuing the tactics of Lenin in 1918 and that he was accelerating the move towards a "classless society." If this desirable aim of Communism were to be achieved, class conflict would have to be intensified so that it could be ended the more quickly. The state would achieve its objectives "not through the weakening of its power but through it becoming as strong as possible so as to defeat the remnants of the dying classes and to defend itself against capitalist encirclement."

This brings us to the most frequently discussed aspect of Stalin's purges: how were they affected by the external situation? Two very different answers have been provided.

The first is that Stalin was obsessed with the fear that the west would smash the Soviet regime before his industrialization programme was complete. It therefore made sense to adopt a pragmatic approach to foreign policy; Germany, the main threat, could be won over by a temporary policy of cooperation. Stalin found it no more difficult to collaborate with Fascism than with any other European system, for he regarded it merely as a variant of western capitalism. The old-style Bolsheviks, by contrast, were profoundly anti-Fascist and saw Hitler as a far more deadly enemy than either France or Britain. According to R. Tucker and R. Conquest, Stalin therefore considered it essential to remove the anti-Hitler element to make possible the accommodation with Germany which eventually materialized in August 1939, in the Nazi-Soviet Non-Aggression Pact.

I. Deutscher puts a different cast. Stalin's main worry was that his regime would be destroyed from *within*—by internal revolt. There seemed little chance of this happening in 1936. Unless, of course, some major external catastrophe occurred, which could lead to a revival of the scenario of the First World War; military crisis could well bring about a revolution. Stalin's solution was therefore to destroy any elements within Russia which could possibly take advantage of such a situation. The show trials dealt with these potential threats by magnifying the charge against them.

Nazism and Communism

Bernard Wasserstein

The leaders and the ideologies of Nazism and Communism appeared to be enemies. However, many observers have noted similarities between the two. In the following selection, Bernard Wasserstein delineates some of their similarities and differences.

CONSIDER: *The ways Hitler and Stalin, as well as Nazism and Communism, were similar; the crucial differences between the two belief systems; why Communism might have survived in power longer than Nazism.*

Stalin and Hitler continue to pose the most elusive challenges to historical understanding of the twentieth century, not only because they were the most destructive political leaders of their time, probably of all time, but also because, terrifyingly for those with any faith in the human spirit, they were wildly popular among their own peoples.

Nor was this merely a matter of their persons. Both Nazism and Communism became deeply attractive belief systems for millions. Both in their day offered emotional comfort to the disoriented, reassurance to the bewildered. Both demanded surrender of self to the mass, offering in return the comfort of suspension of individual moral responsibility. Both dispensed with the rule of law, elevated the secret police to the highest authority in the land, constructed vast systems of slave labour, and killed millions of their subjects. Yet in the supreme test of total war both sustained the morale and adhesion of their followers at least as well as the liberal democracies. Both succumbed on battlefields of their own choosing: Nazism by defeat in war, Communism by its failure to create a classless society free from material want. Yet so long as they could plausibly claim success, most of their subjects willingly did as they were told.

We should not, however, fall into the common error of imputing a false parallelism between the two great warrior ideologies. Nazism, for all its revolutionary jargon, represented in its essence a reaction against the nineteenth-century faith in human progress. It was an attempt to seize history by the collar and frog-march it in a direction determined primarily by the selfish interests and obsessive beliefs of those in power. From the outset it was an anti-intellectual movement, offering its adherents the spurious solidarity of the street gang and the prospective enjoyment of stolen booty.

SOURCE: Bernard Wasserstein, *Barbarism and Civilization* (Oxford: Oxford University Press, 2007), pp. 203–204

Communism, by contrast, was a sophisticated and internally coherent framework of thought. It was not, as it is sometimes portrayed, a manic delusion of the intelligentsia but rather a modern transformation of the utopian chiliasm of the most enlightened elements in European thought since the seventeenth century. As distinct from the cave-man morality of Nazism and from the individualistic ethic of liberalism, Communism sought to achieve a higher collective good that derived from Rousseau's concept of the general will and Gerard Winstanley's idea of the common weal. The source of its special appeal to several generations of European intellectuals, perhaps also one of the reasons why it survived in power so much longer than Nazism, was its (ultimately self-falsified) claim, derived from Marx, to be able to discern and to accelerate the underlying motive forces of history. That both Communism and Nazism developed into mechanisms of brute force and thuggery should not blind us to their distinctive origins and aspirations.

*~ CHAPTER QUESTIONS

1. In light of the evidence and interpretations presented in this chapter about these authoritarian regimes, how would you explain their appeal or relative success in the twentieth century? In what ways should Italian fascism, German Nazism, and Russian communism be distinguished here?

2. Considering some of the theories and practices of these governments during the 1920s, 1930s, and 1940s, would you conclude that "totalitarianism" almost inevitably leads to violence and war, or rather that it happens to involve violence and war because of particular historical circumstances of the times? In this respect, should fascism be distinguished from communism? Why or why not?

3. In what ways do Italian fascism and German Nazism differ in theory and practice from liberal democracy? In what ways does Russian communism differ from both?

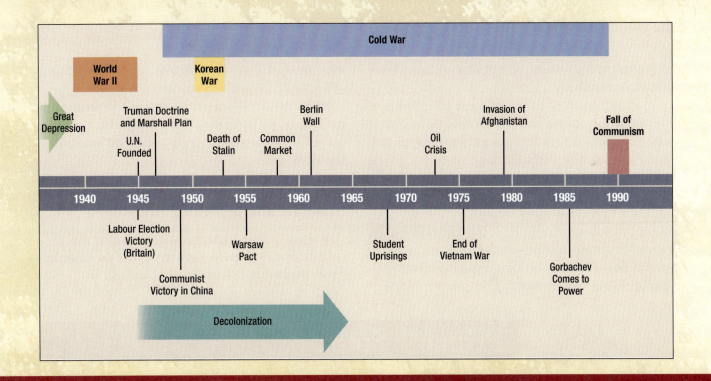

18 World War II and the Postwar World

World War II broke out in 1939 and was even more destructive than World War I. In 1945 Europe emerged from the war facing an overwhelming task of recovery. It had lost her position of dominance in the world, reflected in the successful independence movement among its colonies and the rise of the two new superpowers: the United States and the Soviet Union. Nevertheless, by the early 1960s, Europe had greatly recovered from the war and was enjoying considerable prosperity.

This chapter deals with five developments between 1939 and the early 1960s. First, almost all of Western civilization became embroiled in the war that broke out in 1939 and that did not end until two atomic bombs were dropped on Japan in 1945. What were the origins of World War II? What connections between Hitler, Nazism, and appeasement might have led to the outbreak of the war in 1939? How did people experience the war?

Second, by 1947 the growing hostility between the United States and the Soviet Union became formalized in speeches, policies, and alliances, resulting in a division between Eastern and Western Europe and more broadly between Communist and non-Communist countries throughout the world: The Cold War had broken out. The Cold War remains a controversial issue among American historians as well as between Western and Soviet scholars. Why did it occur? What policies characterized the Cold War?

Third, Europe recovered from World War II more rapidly than expected. By the 1950s most countries were back on their feet, thanks in part to aid from the superpowers. By the early 1960s Western Europe was enjoying unprecedented prosperity and relative political and social stability. What were some of the political and social changes that occurred in this process of recovery? How are they exemplified by the establishment of a Labour government in Britain in 1945?

Fourth, European powers were unable to hold on to all their colonies in the two decades following the war. What were some of the arguments made and the strategies used in the struggle over decolonization? What role did the United Nations play in this struggle? How were problems in the Middle East related to the struggle over decolonization and the actions of the United Nations?

Fifth, several social and cultural developments marked this era. One of the most important of these was feminism. Art and the media took new turns during this period, challenging viewers' expectations. What was the nature of these developments? How did they reflect the rapid pace of historical change during this period?

While these developments have undergone some modification in the last thirty years, they remain part of the present along with other trends that will be examined in the final chapter.

❧ For Classroom Discussion

Hold a debate between the two sides of the Cold War. Use the excerpts by Gormly, Ponomaryov, and the selections from the Truman Doctrine and the Marshall Plan.

Primary Sources

The Battle of Britain

Mrs. Robert Henrey

In July 1940 the Germans unleashed massive air attacks against Britain in preparation for an invasion of the island nation. For almost two months, the Germans bombed London every night. In cellars and subway stations, the British people holed up while their planes and antiaircraft guns fought off the Germans. By November, the British had won the Battle of Britain. The following excerpt is from account by Mrs. Robert Henrey, who lived in London's West End and survived the attacks.

CONSIDER: *The effects of the bombings on the morale of the British people; the symbolic importance of St. Paul's Cathedral.*

Bombs fell by day as well as by night. We became accustomed to the sudden drone of an airplane in the middle of the morning, the screech of a bomb, the dull crash of its explosion and the smell of cordite that filled the air a moment later. The sight of a burned-out bus unexpectedly in Berkeley Square, the ruins of a shop still half-hidden in a cloud of dust, streets that were impassable because of time bombs, enemy planes that burst in mid air sending down large chunks of fuselage, the pilots gliding down with their parachutes, became the normal things of life. . . . Almost every night some landmark near us would go up in dust. . . .

From the very first night of the battle for London [1940], because of the fires in the east which lit up the dome, St. Paul's Cathedral had become a symbol of London's defiance. As long ago as the night of the 12th September a large delayed-action bomb hurtled down south of the granite posts and buried itself twenty-seven feet deep. Everybody knew that if it exploded there would be nothing left of St. Paul's. For three days men worked to dig it out. Then it was driven in state to Hackney Marshes on a lorry under the command of Lt. Davies, a Canadian who became a national hero.

Even for a very ordinary housewife living with her baby in the West End, St. Paul's could never for long be out of her mind. Almost every evening from the flat roof of Carrington House we peered east and prayed that it might stand.

A German Soldier at Stalingrad

William Hoffman

In June 1941 German forces turned eastward and invaded the Soviet Union. The German war machine advanced quickly until the Russian winter and Soviet resistance slowed them down. In June 1942 the Germans went on the offensive again. In August they reached the outskirts of Stalingrad, a crucial industrial city on the Volga River. The battle raged for six months and was so fierce that the city was virtually destroyed. More than a million Soviet soldiers and civilians lost their lives. In the end Russian forces managed to trap what remained of Germany's exhausted Six Army, win the battle of Stalingrad, and turn the tide on the eastern front.

The following are excerpts from the diary of a German soldier, William Hoffman, who lost his life in the fighting.

SOURCE: Mrs. Robert Henrey, *London Under Fire, 1940–1945* (London: J. M. Dent, The Orion Publishing Group, 1969), pp. 43–44.

SOURCE: Vasili Chuikov, *The Battle for Stalingrad* (Chelmsford, U.K.: Grafton Books, HarperCollins Publishers Ltd., 1964), pp. 248–254.

CONSIDER: *Hoffman's attitudes about the war in Russia, German prospects, and Hitler during July and August 1942; Hoffman's view of the Russians; the causes for Hoffman's discouragement and despair during September, October, and November 1942.*

July 3, 1942. . . . Today, after we'd had a bath, the company commander told us that if our future operations are as successful, we'll soon reach the Volga, take Stalingrad and then the war will inevitably soon be over. Perhaps we'll be home by Christmas.

July 29 1942. . . . The company commander says the Russian troops are completely broken, and cannot hold out any longer. To reach the Volga and take Stalingrad is not so difficult for us. The Führer knows where the Russians' weak point is. Victory is not far away. . . .

August 2. . . . What great spaces the Soviets occupy, what rich fields there are to be had here after the war's over! Only let's get it over with quickly. I believe that the Führer will carry the thing through to a successful end.

September 4. We are being sent northward along the front towards Stalingrad. We marched all night and by dawn had reached Voroponovo Station. We can already see the smoking town. It's a happy thought that the end of the war is getting nearer. That's what everyone is saying. If only the days and nights would pass more quickly . . .

September 5. Our regiment has been ordered to attack Sadovaya station—that's nearly in Stalingrad. Are the Russians really thinking of holding out in the city itself? We had no peace all night from the Russian artillery and aeroplanes. Lots of wounded are being brought by. God protect me . . .

September 8. Two days of non-stop fighting. The Russians are defending themselves with insane stubbornness. Our regiment has lost many men. . . .

September 13. . . . The Russians are fighting desperately like wild beasts, don't give themselves up, but come up close and then throw grenades. Lieutenant Kraus was killed yesterday, and there is no company commander.

September 16. Our battalion, plus tanks, is attacking. . . . Barbarism. The battalion is suffering heavy losses. . . .

September 18. . . . The Russians inside are condemned men; the battalion commander says: "The commissars have ordered those men to die in the elevator."

If all the buildings of Stalingrad are defended like this then none of our soldiers will get back to Germany. I had a letter from Elsa today. She's expecting me home when victory's won.

October 10. The Russians are so close to us that our planes cannot bomb them. We are preparing for a decisive attack. The Führer has ordered the whole of Stalingrad to be taken as rapidly as possible.

October 22. We have lost many men; every time you move you have to jump over bodies. You can scarcely breathe in the daytime: there is nowhere and no one to remove the bodies, so they are left there to rot. Who would have thought three months ago that instead of the joy of victory we would have to endure such sacrifice and torture, the end of which is nowhere in sight? . . .

The soldiers are calling Stalingrad the mass grave of the Wehrmacht [German army]. There are very few men left in the companies.

October 28. Every soldier sees himself as a condemned man. The only hope is to be wounded and taken back to the rear. . . .

November 10. A letter from Elsa today. Everyone expects us home for Christmas. In Germany everyone believes we already hold Stalingrad. How wrong they are. If they could only see what Stalingrad has done to our army.

November 18. Our attack with tanks yesterday had no success. After our attack the field was littered with dead.

November 21. The Russians have gone over to the offensive along the whole front. Fierce fighting is going on. So, there it is—the Volga, victory and soon home to our families! We shall obviously be seeing them next in the other world.

The Truman Doctrine and the Marshall Plan

During World War II the Soviet Union and the United States were allied against their common enemies, the Axis powers. Shortly after the end of the war, animosity began to reappear between the former allies. By 1947 that animosity had risen to

SOURCE: U.S. Congress, *Congressional Record,* 80th Congress, 1st Session (Washington, D.C.: U.S. Government Printing Office, 1947), vol. 93, p. 1981.

SOURCE: U.S. Congress, Senate Committee on Foreign Relations, *A Decade of American Foreign Policy: Basic Documents, 1941–1949* (Washington, D.C.: U.S. Government Printing Office, 1950), pp. 1270–1271.

the point where it was formalized in government programs and international policies; the Cold War had broken out. In the United States this was most clearly announced in two policy decisions excerpted here. The first is a speech delivered by President Truman on March 12, 1947, to Congress, concerning proposed aid to Greece and Turkey, which appeared in danger of falling under the influence of the Soviet Union. The principles contained in this speech became known as the Truman Doctrine. The second is a statement made by Secretary of State George C. Marshall on November 10, 1947, to Senate and House Committees on Foreign Relations, proposing massive aid to Europe. This proposal became known as the Marshall Plan.

CONSIDER: *The American perception of the Soviet Union and its allies; the purposes of this foreign policy; how the Soviet Union would probably perceive and react to this foreign policy.*

The peoples of a number of countries of the world have recently had totalitarian regimes forced upon them against their will. The Government of the United States had made frequent protests against coercion and intimidation, in violation of the Yalta agreement, in Poland, Rumania, and Bulgaria. I must also state that in a number of other countries there have been similar developments.

At the present moment in world history nearly every nation must choose between alternative ways of life. The choice is too often not a free one.

One way of life is based upon the will of the majority, and is distinguished by free institutions, representative government, free elections, guaranties of individual liberty, freedom of speech and religion, and freedom from political oppression.

The second way of life is based upon the will of a minority forcibly imposed upon the majority. It relies upon terror and oppression, a controlled press and radio, fixed elections, and the suppression of personal freedoms.

I believe that it must be the policy of the United States to support free peoples who are resisting attempted subjugation by armed minorities or by outside pressures.

I believe that we must assist free peoples to work out their own destinies in their own way.

I believe that our help should be primarily through economic and financial aid, which is essential to economic stability and orderly political processes.

❧

As a result of the war, the European community which for centuries had been one of the most productive and indeed creative portions of the inhabited world was left prostrate. This area, despite its diversity of national cultures and its series of internecine conflicts and wars, nonetheless enjoys a common heritage and a common civilization.

The war ended with the armies of the major Allies meeting in the heart of this community. The policies of three of them have been directed to the restoration of that European community. It is now clear that only one power, the Soviet Union, does not for its own reasons share this aim.

We have become involved in two wars which have had their origins in the European continent. The free peoples of Europe have fought two wars to prevent the forcible domination of their community by a single great power. Such domination would have inevitably menaced the stability and security of the world. To deny today our interest in their ability to defend their own heritage would be to disclaim the efforts and sacrifices of two generations of Americans. We wish to see this community restored as one of the pillars of world security; in a position to renew its contribution to the advancement of mankind and to the development of a world order based on law and respect for the individual.

The record of the endeavors of the United States Government to bring about a restoration of the whole of that European community is clear for all who wish to see. We must face the fact, however, that despite our efforts, not all of the European nations have been left free to take their place in the community of which they form a natural part.

Thus the geographic scope of our recovery program is limited to those nations which are free to act in accordance with their national traditions and their own estimates of their national interests. If there is any doubt as to this situation, a glance at the present map of the European continent will provide the answer.

The present line of division in Europe is roughly the line upon which the Anglo-American armies coming from the west met those of the Soviet Union coming from the east. To the west of that line the nations of the continental European community have been grappling with the vast and difficult problems resulting from the war in conformity with their own national traditions without pressure or menace from the United States or Great Britain. Developments in the European countries to the east of that line bear the unmistakable imprint of an alien hand.

The Cold War: A Soviet Perspective

B. N. Ponomaryov

The Cold War and indeed modern history were seen differently in the Soviet Union than in the West. The following excerpt is from History of the Communist Party of the Soviet Union *(1960), an official publication of the Soviet*

SOURCE: B. N. Ponomaryov et al., *History of the Communist Party of the Soviet Union,* Andrew Rothstein, trans. (Moscow: Foreign Languages Publishing House, 1960), pp. 599, 606–12.

government. Here the focus is on the end of World War II and the early Cold War period.

CONSIDER: *The elements of this interpretation most likely to be accepted by Western non-Marxist historians; how this interpretation differs from Truman's and Marshall's perceptions; how these differences help explain the existence of the Cold War.*

As a result of the war the capitalist system sustained enormous losses and became weaker. *The second stage of the general crisis of capitalism set in,* manifesting itself chiefly in a new wave of revolutions. Albania, Bulgaria, Eastern Germany, Hungary, Czechoslovakia, Poland, Rumania and Yugoslavia broke away from the system of capitalism. . . .

In their relations with the People's Democracies the Communist Party and the Soviet Government strictly adhered to the principle of non-interference in their internal affairs. The U.S.S.R. recognised the people's governments in these States and supported them politically. True to its internationalist duty, the U.S.S.R. came to the aid of the People's Democracies with grain, seed and raw materials, although its own stocks had been badly depleted during the war. This helped to provide the population with foodstuffs and also to speed up the recommissioning of many industrial enterprises. The presence of the Soviet armed forces in the People's Democracies prevented domestic counter-revolution from unleashing a civil war and averted intervention. The Soviet Union paralysed the attempts of the foreign imperialists to interfere in the internal affairs of the democratic States. . . .

The U.S.A. decided to take advantage of the economic and political difficulties in the other leading capitalist countries and bring them under its sway. Under the pretext of economic aid the U.S.A. began to infiltrate into their economy and interfere in their internal affairs. Such big capitalist countries as Japan, West Germany, Italy, France and Britain all became dependent on the U.S.A. to a greater or lesser degree. The people of Western Europe were confronted with the task of defending their national sovereignty against the encroachments of American imperialism. . . .

The radical changes that took place after the second world war substantially altered the political map of the world. There emerged *two* main *world* social and political camps: the *Socialist* and democratic camp, and the *imperialist* and anti-democratic camp. . . .

The ruling circles of the U.S.A., striving for world supremacy, openly declared that they could achieve their aims only from "positions of strength." The American imperialists unleashed the so-called cold war, and sought to kindle the flames of a third world war. In 1949, the

U.S.A. set up an aggressive military bloc known as the North Atlantic Treaty Organisation (NATO). As early as 1946, the Western States began to pursue a policy of splitting Germany, which was essentially completed in 1949 with the creation of a West German State. Subsequently they set out to militarise West Germany. This further deepened the division of Germany and made her reunification exceptionally difficult. A dangerous hotbed of war began to form in Europe. In the Far East the United States strove to create a hotbed of war in Japan, stationing its armed forces and building military bases on her territory.

In 1950, the United States resorted to open aggression in the Far East. It occupied the Chinese island of Taiwan, provoked an armed clash between the Korean People's Democratic Republic and South Korea and began an aggressive war against the Korean people. The war in Korea was a threat to the People's Republic of China, and Chinese people's volunteers came to the assistance of the Korean people.

The military adventure of the U.S.A. in Korea sharply aggravated international tension. The U.S.A. started a frantic arms drive and stepped up the production of atomic, thermonuclear, bacteriological and other types of weapons of mass annihilation. American military bases, spearheaded primarily against the U.S.S.R., China and the other Socialist countries, were hastily built at various points of the capitalist world. Military blocs were rapidly knocked together. The threat of a third world war with the use of mass destruction weapons increased considerably.

The Berlin Wall
Jens Reich

Perhaps the most striking symbol of the Cold War that divided Europe was the Berlin Wall. In 1961, the East German government, under orders from Moscow, erected a 100-mile heavily armed wall in Berlin to keep its citizens from fleeing to the West. Berlin had served as an escape route for 2.6 million people, especially professionals and the well educated who sought a higher standard of living and broader cultural options in West Berlin and Western Europe. In the following selection, Jens Reich, a 22-year-old student in East Berlin in 1961, describes his reactions when the wall went up.

CONSIDER: *What Reich means by "Wall-Sickness"; the significance of the Berlin Wall to people such as Reich.*

SOURCE: Jens Reich, "Reflections on Becoming an East German Dissident, on Loosing the Wall and a Country," in *Spring in Winter, The 1989 Revolutions,* ed. by Gwyn Prins (Manchester, U.K.: Manchester University Press, 1990) (Dist. by St. Martin's Press), pp. 75–77.

I was a student in East Berlin before 13th August, 1961, before the day of "The Wall." I came to Berlin in 1956, as a boy of 17. I had lived in a rather dull provincial town and after Halberstadt, Berlin was like a revelation for me. . . . And then we had West Berlin. What a thrill! Cinemas, theatres, the Philharmonie. . . . I took everybody who came to visit me in Berlin. And I remember the coming of The Wall.

I mention all these details, which I remember so clearly, in order give a sense of the shock that we suffered when The Wall came upon us one night. There we were in Berlin, at the crossroads between East and West, at the juncture of two fundamentally different cultures, and suddenly we were locked up like canaries in a cage. Literally from one day to the next, from being a vibrant and cultured city, Berlin subsided into the drowsy torpor of a midsummer afternoon in the provinces. We were imprisoned in a dull, flat country.

In the first years no foreign earth was available to us at all. Czechoslovakia, Poland and the Soviet Union could only be visited by professional people. Bulgaria and Romania opened for tourists in the mid-sixties; but prices were steep and they were holiday resorts rather than centres of European culture. To reach West Germany was a venture that most probably ended in prison for *Republikflucht*, or worse, for the Border Guards shot mercilessly at people trying to climb over "The Wall."

To call it a wall doesn't really do it justice. It was an entire system of watch towers, barbed wire, searchlights, pierced steel plate (to call it "wire mesh" gives the wrong impression of what was called "The Wire" within "The Wall"), strips sown with land-mines, free-fire zones covered by automatic guns, dog runs with ferocious, hungry dogs, armed Border Guard launches on the river to stop swimmers—all this apparatus of containment as well as concrete walls and passages. . . .

"Wall-sickness" was the eternal, lamenting analysis of our life blighted and circumscribed by *Die Mauer*. It came from being in a cage in the centre of Europe. Wall-sickness was boredom. We felt condemned to utter, excruciating dullness, sealed off from everything that happened in the world around us. Wall-sickness was loneliness, the feeling that you were condemned to die without having ever seen Naples, or Venice, or Paris, or London.

Some people could not stand the prospect of a life of such tedium and literally went mad. People would sometimes do crazy irrational things. You might go to the border, for example, draw your identity card and announce that you wanted "to be rid of this shitty country," a gesture with the guaranteed outcome of years in prison, but done in the hope that West Germany would buy you out sooner or later (often later!). Wall-sickness was the anguish of deprivation of a whole generation born between 1930 and 1950. We knew what we had lost.

British Labor's Rise to Power
Harry W. Laidler

During World War II governments became involved in social and economic activities to an unprecedented degree. Although with the end of the war this changed to some degree, there was still significant acceptance of government involvement in society. In Great Britain this was combined with an increasing acceptance of the Labor party, whose strength had been growing since the end of World War I. In the elections of 1945, this party, made up of a combination of Socialist and trade-union groups, gained a majority and took office, replacing the Conservatives led by Winston Churchill. The new government initiated policies that substantially changed the relationship between the government and the people during the period following World War II. Excerpts from the Labor party platform set forth shortly before the 1945 elections are presented here.

CONSIDER: *The ways in which this platform constituted a major assault on capitalism and laissez-faire; how this platform might reflect the experience of the Great Depression and the world wars; how a Conservative might argue against this platform.*

The Labor party is a socialist party, and proud of it. Its ultimate purpose at home is the establishment of the socialist commonwealth of Great Britain—free, democratic, efficient, progressive, public-spirited, its material resources organized in the service of the British people.

But socialism cannot come overnight, as the product of a week-end revolution. The members of the Labor party, like the British people, are practical-minded men and women.

There are basic industries ripe and over-ripe for public ownership and management in the direct service of the nation. There are many smaller businesses rendering good service which can be left to go on with their useful work.

There are big industries not yet ripe for public ownership which must nevertheless be required by constructive supervision to further the nation's needs and not to prejudice national interests by restrictive antisocial monopoly or cartel agreements—caring for their own capital structures and profits at the cost of a lower standard of living for all.

In the light of these considerations, the Labor party submits to the nation the following industrial program:

1. *Public Ownership of the Fuel and Power Industries.* For a quarter of a century the coal industry, producing Britain's most precious national raw material, has

SOURCE: Harry W. Laidler, "British Labor's Rise to Power," in *League for Industrial Democracy Pamphlet Series* (New York: League for Industrial Democracy, 1945), pp. 24–25. Reprinted by permission of the publisher.

been floundering chaotically under the ownership of many hundreds of independent companies. Amalgamation under public ownership will bring great economies in operation and make it possible to modernize production methods and to raise safety standards in every colliery in the country. Public ownership of gas and electricity undertakings will lower charges, prevent competitive waste, open the way for co-ordinated research and development, and lead to the reforming of uneconomic areas of distribution. Other industries will benefit.

2. *Public Ownership of Inland Transport.* Co-ordination of transport services by rail, road, air and canal cannot be achieved without unification. And unification without public ownership means a steady struggle with sectional interests or the entrenchment of a private monopoly, which would be a menace to the rest of industry.

3. *Public Ownership of Iron and Steel.* Private monopoly has maintained high prices and kept inefficient high-cost plants in existence. Only if public ownership replaced private monopoly can the industry become efficient.

These socialized industries, taken over on a basis of fair compensation, to be conducted efficiently in the interests of consumers, coupled with proper status and conditions for the workers employed in them.

4. *Public Supervision of Monopolies and Cartels* with the aim of advancing industrial efficiency in the service of the nation. Anti-social restrictive practices will be prohibited.

5. A *First and Clear-cut Program for the Export Trade.* We would give State help in any necessary form to get our export trade on its feet and enable it to pay for the food and raw materials without which Britain must decay and die. But State help on conditions—conditions that industry is efficient and go-ahead. Laggards and obstructionists must be led or directed into a better way. Here we dare not fail.

6. *The Shaping of Suitable Economic and Price Controls* to secure that first things shall come first in the transition from war to peace and that every citizen (including the demobilized Service men and women) shall get fair play. There must be priorities in the use of raw materials, food prices must be held, homes for the people must come before mansions, necessities for all before luxuries for the few. We do not want a short boom followed by collapse as after the last war; we do not want a wild rise in prices and inflation, followed by a smash and widespread unemployment. It is either sound economic controls—or smash.

Declaration Against Colonialism
The General Assembly of the United Nations

Most colonized peoples gained their independence from Western powers during the twenty years that followed World War II. This reflected both the weakness of Europe after the war and the strength of anti-imperialist sentiments around the world. Yet the process of decolonization was difficult in itself and was complicated by the ideological differences that divided nations. In 1960, after a bitter debate, the United Nations adopted the following "Declaration Against Colonialism." Although no nation voted against the resolution, Australia, Belgium, the Dominican Republic, France, Great Britain, Portugal, South Africa, Spain, and the United States abstained.

CONSIDER: *Possible reasons these nations abstained; justifications used by nations for not giving up their colonial possessions; what this declaration reveals about the strengths and weaknesses of the United Nations.*

The General Assembly.

Mindful of the determination proclaimed by the peoples of the world in the Charter of the United Nations to reaffirm faith in fundamental human rights, in the dignity and worth of the human person, in the equal rights of men and women and of nations large and small and to promote social progress and better standards of life in larger freedom,

Conscious of the need for the creation of conditions of stability and well-being and peaceful and friendly relations based on respect for the principles of equal rights and self-determination of all peoples, and of universal respect for, and observance of, human rights and fundamental freedoms for all without distinction as to race, sex, language or religion,

Recognizing the passionate yearning for freedom in all dependent peoples and the decisive role of such peoples in the attainment of their independence,

Aware of the increasing conflicts resulting from the denial of or impediments in the way of the freedom of such peoples, which constitute a serious threat to world peace,

Considering the important role of the United Nations in assisting the movement for independence in Trust and Non-Self-Governing Territories,

Recognizing that the people of the world ardently desire the end of colonialism in all its manifestations,

Convinced that the continued existence of colonialism prevents the development of international economic cooperation, impedes the social, cultural and economic

SOURCE: General Assembly of the United Nations, "Declaration Against Colonialism," *Official Records of the General Assembly,* Fifteenth Session, Resolution 1514, December 14, 1960.

development of dependent peoples and militates against the United Nations ideal of universal peace,

Affirming that peoples may, for their own ends, freely dispose of their natural wealth and resources without prejudice to any obligations arising out of international economic co-operation, based upon the principle of mutual benefit, and the international law,

Believing that the process of liberation is irresistible and irreversible and that, in order to avoid serious crises, an end must be put to colonialism and all practices of segregation and discrimination associated therewith,

Welcoming the emergence in recent years of a large number of dependent territories into freedom and independence, and recognizing the increasingly powerful trends towards freedom in such territories which have not yet attained independence,

Convinced that all peoples have an inalienable right to complete freedom, the exercise of their sovereignty and the integrity of their national territory,

Solemnly proclaims the necessity of bringing to a speedy and unconditional end colonialism in all its forms and manifestations;

And to this end

Declares that:

1. The subjection of peoples to alien subjugation, domination and exploitation constitutes a denial of fundamental human rights, is contrary to the Charter of the United Nations and is an impediment to the promotion of world peace and co-operation.

2. All peoples have the right to self-determination; by virtue of that right they freely determine their political status and freely pursue their economic, social and cultural development.

3. Inadequacy of political, economic, social or educational preparedness should never serve as a pretext for delaying independence.

4. All armed action or repressive measures of all kinds directed against dependent peoples shall cease in order to enable them to exercise peacefully and freely their right to complete independence, and the integrity of their national territory shall be respected.

5. Immediate steps shall be taken, in Trust and Non-Self-Governing Territories or all other territories which have not yet attained independence, to transfer all powers to the peoples of those territories, without any conditions or reservations, in accordance with their freely expressed will and desire, without any distinction as to race, creed or color, in order to enable them to enjoy complete independence and freedom.

6. Any attempt aimed at the partial or total disruption of the national unity and the territorial integrity of a country is incompatible with the purposes and principles of the Charter of the United Nations.

7. All States shall observe faithfully and strictly the provisions of the Charter of the United Nations, the Universal Declaration of Human Rights and the present Declaration on the basis of equality, noninterference in the internal affairs of all States, and respect for the sovereign rights of all peoples and their territorial integrity.

The Balfour Declaration, U.N. Resolution 242, and A Palestinian Memoir: Israel, Palestine, and the Middle East

Since World War II, the Middle East has been a center of violent conflict as well as a source of great concern for the world. One of the main sources of conflict has been the struggle over the creation of Israel and the Palestinian problem that resulted. The roots of this Israeli–Palestinian struggle stretch back at least as far as the late nineteenth century when the Zionist movement—a movement to make Palestine the national home of the Jews—began. The struggle over the creation of Israel came to a head in 1948 when the British, who controlled Palestine, left it in the hands of the United Nations. A United Nations resolution and the first Arab–Israeli war resulted in the creation of Israel, a massive number of Palestinian refugees, and decades of conflict between Arabs and Israelis.

The first of the following three documents on this topic is the Balfour Declaration, a 1917 letter from British Foreign Secretary Balfour to Walter Rothschild, the representative of British Jewry. The letter was used by Zionists to support immigration to Palestine and to obligate the British to create a Jewish homeland there. The second document is Resolution 242 (passed by the United Nations in 1967), which recognized Israel's existence and its need for security but at the same time called on Israel to withdraw from the territories captured in the 1967 Arab–Israeli War. The third document contains excerpts from a memoir of a Palestinian exile, Fawaz Turki. He describes the flight from Palestine in 1948, the years of exile that followed, and his continuing sense of Palestinian consciousness.

CONSIDER: *Why the Balfour Declaration was so important and why the Palestinians rejected it; why Israel has been reluctant to accept U.N. Resolution 242; the source and importance of Turki's sense of Palestinian consciousness.*

SOURCES: *International Documents on Palestine,* 1968, Zuhair Diab, ed. (New York, 1971); Fawaz Turki, *The Disinherited: Journal of a Palestinian Exile* (New York: Monthly Review Press, 1972), pp. 43–45, 54, as excerpted.

THE BALFOUR DECLARATION

Dear Lord Rothschild,

I have much pleasure in conveying to you, on behalf of His Majesty's Government, the following declaration of sympathy with Jewish Zionist aspirations which has been submitted to, and approved by, the Cabinet.

"His Majesty's Government view with favour the establishment in Palestine of a national home for the Jewish people, and will use their best endeavours to facilitate the achievement of this object, it being clearly understood that nothing shall be done which may prejudice the civil and religious rights of existing non-Jewish communities in Palestine, or the rights and political status enjoyed by Jews in any other country,"

I should be grateful if you would bring this declaration to the knowledge of the Zionist Federation.

Yours sincerely,
Arthur James Balfour

U.N. RESOLUTION 242

The Security Council . . .

1. *Affirms* that that the fulfilment of Charter principles requires the establishment of a just and lasting peace in the Middle East which should include the application of both the following principles:
   (i) Withdrawal of Israel armed forces from territories occupied in the recent conflict;
   (ii) Termination of all claims or states of belligerency and respect for and acknowledgement of the sovereignty, territorial integrity and political independence of every State in the area and their right to live in peace within secure and recognized boundaries free from threats or acts of force;
2. *Affirms further* the necessity
   (a) For guaranteeing freedom of navigation through international waterways in the area;
   (b) For achieving a just settlement of the refugee problem;
   (c) For guaranteeing the territorial inviolability and political independence of every State in the area, through measures including the establishment of demilitarized zones.

A PALESTINIAN MEMOIR

A breeze began to blow as we moved slowly along the coast road, heading to the Lebanese border—my mother and father, my two sisters, my brother and I. Behind us lay the city of Haifa, long the scene of bombing, sniper fire, ambushes, raids, and bitter fighting between Palestinians and Zionists. Before us lay the city of Sidon and indefinite exile. Around us the waters of the Mediterranean sparkled

in the sun. Above us eternity moved on unconcerned, as if God in his heavens watched the agonies of men, as they walked on crutches, and smiled. And our world had burst, like a bubble, a bubble that had engulfed us within its warmth. From then on I would know only crazy sorrow and watch the glazed eyes of my fellow Palestinians burdened by loss and devastated by pain.

April 1948. And so it was the cruelest month of the year, but there were crueler months, then years. . . .

After a few months in Sidon, we moved again, a Palestinian family of six heading to a refugee camp in Beirut, impotent with hunger, frustration, and incomprehension. But there we encountered other families equally helpless, equally baffled, who like us never had enough to eat, never enough to offer books and education to their children, never enough to face an imminent winter. In later years, when we left the camp and found better housing and a better life outside and grew up into our early teens, we would complain about not having this or that and would be told by our mothers: "You are well off, boy! Think of those still living there in the camps. Just think of them and stop making demands." We would look out the window and see the rain falling and hear the thunder. And we would remember. We would understand. We would relent as we thought "of those still living there."

Man adapts. We adapted, the first few months, to life in a refugee camp. In the adaptation we were also reduced as men, as women, as children, as human beings. At times we dreamed. Reduced dreams. Distorted ambitions. One day, we hoped, our parents would succeed in buying two beds for me and my sister to save us the agonies of asthma, intensified from sleeping on blankets on the cold floor. One day, we hoped, there would be enough to buy a few pounds of pears or apples as we had done on those special occasions when we fought and sulked and complained because one of us was given a smaller piece of fruit than the others. One day soon, we hoped, it would be the end of the month when the UNRWA rations arrived and there was enough to eat for a week. One day soon, we argued, we would be back in our homeland.

The days stretched into months and those into a year and yet another. Kids would play in the mud of the winters and the dust of the summers, while "our problem" was debated at the UN and moths died around the kerosene lamps. . . .

Our Palestinian consciousness, instead of dissipating, was enhanced and acquired a subtle nuance and a new dimension. It was buoyed by two concepts: the preservation of our memory of Palestine and our acquisition of education. We persisted in refusing the houses and monetary compensation offered by the UN to settle us in our host countries. We wanted nothing short of returning to our homeland. And from Syria, Lebanon, and Jordan, we would see, a few miles, a few yards, across the border, a land where we had been born, where we had lived, and where we felt the earth. "This is my land," we would shout, or cry, or sing, or plead, or reason. And to that land a people had come, a foreign community of colonizers, aided by a Western world in a hurry to rid itself of guilt and shame, demanding independence from history, from heaven, and from us.

The Second Sex
Simone de Beauvoir

and

A Feminist Manifesto
Redstockings

It is increasingly recognized that women, both individually and in organizations, have been struggling for changes for a long time. The effort to gain consciousness and understanding of what it means to be a woman—politically, socially, economically, and sexually—has become central to women's struggles for change in the mid-twentieth century. The most important book in Europe and probably all of the West to explore this effort is The Second Sex, *by Simone de Beauvoir, first published in France in 1949. In this book de Beauvoir, a well-known French novelist, social critic, and existential philosopher, argues that women have been forced into a position subordinate to men in numerous obvious and subtle ways. During the 1960s and 1970s women's struggle for change spread and took on a new militancy. Throughout the West, women were arguing for change in what came to be known, especially in the United States, as the women's liberation movement. Numerous women's organizations formed, and many issued publications stating their views.*

The first of the following two selections on the liberation of women is from The Second Sex. *De Beauvoir stresses the status and role of woman as the "Other" in comparison to man. The second selection is an example of one of the more radical statements of feminism. It was issued in July 1969 by* Redstockings, *an organization of New York feminists.*

CONSIDER: *How de Beauvoir relates women to "Negroes" and proletarians; the handicaps facing women according to de Beauvoir; the primary demands of the Redstockings; how this group justifies its demands; how men might react to this selection.*

The parallel drawn . . . between women and the proletariat is valid in that neither ever formed a minority or a separate collective unit of mankind. And instead of a single historical event it is in both cases a historical

development that explains their status as a class and accounts for the membership of *particular individuals* in that class. But proletarians have not always existed, whereas there have always been women. They are women in virtue of their anatomy and physiology. Throughout history they have always been subordinated to men, and hence their dependency is not the result of a historical event or a social change—it was not something that *occurred*. The reason why otherness in this case seems to be an absolute is in part that it lacks the contingent or incidental nature of historical facts. A condition brought about at a certain time can be abolished at some other time, as the Negroes of Haiti and others have proved; but it might seem that a natural condition is beyond the possibility of change. In truth, however, the nature of things is no more immutably given, once for all, than is historical reality. If woman seems to be the inessential which never becomes the essential, it is because she herself fails to bring about this change. Proletarians say "We"; Negroes also. Regarding themselves as subjects, they transform the bourgeois, the whites, into "others." But women do not say "We," except at some congress of feminists or similar formal demonstration; men say "women," and women use the same word in referring to themselves. They do not authentically assume a subjective attitude. The proletarians have accomplished the revolution in Russia, the Negroes in Haiti, the Indo-Chinese are battling for it in Indo-China; but the women's effort has never been anything more than a symbolic agitation. They have gained only what men have been willing to grant; they have taken nothing, they have only received.

The reason for this is that women lack concrete means for organizing themselves into a unit which can stand face to face with the correlative unit. They have no past, no history, no religion of their own; and they have no such solidarity of work and interest as that of the proletariat. They are not even promiscuously herded together in the way that creates community feeling among the American Negroes, the ghetto Jews, the workers of Saint-Denis, or the factory hands of Renault. They live dispersed among the males, attached through residence, housework, economic condition, and social standing to certain men—fathers or husbands—more firmly than they are to other women. If they belong to the bourgeoisie, they feel solidarity with men of that class, not with proletarian women; if they are white, their allegiance is to white men, not to Negro women. The proletariat can propose to massacre the ruling class, and a sufficiently fanatical Jew or Negro might dream of getting sole possession of the atomic bomb and making humanity wholly Jewish or black; but women cannot even dream of exterminating the males. The bond that unites her to her oppressors is not comparable to any other. The division of the sexes is a biological fact, not an event in human history. Male and female stand opposed within a primordial *Mitsein,* and woman has not broken it. The couple is a fundamental unity with its two halves riveted together, and the cleavage of society along the line of sex is impossible. Here is to be found the basic trait of woman: she is the Other in a totality of which the two components are necessary to one another. . . .

Now, woman has always been man's dependent, if not his slave; the two sexes have never shared the world in equality. And even today woman is heavily handicapped, though her situation is beginning to change. Almost nowhere is her legal status the same as man's, and frequently it is much to her disadvantage. Even when her rights are legally recognized in the abstract, longstanding custom prevents their full expression in the mores. In the economic sphere men and women can almost be said to make up two castes; other things being equal, the former hold the better jobs, get higher wages, and have more opportunity for success than their new competitors. In industry and politics men have a great many more positions and they monopolize the most important posts. In addition to all this, they enjoy a traditional prestige that the education of children tends in every way to support, for the present enshrines the past—and in the past all history has been made by men. At the present time, when women are beginning to take part in the affairs of the world, it is still a world that belongs to men—they have no doubt of it at all and women have scarcely any. To decline to be the Other, to refuse to be a party to a deal—this would be for women to renounce all the advantages conferred upon them by their alliance with the superior caste. Man-the-sovereign will provide woman-the-liege with material protection and will undertake the moral justification of her existence; thus she can evade at once both economic risk and the metaphysical risk of a liberty in which ends and aims must be contrived without assistance. Indeed, along with the ethical urge of each individual to affirm his subjective existence, there is also the temptation to forgo liberty and become a thing. This is an inauspicious road, for he who takes it—passive, lost, ruined—becomes henceforth the creature of another's will, frustrated in his transcendence and deprived of every value. But it is an easy road; on it one avoids the strain involved in undertaking an authentic existence. When man makes of woman the *Other,* he may, then, expect her to manifest deep-seated tendencies toward complicity. Thus, woman may fail to lay claim to the status of subject because she lacks definite resources, because she feels the necessary bond that ties her to man regardless of reciprocity, and because she is often very well pleased with her role as the *Other.*

Now, what peculiarly signalizes the situation of woman is that she—a free and autonomous being like all human creatures—nevertheless finds herself living in a world where men compel her to assume the status of the Other. They propose to stabilize her as object and to doom her to immanence since her transcendence is to be overshadowed and forever transcended by another ego (*conscience*) which is essential and sovereign. The drama of woman lies in this conflict between the fundamental aspirations of every subject (ego)—who always regards the self as the essential—and the compulsions of a situation in which she is the inessential.

I. After centuries of individual and preliminary political struggle, women are uniting to achieve their final liberation from male supremacy. Redstockings is dedicated to building their unity and winning our freedom.

II. Women are an oppressed class. Our oppression is total, affecting every facet of our lives. We are exploited as sex objects, breeders, domestic servants, and cheap labor. We are considered inferior beings, whose only purpose is to enhance men's lives. Our humanity is denied. Our prescribed behavior is enforced by the threat of physical violence.

Because we have lived so intimately with our oppressors, in isolation from each other, we have been kept from seeing our personal suffering as a political condition. This creates the illusion that a woman's relationship with her man is a matter of interplay between two unique personalities, and can be worked out individually. In reality, every such relationship is a *class* relationship, and the conflicts between individual men and women are *political* conflicts that can only be solved collectively.

III. We identify the agents of our oppression as men. Male supremacy is the oldest, most basic form of domination. All other forms of exploitation and oppression (racism, capitalism, imperialism, and the like) are extensions of male supremacy: men dominate women, a few men dominate the rest. All power structures throughout history have been male-dominated and male-oriented. Men have controlled all political, economic, and cultural institutions and backed up this control with physical force. They have used their power to keep women in an inferior position. *All men* receive economic, sexual, and psychological benefits from male supremacy. *All men* have oppressed women.

IV. Attempts have been made to shift the burden of responsibility from men to institutions or to women themselves. We condemn these arguments as evasions. Institutions alone do not oppress; they are merely tools of the oppressor. To blame institutions implies that men and women are equally victimized, obscures the fact that men benefit from the subordination of women, and gives men the excuse that they are forced to be oppressors. On the contrary, any man is free to renounce his superior position provided that he is willing to be treated like a woman by other men.

We also reject the idea that women consent to or are to blame for their own oppression. Women's submission is not the result of brainwashing, stupidity, or mental illness but of continual, daily pressure from men. We do not need to change ourselves, but to change men.

The most slanderous evasion of all is that women can oppress men. The basis for this illusion is the isolation of individual relationships from their political context and the tendency of men to see any legitimate challenge to their privileges as persecution.

V. We regard our personal experience, and our feelings about that experience, as the basis for an analysis of our common situation. We cannot rely on existing ideologies as they are all products of male supremacist culture. We question every generalization and accept none that are not confirmed by our experience.

Our chief task at present is to develop female class consciousness through sharing experience and publicly exposing the sexist foundation of all our institutions. Consciousness-raising is not "therapy," which implies the existence of individual solutions and falsely assumes that the male-female relation-ship is purely personal, but the only method by which we can ensure that our program for liberation is based on the concrete realities of our lives. The first requirement for raising class consciousness is honesty, in private and in public, with ourselves and other women.

VI. We identify with all women. We define our best interest as that of the poorest, most brutally exploited woman.

We repudiate all economic, racial, educational, or status privileges that divide us from other women. We are determined to recognize and eliminate any prejudices we may hold against other women.

We are committed to achieving internal democracy. We will do whatever is necessary to ensure that every woman in our movement has an equal chance to participate, assume responsibility, and develop her political potential.

VII. We call on all our sisters to unite with us in struggle.

We call on all men to give up their male privileges and support women's liberation in the interests of our humanity and their own.

In fighting for our liberation we will always take the side of women against their oppressors. We will not ask what is "revolutionary" or "reformist," only what is good for women.

The time for individual skirmishes has passed. This time we are going all the way.

Visual Sources

The Destruction of Europe

The following map (map 18.1) shows the destruction inflicted on Dresden in the Anglo-American bombing raid of February 13–14, 1945, during the last stages of World War II. As in other "area bombings" made by Allied forces during the war, thousands of civilians were killed in this raid. This shows the blurring of civilian and military targets and the growing use of terror in modern warfare. Military targets such as factories, railway bridges, railway marshaling yards, main railway lines, troop bunkers and barracks, arsenals, and command headquarters were

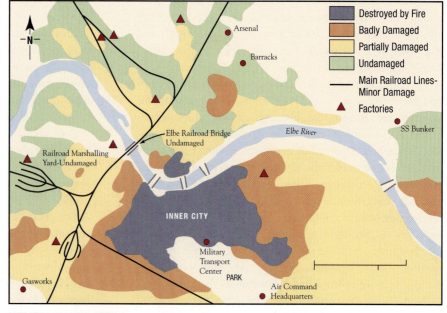

MAP 18.1   Dresden, 1945

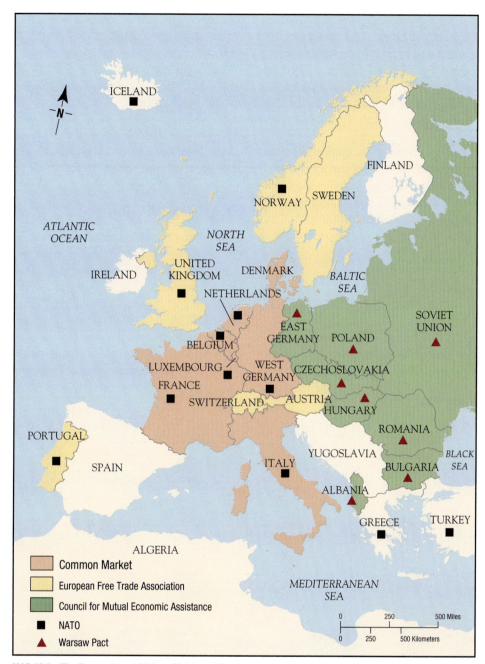

MAP 18.2 The Economic and Military Division of Europe

for the most part not significantly damaged. Instead, the destruction was concentrated on the heavily populated inner city, which was almost completely leveled by fires from incendiary bombing.

CONSIDER: The possible explanations for this raid and its effects; how warfare conducted in this manner seems to contradict the classic ideals of Western civilization concerning the value of the individual and individual rights.

The Cold War and European Integration

Map 18.2 gives some idea of the movements toward the Cold War and toward European integration in the two decades following World War II. Militarily, West and East divided into NATO, led by the United States, and the Warsaw Pact Organization, led by the U.S.S.R. Economically, Western European nations became increasingly tied together through organizations such as the Benelux Customs Union, the European Coal and Steel Community, the European Economic Community (Common Market), and the European Free Trade Association; the East joined in the Council for Mutual Economic Assistance (Comecon). Although military cooperation and economic cooperation were not always linked together, such linkage often did take place.

CONSIDER: The geographic logic, if any, of the political and economic decisions that were made by the various countries; how maps of the world indicating regional economic cooperation, military alliances, political upheavals, and international "hotspots" might show the extent and intensity of the Cold War and regional cooperation even more fully than this map of Europe.

Decolonization in Asia and Africa

Weakened by World War II and faced with growing movements for national liberation, Western imperial powers were forced to start giving up their colonial holdings in the late 1940s. As indicated by map 18.3, the process of

decolonization was in some ways rapid—witness the large areas that gained independence in the few years around 1960—and in some ways delayed—it took some three decades for the process to be almost complete with some areas (e.g., Namibia, Hong Kong) still under external control into the 1990s.

CONSIDER: Possible explanations for some areas gaining independence sooner, others later; possible problems new countries faced following independence.

Televised Violence

Most observers agree that television has had a great impact on the lives of people within Western civilization and throughout the world, but exactly what that impact has been is open to debate. The following picture (figure 18.1) illustrates one of the most controversial issues that have been raised. It shows a television camera crew filming the live action in Vietnam. Here the crew and troops surround a nine-year-old girl burned by an aerial napalm attack in 1972. The images filmed by such crews were displayed on daily newscasts in America and elsewhere, giving civilians a

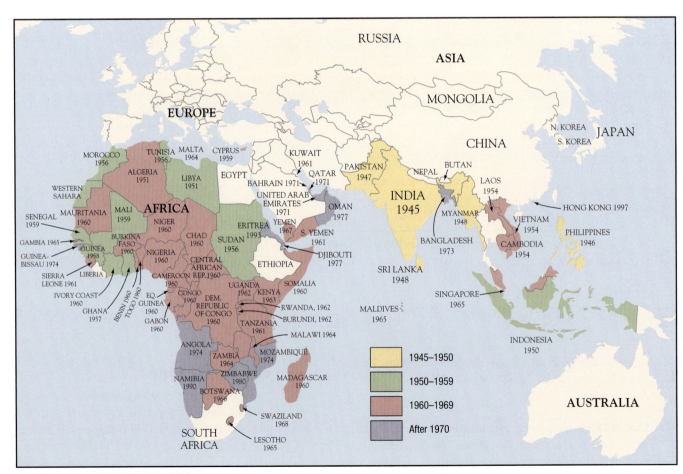

MAP 18.3   Decolonization in Asia and Africa

FIGURE 18.1 (© AP Photo/Nick Ut)

virtual firsthand, up-to-the-minute, perhaps overly realistic impression of what the war was like. However, critics argue that because such images became so common, because they were displayed just before and just after the most mundane of other television shows (typically, situation comedies), and because they were viewed so often from the comfort of a living room, the image of a very real war may have come to seem unreal. Indeed, one must wonder whether this picture itself is not part of a staged scene for a movie (as was the case with a scene the audience sees being filmed in Apocalypse Now, a major movie of 1979–1980).

CONSIDER: Other ways in which the media in the twentieth century have affected people's perception and understanding of war.

Number 1

Jackson Pollock

Twentieth-century artistic styles have tended to become increasingly removed from popular tastes and from what the general public has been used to expecting from art. This was particularly the case

with the style of action painting or abstract expressionism, which came to the fore shortly after World War II. The leading painter in this school of art was Jackson Pollock (1912–1956), who executed this work (figure 18.2), entitled Number 1, in 1948. In 1950 Pollock was interviewed by Francis V. O'Connor, a well-known art critic; a selection from that interview follows.

CONSIDER: How Pollock's statements and this painting reflect some of the trends of twentieth-century history.

Mr. Pollock, in your opinion, what is the meaning of modern art?

Modern art to me is nothing more than the expression of contemporary aims of the age that we're living in.

Did the classical artists have any means of expressing their age?

Yes, they did it very well. All cultures have had means and techniques of expressing their immediate aims—the Chinese, the Renaissance, all cultures. The thing that interests me is that today painters do not have to go to a subject matter outside of themselves. Most modern painters work from a different source. They work from within.

Would you say that the modern artist has more or less isolated the quality which made the classical works of art valuable, that he's isolated it and uses it in a purer form?

Ah—the good ones have, yes.

Mr. Pollock, there's been a good deal of controversy and a great many comments have been made regarding your method of painting. Is there something you'd like to tell us about that?

My opinion is that new needs need new techniques. And the modern artists have found new ways and new means of making their statements. It seems to me that

FIGURE 18.2 (Digital Image © The Museum of Modern Art/Licensed by Scala/Art Resource, NY. © 2010 The Pollock-Krasner Foundation/Artists Rights Society (ARS), New York)

the modern painter cannot express this age, the airplane, the atom bomb, the radio, in the old forms of the Renaissance or of any other past culture. Each age finds its own technique.

Which would also mean that the layman and the critic would have to develop their ability to interpret the new techniques.

Yes—that always somehow follows. I mean, the strangeness will wear off and I think we will discover the deeper meanings in modern art.

I suppose every time you are approached by a layman they ask you how they should look at a Pollock painting, or any other modern painting—what they look for—how do they learn to appreciate modern art?

I think they should not look for, but look passively— and try to receive what the painting has to offer and not bring a subject matter or preconceived idea of what they are to be looking for.

Would it be true to say that the artist is painting from the unconscious, and the—canvas must act as the unconscious of the person who views it?

The unconscious is a very important side of modern art and I think the unconscious drives do mean a lot in looking at paintings.

Then deliberately looking for any known meaning or object in an abstract painting would distract you immediately from ever appreciating it as you should?

I think it should be enjoyed just as music is enjoyed— after a while you may like it or you may not. But—it doesn't seem to be too serious. I like some flowers and others, other flowers I don't like. I think at least it gives— I think at least give it a chance.

Well, I think you have to give anything that sort of chance. A person isn't born to like good music, they have to listen to it and gradually develop an understanding of it or liking for it. If modern painting works the same way—a person would have to subject himself to it over a period of time in order to be able to appreciate it.

I think that might help, certainly.

Mr. Pollock, the classical artists had a world to express and they did so by representing the objects in that world. Why doesn't the modern artist do the same thing?

H'm—the modern artist is living in a mechanical age and we have a mechanical means of representing objects in nature such as the camera and photograph. The modern artist, it seems to me, is working and expressing an inner world—in other words—expressing the energy, the motion, and other inner forces.

Would it be possible to say that the classical artist expressed his world by representing the objects, whereas the modern artist expresses his world by representing the effects the objects have upon him?

Yes, the modern artist is working with space and time, and expressing his feelings rather than illustrating.

Secondary Sources

Appeasement at Munich Attacked

George F. Kennan

The traditional view in the debate over who was responsible for the outbreak of World War II is that Hitler was emboldened by the unnecessarily weak policy of appeasement pursued by the Western democracies during the 1930s. One element of this appeasement was the Munich Conference of 1938 at which England and France agreed to the dismemberment of Czechoslovakia in return for Hitler's promise to demand no further territories. In the following selection George F. Kennan, former U.S. ambassador to the Soviet Union and Pulitzer Prize winner for a two-volume work on Soviet-American relations, presents the traditional view of appeasement.

CONSIDER: *From the point of view of the French and British statesmen actually participating in the Munich*

Conference of 1938 whether Kennan's criticism is justified; the implications of the argument about the causes of or blame for World War II.

The Munich agreement was a tragically misconceived and desperate act of appeasement at the cost of the Czechoslovak state, performed by Chamberlain and the French premier, Daladier, in the vain hope that it would satisfy Hitler's stormy ambition, and thus secure for Europe a peaceful future. We know today that it was unnecessary—unnecessary because the Czech defenses were very strong, and had the Czechs decided to fight they could have put up considerable resistance; even more unnecessary because the German generals, conscious of Germany's relative weakness at that moment, were actually prepared to attempt the removal of Hitler then and there, had he persisted in driving things to the point of war. It was the fact that the Western powers and the Czechoslovak government did yield at the last moment, and that Hitler once again achieved a bloodless triumph, which deprived the generals of any

SOURCE: George F. Kennan, *Russia and the West Under Lenin and Stalin* (Boston: Atlantic–Little, Brown, 1961), p. 322. Reprinted by permission of Little, Brown and Company.

excuse for such a move. One sees again, as so often in the record of history, that it sometimes pays to stand up manfully to one's problems, even when no certain victory is in sight.

The Origins of the Second World War: Appeasement Defended

A. J. P. Taylor

The traditional view attacking appeasement as unjustified and a major cause of World War II has been questioned from different perspectives. Perhaps the most controversial perspective comes from A. J. P. Taylor, a popular, outspoken British historian who has written extensively on modern European history. In the following selection from The Origins of the Second World War, *Taylor argues that the appeasers have been unfairly faulted for their policies.*

CONSIDER: *The ways that Taylor and Kennan would disagree about the legitimacy of appeasement rather than the facts of appeasement; the implications of Taylor's argument about the causes of or blame for World War II; the advantages and dangers of looking at appeasement in the 1930s as a historical lesson to be learned for dealing with more recent circumstances.*

He got as far as he did because others did not know what to do with him. Here again I want to understand the "appeasers," not to vindicate or to condemn them. Historians do a bad day's work when they write the appeasers off as stupid or as cowards. They were men confronted with real problems, doing their best in the circumstances of their time. They recognised that an independent and powerful Germany had somehow to be fitted into Europe. Later experience suggests that they were right. At any rate, we are still going round and round the German problem. Can any sane man suppose, for instance, that other countries could have intervened by armed force in 1933 to overthrow Hitler when he had come to power by constitutional means and was apparently supported by a large majority of the German people? Could anything have been designed to make him more popular in Germany, unless perhaps it was intervening to turn him out of the Rhineland in 1936? The Germans put Hitler into power; they were the only ones who could turn him out. Again the "appeasers" feared that the defeat of Germany would be followed by a Russian domination over much of

Europe. Later experience suggests that they were right here also. Only those who wanted Soviet Russia to take the place of Germany are entitled to condemn the "appeasers"; and I cannot understand how most of those who condemn them are now equally indignant at the inevitable result of their failure.

Nor is it true that the "appeasers" were a narrow circle, widely opposed at the time. To judge by what is said now, one would suppose that practically all Conservatives were for strenuous resistance to Germany in alliance with Soviet Russia and that all the Labour party were clamouring for great armaments. On the contrary, few causes have been more popular. Every newspaper in the country applauded the Munich settlement with the exception of *Reynolds' News*. Yet so powerful are the legends that even when I write this sentence down I can hardly believe it. Of course the "appeasers" thought firstly of their own countries as most statesmen do and are usually praised for doing. But they thought of others also. They doubted whether the peoples of eastern Europe would be best served by war. The British stand in September 1939 was no doubt heroic; but it was heroism mainly at the expense of others. The British people suffered comparatively little during six years of war. The Poles suffered catastrophe during the war, and did not regain their independence after it. In 1938 Czechoslovakia was betrayed. In 1939 Poland was saved. Less than one hundred thousand Czechs died during the war. Six and a half million Poles were killed. Which was better—to be a betrayed Czech or a saved Pole? I am glad Germany was defeated and Hitler destroyed. I also appreciate that others paid the price for this, and I recognise the honesty of those who thought the price too high.

A World at Arms

Gerhard L. Weinberg

The issues involved with appeasement, which have so often been a focus for analysis, lead to the broader questions of why war broke out in 1939 and whether it could have been prevented. To answer these questions, historians often look back to the whole era that began with the outbreak of World War I in 1914. In the following selection, Gerhard Weinberg of the University of Michigan compares the two wars and emphasizes the differences that separate them. He also leaves no doubt whom he holds responsible for World War II.

SOURCES: A. J. P. Taylor, *The Origins of the Second World War*, 2nd ed. (New York: Atheneum Publishers, 1965), pp. 291–292. Reprinted by permission of the publisher.

SOURCES: Gerhard L. Weinberg, *A World At Arms: A Global History of World War II.* Cambridge, U.K.: Cambridge University Press, 1994, pp. 1–2, 43–44.

CONSIDER: *In what ways the causes and nature of the two wars differed; how Weinberg's interpretation compares to those of Kennan and Taylor.*

Although this book contains a chapter on the background of World War II, it defines that war as beginning in 1939 in Europe. While some have argued that the war was merely a continuation of World War I after a temporary interruption created by the armistice of 1918, and that the whole period from 1914 to 1945 should be seen as the age of a new European civil war, a Thirty-one Years War if you will, such a perspective ignores not only the very different origins and nature of the prior conflict but obscures instead of illuminating the special character of the second one. If an important by-product of both wars was the weakening of Europe and its hold on the world, the *intentions* of the belligerents were fundamentally different. It is true that these changed somewhat in the course of each of these lengthy struggles, but a basic differentiation remains.

In World War I, the two sides were fighting over their relative roles in the world, roles defined by possible shifts in boundaries, colonial possessions, and military and naval power. It is true that the Austro-Hungarian empire anticipated the elimination of Serbia's independent status, and Germany very quickly came to the conclusion that Belgium would never regain its independence, but beyond this expected disappearance of two of the smaller states which had emerged from larger constructions during the nineteenth century, the other powers—and most especially the major ones—were all expected to survive, even if trimmed by the winners. In this sense, the war, however costly and destructive in its *methods*, was still quite traditional in its aims.

It is also true that the fighting itself, with its unprecedented casualties, its incredible costs, the appearance of such new weapons as poison gas, airplanes, tanks, and submarines, as well as vast shifts in world economic patterns, ended up completely transforming the pre-war world and doing so in ways that none of the belligerents had anticipated. The effects on winners and losers alike were colossal, and the pre-war world could not be revived even if some made valiant and sometimes counterproductive efforts to do so. But neither side had either intended or preferred the massive changes which resulted from the ability of the modern state to utilize the social and mechanical technologies developed in the preceding two centuries to draw vast human and material resources out of their respective societies and employ them—and thereby use them up—in the cauldron of battle.

In World War II, all this was very different indeed. The *intent* was different from the start. A total reordering of the globe was at stake from the very beginning, and the leadership on both sides recognized this. The German dictator Adolf Hitler had himself explicitly asserted on May 23, 1939, that the war he intended would be not for the Free City of Danzig but for living space in the East; his Foreign Minister similarly assured Italy's Foreign Minister that it was war, not Danzig, that Germany wanted. When Germany had conquered Poland and offered a temporary peace to Britain and France, those countries responded by making it clear, as British Prime Minister Neville Chamberlain explained, that there could be no agreement with a German government led by Hitler, a man who had regularly broken his promises. If Chamberlain, who has often been derided for allegedly not grasping the true nature of the National Socialist challenge, saw the issues so clearly, the historian decades later ought not to close his or her eyes to the reality of a very different war. This was, in fact, a struggle not only for control of territory and resources but about who would live and control the resources of the globe and which peoples would vanish entirely because they were believed inferior or undesirable by the victors.

It was in this way that the two wars which originated in Europe differed greatly from each other even if separated by only two decades. . . .

No appeals from prospective neutrals could move Hitler. He not only would not put off war for one day, he was in such a hurry that he gave the orders to begin hostilities hours earlier than the German military timetable required. To justify war in the eyes of the German public, he shared in the preparation of demands on Poland that might sound reasonable to his people—and that he ordered withheld until after they were no longer valid. He would not again run the "danger" of having his ostensible demands agreed to, or made the basis for real negotiations, or be met with counter-offers. Now that there was no longer any chance of splitting the Western Powers from Poland, his focus of attention was on the German home front in the coming war, a reflection of his belief that it had been the collapse there which had produced defeat in the preceding great conflict. . . .

On the morning of September 1 the German offensive into Poland began. . . . To the thunderous applause of the representatives of the German people, he announced that Germany was once more at war.

Almost every nation eventually participated in the new war, some as victims of attack, some as eager attackers themselves, some at the last moment in order to participate in the post-war world organization. A flood of blood and disaster of unprecedented magnitude had been let loose on the world. If the details of military operations and the localities of combat were often vastly different from those of World War I, the fearful anticipation that a new war would be as horrendous or quite likely even worse than the last proved all too accurate. There would be, however, no agitated discussion this time, as there had been after the crisis of 1914, of the question of who was responsible for the outbreak of war. It was all too clear that Germany had taken the initiative and that others had tried, perhaps too much, but certainly very hard, to avert another great conflict. There would be no second "war guilt" debate.

Life and Death in the Third Reich

Peter Fritzsche

During World War II, the Nazis went to great efforts to murder Europe's Jews. Historians have long investigated why. In the following selection, Peter Fritzsche argues that Nazi Germany carried out its murderous program "in order to realize its utopian project of reorganizing the continent along racial lines."

CONSIDER: *Why the Nazis focused so much on Jews; why the Nazis continued the murder of Jews even after Germany was losing the war.*

Nazi Germany murdered Europe's Jews in order to realize its utopian project of reorganizing the continent along racial lines. The Nazis did not simply consider the Jews racially different or inferior but feared them as agents of social decomposition who threatened the moral, political, and economic health of the nation and its empire. According to the Nazis, Jews would not be allowed to compromise Germany's ability to fight a war, as had allegedly been the case in 1914–1918. Jews were also understood to be the main basis of support for Bolshevism and for international finance capitalism, a contradictory position that was no less firmly held for being illogical. This made Jews across Europe nothing less than enemy combatants to be seized and eliminated. It is important to realize that Hitler genuinely believed that Jews in Germany and everywhere else in Europe presented a direct danger to the new Reich. Without "the extermination of the Jewish people," Himmler admitted in 1943, "we would most likely be where we were in 1916–17."[131]

As Germany began to lose the war, the Nazis tirelessly extended their murderous reach and spread the knowledge of the murder of the Jews so that Germans and their allies would realize that they had burned the bridges behind them. In other words, Nazi propaganda reframed the crime in conventional moral terms and suggested to perpetrators how the Allies perceived them in order to fuel the determination to fight to the bitter end. As a result, the Nazis spared no effort in the spring of 1944 to kill hundreds of thousands of Hungarian Jews who had survived the war until then. Over the course of the war, the murder of the Jews became an increasingly desperate policy in which the "final solution" would not follow a final victory, but rather final victory depended on the "final solution." In the summer of 1941, it was the megalomania of Nazi imperialism which encouraged Hitler and Himmler to abandon the idea that the "final solution" had to wait until the end of the war and to implement it in the Soviet Union immediately. Soon thereafter, the realization that the world war would not be over "next spring" and that German authorities would not be able to deport the Jews whom they had impoverished and ghettoized pushed planners to contemplate killing the Jews under their control. As the war entered its third year and expanded into a world conflict, the Nazis believed that the immediate destruction of European Jews was necessary if Germany was to emerge victorious. And finally, in 1943 and 1944 the "final solution" was regarded as the only way for Germany to hold onto its crumbling position of strength. The logic of the Nazis' anti-Semitism led them to the ultrarevolutionary "position from which there is no escape." . . .

In sum, World War II was not the fearsome context for pogroms and atrocities. It was something even more terrible: an existential war waged by the national Socialists in order to build a new racial order in which the cultivation of the healthy German body rested on the physical annihilation of Europe's Jews and the destruction of non-German nations throughout eastern Europe. What we now know as the Holocaust is what made World War II so awfully different and undermined attempts to establish moral symmetry between victors and vanquished as had been the case in previous wars.

Origins of the Cold War

James L. Gormly

The period between the end of World War II and the mid-1960s was marked by the Cold War between the two superpowers emerging from World War II, the United States and the U.S.S.R. Initially American historians analyzed the Cold War with assumptions not too different from policymakers': The United States was only responding defensively to an aggressive Soviet Union intent on spreading its control and Communist ideology over the world. But by the 1960s other interpretations were being offered, most notably a revisionist position holding the Cold War to be at least in part a result of an aggressive, provocative American foreign

SOURCE: Peter Fritzsche, *Life and Death in the Third Reich* (Cambridge: The Belknap Press of Harvard University Press, 2008), pp. 213–214, 295–296.

SOURCES: From James L. Gormly, *From Potsdam to the Cold War*, pp. 220–223. Copyright 1990 by Scholarly Resources, Inc. Reprinted by permission of Scholarly Resources, Inc.

policy. In the following selection James Gormly describes the competing interpretations and suggests how the controversy might be analyzed.

CONSIDER: *Whether the Cold War was inevitable or could have been avoided; how the speeches by Truman and Marshall support one side or the other; which view makes the most sense to you.*

Those who place the major responsibility for the Cold War on the Soviet Union argue that Stalin, as dictator and leader of a totalitarian system, easily could have moderated the nation's interests to meet U.S. objections and ensure peace. According to this view, if the generalissimo was not an expansionist wanting to overrun central and Western Europe, he should have articulated the defensive and limited nature of his goals to the Truman administration and the American public. Instead, the Russians would not accept the U.S. vision for a stable and prosperous world or trust that Washington accepted the legitimacy of the Soviet Union and recognized its need for some degree of influence over regions along its borders. Moscow needed "a hostile international environment" to maintain control and the integrity of the Soviet state. Thus, Stalin was either an expansionist or unwilling to communicate his aims, and the United States, supported by Britain, had no other option than to react aggressively. . . .

Other analysts place a large amount of the blame on the United States and its unwillingness to accept expressed Soviet needs and to articulate to the Russians and Stalin that Washington trusted them and recognized the legitimacy of their system and state. Some explain U.S. behavior as an outgrowth of the American Open Door ideology, which sought to ensure for the nation's businesses access to world markets. Still others credit U.S. actions to a general arrogance of power that translated the country's tremendous economic and military strength and accomplishments into a moral, ideological superiority. According to this theory, many Soviets feared that the West still hoped to destroy their state. To convince them that America intended to be a friend and thereby avoid the Cold War, the United States should have shelved its presumptuousness and global goals and demonstrated an affirmation of the Soviet Union's right to rule and enjoy the fruits of its victory. To ease fears and mistrust, Washington needed to recognize Russia's new borders, its diplomatic equality, and its spheres of influence in Eastern Europe. Instead, the U.S. government continued to follow the path suggested by Ambassador Harriman, who stated that the administration should supply assistance to the Soviets only if they "played the international game with us in accordance with our standards." . . .

Given the situation, the belief that U.S. actions divided the world into two camps and necessitated a rapid Sovietization of Eastern Europe seems as logical as the view that Russian expansionism forced the United States to institute its containment policy. To evaluate and assess either theory fully and to determine if the Cold War international system could have been avoided requires an examination of Soviet records, but, even without such information, and using existing American and British documents, one can conclude that U.S. policymakers made few efforts after the Potsdam Conference to reassure Moscow that mutual cooperation was possible and that Washington had no intention of seeking the destruction of the Soviet state.

The Collapse of European Empires
John Springhall

During the years after the end of World War II, Western powers rapidly lost almost all of their overseas holdings. Various explanations for this development, from the weakness of the colonial state to the strength of the struggle for liberation, have been proposed. In the following selection, John Springhall analyzes the main interpretations of the collapse of European Empires after 1945.

CONSIDER: *The differences between the "nationalism," the "international," and the "metropolitan" explanations; the legacy of colonial rule.*

One of the problems in writing about decolonization is that we know the end of the story. Whether self-government is seen as either the result of deliberate preparation/abrupt withdrawal by a colonial state ('decolonization') or as a triumph wrested from the colonizers by nationalist movements ('liberation struggle'), the story allows itself to be read backwards in order to privilege the process of ending colonial rule over anything else that was happening in the postwar years. Firstly, those favouring a *nationalist* or – to use Euro-centric terminology – 'peripheral' explanation (Easton, 1964; Grimal, 1978; Low, 1993), emphasize that indigenous upheavals invariably set the pace for decolonization, while the disappearance of collaborative elites also made continued European colonial rule unworkable (see Chapter 8).

Secondly, those historians who favour the *international* explanation of imperial disengagement (McIntyre, 1977; Lapping, 1985) point out that, in the new bipolar world after 1945, both the United States and the Soviet Union were hostile to old-style imperialism, although for differ-

SOURCE: John Springhall, *Decolonization since 1945* (New York: Palgrave, 2001), pp. 4–5, 217–218.

ent ideological reasons. Newly independent Third World states like India and Ceylon (Sri Lanka since 1972) also exerted international pressure through the United Nations (UN) to accelerate the process of decolonization. Thirdly, a focus on the domestic consequences of international relations, the *metropolitan* or domestic constraints approach (Kahler, 1984; Holland, 1985), illuminates how empire was fast becoming too burdensome and served no strategic or economic purpose for the mother country. From this perspective, loss of the 'will to rule' led to a belief that it was not worth expending men and money to preserve what were perceived as colonial liabilities by the middle-class taxpayer.

❧

Empires are now topics largely of interest to the historian, for they do not exist in the present. The collapse and disappearance of European empires from 1945 onwards changed the nature of the world we live in – no longer was mere possession of a white skin, and the scientific, military and technical knowledge it signified, sufficient to authorize command over others. The legacy of colonial rule has cast a long shadow, however: independence often meant multi-ethnic, fragmented states that were too small to be economically viable, and cut off from the rest of the world. While many former European colonies embarked on self-government with high expectations and a relatively healthy bank balance, not many of these hopes were fulfilled. The record of post-colonial Africa, for example, suggests that, judged by Western standards, the commitment of many new states to democratic values and human rights was precarious and soon nearly all were heavily in debt.

The Wretched of the Earth

Frantz Fanon

When discussing colonialism in the decades following World War II, most historians focus on its political and economic consequences. Some observers, however, point to the deeper psychological consequences of colonialism. The best known of these observers was Frantz Fanon (1925–1961), a French psychiatrist from the French West Indies whose writings supported the Algerian rebels in their struggle for independence from France after World War II. In his book The Wretched of the Earth *(1961), Fanon argues that colonialism had its greatest impact on the people physically involved in it: the foreign occupiers (settlers) and the colonized (natives). In the following excerpt from that book, Fanon emphasizes the great physical and psychological gap between these two groups.*

SOURCES: Frantz Fanon, *The Wretched of the Earth,* trans. Constance Farrington. Copyright © 1963 by Presence Africaine. Used by permission of Grove Weidenfeld.

CONSIDER: *What connections there are between the physical and the psychological gaps separating settlers and natives; the attitudes of the settlers toward the natives; the attitudes of the natives toward the settlers and their institutions.*

The colonial world is a world cut in two. The dividing line, the frontiers are shown by barracks and police stations. In the colonies it is the policemen and the soldier who are the official, instituted go-betweens, the spokesmen of the settler and his rule of oppression. . . .

It is obvious here that the agents of government speak the language of pure force. The intermediary does not lighten the oppression, nor seek to hide the domination; he shows them up and puts them into practice with the clear conscience of an upholder of the peace; yet he is the bringer of violence into the home and into the mind of the native. . . .

The settler's town is a strongly-built town, all made of stone and steel. It is a brightly-lit town; the streets are covered with asphalt, and the garbage-cans swallow all the leavings, unseen, unknown and hardly thought about. The settler's feet are never visible, except perhaps in the sea; but there you're never close enough to see them. His feet are protected by strong shoes although the streets of his town are clean and even, with no holes or stones. The settler's town is a well-fed town, an easy-going town; its belly is always full of good things. The settler's town is a town of white people, of foreigners.

The town belonging to the colonised people, or at least the native town, the negro village, the medina, the reservation, is a place of ill fame, peopled by men of evil repute. They are born there, it matters little where or how; they die there, it matters not where, nor how. It is a world without spaciousness; men live there on top of each other, and their huts are built one on top of the other. The native town is a hungry town, starved of bread, of meat, of shoes, of coal, of light. The native town is a crouching village, a town on its knees, a town wallowing in the mire. It is a town of niggers and dirty arabs. The look that the native turns on the settler's town is a look of lust, a look of envy; it expresses his dreams of possession—all manner of possession: to sit at the settler's table, to sleep in the settler's bed, with his wife if possible. The colonised man is an envious man. And this the settler knows very well; when their glances meet he ascertains bitterly, always on the defensive "They want to take our place." It is true, for there is no native who does not dream at least once a day of setting himself up in the settler's place.

This world divided into compartments, this world cut in two is inhabited by two different species. The originality of the colonial context is that economic reality, inequality and the immense difference of ways of life never come to mask the human realities. When you examine at close quarters the colonial context, it is evident that what parcels out the world is to begin with the fact of belonging to or not belonging to a given race, a given species. . . .

It is not enough for the settler to delimit physically, that is to say with the help of the army and the police force, the place of the native. As if to show the totalitarian character of colonial exploitation the settler paints the native as a sort of quintessence of evil. Native society is not simply described as a society lacking in values. It is not enough for the colonist to affirm that those values have disappeared from, or still better never existed in, the colonial world. The native is declared insensible to ethics; he represents not only the absence of values, but also the negation of values. . . .

The Church in the colonies is the white people's Church, the foreigner's Church. She does not call the native to God's ways but to the ways of the white man, of the master, of the oppressor. And as we know, in this matter many are called but few chosen.

❧ **CHAPTER QUESTIONS**

1. To what extent do the trends described in this chapter give further support to the argument that Western civilization has been on the decline since World War I in comparison to the heights it reached in the nineteenth century? What developments might be cited to refute this argument?

2. How might one make an argument that the fundamental historical shift in the last two hundred years did not come with World War I but rather with World War II, as indicated by the consequences of that war and the developments of the postwar period?

3. Do you think the Cold War was caused primarily by developments related to World War II or by the ideological differences between Communist and non-Communist countries? Were there any ways in which the Cold War might have been averted?

19 The Present in Perspective

The most recent years in Western history are particularly difficult to evaluate. They are so much a part of the present that it is almost impossible to gain a historical perspective on them.

While many of the basic trends of the postwar era examined in the previous chapter have continued, some important changes have become apparent—particularly in the last few years. The Cold War between the United States and the Soviet Union waned during the late 1980s and ended with the collapse of communism after 1989. Revolutionary changes have taken place in what was the Soviet Union and in Eastern Europe. For the West, these changes may be so far-reaching as to constitute a historical watershed—a marking of the end of the twentieth century and the beginning of the twenty-first century. The rest of Europe, and indeed much of the world, had already been pursuing increasingly independent courses from the two superpowers. The strife-ridden, oil-rich Middle East

has become an area of great concern and importance to the world community. Certain areas in Asia—like Japan, South Korea, Taiwan, and Singapore—have developed economies that have shifted the economic balance of power in the world. New technological accomplishments, ranging from space exploration to the production of computers, affect our civilization in many ways. Concerns about "globalism" and ecological problems have become more acute. Numerous other recent trends and events could be added to this necessarily brief list.

This chapter is not organized in the usual way, for the sources are so much a part of the present that the usual distinctions between primary and secondary sources are no longer useful. The selections focus particularly on changes in the Communist world, especially the former Soviet Union, and related political changes. Other selections interpret the present era as a whole and suggest problems for the future.

There is much ambivalence about recent developments. Our own involvement makes evaluation of the present particularly difficult. At best, the selections in this chapter can throw elements of the present into perspective.

❧ **For Classroom Discussion**

What are the most serious problems facing the West and the world today? Use the selections by Kolbert, Huntington, Juergensmeyer, and McNeill.

The Short Century—It's Over

John Lukacs

Historians have traditionally been interested in dividing their study and analysis of civilizations into eras or periods that make some sense—ideally that begin and end with some watershed developments and have some unifying characteristics. This is particularly difficult to do for our own time, for we lack some historical perspective. In the following selection John Lukacs, writing in 1991 before the dissolution of the Soviet Union, argues that in 1989 watershed events occurred in the West, bringing the twentieth century to an end and initiating the twenty-first century.

CONSIDER: *How Lukacs supports his argument; whether his argument works as well for the non-Western world; what this might mean for the future.*

The 20th century is now over, and there are two extraordinary matters about this.

First, this was a short century. It lasted 75 years, from 1914 to 1989. Its two principal events were the two world wars. They were the two enormous mountain ranges that dominated its landscape. The Russian Revolution, the atom bomb, the end of the colonial empires, the establishment of the Communist states, the emergence of the two superpowers, the division of Europe and of Germany—all of these were the consequences of the two world wars, in the shadow of which we were living, until now.

The 19th century lasted exactly 99 years, from 1815 to 1914, from the end of Napoleon's wars to the start of the—so called—First World War. The 18th century lasted 126 years, from 1689 to 1815, from the beginning of the world wars between England and France (of which the American War of Independence was but part) until their end at Waterloo.

Second, we know that the 20th century is over. In 1815, no one knew that this was the end of the Atlantic world wars and the beginning of the Hundred Years' Peace. At that time, everyone, friends as well as enemies of the French Revolution, were concerned with the prospect of great revolutions surfacing again. There were revolutions after 1815, but the entire history of the 19th century was marked by the absence of world wars during 99 years. Its exceptional prosperity and progress were due to that.

In 1689, the very word "century" was hardly known. The "Oxford English Dictionary" notes its first present usage, in English, in 1626. Before that the word meant a Roman military unit of 100 men; then it began to have another meaning, that of 100 years. It marked the beginning of our modern historical consciousness.

We know that the 20th century is over—not merely because of our historical consciousness (which is something different from a widespread knowledge of history) but mainly because the confrontation of the two superpowers, the outcome of the Second World War, has died down. The Russians have retreated from Eastern Europe and Germany has been reunited. Outside Europe, even the Korean and the Vietnam wars, the missile crisis in Cuba and other political crises such as Nicaragua were, directly or indirectly, involved with that confrontation.

In 1991, we live in a very different world, in which both the U.S. and the Soviet Union face grave problems with peoples and dictators in the so-called third world. Keep in mind that the ugly events in Lithuania are no exception to this: They involve the political structure of the Soviet Union itself. Even its name, the Union of Soviet Socialist Republics, is becoming an anachronism, as once happened with the Holy Roman Empire.

Keep in mind, too, that no matter when and how the gulf war ends, the so-called Middle East will remain a serious problem both for the U.S. and the Soviet Union. Even in the case of a smashing American political or military victory, its beneficial results will be ephemeral. To think—let alone speak—of a Pax Americana in the Middle East is puerile nonsense.

Not only the configuration of great powers and their alliances but the very structure of political history has changed. Both superpowers have plenty of domestic problems. In the Soviet Union, this has now become frighteningly actual; in the U.S., the internal problems are different but not superficial. The very sovereignty and cohesion of states, the authority and efficacy of the governments are not what they were.

Are we going to see ever larger and larger political units? "Europe" will, at best, become a free-trade economic zone, but a Union of Europe is a mirage. Or are we more likely going to see the break-up of several states into small national ones? Are we going to see a large-scale migration of millions of peoples, something that has not happened since the last centuries of the Roman Empire? This is at least possible. The very texture of history is changing before our very eyes.

Are we on the threshold of a new Dark Ages? We must hope not. The main task before us is the rethinking of the word "progress." Like that of "century," the meaning of that word, too, is more recent than we have been accustomed to think. Before the 16th century, that is, before the opening of the so-called modern age (another misnomer, suggesting that this age would last forever) progress simply meant an advance in distance, not in time, without the sense of evolutionary improvement.

Thereafter, the word "progress" began to carry the unquestionable optimistic meaning of endless material and scientific promise, until, during the 20th century, it began to lose some of its shine, because of the increasingly questionable benefits of technology. At the beginning of the 20th century, technology and barbarism seemed to be antitheses. They no longer are. But technology and its threat to the natural environment are only part of the larger problem of progress, a word and an ideal whose more proper and true application is the task of the 21st century that has already begun.

The End of the Cold War

Raymond L. Garthoff

For over four decades after World War II international affairs were dominated by the Cold War between the United States and the Soviet Union. While there were times—particularly in the 1970s—when tensions between these two superpowers seemed to ease, conflicts persisted until the mid-1980s. In 1985 Mikhail Gorbachev rose to power in the Soviet Union and initiated major reform policies: glasnost (political and cultural openness) and perestroika (economic restructuring). Major changes within the Soviet Union, in other eastern European countries, and in international affairs streamed from these policies. By 1991 the Soviet Union had lost control over the states of Eastern Europe and was itself disintegrating—the Cold War was over. In the following selection, Raymond L. Garthoff analyzes the roles played by Gorbachev and American diplomacy in ending the Cold War.

CONSIDER: *Why, according to Garthoff, Gorbachev set out deliberately to end the Cold War; what sorts of perceptions influenced American foreign policy during the Cold War according to Garthoff; what other factors might help to explain why the Cold War ended.*

SOURCE: Raymond L. Garthoff, "Why Did the Cold War Arise, and Why Did It End?" in *The End of the Cold War: Its Meaning and Implications*, Michael J. Hogan, ed. (Cambridge, England: Cambridge University Press, 1992), pp. 131–32.

In the final analysis, only a Soviet leader could have ended the Cold War, and Gorbachev set out deliberately to do so. Although earlier Soviet leaders had understood the impermissibility of war in the nuclear age, Gorbachev was the first to recognize that reciprocal political accommodation, rather than military power for deterrence or "counterdeterrence," was the defining core of the Soviet Union's relationship with the rest of the world. The conclusions that Gorbachev drew from this recognition, and the subsequent Soviet actions, finally permitted the Iron Curtain to be dismantled and ended the global confrontation of the Cold War.

Gorbachev, to be sure, seriously underestimated the task of changing the Soviet Union, and this led to policy errors that contributed to the failure of his program for the transformation of Soviet society and polity. His vision of a resurrected socialism built on the foundation of successful *perestroika* and *demokratizatsiya* was never a realistic possibility. A revitalized Soviet political union was beyond realization as well. Whether Gorbachev would have modified his goals or changed his means had he foreseen this disjunction is not clear, probably even to him. In the external political arena, however, Gorbachev both understood and successfully charted the course that led to the end of the Cold War, even though in this arena, too, he almost certainly exaggerated the capacity for reform on the part of the Communist governments in Eastern Europe.

As the preceding discussion suggests, the Western and above all the American role in ending the Cold War was necessary but not primary. There are a number of reasons for this conclusion, but the basic one is that the American worldview was derivative of the Communist world-view. Containment was hollow without an expansionist power to contain. In this sense, it was the Soviet threat, real or imagined, that generated the American dedication to waging the Cold War. . . .

American policymakers were guilty of accepting far too much of the Communist worldview in constructing an anti-Communist antipode, and of being too ready to fight fire with fire. Indeed, once the Cold War became the dominant factor in global politics (and above all in American and Soviet perceptions), each side viewed every development around the world in terms of its relationship to that great struggle, and each was inclined to act according to a self-fulfilling prophecy. The Americans, for example, often viewed local and regional conflicts of indigenous origins as Cold War battles. Like the Soviets, they distrusted the neutral and nonaligned nations and were always more comfortable when countries around the world were either allies or the satellites and surrogates of the other side. Thus, many traditional diplomatic relationships not essentially attendant on the superpower rivalry were swept into the vortex of the Cold War, at least in the eyes of the protagonists and partly by their actions.

After Communism: Causes for the Collapse

Robert Heilbroner

The rapid collapse of communism in the Soviet Union and Eastern Europe has stunned most observers. Only in retrospect have reasons for this collapse been presented with any conviction. Scholars are now struggling to interpret what has happened. One of these is Robert Heilbroner, who has written extensively on economics, economic history, and current affairs. In the following selection he focuses on the Soviet economic system, particularly the Soviet's central planning system, as the key to the collapse.

CONSIDER: *Why the Soviet's central planning system might have worked well enough in the early stages of industrialization or for specific projects, but not well enough for a mature industrialized economy; why the collapse of communism in the Soviet Union has such widespread significance.*

Socialism has been a great tragedy this century, its calamitous finale the collapse of Communism in the Soviet Union and Eastern Europe. I doubt very much whether socialism has now disappeared from history, but there is no doubt that the collapse marks its end as a model of economic clarity. Moreover, I suspect that its economic failure may haunt socialism longer than the pathologies of Communism. Early on, one could see that the Soviets were headed toward political disaster, but much of that disaster seemed attributable to the hopeless political heritage of Russian history, not to socialism per se. It was the economic side of the Russian collapse that came as a shock. The prodigies of Russian prewar industrialization appeared to be an incontrovertible argument for the capacity of a planned economic system to achieve growth, and the argument appeared to be confirmed by the spectacular performance of the Soviets during the years of reconstruction immediately following the Second World War. Thus, there may have been discomfiture but there was not much surprise when the Soviet economy during the nineteen-fifties grew twice as fast as the American economy. Surprise did not appear until the nineteen-seventies, when the Soviet growth rate slipped to only half of ours, and consternation was not evident until the middle to late nineteen-eighties, when C.I.A. and academic specialists alike began to report something very close to zero growth. But collapse! No one expected collapse.

There is still no definitive account as to exactly why the Soviet economic system collapsed—one can never find the nail for whose want the shoe was lost. There were undoubtedly elements of this economic disaster with their roots in history: the bureaucrat is well known to Russian literature. Perhaps the final blow was delivered by *glasnost,* which released long-pent-up anger against economic conditions; or perhaps by the Soviet attempt to meet the Star Wars initiative—one hears many such guesses. All we know for certain is that the system deteriorated to a point far beyond the worst economic crisis ever experienced by capitalism, and that the villain in this deterioration was the central planning system itself. The conclusion one inevitably comes to is that to whatever extent socialism depends on such a system it will not work. . . .

The great problem of central planning lies buried in the procedures by which the economy is given its marching orders. As in a military campaign, which central planning resembles in many ways, production is brought about by a series of commands from the top, not by the independent decisions of regimental commanders, company captains, and platoon sergeants. This means that the economy "works" because—and only to the extent that—the quantity, quality, size, weight, and selling price of every nut, bolt, hinge, beam, tractor, and hydroelectric turbine have been previously determined. At the supreme headquarters, the numbers for gross national product are announced. In considerably lower and dingier offices, the numbers for nuts, bolts, and turbines are calculated, but it is apparent that if the plans for the latter are off, the plans for the former may be impossible to attain.

Planning thus requires that the immense map of desired national output be carved up into millions of individual pieces, like a jigsaw puzzle—the pieces produced by hundreds of thousands of enterprises, and the whole thing finally reassembled in such a way as to fit. That would be an extraordinarily difficult task even if the map of desired output were unchanged from year to year, but, of course, it is not: the chief planners change their objectives, and new technologies or labor shortages or bad weather or simply mistakes get in the way. In 1986, before *perestroika* was officially formulated, Gosplan, the highest planning commission in the Soviet Union, issued two thousand sets of instructions for major "product groups," such as construction materials, metals, and automotive vehicles. Gossnab, the State Material and Technical Supply Commission, then divided these product groups into fifteen thousand categories—lumber, copper, and trucks, for instance—and the various ministries in charge of the categories in turn subdivided them into fifty thousand more finely detailed products (shingles, beams, laths, boards) and then into specific products in each category (large, medium, and small shingles). These plans then percolated down through the hierarchy of production, receiving emendations or protests as they reached the level of plant managers and engineers, and thereafter travelled back up to the ministerial level. In this Byzantine process, perhaps the most difficult single step was to establish "success indicators"—desired performance targets—for enterprises. For many years, targets were given in physical terms—so many yards of cloth or tons of nails—but that led to obvious difficulties. If cloth was rewarded by the yard, it was woven loosely to make the yarn yield more yards. If the output of nails was determined by their number, factories produced huge numbers of pinlike nails; if by weight, smaller numbers of very heavy nails. The satiric magazine *Krokodil* once ran a cartoon of a factory manager proudly displaying his record output, a single gigantic nail suspended from a crane.

The difficulty, of course, was that the inevitable mismatches and mistakes could not be set to rights by the decisions of platoon sergeants or regimental commanders who were able to see that the campaign was not going as expected.

✦

I am not very sanguine about the prospect that socialism will continue as an important form of economic organization now that Communism is finished. This statement will come as a wry commentary to those who remember that Marx defined socialism as the stage that precedes Communism. But the collapse of the planned economies has forced us to rethink the meaning of socialism. As a semireligious vision of a transformed humanity, it has been dealt devastating blows in the twentieth century. As a blueprint for a rationally planned society, it is in tatters.

The Rise of China

Rosemary Righter

Since the late 1970s, and particularly since the early years of the 1990s, China's economy has grown at an astounding rate. This economic growth has made China more powerful and influential on the world stage. In the following selection, Rosemary Righter analyzes these changes and the role played by Chinese leader Deng Xiaoping.

CONSIDER: *Connections between the crushing of the Tiananmen democracy movement and the new emphasis on "getting rich"; the benefits and problems associated with China's economic development.*

SOURCE: Rosemary Righter, "Out of the Red," *Times Literary Supplement*, February 1, 2008, p. 22.

Fifteen years ago, that master of political cunning Deng Xiaoping made his famous trip south from Beijing to Shenzhen near the Hong Kong border. It was the moment when he decisively outflanked the Politburo's diehard believers in class struggle and the command economy, men whose "ossified way of thinking" he had challenged on assuming the leadership of China in 1976, and who had made a comeback after his crushing of the Tiananmen democracy movement. Now, under the Orwellian rubric of "socialism with Chinese characteristics", Deng decreed that it was time to let enterprise rip. Out went Mao's "better Red than expert"; in came "it doesn't matter about the colour of the cat, so long as it catches mice".

The pent-up energies thus released generated an economic and social upheaval unequalled in history for scale and speed, as well as unpredictable and potentially unmanageable consequences. The take-off was almost vertical. Within months of Deng's apocryphal injunction that "to get rich is glorious", officially recorded national growth rates soared to five times their post-Tiananmen level, ranging between 7 and 12 per cent thereafter and scoring in double digits for each of the past five years. Industrial output and investment in infrastructure have surged faster still; after more than a year of official efforts to cool the economy, they rose in the first half of 2007 by 18.5 per cent and 26 per cent respectively. . . .

The contradictions are becoming acute. On the positive side of the ledger, when adjusted to take account of purchasing power, China's contribution to global growth has for the past seven years exceeded that of the United States. That bald statistic does not take into account the benign worldwide impact of low inflation, held down in large part by the abundant availability of low-cost Chinese imports. Less benignly, however, China may already be the world's biggest emitter of greenhouse gases. China depends on coal, the unwashed, sulphur-belching variety, to meet 70 per cent of its primary energy demand, and already burns more coal than the US, Europe and Japan together. Already China exports sulphur dioxide pollution as far as Los Angeles. This is just the start: the Chinese Academy of Engineering reports that, in the next fifteen years, China will need as much additional power from all sources as the US developed in the past half-century – even if its industries can be compelled to curb wastage so profligate that each unit of output consumes 50 percent more energy in China than in India, and ten times more than in Japan. According to Zhou Shengxian, China's top environment minister, industrial effluent has turned more than a quarter of China's seven main rival systems into "sticky glue". Toxic fumes blanket its cities, and air and water pollution kill 500,000 Chinese a year, according to the World Bank.

China's phenomenal advance has been socially, generationally and geographically lopsided. This Deng expected: he explicitly said that some people would have to get rich first, although it is doubtful that he anticipated the yawning gulf that would open up between China's wealth-flaunting nouveau riche and the poor at their gates. The rich–poor divide comes as a rude shock in a society where most people over forty remember starting out earning roughly the same pittance as everyone else, with the state providing basic services for free. China's income gap – most spectacularly between town and countryside, but also within cities – now rivals that of Victorian England and exceeds that of the US. An aperitif in a slick Beijing bar costs a month's farm income. Illiteracy is rising because the cost of education is beyond the reach of millions, as is healthcare; rural and urban migrant families can be reduced by a single illness to poverty so abject that they cannot afford enough clothes or food. China has compressed into a few years an industrial revolution and the urbanization of a vast nation, all without the safety valves of political accountability, social security and a fair and accessible judicial system. The dramatic overall increase in prosperity sharpens the resentments of those whose lives are just as poor as before, and considerably more precarious.

FIGURE 19.1 (© Bruno Barbey/Magnum Photos)

Modernization: The Western and Non-Western Worlds

Although almost all areas of the world that were once colonies of the Western powers gained independence during the quarter-century following World War II, the penetration of the rest of the world by Western ideas, values, institutions, and products has been extremely widespread. This is illustrated in the photograph (figure 19.1) showing a citizen of Kuwait, an oil-rich sheikdom of the Persian Gulf, carrying a Western television set across a road. He is wearing Western-style tennis shoes that were probably manufactured in the Far East. In the background are a bilingual store sign and Western automobiles. Reflected in the glass of the television set is a modern building probably designed by a Western architect and built under the direction of an international construction firm using both foreign and domestic labor and materials. This photograph suggests that some of the formerly colonized areas are taking economic, political, and social steps in the same direction as Western industrialized states.

Terrorism and the Clash of Civilizations

Samuel P. Huntington

On September 11, 2001, terrorists struck targets in the United States, killing thousands of people. Scholars trying to explain the causes of these acts often point to other instances of terrorism in recent years and deeper conflicts dividing the Western and non-Western worlds. Samuel P. Huntington is one of the most influential and controversial of these scholars. In an often-cited article that first appeared in 1996, he argued that a fundamental clash of civilizations—particularly between Western and Islamic civilizations—is in the offing. In the following excerpt from a more recent publication that appeared after the September 2001 attack, he stresses that the risk of a clash of civilizations is growing and that we have entered "the age of Muslim wars."

CONSIDER: *How Huntington explains the causes of contemporary Muslim wars; why, according to Huntington, the makings of a general clash of civilizations exist.*

Contemporary global politics is the age of Muslim wars. Muslims fight each other and fight non-Muslims far more often than do peoples of other civilizations. Muslim wars have replaced the cold war as the principal form of international conflict. These wars include wars of terrorism,

SOURCE: Samuel P. Huntington, "The Age of Muslim Wars," *Newsweek,* December 17, 2001.

guerrilla wars, civil wars and interstate conflicts. These instances of Muslim violence could congeal into one major clash of civilizations between Islam and the West or between Islam and the Rest. That, however, is not inevitable, and it is more likely that violence involving Muslims will remain dispersed, varied and frequent. . . .

Overall, however, the age of Muslim wars has its roots in more general causes. These do not include the inherent nature of Islamic doctrine and beliefs, which, like those of Christianity, adherents can use to justify peace or war as they wish. The causes of contemporary Muslim wars lie in politics, not seventh-century religious doctrines.

First, one of the most significant social, cultural and political developments in the past several decades has been the resurgence of Islamic consciousness, movements and identity among Muslim peoples almost everywhere. This Islamic resurgence is in large part a response to modernization and globalization and is highly constructive in many ways. Islamist organizations have moved in to meet the needs of the growing numbers of urban Muslims by providing social support, moral guidance, welfare, health services, education, unemployment relief—all services that Muslim governments often do not provide. In addition, in many Muslim Societies, Islamists are the principal opposition to highly repressive governments. The Islamic resurgence has also spawned a small number of extremists who supply the recruits for terrorism and guerrilla wars against non-Muslims.

Second, throughout the Muslim World, and particularly among Arabs, there exists a great sense of grievance, resentment, envy and hostility toward the West and its wealth, power and culture. This is in part a result of Western imperialism and domination of the Muslim world for much of the 20th century. It is also in part the result of particular Western policies, including American action against Iraq since 1991 and the continuing close relationship between the United States and Israel. It is, more broadly, a reaction of Muslim peoples to their own corrupt, ineffective and repressive governments and the Western governments they see supporting those regimes.

Third, tribal, religious, ethnic, political and cultural divisions within the Muslim world stimulate violence between Muslims. They also promote violence between Muslims and non-Muslims because different Muslim groups and governments, such as those of Saudi Arabia and Iran, compete with each other in promoting their own brand of Islam and have supported Muslim groups fighting non-Muslims from Bosnia to the Philippines. If one or two states dominated the Muslim world, which has not been the case since the end of the Ottoman Empire, less violence would occur among Muslims and, probably, between Muslims and non-Muslims. . . .

These factors are among the sources of the widespread violence involving Muslims. To date, that violence has been largely localized, limited and dispersed. Could it evolve into a major violent civilizational war between Islam and the West and possibly other civilizations? This is clearly the goal of Osama bin Laden. He declared holy war on the United States, enjoined Muslims to kill Americans indiscriminately and vigorously attempted to mobilize Muslims everywhere for his jihad. He has not succeeded in this effort, in part because of the many divisions within Islam. The United States, on the other hand, has declared a global war on terrorism, but in fact there are many wars by different governments against different terrorist groups. The United States is primarily concerned with Al Qaeda; other governments are concerned with their own local terrorists.

The makings of a general clash of civilizations exist. Reactions to September 11 and the American response were strictly along civilizational lines. The governments and peoples of Western countries were overwhelmingly sympathetic and supportive, making commitments to join with the United States in the war on terrorism. . . . The leading countries of non-Western, non-Muslim civilizations—Russia, China, India, Japan—reacted with modulated expressions of sympathy and support. Almost all Muslim governments condemned the terrorist attacks, undoubtedly concerned with the threat Muslim extremist groups posed to their own authoritarian regimes. Only Uzbekistan, Pakistan and Turkey, however, provided direct support to the American response, and among major Arab governments only Jordan and Egypt endorsed that response. In most Muslim countries, many people condemned the terrorist attacks, a small number explicitly endorsed the attacks and huge numbers denounced the American response. The longer and the more intensely the United States and its allies use military force against their opponents, the more widespread and intense will be the Muslim reaction. September 11 produced Western unity; a prolonged response to September 11 could produce Muslim unity.

Religious Terrorism

Mark Juergensmeyer

Terrorism is not new. However, terrorist organizations grew alarmingly in the 1980s and 1990s and adopted bolder tactics aimed at both military and civilian targets. Events during the first years of the twenty-first century, such as the attacks on the United States on September 11, 2001, and those on Spain on March 11, 2004, suggest how deadly terrorism can become. In the following selection from Terror in the Mind

SOURCE: Mark Juergensmeyer, *Terror in the Mind of God: The Global Rise of Violence* (Berkeley, CA: The University of California Press, 2001), pp. 5–6, 11.

of God: The Global Rise of Religious Violence, *Mark Juergensmeyer focuses on religious terrorism.*

CONSIDER: *The meaning of religious terrorism according the Juergensmeyer; the possible causes for terrorism; what enables people to carry out acts of terrorism.*

Terrorism is meant to terrify. The word comes from the Latin *terrere,* "to cause to tremble," and came into common usage in the political sense, as an assault on civil order, during the Reign of Terror in the French Revolution at the close of the eighteenth century. Hence the public response to the violence—the trembling that terrorism effects—is part of the meaning of the term. It is appropriate, then, that the definition of a terrorist act is provided by us, the witnesses—the ones terrified—and not by the party committing the act. It is we—or more often our public agents, the news media—who affix the label on acts of violence that makes them terrorism. (These are public acts of destruction, committed without a clear military objective, that arouse a widespread sense of fear.)

This fear often turns to anger when we discover the other characteristic that frequently attends these acts of public violence: their justification by religion. Most people feel that religion should provide tranquility and peace, not terror. Yet in many of these cases religion has supplied not only the ideology but also the motivation and the organizational structure for the perpetrators. It is true that some terrorist acts are committed by public officials invoking a sort of "state terrorism" in order to subjugate the populace. The pogroms of Stalin, the government-supported death squads in El Salvador, the genocidal killings of the Khmer Rouge in Cambodia, ethnic cleansing in Bosnia and Kosovo, and government-spurred violence of the Hutus and Tutsis in Central Africa all come to mind. The United States has rightfully been accused of terrorism in the atrocities committed during the Vietnam War, and there is some basis for considering the nuclear bombings of Hiroshima and Nagasaki as terrorist acts.

But the term "terrorism" has more frequently been associated with violence committed by disenfranchised groups desperately attempting to gain a shred of power or influence. Although these groups cannot kill on the scale that governments with all their military power can, their sheer numbers, their intense dedication, and their dangerous unpredictability have given them influence vastly out of proportion with their meager military resources. Sonic of these groups have been inspired by purely secular causes. They have been motivated by leftist ideologies, as in the cases of the Shining Path and the Tupac Amaru in Peru, and the Red Army in Japan; and they have been propelled by a desire for ethnic or regional separatism, as in the cases of Basque militants in Spain and the Kurdish nationalists in the Middle East.

But more often it has been religion—sometimes in combination with these other factors, sometimes as the primary motivation—that has incited terrorist acts. . . .

As these instances show, it takes a community of support and, in many cases, a large organizational network for an act of terrorism to succeed. It also requires an enormous amount of moral presumption for the perpetrators of these acts to justify the destruction of property on a massive scale or to condone a brutal attack on another life, especially the life of someone one scarcely knows and against whom one bears no personal enmity. And it requires a great deal of internal conviction, social acknowledgment, and the stamp of approval from a legitimizing ideology or authority one respects. Because of the moral, ideological, and organizational support necessary for such acts, most of them come as collective decisions—such as the conspiracy that led to the release of nerve gas in the Tokyo subways and the Hamas organization's carefully devised bombings.

The War in Iraq
Michael Ignatieff

In March 2003, the United States took a major step in the name of its "war on terrorism." The U.S. military, backed by British forces and the token support of other nations, attacked Iraq. Within weeks, U.S. and British air and ground forces overwhelmed Iraqi defenders and toppled Saddam Hussein and the Baathist Party, which had ruled Iraq with an iron fist for more than 20 years. From the beginning, many debated the reasons and wisdom of the attack on Iraq. In the following selection, Michael Ignatieff analyzes the reasons for the war. Ignatieff is director of the Carr Center at the Kennedy School of Government at Harvard University. He describes himself as a liberal and a reluctant, yet convinced, supporter of the war in Iraq.

CONSIDER: *What, according to Ignatieff, is the most important reason the Bush administration invaded Iraq; what role September 11 played in the invasion of Iraq.*

Human rights could well be improved in Iraq as a result of the intervention. But the Bush administration did not invade Iraq just to establish human rights. Nor, ultimately, was this intervention about establishing a democracy or saving lives as such. And here we come to

SOURCE: Michael Ignatieff, "Why Are We in Iraq?" *The New York Times Magazine,* September 7, 2003, p. 7.

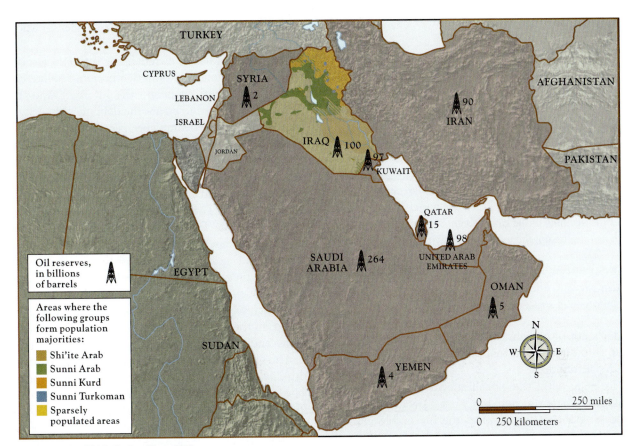

MAP 19.1   The Middle East and Iraq, 2003

the heart of the matter—to where the Bush administration's interventions fit into America's long history of intervention. All such interventions have occurred because a president has believed going in that it would increase both his and his country's power and influence. To use Joseph S. Nye Jr.'s definition, "power is the ability to obtain the outcomes one wants." Presidents intervene because successful interventions enhance America's ability to obtain the outcomes it wants.

The Iraq intervention was the work of conservative radicals, who believed that the status quo in the Middle East was untenable—for strategic reasons, security reasons and economic reasons. They wanted intervention to bring about a revolution in American power in the entire region. What made a president take the gamble was Sept. 11 and the realization, with 15 of the hijackers originating in Saudi Arabia, that American interests based since 1945 on a presumed Saudi pillar were actually built on sand. The new pillar was to be a democratic Iraq, at peace with Israel, Turkey and Iran, harboring no terrorists, pumping oil for the world economy at the right price and abjuring any nasty designs on its neighbors.

As Paul Wolfowitz has all but admitted, the "bureaucratic" reason for war—weapons of mass destruction—

was not the main one. The real reason was to rebuild the pillars of American influence in the Middle East. Americans may have figured this out for themselves, but it was certainly not what they were told. Nor were they told that building this new pillar might take years and years. What they were told—misleadingly and simplistically—was that force was justified to fight "terrorism" and to destroy arsenals of mass destruction targeted at America and at Israel.

War, Oil, and Instability in the Middle East

Map 19.1 shows the Middle East, estimated oil reserves in several nations, and ethno-religious groups in Iraq. The oil reserves suggest one reason why the Middle East might be of such strategic importance to many areas in the world that depend on foreign sources for their energy needs. The war in Iraq, Iraq's internal divisions, the conflicts between Palestinians and Israelis, and the growth of international terrorism stemming from this region also reflect the instability and complexity of the Middle East.

CONSIDER: *The ways war in Iraq might change this region; the problems facing those in Iraq who are trying to establish a stable, unified nation.*

Globalization

Thomas L. Friedman

Scholars looking at Western history since the fall of Communism have tried to come up with terms that best characterize the period. Several scholars have focused on "globalization" as the outstanding quality of this period. While some historians also use the term in descriptions of the post-1945 world and even the world during the decades just before World War I, globalization now refers to something different in quantity and quality. In the following selection from his well-received book, The Lexus and the Olive Tree, Thomas L. Friedman analyzes the meaning of the globalization system by comparing it with its predecessor, the Cold War system.

CONSIDER: *What Friedman means by the "globalization system"; how it differs from the "Cold War system; the three "balances" that structure the globalization system.*

Today's era of globalization, which replaced the Cold War, is a similar international system, with its own unique attributes.

To begin with, the globalization system, unlike the Cold War system, is not static, but a dynamic ongoing process: globalization involves the inexorable integration of markets, nation-states and technologies to a degree never witnessed before—in a way that is enabling individuals, corporations and nation-states to reach around the world farther, faster, deeper and cheaper than ever before, and in a way that is also producing a powerful backlash from those brutalized or left behind by this new system.

The driving idea behind globalization is free-market capitalism—the more you let market forces rule and the more you open your economy to free trade and competition, the more efficient and flourishing your economy will be. Globalization means the spread of free-market capitalism to virtually every country in the world. Globalization also has its own set of economic rules—rules that revolve around opening, deregulating and privatizing your economy.

Unlike the Cold War system, globalization has its own dominant culture, which is why it tends to be homogenizing. In previous eras this sort of cultural homogenization happened on a regional scale—the Hellenization of the Near East and the Mediterranean world under the Greeks, the Turkification of Central Asia, North Africa, Europe and the Middle East by the Ottomans, or the Russification of Eastern and Central Europe and parts of Eurasia under the Soviets. Culturally speaking, globalization is largely, though not entirely, the spread of

Americanization—from Big Macs to iMacs to Mickey Mouse—on a global scale.

Globalization has its own defining technologies: computerization, miniaturization, digitization, satellite communications, fiber optics and the Internet. And these technologies helped to create the defining perspective of globalization. If the defining perspective of the Cold War world was "division," the defining perspective of globalization is "integration." The symbol of the Cold War system was a wall, which divided everyone. The symbol of the globalization system is a World Wide Web, which unites everyone. The defining document of the Cold War system was "The Treaty." The defining document of the globalization system is "The Deal.". . .

Last, and most important, globalization has its own defining structure of power, which is much more complex than the Cold War structure. The Cold War system was built exclusively around nation-states, and it was balanced at the center by two superpowers: the United States and the Soviet Union.

The globalization system, by contrast, is built around three balances, which overlap and affect one another. The first is the traditional balance between nation-states. In the globalization system, the United States is now the sole and dominant superpower and all other nations are subordinate to it to one degree or another. The balance of power between the United States and the other states still matters for the stability of this system. . . .

The second balance in the globalization system is between nation-states and global markets. These global markets are made up of millions of investors moving money around the world with the click of a mouse. I call them "the Electronic Herd," and this herd gathers in key global financial centers, such as Wall Street, Hong Kong, London and Frankfurt, which I call "the Supermarkets." The attitudes and actions of the Electronic Herd and the Supermarkets can have a huge impact on nation-states today, even to the point of triggering the downfall of governments. . . .

The United States can destroy you by dropping bombs and the Supermarkets can destroy you by downgrading your bonds. The United States is the dominant player in maintaining the globalization gameboard, but it is not alone in influencing the moves on that gameboard. This globalization gameboard today is a lot like a Ouija board—sometimes pieces are moved around by the obvious hand of the superpower, and sometimes they are moved around by hidden hands of the Supermarkets.

The third balance that you have to pay attention to in the globalization system—the one that is really the newest of all—is the balance between individuals and nation-states. Because globalization has brought down many of the walls that limited the movement and reach of people, and because it has simultaneously wired the world into networks, it gives more power to individuals to

SOURCE: Thomas L. Friedman, *The Lexus and the Olive Tree* (New York: Farrar, Straus, Giroux, 1999), pp. 7–12.

influence both markets and nation-states than at any time in history. So you have today not only a superpower, not only Supermarkets, but, as I will also demonstrate later in the book, you have Super-empowered individuals. Some of these Super-empowered individuals are quite angry, some of them quite wonderful—but all of them are now able to act directly on the world stage without the traditional mediation of governments, corporations or any other public or private institutions.

Global Warming

Elizabeth Kolbert

For years, various observers and scientists have been cautioning that the global climate is warming, in great part thanks to human activities, and that this global warming will soon have alarming consequences. At first, other scientists disputed these claims; fewer now deny them. In the following selection, Elizabeth Kolbert examines some of the evidence for global warming and its potential consequences.

CONSIDER: *Why global warming might become such a historically important development; why the problem of global warming is already so difficult to solve.*

The retreat of the Arctic sea ice, the warming of the oceans, the rapid shrinking of the glaciers, the redistribution of species, the thawing of the permafrost—these are all new phenomena. It is only in the last five or ten years that global warming has finally emerged from the background "noise" of climate variability. And even so, the changes that can be seen lag behind the changes that have been set in motion. The warming that has been observed so far is probably only about half the amount required to bring the planet back into energy balance. This means that even if carbon dioxide were to remain stable at today's levels, temperatures would still continue to rise, glaciers to melt, and weather patterns to change for decades to come.

But CO_2 levels are *not* going to remain stable. Just to slow the growth . . . is a hugely ambitious undertaking, one that would require new patterns of consumption, new technologies, and new politics. Whether the threshold for "dangerous anthropogenic interference" is 450 parts per million of CO_2 or 500, or even 550 or 600, the world is rapidly approaching the point at which, for all practical purposes, the crossing of that threshold will become impossible to prevent. To refuse to act, on the grounds that still more study is needed or that meaningful efforts are too costly or that they impose an unfair burden on industrialized nations, is not to put off the consequences, but to

rush toward them. Just as this book was being completed, Hurricane Katrina struck New Orleans. Though hurricanes are, in their details, extremely complicated, basically they all draw their energy from the same source: the warm surface waters of the ocean. (This is why they form only in the tropics, and during the season when sea surface temperatures are highest.) It follows that as sea surface temperatures increase, the amount of energy available to hurricanes will grow. In general, climate scientists predict that climbing CO_2 levels will lead to an increase in the intensity of hurricanes, though not in hurricane frequency. Meanwhile, as sea levels rise, storm surges, like the one that breached the levees in New Orleans, will inevitably become more dangerous. . . .

Ice core records also show that we are steadily drawing closer to the temperature peaks of the last interglacial, when sea levels were some fifteen feet higher than they are today. Just a few degrees more and the earth will be hotter than it has been at any time since our species evolved. The feedbacks that have been identified in the climate system—the ice-albedo feedback, the water vapor feedback, the feedback between temperatures and carbon storage in the permafrost—take small changes to the system and amplify them into much larger forces. Perhaps the most unpredictable feedback of all is the human one. With six billion people on the planet, the risks are everywhere apparent. A disruption in monsoon patterns, a shift in ocean currents, a major drought—any one of these could easily produce streams of refugees numbering in the millions. As the effects of global warming become more and more difficult to ignore, will we react by finally fashioning a global response? Or will we retreat into ever narrower and more destructive forms of self-interest? It may seem impossible to imagine that a technologically advanced society could choose, in essence, to destroy itself, but that is what we are now in the process of doing.

Ecological Threats

J. R. McNeill

Over the past several decades, it has become increasingly apparent that modern civilization is exacting a price from nature. Scholars point out that the world's air and water are becoming polluted, the world's species are being diminished or destroyed, and the world's resources are being threatened. In the following excerpt from his book, Something New Under the Sun: An Environmental History of the Twentieth-Century World, *J. R. McNeill looks at the combination of ecological and societal problems facing us and the need for policies to deal with these problems.*

SOURCE: Elizabeth Kolbert, *Field Notes from a Catastrophe: Man, Nature, and Climate Change* (New York: Bloomsbury Publishing, 2006), pp. 184–187.

SOURCE: J. R. McNeill, *Something New Under the Sun: An Environmental History of the Twentieth-Century World* (New York: W. W. Norton & Co., 2000), pp. 360–362.

CONSIDER: *The key causes for the ecological problems we face; how policies have contributed to these problems.*

The reason I expect formidable ecological and societal problems in the future is because of what I see in the past. In this book I have tried to give some measure to the ecological changes experienced in the twentieth century. Only some of them are easily reducible to numbers. They are recapitulated in *Table 19.1*, which is intended as a summary measure of environmental change and some of the factors producing it in the twentieth century. . . .

According to the Hebrew Bible, on the fifth day of creation God enjoined humankind to fill and subdue the earth and to have dominion over every living thing. For

Table 19.1 The Measure of the Twentieth Century

Item	Increase Factor, 1890s–1990s
World population	4
Urban proportion of world population	3
Total world urban population	13
World economy	14
Industrial output	40
Energy use	16
Coal production	7
Air pollution	≈5
Carbon dioxide emissions	17
Sulfur dioxide emissions	13
Lead emissions to the atmosphere	≈8
Water use	9
Marine fish catch	35
Cattle population	4
Pig population	9
Horse population	1.1
Blue whale population (Southern Ocean only)	0.0025 (99.75% decrease)
Fin whale population	0.03 (97% decrease)
Bird and mammal species	0.99 (1% decrease)
Irrigated area	5
Forest area	0.8 (20% decrease)
Cropland	2

most of history, our species failed to live up to these (as to so many other) injunctions, not for want of trying so much as for want of power. But in the twentieth century the harnessing of fossil fuels, unprecedented population growth, and a myriad of technological changes made it more nearly possible to fulfill these instructions. The prevailing political and economic systems made it seem imprudent not to try: most societies, and all the big ones, sought to maximize their current formidability and wealth at the risk of sacrificing ecological buffers and tomorrow's resilience. The general policy of the twentieth century was to try to make the most of resources, make Nature perform to the utmost, and hope for the best.

With our new powers we banished some historical constraints on health and population, food production, energy use, and consumption generally. Few who know anything about life with these constraints regret their passing. But in banishing them we invited other constraints in the form of the planet's capacity to absorb the wastes, by-products, and impacts of our actions. These latter constraints had pinched occasionally in the past, but only locally. By the end of the twentieth century they seemed to restrict our options globally. Our negotiations with these constraints will shape the future as our struggles against them shaped our past.

Those responsible for policy tend to take as their frame of reference the world as we know it. This invites them to think of things as they observe and experience them—the regime of perpetual disturbance as I called it in the Preface—as "normal." In fact, in ecological terms, the current situation is an extreme deviation from any of the durable, more "normal," states of the world over the span of human history, indeed over the span of earth history. If we lived 700 or 7,000 years, we would understand this on the basis of experience and memory alone. But for creatures who live a mere 70 years or so, the study of the past, distant and recent, is required to know what the range of possibilities includes, and to know what might endure.

❧ CHAPTER QUESTIONS

1. The closeness of recent years makes it difficult to know what trends and developments will be the most significant historically. Those selected for this chapter are just a few of the possibilities. What others might have been selected? What evidence would demonstrate their importance?

2. It is possible to argue that most of what is claimed to be new about recent years is not really so new, that it is just our impression that it is new because we have been living through it. How might this argument be supported? How might it be refuted?